CW01621558

OPUS

BY

LEE SHYE

LMN PUBLISHING

OPUS by LEE SHYE

First published in Denmark in 2017
by
Publisher Books on Demand GmbH, Copenhagen, Denmark

Translated to English in 2020

Revised and published in 2025

by

LMN Publishing

A CIP catalogue record for this title is available from the British Library.

Hardback ISBN 978 87 974888 0 5
Paperback ISBN 978 87 974888 1 2
E-book ISBN 978 87 974888 2 9
Target Exclusive Edition ISBN 978 87 974888 3 6

Cover Art by Jem Butcher

Warning:

The book contains elements that may not be suitable for some readers. It contains scenes of murder, execution, personal violence and torture. Additionally, there are consensual acts of a mature sexual nature and dominance/submissive scenes.

Readers who may be sensitive to these, please take note.

Dedicated to Camille

This book supports the following charities:

Galgo del Sol (Dog rescue charity in Murcia, Spain)

VETPAW (Veterans Empowered To Protect African Wildlife), A US registered charity

Information about these charities can be found on the author's website:

www.leeshye.com

"In war there are no winners
only monsters on both sides."

Camille.

Chapter 1

Do you know the feeling of suddenly opening your eyes one day and the first thought that pops into your head is, "What the hell am I doing here?"

Well, that's the way I feel right now.

I am on a cold concrete floor in an empty warehouse in Bosnia. To actually see me you have to have a trained eye because my camouflage clothes blend perfectly in with the grey and white cement collage of rubble and rebars that constitutes the furnishing of the room.

It is autumn or maybe I should say the beginning of winter because I think we are in late November, but I am not sure. It has been a while since I have concentrated on such basic details as what month it is.

The details are some of the first things to disappear. In the beginning I didn't notice them. There was so much to learn and as I did my view of the world changed; including my morals and ethics which were tested to the brink and did I pass? That is hard to say. One thing is for sure – my feelings today are not the same as they were back then. My empathy is almost gone or rather it is suppressed so I can survive.

I know it sounds cynical but nevertheless it is the truth, so why the hell try to cover it up?

It is actually fucking cold here. My body is almost numb. I have to find a jacket and some boots or this could end terribly badly. How the fuck did I lose my boots? Anyway, who the fuck cares.

There is nothing in the room where I am besides rubble, rebars and oceans of white concrete dust that came from the bullet holes as well as the collapsed wall that once separated the room into two. The wall in front of me, facing the street is scattered with holes and it's obvious it has looked like this for a while. My guess is that they were made by grenades during the civil war in the nineties, but honestly it doesn't really matter. What matters is, that it gives cover in case I should be attacked.

I'd better check if it is possible to get out of here because, if not, I have to create an alternative exit path. It is quiet everywhere. No voices or sounds from cars or tanks, no gunfire or grenade blasts. No signs of any kind of physical activity anywhere.

Maybe this is not such a bad place to wake up after all? But I can't stay here because it is neither safe nor very productive. From experience I know that I have to get going which is also what my intuition tells me and who does not listen to that? I know I do. Actually, it is the reason why I am still alive.

Fortunately, I have hidden OPUS. You probably think I am crazy but that is what I call my rifle. We have all given our rifles names. As a matter of fact, we were encouraged to do so on the first day in the military training camp for snipers. Some ended up calling their rifle their best friend, I wouldn't go that far, but without OPUS I am just a hunted animal and not the hunter.

I know that OPUS is here under some rubble behind me because I have my hand on its barrel. It is cold to touch but OPUS makes me feel warm ... safe.

That the name of my rifle became my call name is due to my first sergeant. For some reason he started calling me OPUS and it sort of stuck. In a way it was very convenient because in my line of work no one uses their birth name. It often happens that one's call name becomes such a big part of one's identity that the old name totally disappears. It is really not a bad thing when that happens especially since a lot of the things I have done in no way reflect on what one would expect a quiet catholic schoolgirl to do.

By now you are probably thinking ... 'Oh, no ... another warrior, a patriot, a fanatic that hides behind her identity while she runs around killing innocent people.' But that couldn't be further from the truth.

I am a professional soldier. A sniper who has been trained to kill people without asking any questions. I am for hire to the highest bidder, no matter which side or what conflict we are talking about. I am impartial and do not question the morality of eliminating the targets. I work systematically till the job is done and then I am gone. No sentimentality, no remorse. A clean *cut* and then I am off to the next assignment.

Maybe you are wondering how I can be so cold but it is just the way it is. No feelings, just a cross at the end of my telescopic sight. That is what my target is to me – a cross, a mark.

Is it terrifying to think like this? No – not for me. Practical is more like it and in more ways than one.

You see, it really doesn't interest me who or what the mark is or if the person has family, friends, children or if they will be missed after I have pulled the trigger. It doesn't matter to me. I don't care.

If you think that not caring is something that was gradually learned during my training, you are mistaken because it is not the case. It has always been there in some shape or form. The snipers who do not possess this trait do not last long in this business and often they end up as marks themselves. It is not unlikely that you will get an assignment to kill one of your own but in the last few years such assignments had been given and carried out by special units. I know of them but I am not in contact with them.

In fact, for the last year or so I haven't been in contact with that many soldiers. But I used to be. Some who I have worked with I wouldn't even call soldiers. They were more like warriors – warriors with a cause.

When I am working I am usually based in or near a military camp and my presence has often created rumours. The most experienced soldiers know to leave me alone and if we occasionally meet, they just look and nod, which I interpret as a kind of professional courtesy and recognition. But to be honest it doesn't really interest me. On the other hand the younger soldiers show everything from insecurity to cockiness towards me. I register their behaviour and file it under 'uninteresting'.

For the most part I keep to myself. I prefer it that way because then I don't have to get emotionally involved with anything or anyone. You see, it could cost me my life if I lose focus and nothing or no one is worth my own life. Because even if the life of others has no value to me, I do value my own: I actually value everything about it. From the wind in the trees to the dawning of the sun ... Even the cold concrete floor beneath me gives me a certain mental vitality.

It is nice that it is so quiet here. I have missed the silence.

The cuts on my arms and hands are only superficial and as I sit here yesterday's fight is coming to life in front of me like an old black and white movie. But there was no one on the set that screamed 'Cut' or 'Take two.' It was a quick fight which ended in me putting two bullets in the chest of my opponent. It was a little sloppy of me to use two shots but I was not sure that the first one was lethal so ...

Some would characterize what happened as an execution while others would describe it as a definitive elimination of a mark. To me it was only to make sure the mark stayed down permanently, in other words, a practical measure to secure my own survival.

I may not be absolutely sure what month we are in but I have no doubt that my latest assassination contract is up today so I have to find a place where I can download my next mission.

I receive my assignments through my email which I access by phone. Normally they contain a time, a date and a name but sometimes I only get a name and then I have to figure out the rest by myself. I don't mind. It makes for a nice variation in the job and I enjoy it.

The entire setup regarding all this is really quite simple because I have a fixed tariff. This makes it very easy for me because I then don't have to discuss money issues with the clients and when it comes to carrying out the job I decide how to do it. Every assignment has its own bank account and when a job is done and the money is paid into the account, I transfer the money to my own account and close the other account. This means that for every new assignment I get there is a new account number which I email to the client. It is simple, easy and hard to trace.

This year alone I have opened and closed nineteen accounts.

The concrete wall behind me gives me a comfortable support for my back. I think I could actually sleep for a few hours but it will have to wait because of the way the situation is right now.

Fuck, if you only knew ...

Chapter 2

Maybe I should have taken a different path and followed my dream of becoming an engineer. It would have been simple and it was originally my plan but first I had to do the mandatory military service. It was all so straight forward. Everything was planned, but then I got a rifle in my hands and something awoke in me.

Don't get me wrong. I didn't suddenly become insane or obsessed with guns and target shooting. No ... It was nothing like that. As a person, I have always been a bit competitive, although primarily directed towards myself. It may seem strange, but I was never interested in what others achieved as long as it did not have a direct impact on me which it rarely did.

So sending me to the military was just feeding my competitive gene and honestly, I loved it. I even got the opportunity to combine it with my inner perfectionism and it was probably one of the reasons I stayed in the army.

In the beginning, the training I received was very basic – both in terms of the physical part and in particular when it came to target practice. It did not take long before the significance of the weapon itself caught my interest and I found it quite rewarding how much I could optimize my kill situations by using the for me correct weapon in a given situation. The equipment that would be right for me was not necessarily right for another sniper.

The innate curiosity and competitive gene, which had been noted by my teachers at boarding school, were then developed by my military instructors who nurtured my ability to combine speed and accuracy when shooting.

As time passed, it appeared that I had a natural talent for single task solutions and since I could work in teams as well as an individual operator, I was a very attractive asset. As a sniper you usually work with a spotter who is a soldier whose job is to determine the outer factors such as wind conditions, distance to the target, height difference (if there is any) etc. Given this information the sniper should be able to hit the target perfectly which is what happens in most cases. There is a high level of trust between a sniper and the spotter as the sniper comes to depend on the spotter's information so they are often perceived as a unit and not two individual soldiers. I have worked with spotters especially in the beginning of my military training but it soon became obvious that I didn't really need a spotter and that I actually preferred to work on my own. I've never been used to depend on anybody but myself so to work so closely with somebody was strange to me and not something I cared for. Little did I know that this human trait would be seen as being perfect because a sniper that could work alone and without a spotter was in high demand. I guess being an introvert and a loner gave me that edge.

I was constantly highlighted by the instructors and have lost count of the times my solutions to tactical warfare were praised.

In the beginning, it was nice to get such recognition. I was respected by my fellow soldiers but I have never really understood it. To get respect for taking someone's life still sounds hollow to me.

Killing another human being was, in my eyes, made into something amazing and there were apparently no limits to one's hero status when taking a life. The military officers cheered when I passed them ... and in some cases they praised my deeds so profound that it made me uncomfortable because basically I saw no reason for it.

From my school days, I have learned that sometimes it pays to keep a straight face and that was – and still is – exactly what I do in such situations. I always let them shine in the sun of promotions and the press, while I slowly vanish into the shadows of the dazzled crowd of spectators.

It was really this glorification that made me make my decision of leaving the military with the intention of disappearing. Ideally, I would just have gone into oblivion, but one with my skills does not go unnoticed for long and I was quickly contacted by various agencies who wanted to sign me on.

I said, "No." But then I was approached by a foreign intelligence service and, yes, their offer sounded very interesting.

Forty-eight hours after receiving it I was on a plane with a new name and passport to a Middle Eastern country. And the application to the University? I burned it just before I boarded the plane.

For the next two years I found myself in another training camp – or so they called it. Personally, I thought it was the entrance to hell. The training I had received up till now was one that I later would refer to as basic. For most people it would have been the hardest experience in their military career but for me this was just the beginning.

I was trained in endurance such as how to perform my tasks despite sleep deprivation and lack of food and water. And not only did the tasks get more and more complicated. The extreme weather conditions they put me in also escalated.

I was also taught interrogation techniques. Yes, that's what they call it. Not torture, but interrogation techniques. I quickly learned that the line between those two words is subtle and varies greatly, depending on the person who interprets and executes them.

Being able to resist such interrogation was also part of my training. And in connection with this all female soldiers were advised to have their uterus removed. This was to minimize pain and risks of pregnancy after torture and rapes should they be caught. As one of the few, I said yes to it, and have I regretted my decision? That is a question that will never be answered.

In addition, I learned how to ignore the pain that was inflicted during interrogations. In fact I was eventually so resistant to it that I was the only soldier in many years who did not succumb during a nine-day session.

Another element of the education was close combat training. In principle, it could just as well have been called 'A thousand and one ways to kill a man when you are within a radius of three feet'.

I was taught to kill using knives, poles, ropes, strings and chains and I have lost count of how many ways there are to strangle a human being. As long as it happened swiftly and silently, we were told that crushing the larynx with either a kick or with a tool was the most efficient way. To be honest I didn't really expect that I would ever come to employ these techniques, but as time has passed, I must admit that I have used these techniques several times.

Then there were the various close combat skills. I learned Shidokan Muay Thai – a self-defence technique – karate for direct close combat and I topped it off with kickboxing, which was really just to build up raw strength.

Fuck, I could use some of that raw power now. My body needs to get in gear, but then on the other hand ... maybe I should take this little rest to plan my future action?

Being able to think strategically and creatively is a big part of being a good soldier and even though they give you the tools to do it, it mainly has to originate from within one's self.

Some of the assignments I was given meant that I had to think alternatively about the method that I had to use in order to complete my mission. And one of the factors I had to take into account was whether the job had to be executed with the least or the most collateral damage.

Where I felt most at home was during the weapons training. I obviously had a huge flair for it. Target shooting was my favourite discipline and I preferred targets that were moving. For me the challenge was not just to neutralize the mark but to do it with one clean and deadly shot. I trained relentlessly and in all kinds of weather conditions and with all sorts of different weapons. Pistol, semi-automatic and automatic weapons and of course rifle, which became my preferred choice. I started out with a simple model of an American brand, but later I got Russian, Swedish and Israeli models in my hands. A single German was also tried but it simply didn't appeal to me so it was discarded after the first test shooting.

There is no doubt that it was my abilities as a marksman and a fighter that made my superiors choose me to go on real missions even before my time was up in the training camp. Of course, I had to operate in a military unit and I'll never forget my first assignment. It was a mark that had to be eliminated when 'it' came out of a residential property. The task was straightforward and I solved it quickly, simply and without any problem. I was lying on top of a white concrete building – very similar to the one I am in now – with a distance of approximately three hundred and fifty metres to the mark and when 'it' came into view I quickly and efficiently found 'it' in my telescopic sight.

To this day I remember the mark's face and how my heart galloped away. All sounds were gone. Only the beat of my own pulse was present. In my telescopic sight, I quickly found the spot between the mark's eyes and when the red cross in the sight fell perfectly on it, I pressed the trigger. I saw the mark fall to the ground after which I ducked down and rolled over on my back. I lay there completely still and flat with OPUS across my chest and got my heart rate and my breathing under control. Quickly and efficiently I disassembled the rifle and sneaked down and out of the building. My get-away car had been parked nearby and just as unobtrusively as I had entered the area I disappeared out of it. It was all very simple, clean and straightforward.

The trip back went smoothly and immediately after arrival I was called in to my superior's office to give a report. After this I went back to my barracks where a couple of my team mates were inside the dormitory. They looked at me when I entered and one of them even tried to talk to me but I politely rejected him – of course. It was not because I did not want to talk to him, but because he presumably thought I had a need to verbalize my feelings after my mission. But what could I say?

That I had no feelings for what I had just done? No doubts. No regrets.

How would that have made me appear?

Because the truth was that I really didn't feel anything. I might as well just have gone to the grocery store for a bottle of milk.

That's how I felt. And no, it was not a psychological defence mechanism. It was my honest and sincere feelings. Or rather, some might say, lack of them. In fact, the worst was not to feel anything for my deed. That bothered me for quite some time.

At times I tried to force myself to display just some kind of emotion as

I'm probably not that different from so many others, but I cannot pretend to feel something that I don't. The falsehood and dishonesty that lie in being able to do so are not traits that appeal to me and I prefer to avoid such people. But why didn't I feel anything?

How could I take another person's life without any worries?

I knew that many of my fellow soldiers questioned what they were doing, but not me. I did not have any questions about it. For me it was perfectly okay and I saw it as 'just another day at the office'. You may think that it's cold and cynical to be that way, but that does not change the fact that it was the way that I felt.

After my first assignment my daily programme changed. The training in the camp was combined with the practical execution of tasks on real live missions hand-picked and suitable for someone with my skills. The first couple of assignments were 'assassin-kills' and I soon learned the different types. An assassination can be a toxic-kill, done with poison, either from a distance or by close contact with the mark, or it could be a regular execution by frontal, temporal or neck shots. I always operated within a team consisting of a spotter, a tactical combat soldier and at a minimum one combat soldier. It was seldom the same soldiers in any team and as a general rule we rarely knew our missions until a few hours before departure. Often we were briefed on the way to the mission which sometimes made it very difficult since we hardly had any opportunity to prepare. But even that was a learning curve.

When the twenty-four months were over, I was assigned to a special force unit for a year – primarily to gain experience – and then I was 'recruited' to an elite unit. This unit did not exist officially and neither did the missions we were given. We were three snipers and an eight-man military unit operating exclusively overseas. We got orders from Special Command OPS and the tasks varied a lot. It was everything from very specific target eliminations to massacres of entire sectors. And massacres they were. It was violent, bloody and definitely not pretty.

We killed both men and women. Sometimes by the dozen and often there were children among the dead. We did not distinguish. We just followed orders. No doubt such missions were the worst and so was the aftermath. It was custom that the soldiers who had participated in such missions gather afterwards. It was a form of therapy behind closed doors where only the initiates had access. Do not think it was a social therapy group where we talked about what we had just done. Nah ... We reacted by throwing things, smashing things, kicking objects, shouting, screaming and crying.

Often I was just a spectator to the outbursts and reactions of my team mates. I mostly kept to myself and performed my own rituals, which were to disassemble my rifle, clean it and reassemble it so that it was ready, after which I took a shower. Afterwards I always drank a cup of coffee and then went for a walk to process the events of the day. I always went on the walk alone. Those were my rituals – on the good days. The days when we had particularly gruesome massacres, those days my reaction pattern was very unpredictable and depended on how horrible our actions had been.

I especially remember one day when the whole team had been out on a slaughter and it had been ugly. Forty-two died including two children. We returned to the military camp and as always, went directly to our tent. There was no doubt that the rumours of what we had done that day had reached the camp for as we walked silently and vacantly all the soldiers we passed on our way looked at us with a mixture of horror and disgust. Suddenly one of the young officers said "Child murderers" as we passed him.

Normally none of the soldiers made comments when we returned from a mission because everyone knew that it was not the usual assignments that our team was given but this afternoon was different because of the comment.

Why I reacted the way I did, I have no idea. Maybe it was the team spirit that came over me or maybe it was simply the drop that made the cup overflow, but I turned around, went to the officer, drew my gun, unsecured it and put the barrel against his forehead. I stared into his eyes and could clearly see the panic in his and I could smell his fear. Yes ... fear actually has a smell. It is a very recognizable faint but rancid odour which in this case was also slowly mixed with the odour from urine. It was as if we were the only two people in the world. I could hear distant voices, but they did not reach me and therefore made no sense. They were almost like a buzz that slowly turned into a murmur. I remember feeling a hand on my shoulder and suddenly I was back in the moment.

The voice that spoke to me came from a team mate – in this case my commander. He spoke calmly, and slowly it dawned on me what I was doing. I secured the gun and lowered it without taking my eyes off the officer. And in what felt like slow motion I then turned to face the crowd. The sight that met me was amazing. My team mates had formed a semi-circle around us and stood with their weapons aiming at all the surrounding soldiers to keep them away. Without looking at my commander who stood next to me, I handed him my gun, but he refused to take it and instead I secured it and put it back in my belt.

* * *

After this episode no one dared approach us so, in my eyes, it had not been completely in vain. The rumour in the camp was that the officer I had had at gun-point had been so terrified that he had urinated on himself when

I stood there with the gun to his forehead. He later said he had never seen such cold and numb eyes as mine.

The episode was never reported and we did not see the officer again. Four days later we were off to the next camp and the next mission.

I was in a good team. We worked well together and respected each other's little quirks. We never talked to each other about the missions unless they had a military relevance but never about our feelings which suited me just fine. For basically, what was there to say?

After eighteen months, our unit was split up and I got the offer to join another team, but I declined. I had previously been contacted by a French security company and they had offered me a position where I would have a say in the missions I was assigned to. It suited me fine that I could put the slaughters behind me so once again I got a new name and passport.

The intervening period is probably the one where I healed the most, if you can talk about healing, because I worked a lot. The assignments required that I was alone and it was primarily assassination which suited me just fine.

It was not especially mentally hard on me and the fact that the missions required more preparation in the form of strategic planning before execution was perfect for me. I got to refresh that part of my training and focus on more than just carrying out orders. I flew around the world and each mission required a new passport and a new name.

Everything was always very organized. I had specific extraction points regarding my information and my weapons were always cleared for passing security in the airports. So, all in all, it was a time where I just had to focus on my assignments and, as such, I put the past at a distance.

Strange as it may sound it was actually in this job that I refined my ability to shut everything out. The little empathy I had left gradually disappeared and what was left was a resounding indifference to everything. I acted indifferently to anyone or anything and I loved the mental emptiness it gave me. It was extremely gratifying and liberating.

I had been in this job for three years and was very happy with it but then one day, in one of Bangkok's narrow alleys, I bumped into one of my former team mates. We got talking and it transpired that he knew of an elite unit that lacked someone like me and with my reputation I would fit into it perfectly.

The timing could not have been better because after operating solo for a very long period I had actually been thinking about a change and to return to working in a team seemed like the right thing to do. So, I did and that was how I came to know Jackson.

Chapter 3

It is natural to develop feelings for the teammates in one's unit. Being together twenty-four-seven makes it inevitable. The emotions definitely do not have to be of a romantic kind. In fact, it is something that we try to avoid as it can complicate our work as a team. It is okay to feel responsibility, loyalty and charity, but developing deeper loving relationships can make it difficult to carry out our missions. We are one hundred percent dependent on each other and must function as a unit both before, during and after our missions, so love affairs between the individual team members is something that can create insecurity amongst the others in the team, and it should preferably not happen. There must never be any doubts or unresolved issues when we are out on assignments, because there our lives depend on each other. Loyalty and trust are what make us all come home alive.

But despite that, it happens from time to time that we develop deeper feelings for each other – because after all, we are human and not cold and dead things – even though some perceive us as such.

I have had a relationship with someone from my team. His name was Jackson – JAC – and he was a six-foot-four, muscular, dark-haired, explosives expert. For a while we had been eyeing each other but, apart from short dialogues, we had never really talked. Once in a while we had sent a little smile to one another, but not one that could be interpreted as being flirtatious. It more reflected a mutual kindness and understanding for each other.

JAC was French-Canadian and maybe that was one of the reasons why our relationship developed into something more. I have always had a soft spot for the French ...

On the night before one of our missions our relationship changed into something more.

I was in the tent with my teammates Washington, Knox and Abe who were playing cards. Wizard – our commander – had gone to the mess and Private Snake was in the shower. I was lying on my bed with my eyes closed listening to an Arabic language course on my iPod. Years earlier, it had dawned on me that the best way I could prepare for a mission was by focusing on other things such as learning another language. In this way, not only did I get my mind off what was going to happen the next day, but the concentration that learning a new language requires sharpened my brain and thus also my senses.

With eyes closed and wearing headphones, I was completely lost in my own little world, and it was wise not to wake me up suddenly, because it could have fatal consequences. Once, it had resulted in a fight between me and a team member who had inadvertently touched me on my shoulder while I had mentally disappeared into my linguistic universe. It had not been his intention to trigger anything in me, but he did, and after that incident, everyone knew that you had to touch me on one of my shins if you wanted to get in contact with me when I was wearing headphones.

Therefore, it was also with the utmost caution that JAC that night touched me on my right shin. A little startled I sat up on my elbows and took off the headphones. My eyes caught his and, as there was nothing unusual to detect in his glance, I had no idea what he wanted. His voice was formal as he said he wanted to talk to me outside so, without any objection, I put my boots and jacket on and we left the tent.

The sun had just disappeared behind the far mountain tops and as we started strolling through the camp the darkness slowly descended. I have always liked the dusk. The way the darkness creeps up on the daylight, pushing it from all sides to finally devour it totally seems to me to be the right way to end a day. It is almost like the darkness takes away everything that has happened during the day and swallows it. And when one has digested it a new day dawns: Fresh, clean and untouched just waiting for another chapter of one's book of life to be written.

Whether JAC saw it the same way I doubted very much but then again, I didn't care if he did. As far as I was concerned we were going for a walk and I honestly thought to clarify some things regarding the pending mission, but no. For some reason he started talking about himself, about where he came from and how he ended up here.

JAC was born and raised in Montreal in a small middle-class family. He was the elder of two, and when he was sixteen, first his father died in a car accident and later the same year his little brother died. No one in the family had ever been religious before, but after his brother's death, his mother went to see a crisis psychologist and she suggested a group especially for women who had lost family members. There his mother met Elliene who was a member of a Christian sect and before long JAC's mother was deeply involved in the same church. Slowly JAC had witnessed how his mother was absorbed into the Christian faith community and despite the fact that he had tried to get her out of it, he had not succeeded.

The mother disappeared further and further into the congregation and with her, also all the money that the family had saved and, as well as that, all the accident insurance compensation that they had received after their father's death vanished.

Some of the money had been tied up in an education fund for JAC, but the mother had been the guardian of that fund, so when the time came that he could have had it paid, it too had disappeared. JAC had ultimately been left completely alone with no financial means and no family, and when his mother, at the request of the church pastor, chose to sell their house and move into a small apartment where there was no room for JAC, he had literally found himself without a roof over his head.

It was at that moment that his powerlessness had led to a fierce hatred, which he turned against the Christian faith. In JAC's eyes, it had robbed them of their money – which to some extent was true – and therefore he vehemently detested the whole congregation and the pastor. In time, however, he came to have a slightly different view of it, because where he initially blamed the church for exploiting his mother's grief and its lack of understanding, after losing half of his family, he slowly began to acknowledge that the church in some areas had actually given his mother a reason to live. For as JAC so philosophically said, he was apparently not reason enough for her to do so. Whether it was this realization that led him to hate God – and in general all kind of religions – I don't know – but there was no doubt that JAC had felt that God had taken everything from him: firstly his father and little brother, and then his mother.

He said he had suspected God of wanting him to join the sect as well because He had reckoned that JAC could not do without either a roof over his head or financial means, but that was God's mistake. JAC didn't need Him and to prove that he enlisted in the army for, as he had concluded, if it was souls God wanted, then he would provide them for Him. And provide them by the dozen.

Strange as it may seem, JAC's reason to kill had, for many years, been to avenge God, and in an extremely godforsaken environment as ours at times could be, it seemed completely absurd. But perhaps it wasn't. Perhaps it was one of the most plausible reasons for being here.

It was a completely unfamiliar situation for me to hear such personal things about a colleague, but I felt that it was important to him that I knew all this. Somehow, I knew that there was more to him than just being a soldier. Maybe by opening up and telling me about himself was his way of saying that he wanted to know more about me too and so I became more than just the team sniper to him. I have to admit that it was really very nice to get a new perspective on him and it did make our whole approach to each other a lot more personal in the following weeks and I actually enjoyed it.

As time passed, it became somewhat of a ritual that we, the evening before a mission, went for a walk. In the beginning, it was only him who spoke, but as time went on, it became a dialogue, and for the first time, I got to express some of the things I felt: Like being left at the boarding school at the age of six with nobody to fend for me but myself and how my family's lack of presence in my life slowly disassociated me from them to the point where there was no contact at all.

Not even during holidays did I see them. It was as if they had just placed me there and then vanished. My teachers tried to compensate for it by letting me spend my holidays with them but I never felt really welcome in their homes which is understandable enough. They didn't take me in because they wanted to but merely because they felt sorry for me. I was this poor 'leftover' kid that not even her parents wanted for the holidays. The first four years were awful. I was tossed around from one teacher's home to another and, for the introverted child that I was, this was pure hell. I was constantly introduced to new people and even though I wasn't expected to interact with them I still had to participate in whatever family gathering it was.

At times there were so many new faces that I felt like I couldn't breathe. It was as if with every hand shake and fake smile I put on I was slowly being suffocated. I don't think the teachers noticed it but if they did they didn't show it. I often heard them talking about me and phrases like "she was just left there" or "we felt sorry for her so that's why she is here" rang in my ears over and over again. So, in the midst of feeling alone and forgotten I build up a mental wall so I could distance myself from degrading and overbearing comments. But what I didn't know was that this would slowly become such an integrated part of me that I couldn't break it down. It was meant as a temporary shield that I could use when things became too much for me in social gatherings but what I had not imagined was that this shield in the end would become so strong – so impenetrable – that it would lock away most of my emotions. It was as if I during my school years I learned to perfect this ability and the inner strength it brought to me became my backbone in everything I did. I became so good at suppressing my emotions that in the end they just weren't there. And that is when my indifference started to surface.

My family didn't know all this and I doubt very much whether they would have cared. The last time I saw them was the day I went to the join the military. Although their 'goodbyes' were meant to be heart-warming I never really felt the heat. To me it was obvious that we had become strangers and it was somehow okay because one would not expect anything else. After years of them being absent from my life there was no reason for us to try to bond now. I was no longer their little girl but a full-grown woman in her late teens stepping out in the world on her own. It was too late to attempt to rebuild the family ties. In my eyes they had had their chance and blew it. Funnily enough I had no ill will towards them. We were family by name and not by actions. So, with a 'Bon Voyage' I waved goodbye to what was never really there and stepped into the military world without ever looking back.

Of course I did not tell JAC all of this but I told him enough for him to paint a picture and by doing so I felt to some degree like a little bit of my humanity had surfaced again. It was very strange for me, and when I said it to JAC, he just replied that he believed that it was exactly that – our humanity – that enabled us to survive the things we did. In fact, JAC had many philosophical considerations about why we did what we did and what it did to us.

On one of our walks he told me that a senior officer he had once had, managed to convince him to contact his mother to get some kind of closure. As it turned out it would be the last conversation they ever had because when JAC had told her about his 'vengeance in the name of God', she thanked him and praised him for his deeds. She believed that through his actions he had proved to her that he indeed had become God's instrument and, according to her, he could not have served the Divine any better. He was a true warrior of God because he killed for Him. JAC got so furious with his mother and the fact that she could interpret his actions in such a way, that he broke all contact with her – and from that day on, he did not kill to avenge himself on God, but for the sake of not letting God kill him. However, it was not because he went from hating God to fearing Him. Well, maybe in the beginning, but not anymore. Now he just wanted everyone including God to leave him alone so he could do what he did best, which for most part was to clear people out of his way.

As time went on, these evening conversations with JAC were something I looked forward to. Some days it was almost like a *quid pro quo.* A story for a story and honestly, I enjoyed it. There was nothing sexual about our friendship, but as time passed, we did develop feelings for each other. On some of our walks we went into the mess just to sit in one of the corners and talk. None of the other soldiers –from our own or other teams – interfered when they saw us together, and even though we never physically touched each other, we were completely under each other's skin.

One day when I returned from an assassination assignment, Snake picked me up at the helicopter landing pad. He asked me to hurry to the tent, because there was something wrong with JAC. I ran through the camp and into the tent, only to see JAC lying on his bed staring apathetically at the ceiling. Wizard and Washington stood next to his bed, trying to make contact with him, but no, he did not respond. Abe and Knox stood nearby and it was clear that they were perplexed by the whole situation.

I gave Snake OPUS and threw my backpack on the floor before I sat on JAC's bed. Quietly, I started talking to him while I gently let my hand run over his cheek. He turned his eyes to me, and suddenly he sat up and hugged me. He held me so unbelievably tight that for a brief moment I thought I was going to pass out, but I would not push him away. We sat like this for a long time just holding each other only accompanied by the team's worrying glances at us and an all-absorbing silence. After a while, I could feel JAC's hold loosening, and after he had let go completely, we just sat there looking at each other. Without taking my eyes off him, I asked the others to leave and without so much as a word they disappeared out of the tent. After they left, the tent went completely quiet – in fact the silence was much like the one I am experiencing now. Maybe that's why I remember it so clearly.

It had been nice to be alone with JAC and I think he felt the same way because he started to stroke my shoulder length dark hair very gently. We lay down quietly on his bed, and while we lay there, fully clothed and tightly wrapped around each other, we touched each other's hair and faces. I asked him what had happened, and he told it in short, gasping the words.

JAC and a small group of soldiers from the camp had been sent out to blow up a building. Whether the soldiers had known what kind of building it was, he didn't know, but the fact was that nobody had told him that it was a school that he had to level to the ground. And that was not all. It had to take place when it was full of students. That day he had killed four hundred and twenty-seven children and their teachers. The teachers were really irrelevant, but the kids ....

As he recalled, tears rolled down his cheeks. The children had been blown to pieces and there had been remains everywhere. After the blast from the bomb and the collapse of the building, one could hear children screaming, but fortunately they had quickly ceased.

But the colour ... the colour of the children's red blood on the remains of the shattered white concrete walls ... it had almost been the worst. He buried his face in my sand-coloured camouflage jacket while clinging to me with me stroking his hair and back. We lay like this until he fell asleep.

When I was sure he was fast asleep, I carefully got up and almost tip-toed outside. The team was sitting in front of the tent smoking and drinking Coca Cola, but there was no real conversation going on between them. I looked over at Snake and reached for OPUS. A little dejected, I started walking around in front of the tent with my rifle in my hands. To everyone else this must have looked stupid, me pacing back and forth, but the truth was that I was the only one who knew why JAC reacted the way he did. It was not just because he had killed four hundred and twenty-seven kids. No. It was because his brother had been killed in a school shooting which JAC had witnessed. His brother was just thirteen-years-old and had been shot while playing basketball in the schoolyard during a break. JAC stood twenty metres from him and had seen him fall to the ground, but, despite the fact that he had rushed to him and tried to save him, he died in his arms before the ambulance arrived.

JAC had told me this in the deepest confidence on one of our evening walks and, although it would have shed light on his reaction today if the others in the team had known, I had no intention of telling them. That would be discrediting his and my relationship of trust, and that was the last thing I wanted to do. But deep inside me a small fear appeared: what might this mission have done to JAC? Would it have rekindled feelings of guilt and inadequacy; I had no doubt it would. JAC was strong – and not just physically – but he was still human and a mind can only take so much before it breaks.

After pacing around a bit, I finally sat down next to the others. They did not say anything, but their eyes told me that they were deeply moved by the situation. JAC was, in their eyes, one of the strongest and therefore the one they least expected to break. My only answer to this was that he was not broken. He just needed to rest a bit and then he would be back again. Or so I hoped.

That night I swapped beds with Abe so I could sleep next to JAC. When exactly he woke up that night I don't know, but I was awakened by him whispering in a gentle voice 'Thank you' in my ear. I turned around in my bed to look at him, but I was by no means prepared for the warm and loving smile that greeted me. There was no doubt that there was something deeper than just gratitude in it but it did not bother me.

I got up, slipped into a t-shirt, some pants and my boots and together we went outside in the almost tropical night. The camp was pretty lit up so we went somewhere a little more secluded and ended up crawling into the back of a parked truck. Had it been daylight we would just have found some rocks or even the bare ground to sit on but come darkness scorpions and other creatures could be found on these surfaces and neither of us was in the mood for that. Nor was the mess tent an option as it was obvious to me that the conversation we were about to have was to be conducted solely between him and me. So there we sat in the semi darkness on the seats in the back of the truck staring at each other.

I wasn't prepared for the first kiss but it was nice, gentle and for some reason I was surprised how soft his lips were. The kiss soon became deeper and then it was as if a wild greedy demon possessed us. The speed in which we tore the clothes off each other was unbelievable and within seconds JAC was inside me. There was no foreplay just raw sex and neither of us took the other one's needs into consideration. We fucked to satisfy ourselves and not each other and it was strangely liberating for the both of us. We did cuddle afterwards. When we were done, we put the remains of our clothes on and the t-shirts that had been torn into shreds we dumped in a rubbish bin on our way back to the tent. We didn't hold hands. We didn't even touch each other. But we did send some quirky smiles to each other that said that this was not the last time we would do this.

Whether the others in the team knew that JAC and I were involved, I do not know, but they had no doubt that we had a special bond. JAC and I never shared a bed in the tent nor did we display our feelings towards each other when others were nearby and even though we occasionally touched each other briefly when passing, it didn't make anyone suspicious. We used our evening walks to have sex and it didn't seem that anyone in the team found it strange that we at times were gone for hours. It gradually became more the rule than the exception that we disappeared every night for a long time.

One day our team was enriched with a new member. It was a young guy, American with a square built muscular body. His hair was dark blond, short but not army-cut, above a round face with broad smiling lips and hazel brown eyes. Apparently, he was a close combat expert and from the start it was clear that he had not been part of a special unit before. He was used to the common tone that prevailed in the military camps and he talked incessantly and was actually very noisy, which I found insanely annoying. So to avoid a possible confrontation with him, I mentally shut him out, and continued my daily routines as usual. The others in the team had noticed my reaction to him, and seemed to accept it, so they took care of him and left me to my own devices.

One day, however, his open and brashness took over a bit as he came to my bed with a crooked smile on his face while I sat and fine-tuned OPUS.

"So ... Do you want some young meat?" he asked and cupped his crotch.

There was immediately total silence in the tent and everyone's eyes were on us. My eyes however did not deviate from OPUS and without commenting on what he had just said I continued working on it. When he did not get a response from me, he kicked my bed.

"Hello, babe?" he yelled, "Can't you answer?"

The answer came from behind as JAC put his hunting knife to his throat and whispered something to him. Then JAC released his grip and the guy withdrew. JAC and I gazed at each other and after giving me a little nod he went back to his bed. No one in the tent had said anything and a few minutes later it was as if the situation had never occurred.

But later that evening, the guy came into the tent and his gaze showed a mixture of fear and nervousness. He came straight to me, while I was sitting and playing chess with Abe, and without saying anything, he stood next to us and just stared at me. It was clear that he was afraid to disturb anyone and in particular me. Eventually I looked up at him and signalled if he wanted to say anything.

"I'm sorry for what I did earlier today. I had no idea you were OPUS," he said quietly and with a softness to his voice that was nothing like the cockiness he had displayed earlier.

I didn't comment on it, but just smiled at him and then returned to the game. At the same time JAC came into the tent and purposefully he walked towards me. The look JAC sent the guy was unmistakable. It said 'BEWARE' and in order not to escalate a potential conflict between them, I let my king fall on the board. The game was over – in more ways than one. Quietly I got up and signalled to the young guy that he could take my seat and then I went outside where I waited. As expected, JAC followed shortly after and together we left for our evening stroll.

JAC later told me that the others in the team had told the new guy what I had been through to be qualified to be on the team, and that had made a huge impression on him, but it was only when they had mentioned my name that he had become silent and had hurried inside to apologize. Apparently, I had a reputation of being unbelievably controlled and emotionally cold without any ability to show empathy and compassion, so if you were so unlucky to have me as an enemy, you had as good as secured a one-way ticket out of this world.

We laughed a lot about it that night but deep inside me it had touched something. It didn't matter that they called me a cold-hearted bitch but the inability to show empathy and compassion part was not true. I did have empathy just not when it came to my mark. Otherwise I had plenty of it. And compassion? I had ton of compassion especially for people I knew and fellow soldiers. If I didn't have compassion I couldn't do my job. Every time I went on a mission, every time I locked and loaded and was ready to go to war, every time I pulled the trigger I showed compassion. It might sound hollow but I didn't necessarily have to show empathy to feel compassion. I could be emotionally detached from a problem and still care about it. But not many cared or wanted to understand this and therefore it was easier to label me as they did.

Regarding the new guy there is no doubt that everyone on the team made a strenuous effort to get him to loosen up, for he had an immense fear of me. It was actually quite uncomfortable, for he hardly dared to be near me and especially not if we were alone.

However this all changed one scorching afternoon, when the military camp we were in was subjected to a violent attack. JAC, Wizard and Snake were on a mission outside the camp, but me, the young guy – whom we had christened, The Kid – and Knox, Abe and Washington were at home. Most of the morning had been spent lifting weights in the camp's outdoor gym, and as usual, Knox and I had been sparring partners. Knox was a quiet guy with short dark hair almost black and greyish coloured eyes. He was one point eight two metres tall and had it not been for his sharp chiselled jaw line he would have been an average looking guy. He came from the US and was originally trained in the US Special Forces. I had always liked him, especially because there was an inner calmness about him, which he seemed to pass on to the people who were in his vicinity and that applied a lot to me. Knox and I had a lot in common. We both meditated and read many books, although the genres were very different. Knox was into Sci-fi and Fantasy, whereas I've always had a penchant for the old classics like Homer's Odyssey and La Fontaine.

This day, however, turned out not to be 'a book day', because around three p.m., all hell broke loose.

We were sitting drinking coffee inside our tent when the first blasts from the mortar shells sounded. As a completely natural reflex, we grabbed our loaded weapons and ran outside. It was like a sandstorm out there except the sand had been replaced with bullets and grenades, which literally rained down on us. Total chaos reigned with soldiers from the camp running around like headless chickens trying to spot and eliminate the enemy and, in my opinion, it appeared that there were no orders or commands behind their radical and undisciplined behaviour. It seemed like total confusion and anarchy had taken over.

We, of course, were under a different order of command so didn't have to wait for explicit instructions from anyone and could therefore assess the situation and act accordingly without informing anyone of our plans, which is what we did. Soon after the attack began I found myself behind a wall of sandbags with The Kid in the southern end of the camp. From this position we shot numerous enemy soldiers. However several of them managed to dodge our rain of bullets and suddenly they were all over us.

I threw OPUS next to the sandbags so it was shielded from the enemy. It was useless in this kind of fighting. I reached for my Glock instead. But it was too late. They were everywhere. So we fought with our bare fists. And fight we did – like crazy. I had pulled my knife. The Kid had done the same, but he was faster and better with it than I was. The efficiency with which he sliced the opponents was admirable. And the precision? I was amazed. At one point I was fighting an enemy soldier and The Kid saw I was in trouble. The guy was bigger and faster than me and worse ... he was getting the upper hand. The attack from The Kid came from behind and with such a speed that I didn't even see him cut the guy's throat. Suddenly there was just blood gushing out of him and as a ragdoll he fell to the ground. Limp and lifeless. For a fraction of a second I looked at The Kid. But he had already plunged his knife into another soldier's kidney. The viciously contorted expression on his face as he turned the blade in the guy and sliced him open fed me with so much energy. This guy was a killing machine. Behind his young and innocent face was a darkness of violence. And from the looks of it God have mercy on the ones that encountered it.

A fist from an enemy soldier hit my jaw but I didn't fold. It was as if some of The Kid's energy had sparked my own so in three punches the guy was on the ground and had a bullet in his brain. A bullet from my Glock. With the gun in my hand, I started killing every single enemy soldier I came across. At one point I killed a soldier who was fighting The Kid. The shot had half his head explode and the impact made skull fragments and brain mass hit The Kid's face in a blood splatter. It didn't seem to bother him. He just wiped it off continued fighting the next guy in line.

That day I killed sixteen: nine with Opus, the rest in close combat.

* * *

Later that evening, after the attack had ended and when the camp slowly was returning to normal, The Kid came up to me while I was sitting in the mess eating. He sat across from me and we glanced briefly at each other before he quickly turned his eyes to my tray where my food was. Actually, I did not have any desire to talk, but what we had experienced together today could be the icebreaker between us so ...

The Kid started by saying that he was glad I was on his side and that he hoped I would consider him to be a friend. My eyes were still fixed on him as I calmly put down my fork before answering that I would fight for everyone in the team, but that I would not be his friend. Maybe it was cold and inconsiderate of me to say, because basically he just tried to be nice. But the truth was that I didn't want to be anyone's friend and the reason was solely that then it was harder to deal with when a mission cost a team member's life because once in a while, they did.

Throughout my career, I have lost quite a few teammates, but it was never something that had made me consider quitting. As harsh as it may sound, you can actually get used to losing. The first step is to accept the fact that it can happen. When it has a lot of my teammates needed to talk about it, but I would rather be by myself and deal with it my own way. Grieve my own way.

* * *

Maybe this dates back to my time at boarding school, where my parents enrolled me in at the age of six and thus 'left' me to myself. Whether I saw it as a betrayal at the time, I do not know, but one thing is for sure, I quickly learned how to solve my problems by myself, because no one did it for me. However, it never bothered me to deal with things by myself, rather the opposite. Unfortunately, this attitude did not expand my social relationships with my peers. In fact as time went on, I felt best if I could just be the observer and only step in with a solution to a problem when required. To some extinct I still do this, although the roads to the solutions are often paved with bodies and not debate points in discussion groups.

Of course, I had thoughts on how I would react if JAC suddenly did not come home from a mission alive, but I had deliberately not thought it through, because I couldn't. It hurt too much.

So, to avoid any future pain, I declined The Kid's friendship request. It might have seemed a little cold, but it was the best thing to do for the both of us and in due time it was my hope that he would be able to see that too. In return, I assured him that I would always be there for him as a teammate on the missions, but that was all I could give him.

We sat quietly and ate and then he asked the question that I had dreaded and hoped would never come up, namely whether JAC and I had something going on!

I had no idea how to answer. One thing was for sure – I could not tell him the truth. It was too risky for everyone, so I just got up, took my tray and left. The question was never put forward again.

When JAC and the others returned later that evening, we all went to one of the large bonfires that the other soldiers in the camp lit each night. Usually we did not socialize with them as we kept to ourselves, but it had been a special day so this evening we decided to. It was very nice, and as we sat there by the fire talking, laughing and joking, for most of them it was the first impression they got of me as being more than just an ice-cold sniper.

I was sitting between JAC and one of the combat engineers who was pretty entertaining. However he must have misinterpreted my signals because all of a sudden, he turned to me and kissed me. My reaction to it came swiftly as I grabbed his neck and in a fraction of a second he flew through the air in the direction of the bonfire. The second he hit the ground, I stood over him, ready to hit him, but JAC shouted at me. The laughter and small talk around us stopped and no one moved or said anything. The sapper lay on his back, looking up at me in horror. I wasn't going to hurt him. Maybe teach him a lesson about personal boundaries but that was about the height of it.

However, Wizard, who had been sitting on the opposite side of the bonfire all evening, got up and walked over to us. He and JAC had known each other for a long time and there was no doubt that they were extremely good friends. In fact I think, besides me, Wizard was the one that knew JAC best. Whether they talked about close personal things I don't know but they certainly had a deep understanding and inside knowledge of one another. And it was not just on the battlefield.

Of the two Wizard was definitely the leader but JAC was his wingman and the bond they had was built on a profound mutual trust and respect. Physically they were pretty much alike except JAC was taller than Wizard and strength wise I would put them in the same category. But that is where the similarities ended. Where JAC could come across as very polished and definitely 'army-made' Wizard was more like a diamond in the rough. Without a doubt he was military trained but what military that was I was not sure about. I had had a lot of superiors in my time but not one like Wizard. Because where the others had leadership training Wizard was a born leader. I can't put my finger on what he did differently but he somehow lifted our unit to a whole other level.

Most people in the camp were scared of him but I found him intriguing and seeing him in battle, his ruthlessness and uncompromising approach to problem solving, just made me respect him even more. Whatever lay underneath Wizard's otherwise so calm and collected attitude I was not sure but I had this feeling that if I started to scratch his surface I would not have liked what I would have found. A man who could lead soldiers like he did and kill in the most horrible ways was not to be fucked with.

* * *

The first clue I got that JAC was standing right behind me that night by the bonfire was the shadow he cast on the sand. He wasn't there to help me, of that I was certain, but rather to help the sapper.

"Don't," he said very softly to me. Then he took a step towards me. "Let me."

I took a deep breath before I stepped aside and it was just now I saw that Wizard was standing right next to JAC. As JAC moved in on the sapper Wizard grabbed his arm.

"No," he said calmly, awaiting JAC's response.

JAC hesitated for a moment and then he suddenly bent down and whispered something in the engineer's ear. The sapper's eyes flickered between me and JAC.

"I'm sorry," he muttered, and even though I had a hard time believing it, his words were obviously enough for JAC, because he moved away and let

Wizard take over. What happened to the combat engineer after that, I don't know and I really don't care, but if I read Wizard correctly, the sapper would not go unpunished for his action, which usually meant a lot of violence and blood in the process.

There was no reason for JAC and me to stay so we quietly started walking away from the bonfire. When we had distanced ourselves from the others, I asked JAC what he had said to the combat engineer and, without looking at me, he replied that he had threatened to kill him if he touched me again. Our eyes met and I could see that it was not an empty threat, for JAC's eyes were completely black and without emotion.

It was really weird because he had just expressed feelings towards me and yet he seemed untouched by it. But that was exactly how I preferred it – and preferred him. No questions. No lingering. Just the honest truth.

Suddenly I felt his arm around my shoulders. For him it was a small gesture, but for me it was infinitely more and I was conflicted about how I should react. I really wanted to put my arm around his waist, but I didn't know if that would be a good idea. Not because we thereby would signal that there was something between us – something more than us just being teammates – but because I would admit to myself that I had feelings for JAC. I knew deep down that I had, but I was not sure that mine were the same as his and until I knew, there was no need to display them in public. In some ways his action had forced me to address the issue of him and me and I was not sure I was ready for that.

We went into our tent and it was only when we got to my bed that JAC let go of his grip. I looked at him, but when he wanted to kiss me, I refused. I wanted to make sure we were on the same page before we continued but he looked at me smiling and said I should relax, and besides, Wizard knew that we were more than just friends. His statement was said as a casual remark and made me gape for a few seconds as if I needed to process what I had just heard.

The only way I can describe what happened next is that I exploded in rage and for the next half hour we quarrelled fiercely. It was only when Wizard entered that we stopped. With his hands in his pockets JAC walked towards the door and when he passed Wizard, they briefly looked at each other. Then JAC left and I was alone with Wizard.

"Whatever the hell is going on between you two, whether it's superficial or deeper, keep it up," he said with his eyes focused hard on me, "because lately you have both been easier to be around." Without his eyes softening he put his hands on his hips and continued, "Normally I don't meddle, but because it benefits the team that you two are together – whatever together is – I do. So … get your ass outside so you can kiss and make up and we all can move on."

It was obvious that the situation irritated him. He usually did not like to get involved in such things, but the team had to function, so as the leader he felt obligated to have this conversation. Even though I wanted to, it was not the time to argue with him and it would have been wrong. I felt like a teenager who had been caught red-handed and since I didn't have any control over the situation anyway, I followed his order and left the tent slightly frustrated, knowing that Wizard was right.

Outside I found JAC smoking a cigarette. Normally he only smoked after a mission or when he was stressed, so it was obvious which category this cigarette fell into. After a couple of deep breaths, I went to him and our eyes met. There was no doubt he was surprised when I out of the blue gently kissed him; because not only did I display emotion, but I did it in public and without thinking of the consequences.

After the kiss we looked at each other and it was as if I calmed down when I saw his black eyes. I knew them and what they represented and it made me feel safe. Without any objections I let him grab my neck and pull me in to him and the kiss that followed was so long and aggressive that I forgot everything around me. This was so unlike me, because I never completely indulged, just like I never really let go of my control. But right there, I knew JAC had it, and with Wizard inside the tent I for the first time felt one hundred per cent safe, so I let go.

Our kiss lasted until Wizard appeared in the doorway. Without looking at us he said that we had the tent to ourselves for the next two hours and then he just left.

As if his words were our queue JAC pulled me into the tent and to his bed and we ripped the clothes off each other and threw ourselves on it. Again our sex was hard, merciless and with no thought of anything else but our individual satisfaction. But for the first time, it was also legitimate, and that made it somehow both wilder and more intense. For the first time we lay in each other's arms after we were done and it was somehow nice without being too over-cuddly.

When JAC had fallen asleep, I got up, put on my clothes and went outside. Out there, I saw Wizard sitting twenty metres away and with him were Snake and Washington. They were obviously having a major discussion, but it did not stop me from walking over and joining them. Snake handed me his pack of cigarettes and I took one and lit it. It was several years since I had smoked and it was a nice feeling – even though I got a little dizzy. I took a drag and as the discussion slowly died out, their eyes fell on me. I asked them if we were okay and they nodded.

"Everything is okay," Wizard replied while getting up and brushing off sand from his light-coloured khaki-pants. Washington, a medium sized Afro-American combat soldier with huge biceps and a broad and warm smile, looked down at the ground and said that they had had their suspicions about me and JAC for a long time. Snake, who was somehow Washington's total opposite with his blond hair, pale skin and small blue piercing eyes began to giggle.

"The only reason no one has said anything is because it has not affected the team or the missions and that is how it will continue." Wizard could say things in an unbelievably cold and commanding way and this was one of those times. I nodded and assured him that nothing had changed. Nothing at all.

"And ... no display of feelings between you two in public," he said harshly pointing at me and then the tent where JAC was still sleeping. Of course I promised him that that would never happen and to be honest I wasn't really interested in it myself. I think Wizard knew that but he just patted me on the shoulder before he went into the tent.

It was a relief for me that the others knew about me and JAC because lately I had felt that sneaking around behind their backs was not okay. As a team we should not have such secrets from each other. We were a small tight unit and stuff like this should be out in the open. And now it was.

As I stood there watching Wizard disappear, Washington came up with a clever remark about all this and just to show him that nothing had changed, I stubbed out my cigarette on his bare shoulder. As expected, it made him and Snake laugh and when the laughter had subsided, he proclaimed that I was definitely still the same and thanked me for it.

I didn't show it, but I was unbelievably glad that the guys took it the way they did. Snake, who had been completely convulsed with laughter over my reaction to Washington's remark, lay down on his back and chuckled. And that is when I heard the click. Snake heard it too and he immediately froze and stopped giggling. Washington didn't hear it so I shouted to him to stop laughing and when it dawned on him what had happened he almost catapulted up.

"Get JAC and Wizard," I shouted as I sat down next to Snake, who was lying completely still on the bare sand. I spoke quietly to him to ease his tension and as the words flew from my mouth, I could hear JAC and Wizard running towards us. With a few metres between us they stopped and after a quick assessment of the situation Wizard ordered JAC to run down to the big bonfire where a couple of soldiers still were sitting. With JAC gone Wizard sat down next to me and took over the conversation with Snake. But not for long as within a minute, Snake was surrounded by the professional de-mining boys and their gear. As expected, they ordered everyone away from the area within a radius of fifty metres so several of the nearby tents were cleared and everyone pulled away.

Time went by at an awfully slow pace and at the same time the minutes galloped away. Despite the fact that we had been ordered away, the whole team, except for Wizard, who was still sitting next to Snake, stood together at the safe distance waiting for the final verdict from the combat engineers. When Wizard finally approached us, it was only to confirm what we already suspected – that Snake was lying with his head on a mine, which for some inexplicable reason had been overlooked by the camp's sweeper team on their daily clearing round.

None of us said anything, but we had our fears, and it was as if everyone was holding their breath when one of the sappers shortly after came over to Wizard. They exchanged a few words, after which Wizard pulled us aside. The message was as expected. The sappers could not remove the landmine and if Snake made as much as a tiny move with his head, he would set it off. So basically, it was just a matter of time before Snake would get his head blown off but there actually was a solution to the problem and it was Snake's own idea. Everyone had to be pulled back to a safe distance and then I had to shoot him with OPUS from one of the helicopters. Snake had insisted that it should be me, because then he knew it was going to be swift and precise. He knew my accuracy and had always had one hundred percent confidence in me. Everybody starred at me including the sapper but the answer for me was easy.

"Can you do it?" Wizard asked with a serious look upon his face and I nodded. Of course I could. What the hell did he think? That I would say no to fulfilling a teammate's last wish? Why would I – to protect myself? If so that would be the ultimate selfishness. Snake had asked me for a favour – the first and last – and of course I would honour him by doing it.

But I had one request and that was to be allowed to go over to Snake and talk to him before I took off. Wizard of course allowed me to do that and in the conversation that followed with Snake, he confirmed that he wanted it to be me who did it. We then talked briefly about how it should happen and as we did I remember thinking how incredibly brave he was. There was neither fear in his voice nor any tears in his eyes. It was as if he had accepted the situation and that this was how it was going to end for him.

I asked him if he wanted to talk to Wizard but he said no. He wanted his last words to be with Washington, which was no surprise as they were very good friends, so I called him over and when he was there I ran to the tent.

JAC, who had already been inside to pick up OPUS for me, was standing at the entrance with it in his hands when I got there. He handed me the rifle and I hurried down to the other end of the camp, where the spinning rotors of the waiting helicopter indicated it was ready for take-off. I jumped in and we took off. We circled over the camp a few times and as the helicopter's searchlight aimed at Snake on the ground and I found him in the scope. Washington had left Snake's side no doubt on Snake's order so it was just him and me now. Snake looked up at me and as agreed I waited until he closed his eyes to pull the trigger. It seemed like an eternity before he did, but I didn't mind. Guess we all want to live for as long as possible. When his eyelids finally covered his eyes, I aimed at him.

"Bye, Snake. May God have mercy on you," I said quietly and fired the shot. It was perfectly executed and a few seconds later the mine exploded.

The helicopter flew one round before landing and as I jumped out of it and touched ground, I was surprised to see that both JAC and Wizard were waiting for me at the landing site. We didn't say anything to each other as we walked through the camp and down to the mess tent where the rest of the team was waiting for us inside. I don't know why Wizard and JAC felt they had to take care of me and honestly, they didn't need to. Yes, I had just killed a team member, but what was there to worry about? That I would kill another? If that was the case, they could relax. My quota for killing team members and other soldiers for that matter had been reached for the day. In hindsight, it was probably a good idea they escorted me, because they did not know how I would react both in relation to any well-meaning comments that may come from others, as well as my own reaction to what I had just done.

To be honest I really didn't need their presence at that moment. I just wanted to be alone. Not because I had to process what had just happened, I had already done that and 'boxed' it, but because I had no idea how they would perceive me if I told them what I really felt – which was nothing – nothing at all. When I jumped into the helicopter, Snake was nothing but a mark to me. The difference in the way I killed him to how I normally eliminated my mark was that I knew his last wish and honoured him by fulfilling it. Why I had asked God to take care of him before I pulled the trigger I do not know but somehow it felt like the right thing to do. A last minute of absolution, I guess. Other than that, there really was no difference to any other kill.

No doubt that it was Snake I saw when I looked through my sight, but I felt nothing. No sorrow or sadness. No anger or feeling of revenge towards the enemy soldiers that must have placed the bomb. Nothing. It was like being on a mission. It was impersonal. A job that had to be done quickly and, in this case, as painlessly for Snake as possible.

In fact, it scared me that I felt nothing for him. Was I even able to feel anything for anyone when not even this could do it? It was not because I didn't know Snake. We had been on countless missions together and had saved each other many times from enemy fire. Maybe that's why I asked God to forgive him for his deeds as he had helped and been there for me so I survived? To give him a plus in his life account? Only God and Snake would know how many minuses he had there.

Maybe it was to make sure that if there was something good afterwards, he would now at least get a chance to be there. It was really crazy, because I had never thought like this before – but then again, I had never killed a team member before. It was very uncomfortable to have to deal with these things, because I had never seen myself as a believer, but unfortunately I had to admit that when the time came, I was. But being a believer and then doing what I did wasn't it a bit hypocritical?

"Sorry God, but I'm just filling up Heaven for you and by the way I hope for your forgiveness?" Fuck, that was sick. And if there was a Heaven, then there was also a Hell, or there should be ... maybe the Earth was Hell? Could it be the case that if we behaved 'nicely' while living in hell and repented properly, we would go to Heaven when it was all over? And what if we did not? What if we were rejected at the gate? Where were we sent then? Back to Earth? Maybe ... the thought was less scary than the mental numbness I felt at the time.

Our team had, as usual, hunkered down at a table at the very back of the mess and as Wizard, JAC and I walked through, a wave of silence followed us. Wizard was in front of me and JAC behind me and when we got to our table, I quietly put OPUS on it and sat down. Washington pushed a cup of coffee over to me and I took a sip. Why JAC was standing behind me, I had no idea, but it made me feel uncomfortable, so I asked him to sit down. Knox, who was sitting next to me, moved so there was room for JAC. The Kid was sitting on my other side and I'm sure it was of an honest and genuine concern for me when he put his hand on mine and asked if I was okay. I removed my hand and leaned over towards JAC, who automatically put his arm around my shoulders. To be honest, I was not in the mood for that either so I wriggled myself calmly free of his hold. I replied to The Kid that I was okay and just wanted to sit for a while in silence and everyone respected it. But what they didn't know was that I wasn't thinking about my deed and how I had been able to do it. Nor did I grieve for Snake. What was going through my head was how killing Snake could not mean more to me than it did.

Had I really become so inhuman that I was nothing more than a robot carrying out orders? Where was my soul? Did I have one at all? A huge lump grew in my chest and I suddenly had shortness of breath. JAC managed to turn me around and pressed my head down between my legs while I desperately gasped for air. Knox called out for a doctor and seconds later one stood by my side. I tried to gesture that he should go away, but before I could ward it off, I was given an injection and slowly calmed down. JAC got me up on my feet but they collapsed under me due to the medicine so he carried me out of the mess.

The next thing I remember is that I woke up in the infirmary and, despite the doctor's protests, I put on my clothes and left. It was still dark outside and I had no idea where my team was. Where we had had our tent, there was now a crater after the explosion, so I walked around between the other tents and searched. I had to find JAC. He had OPUS and I had to have OPUS. I could feel my heart pounding. I had to find OPUS. I started jogging and suddenly I saw them. They were all sitting around a small bonfire and the moment JAC spotted me, he got up and came to me.

"Do you have OPUS?" I asked him with desperation in my voice and he nodded while he looked anxiously at me and then everything went black. When I woke up daylight was breaking. JAC had put me in his sleeping bag and he was sitting next to it and was awake. The rest of the team slept. We all lay around the fire, whose scent and crackle brought to mind a camping trip.

A couple of soldiers from the camp were building a shelter for us behind where we were sitting and I could hear they were working hard. As I sat up JAC turned his head towards me and for the first time I had an unwavering desire to just disappear in his arms and feel his calm breathing and rhythmic heartbeat. Somehow, I think he could sense my thoughts.

"Come here," he said, opening his jacket towards me and I crawled in to him. He put his arm around me and ran his fingers through my hair.

I felt so insanely safe with him and yet I felt out of this world. To ground myself I drilled my nails into his thighs but he didn't say anything. He just bent his head down and kissed me very gently.

"Am I a monster?" I whispered to him.

"No," he replied calmly, but then again he did not know the truth: I did not regret Snake. JAC mumbled something about it being inconceivable that I had been able to do what I did and that it was one of the most humane deeds he had ever witnessed, but what a damned nonsensical thing to say. For the truth was that there was nothing humane about it and that it was done without emotion or hesitation. I had not seen Snake as Snake, but as a mark, for even though I knew Snake, in the final minutes he had had the same status for me as a random target.

But what the hell were they expecting from me? I had been selected on the basis that I could tackle such situations without becoming emotionally involved, and I had been trained to act mechanically and without personal involvement as a basis for what I did.

Suddenly I felt JAC's other arm around me and in a soft voice he whispered in my ear that I was in shock and that I did not need to put up a façade. Not to him. But what he didn't know was that it was not a façade. It was me!

* * *

The next day we were sent on a new mission, but the group had become different after Snake's death, and as time went on, it became more and more clear that we were not functioning optimally. Maybe it was because it was someone from the team who shot Snake – by someone I mean me – I don't know – but it all ended the day Wizard told me that I had been assigned to go to Central America. He was serious when he said it and we both knew it was not a dream job that was waiting for me over there. JAC was on a mission and since Wizard had been told that I was to leave immediately, I didn't get to say goodbye to either JAC, Knox or The Kid. I packed my things and put a note with a short message on JAC's bed. Then I took my bag and OPUS and said goodbye to the others. It was all very sudden and I had a strange and not very good feeling of what was waiting for me, and it did not diminish when the helicopter lifted off.

Central America usually meant guerrilla warfare and drugs, and if you were a female soldier, it was not a place you wanted to be sent to. I had never been there, and had never really had the intention of going there, but it was all a bit late now. As I was sitting on the commercial flight, I suddenly began to miss JAC. It was a completely unfamiliar feeling for me to miss someone, but it was good because it showed me that I could feel. I looked out of the window and smiled in relief. JAC had made me feel – and I didn't even get to say goodbye.

Chapter 4

Central America was no bed of roses. If there was any good thing to be said about being there it was that I only had solo assignments. I stayed in small lousy hotels that made the military camps look like The Ritz but even though that was to be expected I grew tired of it from time to time.

I received my assignments from a Special Command OP which I supposedly was affiliated with, but the truth was that I rarely saw them. In fact, they had assumed I was a man, so they were somewhat shocked when they met me the first time. A meeting had been set up in a disused warehouse and everyone had arrived when I entered. There was a gasp through the group when I was introduced. The famous OPUS was a woman.

After the meeting one of the officers pulled me aside and asked me if I knew what capture of a woman on this continent could mean. I had heard rumours of special female torture and brutal interrogation methods where gang rape and mutilation were common, but to afflict that on me they would have to catch me first.

While I was in Central America, I often thought of JAC. I had no idea where he was, but rumour would have it that the team had been split and that he and Wizard had been sent to the Far East, but I was not sure if that was true.

During this period, I was constantly moving around Central America. Sometimes I was only in a country for ten hours and then it was off to the next. It was tiring with all that travel and the assignments were very monotonous as it was always officials who had to be eliminated. The only thing that varied was whether it was a police officer or a judge who was to be removed. But it actually had one advantage. I got away from all the brutal massacres that I had seen elsewhere, and I needed that.

And just as I thought it was a thing of the past, I was given an assignment that was to turn everything upside down and meant that I was not to be back in the Balkans until three years later.

Chapter 5

I had been to the Balkans a few times before and knew that what was going on there was very brutal. The Balkan War was officially over – and had been for many years – but ethnic cleansing was still taking place in certain regions, although nobody talked about it. Personally, I had participated in a few of them myself.

I was picked up at the airport by a somewhat shabby looking guy. I don't know why it surprised me but it did. After my last assignment in Belize my employer had transferred me to another division within their agency so I kind of expected to be greeted by a more official looking person but that was definitely not the case.

I was driven to a secluded country estate that undoubtedly had seen better days. When I entered what was once a vestibule, but now was really just a small room without any furniture, I was greeted by an officer and what I suspected were a couple of senior ranking sergeants. As usual, my reputation had preceded me and the awe and obvious relief that I was now part of their unit, at least for a while, was unmistakable.

After a short briefing I was shown to a room where I could put my stuff. My mission was not to start until the next day so, as so many times before, I put in my earplugs, started the iPod and lay down on my sleeping bag with my eyes closed.

While French verbs filled my head I suddenly felt a hand on my shin and, as if I was a vampire just awoken after a thousand years of hibernation, I opened my eyes. Slowly, which was in stark contrast to the speed with which my eyelids opened, I removed the earplugs and to my surprise, I saw The Kid standing at the end of my sleeping bag with a big smile on his face. In so many ways it was completely unreal to see him there, but at the same time also very nice. As I got up memories from the last time I saw him flashed before my eyes but as I gave him a hug they quickly disappeared again. In reality, it was more like The Kid was hugging me, but I immediately reciprocated his gesture, although with a little less enthusiasm. A couple of soldiers who were in the room got into a quarrel about something, but it did not seem to bother The Kid. In fact, I think he was totally indifferent to it. His focus was solely on me.

The intensity of the soldiers' argument quickly rose to a level where it was becoming annoying so it was kind of a relief when The Kid asked me if I had had coffee. I smiled as I answered no and as he went to the door, I slung the leather straps on the metal case that contained OPUS on to my back. Had I been with the old team or even just professional soldiers I would have had no problems leaving it behind but these guys, these patriots fighting for whatever their cause was, I did not trust. I had no doubt that they would be roaming through my stuff as soon as I turned my back on them but they wouldn't find anything of interest except for a couple of cartons of bullets and a few packs of cigarettes.

The Kid was actually the perfect guide around the premises. Not only did he provide me with a cup of steaming hot black coffee but he also gave me a tour of 'The Farm', which the soldiers had named the place. When we were done, we sat down in its enclosed courtyard and as I sipped my second cup of mocha he told me about the missions he had been on since I left. When he had finished talking, there was a much-needed break. I didn't tell him anything about Belize except that it was mostly assassination assignments I performed and there was no need for me to elaborate as he knew only too well what that meant. So, there we sat absorbing the surrounding sounds of the low voices coming from the various soldiers scattered around in small groups that like us had found their way into the sunny courtyard. Their voices were almost like a constant humming and combined with the singing from the birds high above in the surrounding trees it was like music. I was yanked out of this natural choir as The Kid suddenly said,

"JAC broke completely when he came back from the mission that day and found you gone. He smashed all the furniture in the tent and Wizard had to stop him by force. They fought so hard that they both ended up in the infirmary for two days," The Kid paused and looked into his half-cold cup of coffee while swirling it around, "He must have read the message you left him a thousand times, but he would never say what you wrote. What did you write to him?"

"You know better than to ask me that," I replied taking a sip of my now lukewarm coffee.

The Kid did not answer and we let the topic go.

"What has become of JAC and Wizard? Is it true that they have left the 'organization' and gone solo?" My voice was low as I stared straight ahead. The wind had taken hold of the large trees that stood behind the building directly opposite us, and its play with the leaves made it almost sound like water flowing through a stream at full flood. It was so loud that it totally drowned out the beautiful bird song.

"Yes," he replied shortly, "the last thing I heard was that they were somewhere in the Far East." We both knew what 'solo' meant. They had become contractors – mercenaries.

I closed my eyes and enjoyed the rays of sun against my face while The Kid fetched us some more coffee. It was a good day. The sun was shining, the birds were chirping and JAC was most likely alive and with Wizard. I smiled. It was definitely a good day.

* * *

The night came and it went relatively calmly. A bit of shooting in the distance was the only thing, so nothing alarming. The Kid had moved his sleeping bag into the room where I slept and there was no doubt that my presence had given him a boost. Him knowing me had obvious earned him some valuable points in relation to his fellow soldiers and I found it very sweet so I let him bask in the fame that it gave him. He seemed to enjoy it. To me, it was irrelevant but fun to watch and also it was very nice to have a 'family' face nearby. His immediacy yet relaxed demeanour, had a contagious effect on me, and for a while it actually took away a bit of the hype regarding my presence in the camp. Usually, it was one of those things that I 'boxed', if not completely deleted from my memory, so it was good fun, just for once to let it be and become the observer. After a few hours though, I began to find it a bit trivial so I turned to my language course on my iPod and was soon asleep.

The mission the next day was with The Kid and it was nice to be working with him again. We went deeper into the region and ended up on a ridge where we had to wait for a convoy to arrive. It took a few hours before that happened, but when it did, the action started. We took one prisoner and the rest of the soldiers in the convoy were slaughtered, so according to our superiors it had been a success.

When we got back I performed my usual rituals, though without taking a shower. The only water at 'The Farm' came from one tap and it was for drinking and not bathing, so there was no shower. Instead, I sat in the courtyard, where the other soldiers had already camped down and lit a fire. A dead sheep was turning on a spit and it was meant to be our dinner at some point.

As always, we were scattered around the yard and since I was starting to feel the cold, I had placed myself near the bonfire. On the opposite side of it two soldiers had bunked down presumably for the same reason as me – to get warm but much to my surprise one of the soldiers suddenly asked if it was true that I had killed one of my teammates? There was a strange silence in the courtyard and despite the fact that everyone was waiting for my answer I kept looking into the flames. As if heaven sent, The Kid appeared in the courtyard and a quick exchange of glances between us made him walk over and stand behind me. He was so close that when I leaned back slightly I touched his lower leg. He hadn't heard the question but it didn't matter. His presence alone radiated that whatever it was he had my back. It was clear to me that I had to weigh my words very carefully, so when I finally spoke, they came slowly and clearly from my lips.

"It was a 'mercy-kill' and, if I was put in the same situation again, I would not hesitate to do the same."

I think The Kid knew what we were talking about because even though the following silence was to be expected, it was somehow nice that he suddenly broke it.

"That's how it is to be in a 'real family' and OPUS will always be a part of mine. We have each other's back no matter what and I'm proud of what she did. Few people could have done it. She will always have my trust and total support. Knowing that she has my back when I'm out there makes me feel safe and so it should with you."

I smiled. All this was just getting a little too theatrical for me, so to get the whole situation down to earth again, I looked up at The Kid.

"So long as you do not kick my bed, we should be all right," I said and we winked at each other. I let The Kid have the honour of telling the story to his teammates and went to bed. I could hear their laughter and I knew that The Kid had once again risen in their esteem. Good for him, I thought and smiled as I closed my eyes.

* * *

Later that night, I was awakened by the blast from a mortar grenade. The impact was five hundred metres away and it shook the masonry construction of the entire farm in such a way that loose plaster fell from the walls and ceiling in the room where I slept. Automatically I grabbed the case containing OPUS as I jumped out of my sleeping bag.

The impact was followed by complete silence and while no one in the room said anything I quickly opened the metal box and assembled OPUS. I had practiced doing it blindfolded and in the dark so it didn't even take me a minute to do it. One of the senior officers stuck his head inside the door and signalled if everyone was okay, which we confirmed we were. Then another ten to fifteen seconds passed and I used the time to put on my combat boots, lace them up and grab my jacket. As always it was stuffed with the most necessary things like bullets, knives, first aid kit, a pair of half finger gloves that I used for close combat fighting, a lighter and cigarettes.

My credit cards were in the back pocket of my pants which I slept in and the tank top I was wearing was a part of my combat gear. As the soldiers began to quietly exit the room, I grabbed my Glock from under my sleeping bag. Then I was ready. I glanced at the door and saw The Kid standing with his back to the door frame sending the individual soldiers out one by one. Since I was the one who had been furthest away from the door, I was also the last to reach it and it gave me a few seconds alone with The Kid. As he scouted the terrain outside I grabbed his forearm. He looked at me and I signalled that I was going to the roof. He nodded and then I disappeared out the door and into the darkness.

The roof was sloping and covered with loose tiles, which made it relatively difficult to move on without being detected. I managed to reach a chimney and as it turned out its dimensions made it possible for me to climb into it and stand tensed. So having crawled into the chimney it was now just a matter of waiting. The silence that followed was one of suspense and not in a good way. It was ominous and as I looked over the concrete edge of the chimney I could sense the tension in the soldiers in the courtyard.

It was hard for my legs to stand strained like that, but since I knew from experience that the muscle cramps would not occur until after about eight minutes, there ought to be enough time. And there was. A few minutes later I heard a brief hiss and a pop, and then the sky was illuminated by a flash grenade. I waited a moment before I had a quick look over the terrain and the glance revealed that there were enemy troops everywhere outside 'The Farm'. The distance to them was fifty metres and closing, so now I knew what to expect. I waited for the sound of the first gun shots to break the silence and they came three seconds later. A fierce firefight started and I did what I was best at. I eliminated marks.

It was like being in a shooting gallery at an amusement park except the targets here moved more unpredictably but in my eyes it just made the challenge more interesting. It was like being a live participant in a game where the first prize was to avoid being killed yourself. But had I been a betting woman I would have said that the odds were against us as we were outnumbered by the dozen.

A sniper who had positioned himself in one of the trees on the opposite side of the building caught my attention. He had placed himself pretty well – actually better than me – but his cover was lousy, so I just aimed OPUS at him and down he went: Like a winged duck, he fell through the branches and I knew that not only had my shot killed him but our odds had just slightly increased for the better. I disappeared down the chimney again and for a brief moment, I closed my eyes and took a deep breath. I needed to get back into the fight because ... But then something inside me said, 'get out of the chimney'. It was not because my life was in danger. It was more an inner voice that dictated it and when the voice did that I listened. I therefore strapped OPUS to my back, took another deep breath and slid down inside the chimney. Just before I reached the bottom I stopped. I took my Glock from the waistband and on a deep inhale I gathered my legs. I landed in the fireplace on the exhale with the Glock directed into the room. And just in time.

In front of me stood an enemy soldier with his back to me and he was fighting with The Kid. I did not register whether The Kid had the fight under control or not. I just took a step forward and shot the enemy soldier. It was a clean neck shot. The Kid did not pick up that it was me and it was only when the enemy sank to the floor that we stood face to face.

A crooked smile spread on his lips followed by a small nod, and then we left for the courtyard. Whether I rescued The Kid from the other soldier or he would have killed him himself didn't matter. The main thing was that The Kid survived.

When we reached the door to the courtyard, I gave The Kid cover until he was out of sight and five kills later I once again found myself on the first floor this time by an open window. As so many times before, I had exchanged the Glock for OPUS and I was now set for another kill, but stopped when I got Wizard in the sight. My pulse raced uncontrollably as I stepped away from the window. I put myself in a position where my back was against the wall next to the window and then I exhaled. What the hell was he doing here? Hadn't The Kid just told me he was in the Far East? This was some real shit. I could not kill him, I was fully aware of that, but what should I do? Did he even know that The Kid was here?

The thoughts went through my head at lightning speed and then I made a decision that I never thought I would have to make. I would go AWOL. Go against my orders and fight for my own agenda. Fight my own battle, which in this case was to get Wizard, The Kid and me out of this scenario alive.

I had no idea where The Kid was so I decided to go with Wizard first since I already knew where he was. I therefore returned to the window and it seemed like he had not moved from his position at all, for he was in exactly the same place as I had spotted him a few moments ago. He was facing me and was in the middle of a fierce battle with a soldier from 'my team' so I aimed at the soldier and shot him in the neck. He immediately fell to the ground, and whether Wizard was surprised that his opponent suddenly fell dead in front of him, I could not tell, but at least he looked up and caught a glimpse of me. For a brief second he stood still then a soldier was about to attack him from behind, but I shot this one too. Wizard turned around and looked at the dead man, and then he looked up at me again. I hoped he had understood my message and I decided to give him a couple of minutes to find me.

It did not take long before he stood in the doorway of the room I was in. It was nice to see him and we both smiled. However, everything changed when one of my 'teammates' appeared behind Wizard. Immediately I pulled my Glock and shot him, but I should have realized it was not the smartest thing to do: to pull a gun in front of Wizard would obviously provoke a reaction and it did. Despite the fact that the bullet was not intended for him, I found myself standing with his pistol against my forehead. Oddly enough, I wasn't scared. If Wizard had really wanted to shoot me, he would have already done so. I raised my eyebrows and dropped my Glock on the floor hoping he would realize that he in no way was my target and never had been.

"Are you crazy, OPUS?" he said quietly, "You will never do that again. NEVER. Do you hear? I could have shot you."

"I know," I replied almost whispering, "but it was you or him." I nodded towards the soldier and without removing his pistol from me, Wizard looked over his shoulder at the dead man.

"Hell, OPUS ..." it came from him, looking at me again. Then he secured the safety on his gun and lowered it. Words were unnecessary. We both knew what this meant. I picked up my Glock and then I told him that The Kid was here.

There was no doubt that he had heard what I had just said, but he didn't respond, so I left it at that. Wizard was my safest card to get out of this hell hole and I think he felt the same way about me, because we both put full magazines in our guns. We needed to get out of this inferno and as soon as possible, so we started shooting our way out. It was a strange feeling not to fight for anybody other than ourselves, but somehow it felt better and more correct. More true. More genuine.

We fought like crazy and we only stopped when we were two hundred metres outside 'The Farm' and the worst of the battle seemed to be behind us. Then we fled.

We ran through the barren terrain and on the way we climbed cliffs until we finally ended up in a cave. We had been running for a few hours and were obviously out of breath, so a rest was needed. With our backs to the wall of the cave we squatted to catch our breath. We knew that soon we would be 'wanted for desertion' by both sides of the conflict but somehow, it was okay. Perfectly okay.

* * *

Wizard leaned his head up against the cave wall and laughed. Then he said he was happy to see me and that he had missed me. He mumbled a lot of praiseworthy phrases about me and us and ... I could not bear to listen to it, because there was basically only one reason for all this. I therefore crawled over the sandy floor of the cave and put a finger on his lips to silence him. He immediately stopped talking and I then said the three words that were the cause of all this.

"We are Family." We looked at each other and he understood.

"We are Family," he repeated quietly, "We are Family."

I crawled back to the opposite side of the cave and for a while we sat in silence because basically there was nothing more to say.

Eventually Wizard broke it. He said that he hadn't slept for three days and I reassured him that he could relax now that I was here so he should try to get some sleep. He closed his eyes and smiled and then he fell asleep.

I positioned myself in the opening of the cave so I had a full view of the surrounding area and here I watched an amazing sunrise over the barren cliffs. For some reason this dawning was different from the ones I had so far seen and I think it was because for the first time in a long while, I felt that there was a reason for what I was doing; and it was the team – Wizard, Knox, Washington, Abe, The Kid and JAC. It was a nice feeling to finally have a good reason to fight and kill and all of a sudden it dawned on me that this was what I had been looking for. A reason. In all these years I had killed because others had asked me to. It had been so easy – no reason, no emotion.

But then suddenly I felt insecure. Would I now be able to kill without reflecting on this? Without being affected emotionally? Without thoughts before and during the deed? All these questions that once had been so easy to answer had suddenly become difficult, and the unfamiliar territory it brought me to was very uncomfortable. It was so easy to kill without thinking and suddenly I doubted if I would ever be able to kill again!

I looked at Wizard, who was in a deep sleep. I would give him a few more hours but then we would have to move on so I took a deep breath, closed my eyes and began to meditate. However, it was purely to empty my mind, so I hopefully would get rid of all these new and unpleasant questions. They would have to be resolved at a later time.

Wizard's voice interrupted my meditation.

"He is in Kosovo. JAC," he said quietly, "or rather, he was two weeks ago." I turned my head and looked at him. He sat with his head up against the wall and his eyes were still closed.

We both knew that a lot could happen in two weeks so there was no guarantee he was still there.

"How bad is it with you?" I asked.

Wizard opened his eyes and gazed at me. I nodded towards his arm and he looked down. The sleeve of his jacket had crawled up during his sleep and there were visible traces of needle marks on his arm. Again, he leaned his head back and closed his eyes.

"Morphine. Four times a day. Have been on it for a year." He sighed lightly, "I get it from a courier who has a connection to a military hospital." He took some ampoules out of the pocket of his jacket.

"JAC's got it really bad. He is on smack (heroin)." I could see some small drops of sweat on Wizard's forehead, and in the light of what he had just told me, there seemed to be no doubt as to why.

"Is it time for a fix?" I asked trying to tone down my emotions, but the disappointment of seeing him like this had unintentionally shone through in my voice.

He nodded. I lit a cigarette from the pack I had in my pocket, turned my head and told him to hurry up so we could get moving.

As I sat there with my back to him and heard him tighten his belt around his upper arm, I suddenly felt an intense sadness. It washed over me and made me both bitter and slightly sour. Damn it, Wizard. I had seen many soldiers who had succumbed to drugs, but I had never expected him to become one of them. He was one of the mentally strongest people I had ever known, and now he was sitting a few metres from me fixing himself into an escape from reality instead of confronting it and the problem – whatever the hell the problem might be. Thoughts whirled inside my head, but like so many times before, they ended up being tucked away in one of my mental drawers so I could get some peace of mind.

How long it took, I do not know, but my cigarette was long gone when he came over to me and said that we were going to Pristina. I got up and without further discussion took OPUS and we left the cave. It was clear that Wizard knew the area and the terrain well, and his local knowledge paid off when we needed something to eat. We got food from a local farmer who voluntarily opened his home to us. It had never occurred to me to ask Wizard about his nationality and now it gave itself away, for he spoke fluent Croatian. After the meal, we thanked the farmer and with a couple of sandwiches in our pockets made by the farmer's wife we left as abruptly as we had arrived.

And this is how the next few days went. We walked; when we were hungry we were fed by locals and when we were tired we slept either in a barn or in the wild.

Our conversations were relaxed, but my time in Central America was never discussed and it suited me just fine. I did not really want to talk about it and Wizard obviously did not want to hear about it. Next to Somalia, Central America was the worst place to be sent – and especially as a woman. I had got a lot of scars on my soul over there but I had decided to lock that part of my life in a box and throw away the key. It should never be opened again. NEVER. Whether that was the right decision, I do not know. At the time, it was.

The last seventy miles we got a lift with some UN forces and not long after we were dropped off near the Belgian embassy in Pristina. We thanked them for the trip and hurried towards 'downtown'. We moved through small narrow streets and ended up disappearing through an open faded green wooden door. We went up some half-broken stone steps to a door that had white paint peeling off and two smoky glass panels to prevent curious minds seeing what was going on behind it, bore witness to better times in the area.

The door was promptly opened when Wizard knocked. On the other side stood a tiny man with a dark moustache and after exchanging a few words with Wizard, we were allowed to enter the apartment.

Wizard had told me that the place was called 'Heaven' and that the apartment was a so-called safe zone for us, but despite this I felt uneasy. Something didn't feel right there. I took a firm grip on OPUS and was on high alert. There were several men and a few women in the apartment, and while Wizard spoke to some of the men, I took the opportunity to check out all the rooms. If this was 'Heaven' I would certainly not want to see Hell.

The filth in this place was unbelievable. Overfilled bins and plastic bags with garbage had created a true paradise for various fungi, insects and rodents. Stacks of half empty pizza trays, beer cans either empty or with leftovers in them and overfilled ashtrays made the place stink even more. Dirty glasses, plates with rotten food crawling with mites and pots that had been used for pissing in were just some disgusting features of this horrible place. And then there was the filthy bed linen with traces of dried unidentified substances that lay scattered on the floors and beds in the various rooms. The place looked like a drug den where a party had been going on for several weeks. Normally it wouldn't have bothered me but for some reason there was something about this place that felt terribly wrong. So I tracked down Wizard in one of the rooms talking to a tall red-haired guy and whispered to him that we were leaving immediately. He didn't look at me but finished the conversation and one minute later we had left the building.

We walked down the street and, as we turned right, heading for one of the main boulevards, Wizard demanded an explanation as to why I wanted to leave. But before I could answer him, there was a deafening explosion behind us. We both stopped for a second looking at each other. Then we turned and ran back to where the sound of the explosion had come from. As we turned the corner into the street where the apartment was located, we both stopped abruptly. All the windows in it had been blown out and a thick black pall of smoke came out of where they had once been. Wizard stood gaping for a moment, but then we heard the sirens from the fire trucks and we quietly withdrew from the scene. As we started to walk down the street again neither of us spoke of what had just occurred but we both knew my intuition had saved us.

Chapter 6

That evening we met up with some of Wizard's 'colleagues' at a small café. The place was old fashioned, but cozy with its small wooden tables surrounded by mass-produced café stacking chairs. On the walls hung wooden barrels and old brooms side by side with lanterns and old rusty axe heads. Wizard's 'colleagues' were all professional soldiers, and when they learned who I was, smiles spread across their faces.

"So, you're the legendary OPUS," one of them said. "It's an honour to meet you – and still alive."

Very few things could baffle me, but the remark 'and still alive' was one of them. Saying it meant that he had to know the only person I trusted in Central America. They all laughed heartily and were subsequently able to inform me that I was in the top fifty of the most wanted AWOL's. The laughter increased and one by one they shook my hand and said the number they were on the list.

The only one who did not say his number was a medium-height dark-haired guy, with a rather indeterminate British accent. He seemed calm and well-balanced on the surface, but the look he gave me: At first he just stared at me, and there was no doubt that he was trying to read me. What conclusion he came to I don't know, for I had a hard time decoding him.

Later in the evening we changed location and I found out that the dark-haired guy was called Liam and we continued the party in his suite at The Ritz. That night I slept in Liam's bed.

It was definitely not a given that we should end up together that night, because we had not exchanged more than a few words. It was like we were avoiding each other. And yet we were always within touching distance. A few times we caught each other's eye, but it was only in the early hours that Liam pulled me aside. Somehow being so close to him made me very uneasy but, the worst of it was, I could see that he was aware of it. He smiled at me, but the smile did not reach his hard and coal-black eyes. It was as if he deliberately stopped it halfway, and that in itself, sent a shiver down my spine. A man who was able to control his emotions like that was dangerous and yet I could not help but find him unbelievably fascinating and attractive. Behind his façade, behind his eyes, there was something else and as he stood there, he almost engulfed me without words and it was both scary and breath-taking. And then it dawned on me why I was so attracted to him. We were each other's mental reflections and he had undoubtedly seen it from the start. It was as if this realization facilitated my approach, because now I knew who he was and how I should act around him. His raw masculinity and coolness almost forced me to my knees and before long we were lying in his bed.

Here I discovered that his status as an Alpha male did not only apply to the group of contractors but certainly also when it came to him between the sheets. He was a rough but also talented lover who knew what he wanted and how to get it. But what he hadn't taken into account was my traumas from Belize. And how could he. He didn't know about them. I tried to conceal the disgust I felt when he touched me certain ways but I didn't do a very good job of it as he read me like an open book. But where others would have stopped and given up he didn't. He simply just adjusted his touches to where on my body I felt pleasure and then moved on from there. It was almost as if he drew himself a road map of where his hands, mouth and cock could go with a minimum of discomfort for me and a maximum of pleasure for him. Never once did he overstep my boundaries and the times he was close I simply just showed him that it was time for another move. I could feel his respect when I did that but, although it was okay that I guided, he would never let me take over. Several times in those few hours I had flash backs to Belize but with Liam I could just keep pushing forward and never let them take over my mind. I knew I had to work through them and this was a good beginning. And to be honest I don't think I could have had a better first time lover after Belize than Liam.

* * *

It was late in the afternoon when I woke up the next day. The suite was marked by the evening's drinking, but all the participants were missing including Liam. On the table in the living room was a note from Wizard saying 'Gone to get medicine' and it made me smile to myself. Next to the note stood half a bottle of JD – Jack Daniels whiskey – and with a firm grip on it, I went into the bathroom.

As I lay there in the bathtub with my bottle of JD in one hand and my Glock lying on the edge of the tub, a warm content feeling washed over me. I was going to be alright and last night proved it. Belize had given me scars but not so I could not mend them. And if anybody had ever thought they had broken me they couldn't have been more wrong. If anything, Belize had made me stronger.

I heard the door to the suite close and I could recognize Wizard's and Liam's voices and then I froze. JAC was there too.

Before I could get out of the bathtub the door opened and there he was. I could see that he could hardly believe his eyes.

"Damn it, OPUS," he said slamming the door and locking it from the inside.

He just managed to throw his Glock on the floor and tear his clothes off as I pulled him down into the bath and, surrounded by a sea of citrus flavoured bubbles, we disappeared into each other. It was nice to have someone touching me in a familiar way and JAC was, if anyone, the right one to do it. There was nothing sentimental or careful with his touches. He was just the way I remembered him: Selfish. But for the first time it dawned on me that he might seek out personal gratification but he wasn't dominant. He let me lead and that suited me just perfectly. So, I guided him the way I had done with Liam but by keeping the control I could simultaneously push my own boundaries even further. I never for one minute let JAC decide what the next step would be and because of that I was able to climax with no consideration for him. It was selfish but just what I needed to be able to say,

"Fuck you Belize. You didn't get me."

* * *

When we got out of the bathroom, Liam was gone and Wizard was sitting on the couch in the living room far away in a drug-rush.

JAC went over and took two cigarettes from a pack of Marlboro on the table and lit them before he went into the bedroom. I had laid down on the bed wearing nothing but wet hair and a towel. He handed me one of the cigarettes and before he lay on his back next to me he dropped his white towel on the floor. With little drops of water still lingering on to his six-pack making them look like they had been sprayed with diamonds he took a puff of his cigarette.

"I have missed you," he said looking up at the ceiling.

"I missed you too," I replied casually but truthfully.

"Shall we confess our sins?" he asked suddenly.

I took a puff of my cigarette.

"No," I replied firmly and he smiled. For a minute, there was a silence between us and it was not an unpleasant one just a thoughtful one.

"I don't want to be second," he said, alluding to any other men that might be in my life. His comment was legitimate enough and I had by no means intended him to be so. On the contrary.

"As long as you are here, you will never be second. NEVER."

He rolled over onto his side so we were looking into each other's eyes. Then he brushed a couple of locks of hair from my forehead and when our eyes met I knew that I meant the word NEVER. We both stubbed out our cigarettes and continued from where we had left off earlier in the bathtub. And in a selfish and uncompromising lovemaking we both climaxed this time.

* * *

It was dark outside when I woke up and the suite was deserted. The only light came from the bathroom and I could hear JAC was in there. Quietly I got up and went in, but it was only to see him sitting on the floor. He was about to loosen the belt from his arm and the syringe with traces of blood lay on the floor next to him. We looked briefly at each other before I went into the shower and turned it on. JAC closed his eyes and while I was washing him off me, he disappeared into his world of intoxication.

It may seem strange that I did not respond to what I saw, but I did not consider it to be my problem. It was JAC's choice if he wanted to drug himself to death. Personally, I wouldn't. Why escape from a reality that you have helped to create? If you were not satisfied with it or could not stand it, why junk through it? Why not just stop and leave. Go back to being a civilian in the normal world, instead of staying here in our real world with people like me? I know that it is easy to say, because the reality is that it is rarely possible. We had each sealed our fate many years ago, and for some, the only way to survive was through drugs, however tragic it may seem.

A few hours later, JAC and I were having dinner in a nearby restaurant. It was incredibly cozy and it was in fact our first real date in public. We told each other about what we had experienced in the time that had passed since I left camp and as expected we skated over the hard and heavy things and laughed at all the fun and easy stuff. It was wonderfully liberating to be with him again and as we went back to the suite, for the first time, we walked hand in hand.

Back in the suite it was obvious that not only had Liam, Wizard and a few other guys been back for a while, but also room service had been there, making it look completely habitable again. Liam and I exchanged a few glances, but there was not the same message in his eyes as there was in mine. His was like a rival watching his first prize go to another, while mine was a subtle indication that he should see the events of the previous night as purely physical. Actually, it was foolish of me to think that JAC had not already sensed that something had happened between Liam and me, and it should therefore not have come as a surprise, when he pulled Liam aside. Through the crack in the door to the bedroom I could hear that they had a short exchange of words – nothing loud or threatening – and a few minutes later they returned together. This time there were no glances between Liam and me and when I caught JAC's eyes he just smiled and winked at me. In my heart I smiled, because it appeared that the two fighting cocks had reached some sort of agreement regarding me, so I calmly took a mineral water from the tray on the table.

While I was standing there, looking at the lid of the plastic bottle, Liam signalled to one of the guys, who immediately got up and began checking if all the windows and doors were closed. Wizard subsequently swept the room for any microphones and other electronic equipment that were not ours and Liam called the front desk and asked them to hold all calls until further notice. JAC, who had disappeared into the bedroom, now reappeared with a large bag and he emptied its contents on the table. It was filled with 'equipment' we might need to perform the assignments that lay ahead of us.

With the room swept, everyone sat down and the meeting began.

Liam began by describing the different requests that had dropped into his email and despite the fact that there had been a good number of inquiries, he had selected the following: Sarajevo, Gaza, Riyadh, Sudan and Ukraine. Also, Afghanistan was back in the picture, but there one had to participate in unspecified military operations led by the Americans which could mean anything. Liam described briefly each assignment and then it was up to the individual contractors in the room to say which one they wanted and their price. The missions were quickly distributed and the prices were sent to customers via email. Then it was a waiting game. I used the time to call the front desk and order two jugs of coffee, and when I got back to the couch, JAC sat down beside me.

I was now to be introduced to a life as a professional contractor by Liam. In a calm and serious voice, he explained to me how we got the missions, about prices and money transfers, about the code systems they used to communicate with each other when out on assignments and finally about the security regarding oneself.

When you were on a mission, you were usually alone and your client usually perceived you as a one-man army. For me, this was not really something new, and I therefore answered briefly that this was how I had operated for many years and that the biggest difference for me was that now I could decide which assignments I wanted and how much they should cost. Everyone in the room smiled because it really summed up the essence of the life I was now entering which most of them had been living for a while.

Wizard leaned back and with his hands folded behind his head, he said that one must definitely not forget all the perks that came with the job, such as: We usually constituted the 'first wave of attack'; we could risk being wanted by various agencies and thus become hunted by all sides even those we had to 'work with' on the assignments. Pension schemes and dental care were 'non-existent' and, last but not least, that we were not covered by any conventions and therefore were not protected if we were captured by the enemy. Everyone in the room laughed at his summary, but then Liam's phone started to beep, and the laughter died out.

The first offer was accepted. It was Wizard. He was going to Riyadh. Departure tomorrow at zero-six-hundred.

After that, the beeps kept coming, and within half an hour the assignments were distributed.

Liam was going to Sarajevo and JAC to Gaza. No one accepted a mission in Afghanistan this time.

When everyone had been given their assignments, Liam looked at me and said that now it was my turn to be introduced on the market. The subsequent silence, while Liam wrote an email stating that OPUS was available, I attributed to the excitement of introducing a new contractor and one with my reputation. He sent the email to the 'network' and then it was just waiting. It didn't take long. Nineteen missions in less than three minutes and Liam's only comment was "WOW". They were from all over the world and I was free to choose, so I took four assassination missions. Then there was the matter of the price and I had no doubt – one million per assignment. Liam looked up at me. I nodded.

"It's double what they usually pay," he said but I asked him to press 'SEND' which he did without hesitation. Within a minute, all four of them had accepted. Liam leaned back on the couch and, without taking his eyes off the screen, he raised his eyebrows in recognition.

"Four passports must be arranged," he said looking at JAC, who nodded and left the room with his phone in his hand. Then Liam looked at me and started explaining what to do in terms of customer's account numbers and prepayment. He then showed me how to send the account numbers to the customers.

My account would be at an overseas bank. When I had finished my assignments, one of them could fly with me to the bank's head office, so I could be introduced – if I wanted to – he said, but judging by his tone, he was not the one who would be accompanying me. To sort out all the paperwork, he had a lawyer who lived in Geneva, so everything was done legally and by the book.

JAC came back and nodded acknowledging the arrangement for the passports, and then there was a knock on the door. It was room service with the coffee I had ordered.

After a cup of coffee, Wizard left. He had to leave early the next morning and had some things to sort out beforehand, so we didn't see him again. Slowly the others began to leave and eventually only Liam, JAC and I were left in the hotel suite.

JAC's phone beeped and it was a message confirming that the passports were ready. Liam got up and handed me a phone and four SIM cards.

"Good luck," he said, "See you back here in two weeks' time." He had touched my hand briefly as he gave me the SIM cards and our eyes had met, but they radiated more recognition than actual personal feelings. It was very nice that there was nothing emotional in the touch, but whether there was a hidden agenda in his gaze, I had a hard time interpreting. I pulled my hand back and walked over to JAC, who was waiting by the door. It was as if Liam had sucked all the air out of me and the shortness of breath I felt was by no means pleasant.

"See you, Liam." JAC said smiling confidently and, with his arm around my shoulders, we left the suite. We caught a taxi in front of the hotel which took us to the other side of town. When we had been dropped off, we walked for approximately ten minutes through some very dark and gloomy streets until we reached a street corner where a young girl was waiting.

With hardly any conversation, she and JAC exchanged envelopes, and then the girl disappeared down a dark alley.

Quietly, and holding hands, we walked towards the city, and it was only when we had come halfway that we hailed a taxi, which drove us to JAC's hotel.

That night we made love more intensely than ever before. It was as if we were afraid we would never see each other again. Maybe it was because we were not given the opportunity to really say goodbye the last time we were separated. Maybe it was just to reassure each other or maybe it was because it was the purest and most honest kind of humanity we knew. The closest thing to true love we could experience.

Chapter 7

Two weeks later I knocked on the door to the suite again. I heard a click signalling that it was now open and noted the electronic addition to the lock as something Liam had organized while I had been away. I walked in and immediately saw that there was a stranger sitting on the couch next to him. Liam was working on his laptop and as I entered he looked up fleetingly.

"Hey," he greeted before returning to the laptop, "OPUS, this is Aussie – Aussie meet OPUS," he said without looking up. Aussie stood up and smiled genuinely.

"OPUS, fucking A," he said with a thick Australian accent and we shook hands. With a grip like a vice he squeezed my hand uncomfortably hard. Without looking up, Liam asked if everything was okay.

"Yep," I replied, "I haven't slept for days, so is it okay if I ..." I didn't get to finish the sentence before Liam interrupted me and nodded towards the bedroom.

"Of course," he replied, "You know the way."

Aussie blinked a few times, after which his gaze went slowly from Liam to me and then back to Liam. Liam had noticed it, but he just kept working on the laptop, and like him, I chose to ignore Aussie.

"Nice to meet you, Aussie," I said, walking into the bedroom, where I tossed my bag on the floor before closing the door. A few minutes later I was standing in the shower under the hot jets of water. Washing away the past weeks' travels felt wonderful. Despite the fact that I was completely naked and vulnerable as I stood there, I felt unbelievably safe. With Liam on the other side of the door, I was able to relax. It was actually a little weird, because I did not know him that well, but there was just something about his being there that gave me this feeling. I turned off the shower, dried myself, and went straight into his bed.

Six hours later I woke up. For a little while I just lay in the dark enjoying the fact of being there, but the sound of voices interrupted my flow of thoughts. They came from the living room and it sounded like there were quite a few people in there.

I pushed the beige coloured quilt aside and on my way to the sound of voices, I put on a pair of panties and one of Liam's long white shirts. Slowly I opened the door to the living room and there on the sofa which was facing me were JAC and Wizard.

At the sight of me, they both smiled and I felt an unmistakable joy at seeing them. It was a little strange, because if they had not been there, I wouldn't have been sad or missed them. It would have been the most natural thing in the world if they had not been there, but the fact that they were just made my return that bit more pleasant. I walked towards the couch they were sitting on but instead of sitting down between them I walked around to the back of the sofa and as I placed my hands on each of their shoulders I squatted down so only my face, hands, and upper torso were visible.

"Hey, boys," I said with a big smile. It was nice to see them again and not least to touch them.

"Hey, babe." Wizard replied in such a sexy voice that even the biggest crooner in the world would have been envious. JAC began to laugh, but Liam just smiled wryly before returning his gaze to his laptop, which he was still working on. Poor Aussie had no idea how to react to the whole situation and it was clear that he didn't get any less confused when JAC tilted his head slightly backwards and he and I kissed. When we were done, I took his cigarette out of his hand and took a puff.

"Did you have a nice trip?" I asked with a hint of irony in my voice because who says that to people who have just returned from killing somebody. Wizard responded to my question with a laugh and out of the corner of my eye I noticed that my question even made Liam chuckle. JAC put on a smiley face and with a determined grip, he suddenly grabbed my neck and the second after, I lay in his lap.

"Of course." JAC replied, winking naughtily at me. I reciprocated his smile and then turned over so I was lying on my stomach across JAC's legs, with my elbows resting on Wizard's thigh. I put on JAC's sunglasses, which were lying on the table, and turned my head towards Liam and Aussie, who were still sitting on the sofa across from us. I could feel JAC's hand move up under my shirt and as it reached my butt, it stopped. I took another puff on the cigarette. Liam, who had been sitting with his eyes fixed to the screen of the laptop, now looked at me and smiled crookedly.

"Do you fancy a trip to Tehran?" he asked.

"When?" I answered.

"Tomorrow."

I turned and looked up at the ceiling. There was silence in the living room and while I felt JAC's hand now lying on one of my thighs I blew a smoke ring into the air.

"Yes, why not?" I replied, taking one last puff of the cigarette before putting it out. Quietly, I got up and grabbed JAC's dog tag chain and pulled it. My action made him stand up, and it was only when we stood right in front of each other and with our eyes fixed on one another that I let go of the chain.

Quietly I told him I needed him for sex and JAC smiled willingly.

"I am all yours," he replied, spreading his arms, "All yours." Aussie stared first at us then at Liam and then at Wizard before a "Fucking hell" left his lips.

"You have your very own sex bitch here."

Liam looked up from the laptop and he and Wizard exchanged a quick glance.

"You got it all wrong, Aussie. We are her bitches," he said grinning, looking down at the laptop again.

"Oh yeah." JAC replied and with these words hanging in the air, I dragged him into the bedroom and he closed the door behind us. Later I was told that Wizard had told Aussie that I always had sex before a mission and preferably with JAC. Aussie had answered that he would like to make himself available if JAC was not there, but Liam had replied that he did not need to think about that, because that problem had already been solved and then he had winked at Aussie. Wizard had smiled and nodded, and Aussie had reciprocated with the words 'Fucking hardcore'.

When I woke up, it was still dark outside. JAC was lying on his stomach, next to me, sleeping and there was silence in the suite. The door into the living room was half open and the light from one of the lamps hit the bedroom floor in the shape of a light cone. I looked over at the closed bathroom door and there was a faint yellowish streak of light beneath it. Silently, I freed myself from JAC's arm that lay across me and crawled out of the bed. In the heat of the battle, Liam's shirt had ended up on the floor, and after picking it up and putting it on, I went into the living room. The first thing I saw was Wizard and Aussie, each lying on a sofa – asleep and snoring. I could not help smiling, because despite their physical size, there was something incredibly boyish about them. Behind me I heard the bathroom door opening and shortly after Liam entered the living room.

"You can have a few more hours of sleep before you have to leave," he said while stretching.

"No, it's okay," I replied, nodding towards Aussie, "Who is he?"

"An insane Australian I have worked with several times. He's all right."

Liam went to his desk and sat down. Obviously he wasn't finished working on the laptop. Almost like a reflex action I picked up the phone and ordered the front desk to bring up a pot of coffee. Then I went and stood behind Liam and watched what he was doing.

Without further introduction, he began to explain how the money transfers worked: We each had a master account and a set of sub-accounts some of which had multiple account numbers. He explained how the money was channelled around according to who should be paid what percentage. The unremitted percentage serviced all this, without the intervention of any authorities. So that deduction meant that each contractor paid for their management.

To my question about what he did with all this information, he replied that he stored it on a USB so that the laptop was empty at all times. Even when he sat and worked on it, there were security measures so he had to confirm his identity every fifteen minutes via a code, otherwise all files including the USB would be deleted. Also, if the USB was removed unauthorized from the laptop, then everything on it would automatically be deleted. As he sat there talking, he did not seem like a "merc" – a mercenary. He spoke calmly and thoughtfully and was totally engrossed, however we were both torn out of this financial world by a knock on the door. It was the coffee.

After receiving it, I poured two cups for us and Liam closed the laptop and leaned back. I handed him a cup, and with mine in my hand, I went over to the window and looked out. The sky was pitch black. Not a single star or a hint of moonlight was to be seen. The few cars that passed under the streetlights below us seemed out of place as the city was still asleep.

"How long have you been in the game?" I asked quietly, taking a sip of the coffee. Liam sat with his eyes closed.

"Twenty-nine years," he replied, and his response made me face him.

"Jesus, how old were you when you started?" He opened his eyes.

"Fourteen," he replied, snorting. "One car bomb – two dead."

"Shit, Liam." He smiled.

"Yes, the IRA recruited early."

"And how long have you been a merc?"

"Too long," he replied quietly and I caught a hint of sadness in his voice. I didn't expect it and to be honest I didn't want to know why. Actually, I would prefer not to know too much about him, at least not when it came to his feelings. That could complicate things ... for all of us. There was a pause, which gave me the minutes I needed to mentally box all this.

"Do you ever think of quitting?" I asked then, and the second that I had asked the question, I was aware of how foolish it was.

Liam looked at me.

"This is not an industry you quit," he said seriously.

"I know," I replied, taking one more sip of my coffee before putting the cup down on the edge of the desk. I walked past him and, as I passed, he grabbed my wrist. We looked at each other and I could see that he was just about to say something, but I beat him to it.

"Don't, Liam," I said, "I am not the right one to confess your sins to."

I looked away and he let go of me. Whether it was the right thing to reject him that way, I do not know, but I felt I had to. He mustn't get too close to me and the best way to avoid that was by not involving myself too deeply in him. It was so strange to be near him, because despite his unmistakable calm and well-balanced aura, there was a smouldering rage just below the surface that made me insecure. Unfortunately, I had to admit that this was also exactly what attracted me to him, and even though I had tried to see through him, I had not managed to get behind the cool self-controlled arrogance that surrounded him like armour. So I had chosen to take a step back, and it was my intention purely to let our blades cross professionally and not emotionally.

I went into the shower and twenty minutes later I was fully clothed and fastening my belt. Liam had turned on the laptop again and was sitting as usual, working at the desk.

"Your passport, SIM card and ticket are over there," he said, neither gesturing in the direction nor looking up. I looked in the direction of the dresser and I could see another set of tickets and passport beside mine. Apparently, I was not the only one who was leaving.

Liam took the USB out, closed the laptop and looked at his watch. Then he got up. The suite was quiet and the only sound to be heard was a soft snoring coming from Aussie. Liam walked over to the couch where Wizard was lying, and shook his shoulder to wake him. With two fingers he tapped on his watch to indicate it was time to get up. Wizard sat up, yawned and stretched his arms as he slowly began to wake up.

"I'm just going to take a few hours." Liam said referring to getting some sleep and Wizard signalled 'okay' to him while yawning once more.

"We have to talk about OPUS when I get back," I said to Liam and the remark caused a little smile.

"Okay. New gear?"

"No, fine-tuning."

Liam yawned, nodded and as he passed me, he patted me on the shoulder. He walked straight into the bedroom and threw himself on the bed next to JAC. But just before he did it he clicked the safety off on his Glock and put it on the nightstand next to him. I followed each and every one of his moves. It seemed completely insane, but for him it appeared a natural thing to do which I couldn't quite believe, but I kept my thoughts to myself.

I went over to the dresser and took one of the passports. It was Wizard's and the ticket said Moscow. I put the passport back and took my own. I could hear Wizard moving and shortly after he was over by the desk pouring himself a cup of semi-cold coffee.

The light fell on his muscular naked broad back and I could clearly see all the scars on it. Had I now been a human being who belonged to the 'normal world', I would probably have been shocked and asked about them, but he and I belonged to the 'real world', and therefore I did not need to know the answers to his surrealistic back painting. In fact, I probably knew them only too well, for some of them were identical to those which both JAC and I had on our own bodies. Wizard walked back to the couch, took his t-shirt and tossed it casually over one shoulder and disappeared into the bathroom.

I followed him with my eyes and when he had closed the door I went into the bedroom. JAC and Liam slept, and next to them on each of their bedside tables lay their Glocks, but only Liam's was unlocked. I smiled.

My two men, side by side in the same bed. It was almost too good to be true. I looked at my watch. I had one and a half hours before I had to leave. At the same time, Wizard came out of the bathroom and went – without looking at me – back into the living room. A thought struck me and quietly I closed the door to the living room behind me. The only light now in the bedroom was from a dim street lamp outside. Quietly I walked to the bedside table where JAC's Glock lay and clicked the safety off. At the sound of the click, he opened his eyes and grabbed my hand.

"What the hell are you doing?" he whispered and frowned. Liam, who of course had also heard the click, raised his head and looked at me.

"I just want to make sure the odds are even now that I am going to lie down between you," I said, awaiting their reaction.

I knew that JAC, deep down, didn't like the idea of this threesome, because he couldn't bear to share, so there was a real possibility that he would snap. And Liam? I didn't know him that well but he would definitely defend himself at any time.

JAC looked at me, then he looked at Liam, and the two exchanged a brief glance. To show them exactly what I had in mind I took off Liam's shirt so I stood in front of them completely naked awaiting their decision and I didn't have to wait long. With the speed of a snake that launches for its kill JAC grabbed me and rolled me into the middle. As I lay on my back I closed my eyes and stretched my body. I wanted them to touch me, to kiss me, lick me, scratch me and bite me all over. I wanted it rough and I knew these two enormous contractors would be able to deliver. I could feel JAC's soft lips kissing my neck at the same time as Liam's worked their way over my stomach towards my groin and although it was so unbelievably sensual and intense I needed it to be harder and more uncompromising. I grabbed the hair in the back of JAC's neck and pulled his head back so we were starring each other directly in the eyes.

"No mercy, JAC. Do you hear? No mercy," I whispered letting go of my grip. To my surprise his eyes didn't flinch as he answered okay and then I looked down at Liam. With the sound of my voice, he had stopped kissing me on my inner thighs and when our eyes met, I could see that he had heard what I said. I leaned back again and this time their touches felt hard and rough. As JAC started licking and biting so hard that my nipples were bleeding Liam did the same to my clit and labia and the pain they both inflicted on me made me arch my body as if it was a bow. The pleasure of it was out of this world and made me crave for more. Not just in the sense that I wanted sexual relief but I needed to find my boundaries and break through them. I needed to cross that line where Liam's road map and JAC's familiar touches became one. Where my two men melted together in my mind and pushed away the memories from Belize. So as they took their turn plunging deep into me while I sucked the cock of the one not inside me, tasting my own juices, the images from Belize faded away completely. And then and only then did I let myself climax.

The fact that our sex could have ended fatally at any time because of JAC's jealousy, was definitely a key factor to why I came so hard. Because secretly, it turned me on that I had him on a limb between his own life and my desire. Just thinking about it was such a kick that I could hardly breathe. At no point was I afraid for my own life, but the thought that this could cost them theirs was absolutely out of this world.

When we were finished, I got up, put on my clothes, kissed them both, took my bag and went into the living room. Wizard was long gone, so with the ticket, the SIM card and the passport in my pocket, I closed the door to the suite behind me and walked down the hotel corridor. My horrible past in Belize had been conquered and as I looked at my watch I smiled. It showed six a.m. precisely.

Chapter 8

In the taxi on the way to the airport, I put the new SIM card in my phone and a scarf around my head. I had a hijab in my bag but there was no reason to put it on before the plane landed.

* * *

Tehran was like most other large Middle Eastern cities. A jumble of architecturally modern buildings created to insure the largest possible wow factor for the tourists and with the least possible interest for the general part of the population, who for the most part did not live in the large fashionable glass skyscrapers, but instead in smaller whitewashed houses. Most foreigners lived in newly built urbanisations that were gated and fenced, and with concierges and guards, so, when driving around in these areas, one could be anywhere on the Arabian Peninsula.

My assignment was one of the easier ones and since I had a few days beforehand, I took the opportunity to do some shopping. It was an extremely rare opportunity, as my missions were primarily done and over in thirty-six hours, but this time it suited me really well. Since marketplaces and bazaars were obvious targets for assassinations and suicide bombers, I always stayed away from them and therefore it was almost automatic that I cruised down the small side streets to use the local shops. In fact, it was usually here that one could find the best bargains and since my Farsi was quite good, due to my many Middle Eastern missions and the language courses on my iPod, I got some good deals on a pair of hijabs.

I stayed at a small, local hotel that was not mentioned in any tourist guide. The décor of the room was very spartan, which suited me just fine and the place was one where no one asked questions and no one interfered in my coming and going. So I felt quite safe as I paid for my room in advance and in cash, of course.

The evening before the assignment, I was sitting on my bed, and as usual I was getting OPUS ready when I suddenly heard American voices in the hallway. I immediately grabbed my Glock and slipped to the door and listened. There were probably three people and they were relatively loud as they opened the door to the room opposite mine and went in. For a moment I stood and listened, but there was complete silence. All my alarm bells were ringing because there was something about this scenario that was not right. What would three Americans be doing here in this dump? I went back to the bed, packed all my things, and disappeared out of the hotel as anonymously as I had arrived.

A little further down the street there was a local café and here I placed myself in a corner from which I had a full view of the hotel entrance. I sat there for several hours just watching the hotel door and around midnight it paid off. A tall western looking guy came out of the hotel. It was clear that he was ex-military of some kind, as he stood there, scanning the terrain. A car drove down the street and the light from its headlights lit him for a brief second. But that was just long enough for me to take a picture of him with my mobile phone. I immediately sent it to Liam and then proceeded to observe the westerner. He started walking down the street in the opposite direction from where I was sitting, so I let him get a head start before I got up and followed him. A few minutes' walk through some narrow and winding streets and we arrived at a large open square and here I just managed to catch a glimpse of him hailing a taxi. At the same time a message arrived on my phone. It was from Liam. The message was 034 –code for – distress, wait for orders.

I hailed a taxi and gave a destination at the far end of town. It was only to buy myself some time so I could hear from Liam and after just three minutes in the taxi the message came. 001AG – Abort mission immediately and get out – followed by a French address and a six-digit code.

Immediately I diverted the taxi to the airport and a few hours later, I was sitting on the first plane out of Tehran heading for Europe. The plane landed in Frankfurt where I rented a car and turned on the GPS.

The address that Liam had sent was an apartment in Paris and after a few hours driving I handed over the car at *Charles De Gaulle* airport and took the metro to the *Arc de Triomphe*. From there I walked into the Latin Quarter and it didn't take me long to find the old property in a small narrow street.

I went in by the front door and up the wide staircase to the first floor. It looked odd that there was an electronic door lock on the otherwise beautiful Victorian door, but there was. Without further speculation I entered the six-digit code and the door clicked open. For safety I pulled out my Glock before slowly pushing the door wide open until I had a full view of the interior: it was a long hallway with rooms on each side. It was dimly lit but I could see a rather bright light coming from one of the rooms further down. A young woman came out of the lighted room and walked directly towards me. She signalled for me to lower the gun, and even though she didn't seem like a threat I only did when she was right next to me. With a smile on her face, but without saying anything, she walked past me and closed the door behind me. Then she turned to me.

"My name is Patrice," she said with a strong Irish accent and still smiling, "Come. Liam is going to be here soon."

Pretty surprised by the whole situation I followed her and she showed me into a bedroom where clean linen had been put on the bed. I put my bag down and looked around the room which appeared to be unaltered since the property was built but it was cozy and inviting, so who cares.

"Are you hungry?" she asked in a friendly tone. I shook my head and continued looking around the room. Suddenly the front door clicked and I recognized Liam's footsteps down the hall. He stopped at the door to my bedroom and looked at Patrice, who without a word, immediately left the room. Liam entered and his facial expression was serious and did not encourage conversation. He closed the door and, with raised eyebrows, I asked him what was going on.

"It's shit," he replied coldly and mechanically, putting his hands in the pockets of his trousers.

"The picture you sent me ... How did you come across the guy in it?" Liam stared at me and even though he was trying to seem kind, he did not really succeed in hiding the coldness and mistrust in his eyes. I told him about the events of the evening and night and, while I was talking, he leaned against the dresser with his arms crossed while watching me.

"It was good that you sent me that picture. Do you know who the man is?" I shook my head but said nothing. "His name is Greg and he belongs to a joint venture elite unit known for locating, kidnapping, torturing and killing 'dangerous' mercs. Why he was near you, I don't know yet and, to be honest, I don't think that you were the target, because there is no contract out on you yet, at least not a contract that is so big that he would bother to take it," he added, "Furthermore, it is not like him to be so visible and definitely not if you were the target. Personally I think that it's a coincidence but, hopefully, I will know more later on today."

"What about my assignment? It was scheduled for today. In seven hours," I said as I looked at my watch.

"The money has been returned and the customer has been notified. I have re-assigned it."

I looked at him sceptically. This was really shit. It would be a huge problem if I had become a mark for an elite unit, but I was inclined to agree with Liam. It was not me who was the target, but why of all the hotels in Tehran, did they stay at that one? And if it was because the hotel was used by mercs, then it was not safe anymore. Greg had done nothing to hide his presence at the hotel, which in his industry was highly unusual, and especially if he was on a mission. If I had been the target he would not have acted the way he did and even without knowing him I refused to believe that his intelligence would be so bad that he did not know that I was at the hotel. I did not know him – for good reason – and could only imagine what means he had available, but I would think that they were relatively unlimited. Liam straightened up.

"We will stay here for the time being and wait for the others to arrive and I reckon that by then we will know more."

Without further comment, he left the room and went down the hall while I sat on the bed and looked down at my thighs. All this seemed completely crazy. CRAZY.

* * *

Liam spent most of the day in front of the laptop with his Bluetooth glowing in his ear.

Patrice looked after us and without getting in the way of a frequently pacing Liam. At one point I went into the kitchen where Patrice was cooking because there was nothing I could do in this situation. As I sat down in front of the massive wooden dining table, she looked at me and smiled.

"Sorry about all this," I said. It was not really because I was sorry, but I just felt I should say something to her. I had no idea who she was, but it was clear that she was used to being in the apartment and that Liam had her full trust and confidence as there were no closed doors and we could therefore hear everything Liam said. It didn't seem to affect Patrice, who calmly carried on working.

"I'm so used to it," she replied and then she nodded in the direction of a plate of freshly baked croissants on the table, "Help yourself."

They smelled insanely good, so I snatched one and nodded appreciatively while chewing.

I heard the front door opening and I leaned back and looked out into the hallway. It was Wizard and he walked very fast. Without seeing me, he disappeared into one of the rooms, where I could hear him throwing his bag on the floor.

Then he came towards us and when he was almost by the door to the kitchen, I handed a croissant out through the doorway to him. I could feel him taking it out of my hand and then he came into the kitchen.

"Hey, babe," he said cheerfully, ruffling my hair with his hand.

"Patrice. *Mon chére*!" he shouted excitedly, as he almost skated over to her and lifted her up from behind. Patrice chuckled while Wizard swung her around and kissed her on the back of her head. Then he put her down and dipped his croissant in a *bouillabaisse* that stood bubbling on the stove. Patrice slapped him across the wrist.

"Pig," she said and Wizard laughed and turned to me as he chewed eagerly.

Suddenly Liam shouted from the living room and his voice made both Wizard and me stop and look in the direction of the sound. It was the first time I had heard Liam get so upset and apparently it concerned Wizard as well as he frowned which made him look very serious.

I raised my eyebrows and our eyes met.

"How long has he been like this?" he asked.

"All morning." Patrice replied without looking up from the stove.

"Hmm." Wizard went and stood in the doorway and looked into the living room. I turned my head and just managed to catch Liam's gaze, which clearly indicated that none of us should get near him right now. I immediately turned my attention to the plate of croissants again, and Wizard, who had also read the warning in Liam's eyes, retreated as well. As he sat down on the other side of the table he took a second croissant.

"Well as long as we're sitting here, I need to know who you are, Patrice?"

Wizard stopped chewing and Patrice turned around and wiped her hands on her apron.

"Yes, of course, and I'm sorry. I'm Liam's sister," she said, and my facial expression must have said it all, for Wizard almost collapsed in laughter.

"Patrice lives here. She is married to Killian. If you haven't met him yet, you will later; A mad red-haired Irishman with a hell of a temper. But under the façade he is ..." Wizard hesitated, "No, not even under the façade, is he okay." He laughed out loud again and as Patrice threw a tea towel at him she stuck her tongue out.

Suddenly, Liam slammed the door to the living room, and with such a bang that we all stopped what we were doing and looked at each other. Slowly I put my palms on the table and got up.

"I'd better go in there before all the windows go," I said quietly looking at Wizard, whose facial expression questioned whether this really was a good idea.

"Are you sure?" he asked seriously and I have no doubt that if I had asked him to join me he would have done so without hesitation. But I considered it best to deal with Liam alone so I just nodded to Wizard and left the kitchen.

I slowly opened the door to the living room to check Liam's mood, but the silence that met me immediately told me that there was no danger. Quietly I closed the door behind me and knowing that Liam had heard me

I went and stood behind him. He was sitting on one of the couches with his face buried in his hands and to be completely honest, it actually made me a little uneasy. Gently I put my hands on his shoulders.

"Speak to me, Liam. What's going on?"

Liam took a deep breath.

"I have to think and get a handle on all this before I tell you. Besides, I would prefer it if we were all here."

"Okay," I replied, but I did not think that was it. The information I had received from him so far was very sparse and despite the fact that we all seemed to be involved, I could not shake the thought that Liam right now was buying himself some time in relation to it – whatever it was.

"I saw Wizard is back," he said.

"Yes, but he's the only one," I replied, just to indicate that if it was time he wanted, he had a little more.

Liam nodded a few times. Then he got up and went to the window and looked out. He stood there for a long time without saying anything, but then suddenly he turned around and went over to the phone and made a call. It was clear that he did not need my presence, so I retreated to the kitchen, where I was met with the sight of Wizard standing with his head inside the refrigerator, looking for a bottle of white wine. When he had found what he was looking for, he poured two glasses and handed one to me and one to Patrice.

"In the absence of red wine," he said as he lifted his own glass towards us. It came as no surprise to me that it contained JD and not white wine but I was surprised that he didn't offer me any! Normally I would drink JD with him so for him to hand me a glass of white wine was totally out of context both for him and me. It was not that I minded but I was used to being 'one of the guys' and now suddenly it felt like I'd been put in the category with 'the girls'. It felt a little weird but we toasted and drank.

"Everything okay in there?" he asked referring to my brief meeting with Liam but honestly, I could not say that it was. If I had thought I would have become wiser about it all by going in there, that had definitely not happened, and whether or not my presence had spawned a lasting peace, I doubted very much. So as an answer to Wizard's question I raised my eyebrows and shook my head, so Wizard could think whatever he wanted.

* * *

At 5 p.m. the front door clicked open. In came a giant red-haired guy who, based on Wizard's description, could only be Killian. As he stood there in the kitchen wearing a suit and tie, he looked like an overgrown office manager and not someone who in any shape or form would have connections to mercenaries. He was at least two heads taller than Patrice and when he subsequently lifted her up and kissed her, she seemed to be as light as a feather in his large muscular arms. After the welcome greetings to Patrice, he looked over at us and immediately a smile spread across his face.

"What the hell Wizard! What are you doing here? Aren't there any more out there for you to kill?" The sarcastic remark came from him in a thick Irish accent followed by a little wink of his left eye. Wizard and Killian laughed and hugged and it was clear that they liked each other and were good friends. Then Killian turned and looked at me.

"And yourself?"

"OPUS," I replied.

"Yes, of course." He laughed as he shook his head a little, "Where is my brother-in-law?"

Patrice stood leaning against the kitchen table and, where before there had been nothing but love in her eyes, it now changed into worry.

"He is in the living room, but be careful. He is not in a good mood."

Killian's facial expression changed immediately and he now suddenly appeared to be very serious. It was a relief for me to see this change in him, because it somehow confirmed to me that he was 'one of us'. Everyone can change their mood even from second to second, but over time I have learned that even in such situations, you can see the difference between ordinary mood swings and then the intense – almost dangerous – ones. And the latter was exactly what Killian displayed.

Forcefully, he walked to the living room door and after a few hard knocks on it, he went in. For the brief moment, the door was open, I managed to get a glimpse of Liam who was on the phone but then the door closed.

It was as if the sound of the door being closed was a starting signal for Wizard, for the very moment it clicked, he got up from the table and took his cigarettes.

"I think I'll go and rest for a bit," he said, winking at me and I knew what that meant. It was 'medicine time', "Wake me when we are going to eat."

"Of course," I replied, smiling, "Sweet dreams." I chuckled while winking at him.

Wizard gave me an affectionate pat on the back of the neck before walking down the hall and disappearing into his room.

The silence in the kitchen was only interrupted by the little bubbles from the pot of fish soup still simmering on the stove. Patrice sat down at the dining table and sipped her wine.

"How long have you lived in Paris?" I asked quietly, out of curiosity about her and the setup. That she was a part of it, intrigued me.

"Liam bought the apartment eight years ago; I moved here a year later so ... for seven years. The location is perfect – especially in relation to Killian's work."

"Yes, please forgive me for asking, but I had no idea that Liam had this place or that he had a sister," I replied with a hint of indulgence in my voice. Patrice smiled,

"It's not something he tells a lot of people. Do you really know anything about his past?"

"Yes, he has told me a little," I replied, suddenly not wanting to continue the conversation. If I wanted to know anything about Liam, I would want it to come from him and, even though Patrice was his sister, it felt a bit wrong. Whether Patrice could sense it in my answer, I don't know, but she didn't comment further on it but simply took a sip of her wine.

"I only love two people in this whole world and they are Liam and Killian," she said with sincerity that showed that the words came straight from her heart.

I did not know how to respond and I therefore chose to change topic.

"What does Killian do for a living?"

"He is a political adviser in Brussels. He is a member of Sinn Fein."

Her answer immediately made me smile because yes, of course he was. Why had I not even considered that? I poured more wine into our glasses and, like a small child, Patrice took her glass with both hands.

"It was actually Liam who introduced Killian and me to each other ten years ago," she suddenly said in a slightly dreamy voice while smiling wryly, "But we only got married two years ago."

I was pretty surprised by this information; quick arithmetic told me that Liam and Killian, who looked the same age, must have known each other while Liam was in the IRA, and judging by Patrice's appearance, she was not a day over twenty-five so ...

My thoughts began to revolve around this whole scenario and suddenly it hit me. Liam had presumably bought this apartment with some of the money he had earned as a contractor and then installed his sister. There could be many reasons for this, but I was sure it was not out of brother or sister love. Liam seemed to me to be way too much of a strategist for that. Maybe it was a pleasant bonus that he knew where his sister was, but he had not bought the apartment for either her or for their common good. It was an asset – a temporary base that, if necessary, could be wound up quickly and replaced with a new one.

It would not have surprised me if Liam had been the mastermind behind Patrice and Killian's marriage, if not directly then indirectly, because somehow it was very practical that Patrice was married to a political official who was fighting for the same cause that Liam was – just with slightly different methods. Maybe Liam had even had a hidden agenda with it? That could well have been the case.

I leaned back in my chair and lit a cigarette. I wondered how many 'bases' Liam had. I exhaled the smoke and smiled. Time would tell. One thing I was sure of now was that as long as Liam could see an advantage in having me close, that was as long as he would hold on to me, just like he was doing with this apartment.

So, I had to be careful. While we had a mutual need for each other nothing would happen. But what about when the need was no longer there? Would we then look into each other's gun? Right now I needed Liam, because he had the contacts to get us out of this, whatever this was. One thing I hadn't really been able to figure out was how I fitted into his plans? Oddly enough, it didn't make me uneasy. I just had to be on guard because one day the bill for all this would come, I had no doubt about that. The question was just how it was to be paid.

I took a puff of the cigarette and stubbed it out in an ash tray as I exhaled the smoke. I needed some time to myself to gather my thoughts so I got up and went into my room and threw myself on the bed.

How long I lay there I don't know but suddenly Liam appeared in the doorway and looked at me.

"Come into the living room," he said coolly and then disappeared. As I got off the bed I could hear him knocking on Wizard's door. I began to walk down the hallway, and as I passed Liam I could hear Wizard raising his voice. I continued down to the living room.

Killian was standing in the kitchen talking softly to Patrice, so I went into the living room. I could hear footsteps and shortly after Liam entered. Thirty seconds later Wizard appeared in the doorway, looking slightly annoyed. Killian joined us and with a single nod from Liam, Wizard closed the door. Liam didn't waste any time. He began immediately to explain the situation for us.

"This is on a need-to-know basis only," he said as his eyes focused on each of us in turn, "And you must all trust that what I say and do now is to minimize the damage."

"Okay." Wizard replied, but I could sense a clear distrust in his voice.

It was seldom that we trusted anybody, even someone who we knew well and whom, under normal circumstances, we would have had full confidence in. In our job we were constantly surrounded by people who did not see lives to be worth anything, and we all knew that the only reason we were still alive was because we were good at taking care of ourselves and that each and every one of us provided a service that others needed. Our allegiance to these people could be bought, and if the price was right, we were for a short time connected. Once the missions were completed, the contact was terminated, and we were nothing but the person they had needed for a short time to achieve a goal. What that goal was did not matter to us. The goal for us was to complete the assignment and disappear. So that's why we only trusted ourselves and that's why what Liam asked of us was so infinitely big. Liam knew this, but having said that, I also had no doubt that what Liam was doing now was not only for us, but just as much to save himself.

"Killian and Patrice are leaving the apartment now and going to Brussels. They will relocate in one of Sinn Fein's apartments to be under their protection."

Liam looked at Killian, who nodded briefly and left the room. It was clear that Liam did not want Killian to know about the rest of the plan, and Killian had no intention of wanting to either. What you do not know, you cannot tell anybody.

Liam waited until Killian had closed the door before continuing and in the meantime, Wizard had sat down on the sofa and was now staring very sceptically at him.

"The situation is this; the FSB has a contract out on OPUS for the murder in Moscow that you carried out." Liam said looking at Wizard.

"What the hell?" Wizard interrupted and he was about to make various verbal outbursts when Liam's look stopped him.

"The FSB had ordered the assassination of the political opposition leader – the assignment that you carried out, but they subsequently decided that all the loose ends should be terminated so that nothing could be traced back to them. It therefore meant that the sniper had to be killed. Apparently a mix-up occurred, for somebody in the FSB thought that it was OPUS who had performed the contract, so when the FSB contacted Greg, to get him to take the contract on OPUS, Greg subsequently received information from his own intelligence indicating OPUS being in Tehran when the murder took place and therefore it could not have been you ..." Liam stared directly at me as he said this, "who was the shooter. It was therefore no coincidence that Greg was at the hotel in Tehran and the taxi you saw him get into was to take him to the Russian embassy to inform the FSB that they had the wrong sniper and that he therefore wouldn't take the contract. So far, the FSB does not know who actually performed the assassination however they have chosen to uphold the contract on OPUS. There is no doubt that it is only a matter of time before they find out that it was you, Wizard, and when that happens, a contract will be taken out on you as well. And you can be sure that Greg will take that contract."

Liam paused for a moment as he glanced between Wizard and me. I felt totally empty and I could feel a slight panic spreading, which was unfamiliar to me. Normally I had everything under control, but ...

"That's not all," Liam said, "We all know that the FSB does not stop until the corpses fill the streets and neither will they cease until they find the real shooter, even if OPUS is their official target. That's why I've put Patrice and Killian under the protection of Sinn Fein. It's ex IRA people who are responsible for their security and people I know well, so they are safe. Aussie is in Ukraine and if the FSB finds him, we will probably not see him again. As far as I know, Aussie does not know who had the Moscow contract, but before the FSB finds out about that, well ..."

Liam looked at Wizard and me with raised eyebrows and we both knew what he meant: Aussie was virtually dead.

"Do I understand this correctly? There is currently a contract out on me and it's just a matter of time before there's one on Wizard too, and Aussie is 'wanted' because he might know something about all this, which he probably doesn't?" I said this with such astonishing calmness in my voice, that even I was surprised by it, for I was in no way calm about the situation.

Liam nodded. "Yes, that's right."

"But if Greg has not taken the contract on me, who has?"

"I don't know. The FSB works with a lot of outside contractors, and they may also have given it to an internal division of their militia. None of my contacts knew anything."

"And you're sure none of your contacts have taken the contract?"

Liam took a deep breath.

"I don't know."

I slid slowly down the wall which I was leaning up against, staring blankly into the air. No one said anything until Wizard broke the silence.

"How the hell do you know all this?" he said with the deepest mistrust in his voice, scowling over at Liam.

Liam looked at him.

"Because OPUS sent me a picture from Tehran of Greg who had stayed at the same hotel as her. She had no idea who he was or what he was."

I interrupted Liam.

"There was just something about the whole situation in Tehran that did not feel right and he was the trigger. That's why I took the picture and sent it to Liam." I leaned my head back and looked up at the ceiling.

Wizard, who had been sitting with his eyes fixed on Liam, diverted his gaze and looked down.

"We are not safe while we don't know who has the contract on OPUS and as long as we don't know, we are 'sitting ducks'," said Liam with the utmost seriousness in his voice, "The FSB will do anything to get hold of just one of us who can provide them with information. And whether the information is about OPUS or you doesn't matter to them, as long as they get their shooter. And even if they get hold of you first, they have to eliminate OPUS too, because officially ..."

"It was me who took the contract," I said finishing Liam's sentence.

Liam nodded.

"Exactly," he said.

Wizard suddenly swept everything off the table in front of him.

"Fuck," he shouted and his unfocused eyes darted from side to side, "Fuck, fuck, fuck."

Liam had sat down on the couch opposite Wizard and with the most monotonous voice imaginable, he continued.

"My suggestion is that we go to Afghanistan and disappear for a while until we can find out who has the contract on OPUS."

"Have you lost your mind, Liam?" Wizard shouted. "Afghanistan? Where the hell are we going to hide in Afghanistan? If you say on an American base I ..."

With lightning speed, Wizard pulled his Glock, leaned over the table, and put the gun to Liam's forehead.

"Wizard," I said firmly, "Drop it. We are all in shit up to our necks." There was a long pause and neither Wizard nor Liam moved.

"What did you mean by Afghanistan?" I asked, turning to Liam.

It was as if time stood still for a moment, but then Wizard slowly removed the Glock a few centimetres back from Liam's forehead.

"We're going to go to one of the European Camps." Liam continued in the same calm and monotonous tone of voice, but without taking his eyes off Wizard.

Slowly Wizard lowered the gun while his eyes were still locked on Liam, who turned his head slightly and looked at me. I was still staring up at the ceiling.

It made sense what he suggested. In a European Camp we would not be so vulnerable. In an American Camp, Greg would have easy access to us, and we would never be safe there – we would be 'sitting ducks'. We would at least have a chance in a European Camp because it would be more difficult for Greg and his team to get to us.

Wizard had now lowered the gun completely and just to distance himself Liam got up and started to walk around. But his eyes were still fixed on Wizard.

"But we still have a problem ..."

Wizard snorted and looked at Liam while he shook his head.

"Bring it on," he said, waving his gun.

"Even though we are better off in a European Camp, there are the legionnaires and mercenaries from other private security companies to take into consideration."

Wizard laughed a little and swung faster with the gun.

The legionnaires were known for their code of honour, but it was a code that only applied within their own ranks and therefore, had no direct influence on contractors like us. For the same reason, they could be extremely unpredictable in situations like this and, despite my so far sparse contact with them, it was my impression that for them life was primarily about two things: Money and brutality – and not necessarily in that order. Although they were attached to the French army and often constituted the front line in conflicts around the world, it was also my impression that if the cheque had enough zeros on it, friends were suddenly enemies and vice versa – as long as they were not legionnaires or from the French army.

But ... on the other hand, they also had the reputation of completing their missions to perfection so the fact they took on 'extra orders' was somewhat ignored.

The private security companies were not so bad, but here too it depended on which company it was.

"I had no idea there were legionnaires in the European Camps," I said, "I really thought they were just called in for special assignments and then they were gone."

"There is usually at least one permanent division in a Camp." Liam replied still looking at Wizard.

Wizard abruptly stopped waving his gun.

"Is Luc's division one of them?" he asked looking at Liam.

"Yes." Liam replied.

Wizard secured his Glock and put it into his waistband behind his back.

"Then we have a chance," he said firmly with a bit of optimism in his voice which actually rubbed off on my otherwise pessimistic mood. To be honest, I had no idea what he was talking about, and at the moment. I did not really care. If they could give us just a little protection, that would be okay. I got up from the floor and walked to the coffee table.

"What about JAC?" I asked, lighting a cigarette. Liam looked at me and I was well aware that he was trying to figure out if my voice was hiding something emotional or if the question was really just to get a practical status update on him. The truth probably lay in the middle, but I did not let myself be caught up in it and what conclusion Liam came to did not interest me. JAC was a part of the group and therefore his status was important to us – and to me.

"He is in Pakistan – close to the Afghan border and is waiting, as is

Aussie, to hear from me. If we agree to go to one of the camps, we will all meet there."

"What if we split up and disappear in different directions?" The question came from Wizard and actually he had a point.

"It's a possibility too," Liam said, "but our odds are better if we stay together."

Wizard pulled his Glock again and aimed it at Liam, but this time Liam was prepared and they both ended up aiming at each other.

"What keeps you from eliminating OPUS and me right now? Then all the problems would be solved."

"Nothing," Liam replied unemotionally and without any facial expression at all, "Nothing."

The thought had crossed my mind too but I had come to a conclusion that it did not require a Glock to answer that question, so therefore I went over and stood next to them.

"Stop this," I said, "Wizard, think about it. Liam has had the opportunity to kill us the entire time. In fact, he would have been able to kill us without us being able to do much about it. We have had no idea about all this until now. Liam is the only one who has been in possession of the information. The question is, Liam, what has kept you from killing us?"

I looked at him, but Liam's eyes were fixed on Wizard, "Because I do not kill mercs," he said softly and calmly.

There was complete silence in the living room and time seemed to have stalled, but suddenly Liam secured his gun and slowly put it back in his waistband.

Very, very slowly Wizard also lowered his Glock, secured it, and put it behind his back. I took a deep breath as I looked at them both.

For a while, peace was re-established, but I knew the ceasefire was very fragile. But at least for now it was there.

"Good," I said, trying to sound positive, but the word came to sound more hollow than honest, "Do we then agree on Afghanistan?"

Wizard nodded and with his acceptance the plan could be put into action. And there was no time to waste.

Liam walked over to one of the window sills and picked up a cell phone. Like a hawk, I could not help but observe the two fighting cocks, for even though Wizard had agreed to Liam's idea, his trust was in no way restored. My eyes flicked between them, but they did not look at each other, so I took it as a positive sign of their mutual acceptance.

Suddenly, Wizard got up, opened the door, and went out into the kitchen. From the silence in the apartment I concluded that Patrice and Killian had already left.

A moment later Wizard returned with three beers. He handed one to Liam and they exchanged a brief glance, after which Liam accepted the bottle. Then Wizard turned and walked over to me and gave me one. Then he clinked bottles with me, and as he put his beer bottle to his lips he turned away. It took him exactly one minute to finish the bottle. Not a record but good enough. Wizard's rather aggressive attitude made me a little anxious, but for all intents and purposes I tried not to let it show. The last thing we needed was to mix the already explosive cocktail that the two gentlemen had stirred together with my suspicions. Carefully I put my beer bottle down on the coffee table, and out of the corner of my eye I could see that Liam had put his on the window sill – and just like me without as much as having consumed a drop. His phone beeped a few times and after reading the messages, he broke the silence.

"JAC and Aussie are meeting us in Afghanistan," he briefly stated and I could tell by his voice that this was pure information and nothing else.

I was going to ask Liam what time we were leaving, but he got ahead of me and said, "Tomorrow at 8:10 am."

"Okay," I replied and from his tone of voice it was clear that he was not willing to answer any more questions so I kept quiet. He was on his laptop again, which was on the desk, and he stood bent over it as he typed. When he was finished he connected the small portable printer and printed out three tickets. Calmly I went over, looked at them and smiled. It was the first time I had been a Swedish citizen.

The sound of the living room door slamming hard made me turn around and I could immediately see that Wizard was gone. For a brief moment, I considered whether I should stay and smoke one last cigarette, but I quickly let the thought go as I really wanted to follow Wizard's example.

"I'm going to bed," I said, "Wake me if there is anything."

Liam answered with a "Mmm" that signalled a yes, and on that note, I went into my bedroom and went to bed.

I don't know how long I slept, but I woke up to the sound of Liam's Glock as he laid it on the bedside table next to me. He was sitting on the edge of the bed fully dressed with his back to me and even though I was facing him, he just sat there completely still. Suddenly he lay down with his back to me and I could not help but put one arm around him.

"Thank you, Liam," I said softly, squeezing him a little. For some reason I had expected him to react to my touch but he didn't. He just lay there.

"For what?" it came monotonously from him.

"For not killing me."

My answer made him turn but it was to lie on his back and even though I had my arm resting on his chest he still didn't touch me. He just turned his head so we looked into each other's eyes.

"You're welcome," he said and smiled a little, "It makes me sad that Wizard is hooked on that shit," he continued in a low voice.

It was the first time Wizard's drug issues were mentioned and I didn't like talking about it. Maybe that's why I removed my hand from him and rolled over on my back. Somehow I did not feel that he should be the one addressing this. It was Wizard's problem and if he wanted to share it with us, it should come from him and no one else.

"He wouldn't have pulled the trigger," I said with the greatest certainty in my voice, alluding to their little intermezzo with the Glocks earlier.

"And if he had?" Liam asked now starting to cuddle one of my upper arms.

I was quiet.

"He's just like you, Liam. He doesn't kill mercs."

"Maybe," Liam replied, "But all in all ... How the hell do you think he got his nickname as being one of 'The Butchers from The Balkans'?"

I sat up in the bed. This information was new to me and for some reason it surprised me.

"Is he ...? Fuck, Liam."

I had heard of 'The Butchers from the Balkans' but never imagined that Wizard could be one of them. What 'The Butchers' did over there during the war was horrific but then war is horrific. It can bring the worst out in people and even though I didn't condone war crimes I who was I to condemn? I had killed people that were not even in war zones. Did that make my deeds better? I couldn't even excuse my killings by saying they happened during a war because often they didn't. So who was I to talk?

"He is on The Hague's list of international war criminals then?"

Liam did not answer the question but breathed deeply and, suddenly, the seriousness of this dawned on me. If Wizard really was one of 'The Butchers from The Balkans', then he was wanted by the CIA, MI6 and Interpol, in addition to being on The Hague's list of the most wanted war criminals in the world. That made him a highly coveted target and the price on his head would increase tenfold.

Presumably he already had one, but now – after the murder in Moscow – it had undoubtedly got bigger. But it was not only Wizard, whose head was in danger.

It was as if Liam had read my mind because he interrupted my thoughts.

"The word you are looking for is FSB. If they find out that he was behind the killing, then they will most likely say that it was a hit ordered from the Balkans and thus try to ignite the Balkan conflict again. The UN will suffer a betrayal and Wizard will of course be at the top of everyone's list. Especially

FSB's because they have to protect themselves nationally and Russia's reputation internationally. The UN will hunt Wizard because he will be able to expose the FSB for what they are, and last but not least so will the CIA, because they need him to testify who is really behind the assassination in Russia and thus have a means to pressure Putin in the 'fight for Ukraine'. If it becomes known that Wizard is one of 'The Butchers from the Balkans', then the former chief of the armed forces in Sarajevo, Mr. Karadžić, the bastard, his loyal supporters will be chasing him indefinitely, because he can point out several of their senior officers and politicians and expose them for what they really are and for what most of them did during the war. And let us not forget all the militias and other opportunists in the industry who are just waiting for Wizard to surface one day so they can kill him. In other words, it was not really that bad that some idiot in the FSB got you signed up as the one who performed the assassination. The problem arose when Greg was able to prove otherwise."

"Better me than Wizard," I whispered.

Liam sat up.

"No, but we could have dealt with Greg, Christ ... I could have blown his head off myself, and I would have done it without hesitation, but the FSB is a completely different matter. They are a mix of simple patriots and super capitalists. They have access to one of the world's best intelligence networks and have unimaginable financial means behind them. They make Al Qaeda look like a holiday camp for autistics."

Liam grabbed my neck and pulled me hard towards him so that our foreheads almost collided.

"Do you now understand how dangerous this situation is?" His patronizing remark, made me instantly pull myself free of him, but he seemed indifferent and just kept watching me, "I do not approve of the things that Wizard has done in his past, but it is 'his' past and we all have one – whether we want it or not," he continued, however, his voice had become less cold and I detected a little emotion as he completed the sentence.

I did not like this little emotional shift in him, so it was almost a relief when I found the emotions were not to be found in his eyes. They were still completely black and icy cold. I let my fingers run down over his narrow lips and while I touched them I could feel his jaw clench.

What Liam did not know was that it was exactly those very things that turned me on completely and I suddenly kissed him aggressively and he reciprocated. Within minutes we had torn off our clothes and naked we delved into each other on the bed. His hands were everywhere and I found that the road map he had drawn earlier was no longer needed.

Never had I made love so wildly and intensely as I did that night with Liam. We made love in the bed, on the floor, up against the walls and in the shower. It was as if we were both set free by it. Free from our past and for the future that we were not even sure we had. And it was amazing, amazing to be so close to a human being whom I, in every way, was so far from. And then again maybe I wasn't. Wouldn't I have acted the same way as him if I had been in his place? The question would not be answered at this point in time, because I was not in his place, so I let go of the thoughts and let the morning hours come.

Neither Liam nor I got much sleep that night because after we had made love it was time to get up and get ready to leave.

* * *

The first cup of coffee of the day I drank in peace in the kitchen but the solitude was broken when Wizard suddenly showed up. Automatically, I poured a cup and handed it to him. He took a sip of it as he looked out of the kitchen window at a menacing grey sky that heralded rain. I patted him on the shoulder and smiled at him.

"For what it's worth, Wizard, I'll be here for you. You are not going to stand alone. No matter what happens." My remark made him look at me as I walked towards the door. I could hear him as he put his cup down but I just continued walking.

"And you just decided that?" he said coldly. I was pretty surprised by his reply and even though I was half way across the kitchen I stopped and turned to face him. Who the hell was he to question my loyalty? He had always had it and he knew it.

"Fuck you, Wizard. You know I've always been there for you and nothing has changed. Nothing." My voice was calm but reflected the inner smouldering aggression that he had seen a few times but never had directed at him. He stood calmly with his back to me, still looking out of the window, and it was as if he was trying my patience for how long he could hold me before he answered. I guess he decided that enough was enough because suddenly he turned and when our eyes met he smiled at me. Then he walked casually to me and whispered in my ear.

"I know, babe." And then he continued straight on and into the living room. I hated when he was like this. This unpredictable aggression that just lay right under the surface waiting to be provoked so it could poke its ugly head up. It was almost like Wizard tested me – tested us – every time he opened his mouth and with the situation we were in and in the company we were keeping – mercs and God knows who else was hunting us – it was just so dangerous.

“Are we ready?” I could hear him asking Liam, who was sitting on the sofa lacing his boots.

“The tickets are over there.” Liam said, nodding toward the desk, but without looking up. Quietly Wizard walked over and took them, and then a faint knock sounded at the front door. Out of pure reflex, we all drew our guns.

Silently, Liam got up and went to the front door which he carefully opened. It was the French concierge with an envelope for us. Liam thanked him and closed the door again. We put our guns away and Liam threw the envelope over to me.

“The passports,” he said and put on his jacket. I opened the envelope and distributed its contents between us, after which Wizard gave each one of us our ticket. Without further conversation, we grabbed our bags and left the apartment. The time was 8:10 am.

Chapter 9

We were picked up at Kabul airport by Aussie and a soldier from the camp.

"Welcome to Sunny Beach," he laughed, pointing to the jeep.

"And then under NATO's protection," I commented in a dry tone of voice, referring to the soldier sitting behind the wheel in the car waiting for us, wearing a light blue helmet.

"Yes, it's incredible what you can get for a few bottles of JD and a little smoke." Aussie replied, knocking on several of the wooden boxes that were stacked in the back of the car.

We immediately threw our bags in the jeep and quickly jumped in. There was no need to waste any time. We were in a hurry and that in more ways than one. First, we had to set up a temporary base and then we could concentrate on solving all this mess.

The young soldier looked at us briefly, and Aussie, who had placed himself in the front passenger seat, knocked hard and firmly on the dashboard.

"Get us to the Camp and preferably before the JD gets too hot," he said to the driver in a rather commanding tone of voice, referring to the delay in leaving. The soldier tried to find first gear but his eagerness and nerves to get back to base caused him to struggle to find it.

"Hey," Aussie shouted annoyed, "Today, please." The young soldier found the gear but when he let go of the clutch, the car jumped forward and stalled. The incident didn't exactly help the poor guy's nerves and neither did the look Aussie gave him.

"When did you arrive, Aussie?" Liam asked while having a firm grip on one of the jeep's roof handles so he did not fall out of the seat, due to the somewhat erratic driving now that the soldier had got the car up and running. Aussie looked at his watch.

"Three hours ago. I got a lift with a UN Hercules that was heading this way anyway. "

"Everything okay in Ukraine?" The question came from Wizard, who was sitting in the back with his upper body turned half away from us.

Aussie turned his head towards Wizard but the noise from the jeep's engine was so loud that he had to shout.

"Same as usual, you know. Fucking lot of bodies everywhere."

The young soldier was very focused on the road and it was clear that he was uneasy about this whole scenario. I don't think he feared the possibility of hitting a roadside bomb. No. He seemed more afraid of us. I leaned forward and whispered in his ear that he should relax,

"We will take good care of you, if you take care of the driving." Whether my words helped, I don't know, but no one commented on his driving afterwards.

Liam reached for his Glock and secured it and despite Aussie seeing it he didn't comment on it.

"We're there in fifteen clicks," he said casually, "You are going to love it. It's a fucking beach holiday."

We drove out of Kabul and as I leaned back in the seat, I could see the raw desert landscape passing by. It was not even noon and it was already unbearably hot. Normally I did not mind the heat, but that day it seemed suffocating to me, and if a cloud had turned up I wouldn't have minded at all. The dust from the desert sand stood like cascades around the wheels of the car, and even though I had my sunglasses on small grains of sand still crept under them and made my eyes itch. Therefore, in more ways than one, it was wonderful when we finally reached the camp. At high speed we drove down the camp's main street. We passed the mess tent, the infirmary and dozens of barracks and tents before coming to a stop. The first one to touch the hot desert sand with his boots was Wizard. Liam and I followed at a slower pace and, for a brief moment, both of us stood still scouting the terrain that surrounded us. Aussie was already busy distributing the boxes of JD and cigarettes to various customers, and it didn't take long before the car was empty. Four boxes of JD went to the mess, one box went to Command OP, one box to one of the officers' tents and minus one box for us, the rest went to the legionnaires.

When everything was distributed Aussie took a bottle of JD from our box and unscrewed its lid. He drank half of it and after looking at it and his accomplishment he handed it to Liam, who with a slight shake of his head refused.

"Wizard?" Aussie threw the bottle to him and without saying a word Wizard tasted the golden fluid in it. After Wizard it passed on to me and I swallowed a third of the contents before giving it back to Aussie who emptied it. A couple of soldiers with bare torsos and with their t-shirts wrapped around their heads glanced at us as they passed.

"More mercs," I heard one say as he snorted, and luckily for him, we treated his comment with the indifference it deserved.

We grabbed our bags and with Aussie leading the way we went to our tent.

"Has it been swept?" Liam asked as we approached it. Aussie looked surprised at him.

"No fucking idea," he replied, but if he had thought that was the end of it, he was terribly wrong.

"Then find out." Liam said soberly, taking off his sunglasses and putting them in one of his shirt pockets. Aussie was about to protest, but before he could even utter as much as a single word, Liam had grabbed him by the throat. While he squeezed, he said very quietly to Aussie,

"Just fucking do it, Aussie. Please." Somehow, the word 'Please' was completely wrong in that context, because there was nothing about Liam's action that indicated that Aussie had an opportunity to refuse the otherwise 'fine' offer. None of us said anything and after half a minute, Liam removed his hand from Aussie's throat. If I had been in Aussie's place, I would have immediately started a fistfight with Liam, but not Aussie. He just stood there coughing a little, with one hand on his neck where Liam had strangled him.

"See you in fifteen minutes." Wizard said and he and Liam began walking down the camp in the direction of the mess tent. Aussie looked like a big question mark as he stood there looking at them strolling away and then suddenly he turned to me.

"What the hell was that all about? I'm no fucking ..." He was about to run after them, but I managed to grab his upper arm, which made him stop immediately. I don't think he expected my interference but as things were at the moment there was no reason to start anything – and especially not with Liam. Because even though Aussie was both bigger and stronger than Liam, Liam had just shown me that he was lightning fast and I had no doubt that it also applied to his trigger.

"Aussie, just do it okay? It's important." I gave him my most pleading look, and I really think it helped. At least it stopped his venture. For a second he stood and looked in the direction Liam and Wizard went and it was only when I was completely sure that he would not follow them that I slowly let go of my grip.

"There better be a damn good explanation for all this shit," he snorted and without further conversation he disappeared between the tents.

* * *

Fuck, it was hot, and in my eagerness to find just a little shade, I spotted a place by the tent opposite ours. I walked over and sat down with my back up against its cloth. It was nice to get out of the scorching sun even though it was still hot to sit in the shade. There was no wind not even a small breeze but it didn't really matter to me. My refuge was perfect because not only did I have a full view of our tent but also to large parts of the camp. I found it very relaxing and reassuring to be able to follow everything that was going on but the peace was over the moment Aussie came staggering back with a young soldier. They disappeared into our tent, and a few minutes later, two more soldiers arrived. They had a lot of gear with them as well as a bomb dog and after preparing the equipment, they went into the tent.

It seemed like Aussie had everything under control, so I leaned my head back and closed my eyes. But what I thought was going to be a little relaxing time for me was quickly disturbed when a soldier, wearing nothing but black tight underwear, opened the door to the tent I was sitting up against. In his eagerness to see what was going on at our tent, he apparently didn't see me.

Aussie was quite loud in his commands to the three guys, and from the words he used it was clear that he was not happy with their work. Suddenly the door to our tent opened and with the pace the three guys came out it looked like Aussie had physically kicked them out. A second later a furious Aussie came out shouting that the only one qualified to perform the task was the dog, so he would keep that and the rest of them could fuck off. As he disappeared into the tent again, I could not help but smile. However, the soldier in the black underwear quickly made my smile disappear as he said something in Scandinavian and ended the sentence with "Fucking mercs". I was so damn tired of hearing comments like this, so I quietly pulled my hunting knife and made its blade gently touch his Achilles tendon. My strokes up and down his right ankle and calf were just hard enough for him to feel it as strokes and not as a slight irritation from the non-existent wind.

He instantly froze and looked down, and that is when he caught sight of me.

"I didn't quite understand what you said? Would you like to repeat it, and this time in English? Please?" I said calmly, without removing my eyes from the blade of the knife.

He stood completely still and stared at me and out of the corner of my eye I noticed that Liam and Wizard were coming back to our tent. Liam went directly into it while Wizard remained outside finishing off his cigarette before following Liam. But, seeing me and the soldier he began to casually stroll over to us. As he got closer, he caught sight of the hunting knife's blade, which I had tilted slightly so that the sun's rays hit it. Wizard's lips transformed into a crooked smile and he removed the toothpick that he was now chewing on.

"What the hell have you done to deserve this treatment?" he said sarcastically to the soldier without the smile on his lips fading. As expected there was no response from the soldier.

"Hey, pretty boy." Wizard slapped him on the cheeks a few times – just to wake him up. The soldier then repeated in English, almost whispering, what he had said, and Wizard immediately stepped right up to him and whispered,

"Speak up." The soldier looked past Wizard in fear as he repeated it,

"I wish they would go to hell the fucking baby killers, fucking mercs."

Wizard acted surprised.

"Baby killers?" he said, taking a few steps back, "Baby killers?" he shouted in a slightly shrill voice bordering on psychotic while lifting his arms. "He says we're baby killers," he shouted even louder as he slowly turned around. The scene began to attract quite a few soldiers who, wisely enough, stood at a distance from this totally theatrical performance. As the crowd grew, Wizard began doing pirouettes like a ballerina and laughed hysterically. In a way, this scene seemed completely insane and on the verge of the psychotic because the combination of the knife moving up and down the soldier's Achilles tendon in a very calm and steady pace was in direct contrast to the somewhat erratic parody Wizard displayed. And then just as suddenly as Wizard started his world premiere of 'Swan Lake', he stopped it, but only to position himself so that there were five centimetres between his and the Scandinavian soldier's nose. The soldier immediately lowered his gaze, which actually was the best thing he could do in this situation. A direct stare into Wizard's eyes would have triggered a fight that he undoubtedly would have lost.

"You bet we are." Wizard hissed without the slightest emotion in his voice, "But it's only because our fucking governments haven't got the balls to send their own troops in – and that fucking includes you, pretty boy. They send us to do YOUR dirty work – which sometimes includes killing children. Actually, instead of condemning us, you should thank us for doing it, so you can go to sleep every night knowing that at least you did not do that." Wizard grabbed the soldier's neck with one hand, "You know, soldier, I think that if you had to do what we are doing for YOU, you would probably lose your fucking mind and would end up torturing and raping the kids so really we are doing the children a favour by killing them and that's why we classify them as mercy-kills, you fucking asshole."

By now Liam and Aussie had come out of the tent but I had signalled to them not to interfere. So they stood – like many others by now – just watching the course of events. A couple of officers wanted to intervene but luckily Liam got hold of them before they did. The last thing we needed was an escalation of the conflict, and that would no doubt have happened if they had come near us. Suddenly Wizard stepped back and while studying the soldier he tilted his head in a slightly crooked way.

"You know, babe," he said with the words directed at me, "I don't think this shit head really knows what I am talking about. I think we better show him."

Wizard's eyes turned black as he stared at the soldier.

"Are you in need of another bitch, babe?"

"Always," I replied coldly without taking my eyes off the blade of the knife.

As if it was rehearsed, Wizard took a step towards the soldier and with a firm grip on his neck threw him over towards our tent. Calmly I got up, put the knife back in its scabbard and casually brushed sand off my trousers. In my opinion the entire display could well have ended here, but I guess Wizard had other things in mind and, for what I had been able to read from his facial expressions, it was all a joke to him. And a joke he would take as far as possible. Liam had definitely read this too because otherwise Wizard would never have been allowed to pass him and Aussie who were standing at the entrance of the tent.

A couple of the officers stormed to the door to rescue the soldier and to be nice Aussie addressed them as they passed him.

"I would not go in there if I were you," he warned them but the officers ignored him and continued into the tent. Less than a minute later, they were walking backwards out of the tent with their hands slightly raised.

"I tried to warn you." Aussie grinned as he scratched his chin. It was as if his otherwise straightforward attitude, for a brief moment, had been replaced by a wise guy, and considering what had just happened this seemed to me quite justified.

By now I was standing next to Liam and Aussie, who had been joined by one of the legionnaires, who I subsequently learnt was called Luc, and, after the officer's exit, I took a deep breath that ended up in a sigh.

"Well," I said, "I guess I'd better go in there and test drive the guy."

Luc started to chuckle and to the sound of his laughter I walked into the tent.

Half a minute later the soldier stormed out of the door and ran as fast as he could down through the camp, and this to the laughter of Luc, Liam and Aussie. Their polyphonic sound was in no way over, when a few moments later they entered the tent.

Since Wizard was the bass in the boys' choir, it was me who had the honour of telling them how the soldier had panicked when Wizard had commanded him to get on the bed and the poor guy had obviously thought that we were going to rape him and when I began to undo my belt, he ran. In fact, nothing could have been further from the truth when it came to our intention with him. He would have had a good spanking and may have become a few layers of skin thinner but nothing more.

When Liam, Aussie and Luc came in, I was therefore standing and wiping my knife blade while Wizard was lying on his bed petting the bomb dog while laughing.

For a brief moment, I could see that Liam was trying to be serious, but it was clear that it was very difficult for him.

"He was a jerk," I said in a slightly annoyed voice, "Not a type that had the guts to either suck or swallow." My choice of words was extremely carefully chosen, and as foreseen the whole tent collapsed in laughter, "As if he would have been the only one here who had chalked his knees and breathed through his nose. What an asshole."

There was not a dry eye in the tent and suddenly Liam put his hand on Luc's shoulder and said weeping with laughter.

"May I present Luc."

Luc gave me his hand and we shook.

"For all of us who haven't chalked our knees and breathed through our noses, *enchanté*," he said in a voice with a strong French accent. Then he winked at me.

For some reason, this was just what we all needed. A good laugh. I knew very well that the show had not come at the most appropriate time, when we were supposed to be here 'incognito', but as long as no names were mentioned, it did not really matter. All of us mercs were perceived as being totally erratic anyway, so in principle the incident could have been by any of the merc groups in the camp. And with all the tensions that had been in our group in the last twenty-four hours, this was a nice way to gain some normality, because this kind of behaviour was actually not unusual to us.

Chapter 10

Despite having been in the business for several years, it was not often that I came across a soldier of Luc's calibre. He was educated in the Foreign Legion and had, before his debut there, had a brutal criminal career in murder, kidnapping and extortion. That he should end up in the French Foreign Legion was written in the stars because his profile fit perfectly with the type of people who served. One can say a lot about The Legion, but they have managed to get even the worst people like Luc under control, and things that such people would have been sentenced for in the normal world, were in The Legion either totally prohibited or totally legal.

The Legion had repeatedly shown that they could get even the most rough and antisocial criminals to function, and in some cases even gave them a career that legalized what they would otherwise be in prison for. Basically, I would have had nothing against soldiers from The Legion if it were not for the fact that they were so fucking unstable, especially when they were not on missions. In recent years, the Legion had – at least officially – acknowledged that turning an officer into a killer was easy enough, but it had its challenges when turning a killer into an officer. Whether that was why it had become considerably more difficult to be admitted to The Legion, I don't know, and from what I could figure out Luc was 'before that time' and therefore part of the 'old elite'.

Luc was the leader of a division of thirty men. On paper, they were all highly trained, professional soldiers, but if you scratched a little deeper, they were all a bunch of complete egoists who had not got much beyond the puberty stage – except when they were on missions. There they were extremely disciplined and worked precisely and efficiently. A division like Luc's was like a well-oiled tank. Massive, impenetrable and bulldozing over everything it encountered on its way.

But when it came to their behaviour in the camp, it was a slightly different matter. They had their own rules and didn't give a damn about anything or anyone, which we got a taste of later that afternoon when we were invited into their tent.

Wizard had declined the invitation as he did not feel safe in their company, because despite the fact that Luc was okay, there was no reason to tempt mercs from the other private companies and especially not when there was a risk of one of them having accepted the contract that by now was on his head. No doubt they all knew he was in the camp, but the mouse did not exactly have to go to the cat. I could understand where Wizard was coming from, but I did not feel that I could let Liam and Aussie go alone into a tent with thirty legionnaires, no matter how well they knew them, so I arrived at the 'lion's den', as the last of the three of us. Had JAC been there, I would have let him go instead so I could have stayed in the tent with Wizard, but he had not arrived yet, so ...

Luc's division had a tent behind ours. They had their own shower and toilet and at the bottom of the tent, two very lightly dressed Asian girls were sitting on a bed. They whispered and giggled to each other as we entered, but it did not seem to bother anyone. Luc seemed very relaxed as he opened his arms and greeted us.

"My friends," he proclaimed loudly and almost sincerely, "Welcome to the *Moulin Rouge*." He gave Liam a friendly hug without taking the cigarette out of his mouth.

"Aussie, my boy," he almost sang as he patted him on the shoulder, "Frank sends his warmest greetings to you from Ukraine. I hear you had a bit of a party over there." Aussie chuckled a bit. I had not heard Aussie mention a 'Frank', but then again, I had not had a chance to hear about his trip to Ukraine. It struck me all of a sudden that Aussie, who usually chatted away when he came back from a mission, had not said a word about this one. Luc looked at me and raised his eyebrows.

"I didn't catch your name before?" he said, taking the cigarette out of his mouth.

I exchanged a quick look with Liam and luckily Liam caught my 'not-a-word' message and immediately took over.

"Who are they?" he said, nodding down towards the two Asian girls.

"They are a part of the mystery of the East," Luc replied poetically while resting his arms on Aussie and Liam's shoulders. "Therapy, relaxation, pure Zen. Right girls?"

The girls giggled and in their little spaghetti strap tops and short skirts that only just hid their tiny bottoms, they most of all looked like two immature teenage girls.

"You are welcome to use them." Luc said hospitably, patting Liam and Aussie on the shoulders.

"It won't be necessary." Liam replied calmly while sending a little smile in my direction.

"I can see you have brought your own relaxation," Luc laughed and nodded towards me, "If the four boys are more than you can handle, honey, just send them to Miss Lai and Miss Lou. They are used to us, so I think they can handle your guys as well."

His comment seemed so infinitely silly that I, without further thoughts of any consequences, stepped in front of Luc and stuck my Glock into his mouth. As expected, the security clicks on the legionnaires' guns were heard everywhere in the tent and without taking my eyes from Luc's, I knew that they had me at gun-point. The move I had just made was probably not one of my most thought through ones, but now the deed was done and I had to try to get out of it in the best possible way. That is why I said in a calm and clear voice:

"I swallow everything that comes in my mouth. Do you, Luc?" My eyes were emotionally cold, and as I stood there, I would not have had the slightest problem in blowing his head off – though it would have been unbelievably stupid of me. I certainly would not have escaped the tents occupants if I had done so.

"You know I would swallow anything for you," a clear voice said from the back of the tent which immediately led my thoughts back to Belize.

I blinked a few times, as if I had to comprehend the memories the sound of the voice brought to me, and then I pulled the Glock out of Luc's mouth. The voice I had just heard meant infinitely more to me than a silly little incident with the legionnaires did. To signal that the whole thing was over – for my part – I held the Glock up in the air and awaited the tent's reaction. Slowly the guns were lowered, but if I had thought the story would end there, I was horribly wrong. As a smile transformed my lips I began to turn around and from the darkest corner of the tent, a little guy stepped forward.

"Kafka?" I was about to walk to him when Luc tackled me from behind. We ended up in a huge fight over three beds, which however stopped as abruptly as it began when a click sounded.

Kafka stood with his gun at the back of Luc's head.

"Luc, I do not have much conscience and morality, you know that, so, I assure you, I would have no problem putting a bullet through your brain if you harm her in any way."

In slow motion Luc raised his hands, signalling that the fight was over. Quietly Kafka secured his Glock, and Luc and he exchanged brief and respectful glances. As Kafka gave me his hand, he looked at me and then pulled me off the bed. Without any thoughts of the others in the tent, we gave each other a long, warm and sincere hug.

"Damn it, Kafka." I took a step back. It had been quite a few years since I had last seen him, and I could not hide my surprise over the fact that he was here.

The legionnaires in the tent went back to their card games, reading or shaving, and Liam and Aussie turned to Luc.

"So ... Luc? What happened to that whiskey?" Liam asked and that question caused Luc to turn his attention to him and so the atmosphere in the tent calmed down.

"Coming right up, my friend," he said cheerfully, fetching a bottle of JD and four glasses. As the first thing he did, he poured two glasses and handed one to me.

"Forgive and forget," he said raising and clinking his glass with mine.

"Forgive and forget," I replied and we both downed our drinks.

"Damn, it's been a long time," Kafka said, smiling at me, "Great to see you ...," and simultaneously we both said, "and still alive."

We had so many things to talk about but before we started we were interrupted.

"Where do you two know each other from?" The question came from Aussie and he was obviously not the only one curious about this, because both Liam and Luc immediately turned their full attention to us.

"Shall we tell them?" Kafka asked, sending me a look that said – you decide the level of details you want them to know.

"We ran into each other in Belize," I said, and it was as if the word 'Belize' had a magical power, because suddenly everyone in the tent stopped whatever they were doing and there was complete silence. One of the legionnaires sitting at the table playing cards looked at me.

"You've been to Belize?" he said almost whispering and with raised eyebrows. It was as if something suddenly dawned on him because he laid down his cards on the table and stared quizzically at me. "Shit, you are OPUS."

When he said it, I glanced at Liam. I had no doubt that he had his finger on the trigger of his Glock. Aussie had also interpreted the mood as potentially dangerous, because slowly one of his hands disappeared behind his back and no doubt round the grip of his Glock.

"Yes," I replied and I was actually surprised. At the time I was not aware that it was common knowledge that I had been to Belize, but the fact that an ordinary legionnaire knew it said something about my impact.

"Jesus," he said, and unexpectedly he got up from his chair and walked over to me, "Very few people are allowed to shake my hand, but it will be an honour for me if you will? Not many foreign female soldiers survive Belize after being captured, so ..." He stuck out his hand and waited to see if I would shake.

I by no means felt safe in this situation, but I shook his hand. Then he went back and sat down at the table and poured whiskey into his glass and drank it all in one go. I looked at Kafka again and took a deep breath.

"We met in Belize. Kafka was my mark." If I had not had everyone's attention before, I certainly had it now because one could have heard a pin drop on a duvet, that's how quiet it was in the tent.

"I was a transporter and needed to get something out of Belize," Kafka continued, smiling sympathetically at me.

"But my employer had no intention of letting him leave the country alive and as my mission progressed, it became clear that neither would I. It was a crazy assignment, and one night I chose to look up Kafka to find out what the hell was going on."

"It was a mess," Kafka added, "It took us all night to make a plan which we executed the next day. What I needed to get out of Belize was so important that OPUS chose to get caught so I could get away."

It was as if the sentence sucked out all the air in the tent.

"So ... To make a long story short. I was tortured for eighteen days in the most bestial ways you can imagine. The rapes were not really the worst. It was the hooks, which they used to drag my body over spikes with ... and then there was the water .... They tried to drown me and when that didn't work, they submerged me into a tub before electrifying it. They wrapped chains around my neck ... sometime my feet ... and dragged me over shards of sharp stones and glass or simply just used them to keep me restrained while beating me. They never beat me on the same place twice. Some days it was the soles of my feet, some days my back, and others the front and back of my legs. They ... burned me and cut me with ..." I took a deep breath and could feel the shivering in the way I blew the air back into the room. I needed this breath to gather myself before I could continue. I would have told them more, given them more details but as I looked at the disgust and horror in the faces around the tent it was clear that I didn't need to. My message had come across so I decided to wrap up my little 'stroll down memory lane'.

"In short: They beat my body to pieces – in my face alone I had fourteen fractures." I paused and only now did I notice, that everyone seemed to be holding their breath, "They thought I was dead when they threw me in a roadside ditch, and I was pretty much dead too. Incredibly, a farmer found me and drove me to a nearby hospital, and how the hospital could find my pulse is a mystery to me, but they did. I could not be identified as they had ripped a lot of my skin off including my fingerprints. I overheard one of the nurses say that 'they had peeled me like you would peel an orange'." I paused to assess the mood and while I once more gazed around the legionnaires, I noticed that they sat so perfectly still that they almost looked like a collection of stone pillars. Stone pillars with eyes staring at me. I smiled to myself, for never had I had an audience that seemed so captivated by me, "One day I was flown to a military base in the US and there I spent the next two years undergoing twelve major and minor reconstructive operations." I took another deep breath but this time the shiver was gone when I exhaled. Although it was quite a few years since Belize, this was the first time I said out loud what I had been through over there.

"Who picked you up?" Aussie asked and his words cut like knives through the silence in the tent.

"Mossad," I replied looking at him.

"You have connections to Mossad?" Luc asked with a mixture of wonder and scepticism.

"No, but I have," Kafka said as he looked at Luc.

"My own organization would not pick me up as I had not completed the contract on Kafka, so Kafka persuaded Mossad to get me out. No one knew how badly I was hurt and what it would take to get me back on track. If they had known, I doubt very much they would have helped," I said with a little smile on my face as I winked at Kafka.

"Yes, they would," he replied, "Because I held back the cargo until you left the US."

Now it was my turn to be speechless. It had never occurred to me that he had had a hand in my recovery nor that he had 'sat' on the cargo for two years.

"What was the cargo?" one of the legionnaires asked and, taking everything into account, he was probably not the only one in the tent who was curious about that.

Kafka and I looked at each other. We both knew the answer.

"It's classified information and always will be." Kafka replied without taking his eyes off mine.

I shifted my gaze and looked over at the legionnaire.

"And it won't help to torture me to find out. That has been tried and failed." I winked at him and smiled.

"It must have been something very special since you chose to do what you did. You pretty much sacrificed your life for it. And voluntarily."

"You almost died for Kafka," another legionnaire said.

"No, I almost died for the cargo. Not for Kafka." I corrected him and this time my voice was harsh and serious. There was a world of difference for me in why I did it, for I would never die for a stranger, and at the time Kafka was a stranger to me.

“And yet you did it? Why didn’t you just kill Kafka and transport the cargo out of the country yourself?” The silence in the tent returned because really it had been the most logical way out of the problem and trust me the thought had crossed my mind several times when Kafka and I made the plan but ...

“Kafka was the only one who could get the cargo out and besides ... I do not kill mercs.” I sent a little smile to Liam and it was as if it woke him up because he appeared startled.

One of the legionnaires got up from his chair and with determination and steady steps he walked over to me.

“I would go to war for you,” he said, accompanied by a small nod that indicated his approval and respect for me. Then he gave me his hand to shake. I first looked down at it but then I decided to take it.

After all, those were rare words from a legionnaire, so I could hardly deny him my sealing them with a handshake. To my surprise, the rest of them followed his example and lastly, Luc came over.

“You can count on me at any time,” he said quietly, shaking my hand followed by a serious look.

“Does this also apply if the price on my head is higher than what you have in your accounts in the Bahamas?” I asked.

“Yes,” he replied, “And I speak for all of us when I say that.”

While the legionnaires had honoured me, Kafka had risen and quietly packed his things.

“I have always said, that I owe you everything and I mean that. In this case, the amount on the cheque would never be large enough for me to take it,” he said as he again stood in front of me this time with his bag over his shoulder.

I smiled at him and two seconds later, he had left the tent.

“Damn, I think we just lost Kafka to you,” Luc said and his comment was followed by a little snort, “Then it’s a good thing that he is an individual contractor, otherwise he would have had hell to pay.” Luc looked at Liam, who had quietly walked over to me and put both his hands on my shoulders.

“Come,” he said and without the others noticing, he squeezed my shoulders a little, “We are leaving.”

With his arm around my shoulders we walked towards the door, and even though I could never dream of telling him, I thought it was nice to feel his arm round me. Why, I do not really know, because under normal circumstances I wouldn’t care, but in this situation, it somehow evoked a strange sense of togetherness, one I somehow had been longing for but certainly was not prepared for. As we walked, I noticed that people once again had started moving, and when we reached Luc, it seemed that the legionnaires were back to normal. Liam stopped when we were next to Luc, released his hold on my shoulder, and while he remained talking to Luc, I continued to the door.

"Hey!" I suddenly shouted to Luc and Liam and they both turned their heads towards me.

"It was secured," I said to Luc and put my hand on my Glock in my waistband.

"I know," he replied before continuing his conversation with Liam completely unaffected by what I had just said.

Slowly I spun around to get out of the tent, but a not so tall Arab-looking legionnaire, who was standing leaning against the door frame and drumming with his fingers on the stock of his FAMAS rifle, caught my attention.

"No, he didn't," he said very, very quietly, referring to the reply Luc had just given me. As I passed him our eyes met for a brief second. For good reason, neither of us acted upon the comment, but I took note of it and stored it in one of my mental boxes.

Knowing that Aussie was waiting for Liam, I continued to our tent and as I opened the door I was met with a sight that I should have expected. Wizard stood in the middle of it and had Kafka at gun-point. Neither said anything and honestly, I could not endure giving more explanations that night, so I just went to Wizard and patted him gently on his shoulder.

"If you pull that trigger, I'll kill you," I said wearily before throwing myself on my bed convinced that Wizard would not make any more out of it.

And I was right. Wizard slowly lowered his gun and, as if nothing had happened, Kafka continued walking down the tent. He went to the empty bed opposite me and he threw his bag on it. Before the bag hit the mattress, the small incident between them had already been forgotten, and I closed my eyes. It was nice just to lie down and slowly my mental exhaustion sneaked up on me and I dozed off.

* * *

Whether it was the heat in the tent or the recapitulation of everything that had happened in Belize, I do not know – maybe it was a combination – but I woke up in the middle of the night and couldn't sleep any more. There was no reason to stay in bed just to toss and turn, so I got up, put on my jacket, and went out into the Afghan night.

It was relatively cool and a bit windy, but it didn't bother me. In fact, it was rather nice. I lit a cigarette and in the glow of the lighter I saw Liam sitting to my right leaning against the tent. It was actually a little strange that he was just sitting there, without saying anything, because if I had not seen him in the glare, then my reaction to his silhouette could have been fatal for him. As he sat there, with his knees bent and his arms resting relaxed on them, he most of all looked like a stone pillar. The expression on his face was not one I had seen before and it could almost be described as thoughtful with a touch of annoyance in it.

I squatted down next to him and watched him quietly as I smoked my cigarette.

For a long time we just sat there in silence and with the glow from my cigarette as the only proof that we were there.

Suddenly he took his Glock, which was lying next to him, and got up. He secured it, put it in the waistband of his trousers and then he bent down and held out his hand towards me. I shoved my cigarette in the sand, took his hand and stood up. We stood for a while and just looked at each other. Then he turned his head and looked up at the night sky.

"I should have known the way you flinched when I touched you in certain places." The way he continued looking up at the stars as the words left his mouth seemed odd. As if he was searching for an answer in them. I looked up. They were beautiful those stars but they held no key to unlock the Belize box. I was the only one who did that.

"It was just .... When you touched these ... spots ... it brought back memories ... flashbacks if you want ... of what they did. Like when you touched my neck I could feel the chain around it." We both lowered our gaze but instead of finding each other's eyes we stared into the dark in front of us. I turned to face him, saying,

"But if it is any consolation that night meant something to me. Something ...." I didn't get to finish because the look he sent me was not one I could reciprocate. It reflected a fear and suffering I had never known – not even when I was in Belize.

"Promise me you'll never love someone like me," he said suddenly, and the remark came as an unexpected bombshell to me. Since when was love a part of the picture? I looked at him and smiled.

"You don't have to worry. It's not going to happen," I replied quietly, trying desperately to hide the slightly contemptuous tone in which the words unfortunately came out.

"Good," he replied, "Because it will kill you ... one way or another."

There was a strange vulnerability in his voice when he said it and I suddenly regretted that I had walked out of the tent that night. I did not want to know anything more about him than I already did, but it was as if he hoped that I would ask him what he meant by what he had just said.

But no ... I remained silent.

"When all this is over, I'm gone, OPUS," he said quietly, closing his eyes.

"Okay," I replied almost whispering, "And where is that promised land where you think you can hide?" He didn't answer and strangely enough, I suddenly had no doubt that he had found it.

I closed my eyes and could feel his warm wet lips touching mine. It was wonderfully life-affirming but not enough for me to forget who he was.

Chapter 11

The activity in our section of the camp increased rapidly during the next few days, unlike elsewhere, where nothing happened.

Based on the first day's incident between Wizard, the soldier and me, Liam had managed to convince the person in charge, an English colonel, that it was probably in everybody's best interest, that all of us 'mercs' had our own section in the camp. The colonel had wisely agreed and we had been given an area at the very back.

Luc, who had been very eager to see this happen too, had together with Liam designed a temporary outdoor office, which was to serve as the headquarters for the construction site and how Liam had managed to get the UN to assign one of their engineers and a carpenter to us I had no idea, but the fact was that we had them for seventy-two hours. So we were now struggling to build three barracks. Liam spent most of the time with his head buried in drawings while Luc was in charge of us contractors as well as his own legionnaires.

But it had not been easy to get to our current position. Despite my otherwise distinct sense of communication, Liam's diplomacy impressed me as he had several times had to act as mediator between us and Luc's division, and when the other group of private contractors, who were in the camp, joined in, it almost ended up like the peace process in the Middle East – an insoluble hard node. All the parties involved made demands on how things should look and how they should be carried out – and no one would give in.

There was also the question of trust; none of us trusted each other completely, so the meetings always started with all the weapons being placed on a large table and then each participant was scanned from head to toe. There was always an equal number of soldiers present at these 'building meetings' and only the 'chiefs' were allowed to speak. We had appointed Liam to speak for us, and Aussie was his 'wingman'. The spokesman for the third group was a Finnish guy named Halo and it was clear from the start that neither Luc nor Liam could stand him.

It didn't improve the situation that Halo was not the sharpest tool in the box so the negotiations soon became even more tense, as Luc's irritations with him grew. But despite that, all three of them magically managed to reach an agreement on the project, so now the train was on track and speeding up.

Personally, I was okay with doing the hard physical work, because it was a welcome change from the daily tasks, and at the same time I kept in shape. We worked incredibly hard and after two and a half days the barracks were raised and only the last finishing touches were missing.

It was actually quite impressive considering how often Luc had had to separate the legionnaires and contractors even though Liam had made sure Halo had a few special tasks outside the camp during the day, so Luc could be in charge without coming into conflict with him. When Halo returned in the evening, Luc usually went on night missions and Halo officially took over Luc's post as foreman.

Already on the first night it was clear that Halo was not up to the task, but his pride and ego prevented him from stepping down, which had led to two soldiers ending up in the infirmary after he had resolved a conflict between them, by shooting them in their legs. Fortunately they were from his own division, so we did not have to speculate on Luc's reaction when he returned to camp. I hate to think what would have happened if one of the wounded had belonged to either our or Luc's group. Luckily neither of them did.

That we were able to work together for the three days it took us to get the barracks completely finished, was in itself an achievement and, that the standard of the individual barracks was above average compared to the rest of the camp, was quite incredible. Each barrack was equipped with its own toilet facilities, microwaves, stereos with surround sound and gas burner for hobs. Luc had used some of his connections in Kabul to get the majority of these things and Liam had had the rest flown in on transport planes from Germany.

When all the barracks were ready, we moved location from our tents in the middle of the camp and down to 'Mercy Land', as one of Halo's contractors, had aptly named our section in the camp.

Luc's and Halo's barracks had their own housewarmings with booze and whores, both of which were brought in from Kabul and for courtesy reasons we briefly attended their parties, but quickly retreated to our own barrack. We had arranged ourselves so that we could screen off every single bed if we wanted a little privacy and Kafka had already pulled his screen because he wanted to sleep. Liam sat at the table typing on his phone and Aussie was in the shower.

Wizard was sitting on his bed cleaning his AK 47 and at his feet lay the bomb dog, whom Aussie had named 'Sweeper'. Incredible though it may sound, it seemed that the dog had fallen in love with Wizard.

I lay on my bed with my eyes closed and listened to a downloaded Thai language class, so all in all there was peace and quiet until the door opened and JAC entered.

Liam looked up and as he got up from the chair a big smile appeared on his lips.

"JAC, bloody hell," he said and they gave each other a friendly hug.

"Damn!" JAC looked around the barrack, "And you called me back from 'Mecca' to live here in this 'shit hole'?" he stated sarcastically.

It was nice to hear his voice again and while Wizard held up his hand as a greeting, I jumped off my bed and ran to him. Immediately he threw his pack on the floor and we hugged each other for a long time. I think he had missed me because he held tight and let his arm rest around my shoulders after we let go of each other. Aussie appeared from the back of the barrack with a towel around his waist.

"JAC-man," he yelled cheerfully and his voice instantly made JAC let go of my shoulders. As they met they greeted with a handshake and a man hug. In the meantime, Liam had retrieved six glasses and a bottle of JD from one of the cupboards in the kitchen and had now placed them on the table.

"I have to say," JAC threw his jacket on the bed next to mine and once more he glanced around the barrack. He continued cynically, "We should be working for a regular army. Private bath and B&O stereo. Not bad. Do I sense some merc connections?"

Wizard scowled over at him and snorted loudly.

"You have no idea," he said dryly beginning to assemble his weapon.

"And you've got a boyfriend, I see," JAC said slightly teasingly, nodding down at Sweeper, who began wagging his tail eagerly, "You just could not wait for me, honey? Could you?" JAC grinned and sent Wizard an imaginary kiss.

Wizard shook his head while smiling and then he threw the dirty cloth he had been cleaning the rifle with towards JAC, who just managed to duck as it came flying. Still grinning JAC took his bag and put it on his bed. He opened a side pocket and pulled out a small package, which he tossed over to Wizard.

"Greetings from northern Afghanistan," he said and then returned to rummage through his backpack. Wizard took the box, opened it, and looked. Then he poured its contents of small glass ampoules onto the bed.

"Specially made for you," JAC said and a smile spread across Wizard's face as he looked over at JAC. JAC stopped unpacking and their eyes met, "Don't worry, I've tested the quality," he said as Wizard held one of the ampoules up against the ceiling light.

JAC looked over at the curtained bed and then sent me a look that said 'Who is that?'

"Kafka," I said, but I could see that it only spawned more questions in him than it answered. Before I could elaborate, Aussie stood next to JAC and with a teasing smile on his lips he bent down to him.

"You know. Wizard has Sweeper. OPUS has Kafka," he said very quietly as he winked at JAC.

"Vuf Vuf," it came from Kafka behind the screen, but that was all. He didn't seem to want to participate in the conversation any further. I glanced behind the screen and he was lying fully clothed on his bed with his eyes closed and his hands folded over his chest, he looked like he was dead. I smiled and noted that Kafka must have super hearing since he had been able to hear Aussie's whispered comment to JAC.

Strange as it may seem, I knew very little about Kafka – even though he had been the cause of the biggest life changing factor in my life. After Belize, my life was different. Not my work life, no ... that continued as usual with unchanging demands and the strength they required came from within me. It was as if for every bone that had been broken in my body, I had become mentally equally stronger, and that strength carried me through the first long while after being back in the field again. I had been aware from the start that I had to heal one hundred percent physically before I could heal mentally, but I had honestly thought that there would be more psychological consequences, after all that I had been through. But it was not the case.

Of course I had had an idea of what I could be getting myself into when I had let myself be apprehended, so the abuse that I had been subjected to was not exactly a surprise to me. But I was actually expecting some kind of mental reaction afterwards. It just never came. I think many would have ended their military career if they had been exposed to what I experienced in Belize, but I knew right away that I had to return to the field. Back to work ... so I could heal ...

I looked at Wizard who had already put the ampoules away and, as he got up grinning from his bed, the door opened.

In all our excitement over JAC's arrival, Liam had quietly slipped out of the barrack and now he came back, carrying two large wooden boxes, a smaller black metal box as well as four assault rifles. He carefully placed the boxes on the table and hung the rifles on the back of one of the chairs. Like moths to a flame, we all, except Kafka, gathered around the table and as I passed Liam, he handed me the metal box.

"It's for you," he said without having any eye contact with me. The box was relatively light but even so I had a good idea of what was in it.

Calmly and systematically, Liam began to empty the contents of the wooden boxes onto the table and while we stood and watched him slowly filling up the entire table, JAC began to lift some of the items up to study them. A few times he looked at Liam, who calmly continued to empty the boxes. When both boxes were completely empty he put them down on the floor and stepped aside so we could take a closer look.

What we were looking at was a table full of all kinds of explosive devices. None of us said anything. It was a bit like the silence before a storm ... although in this case the storm was more like a bang judging from the contents on the table.

While we were inspecting all the equipment, Liam signalled to JAC to come with him, and together they went to Liam's bed. Here he pulled out a large metal box from underneath it and placed it very carefully on the mattress. The lock was electronic and upon entering the code, the box clicked open. JAC squatted down on the floor next to the bed and began inspecting the contents of the metal box.

"Liam," he then said very quietly and without looking at him, "Where the hell did you get this from?" He turned his head and looked up at Liam and there was no doubt that the contents of the box worried him. Kafka, who had just got up from his bed, walked towards them while putting on a clean t-shirt. When he reached Liam and JAC, he stopped and looked briefly at the contents of the metal box.

"Nice," he said coolly, nodding appreciatively, "Russian?"

JAC looked at him and then he saw Liam nodding back. Kafka yawned and stretched his arms before nonchalantly walking over to the rest of us to inspect the contents of the table. I could see that JAC was looking at Liam and the only sound that could be heard was the faint beat of techno music coming from Luc's barrack. Wizard had retreated and stood like a dark stone pillar by the kitchen counter. His dead pan eyes were fixed on Liam as he crossed his arms in front of him. It was a pretty uncomfortable to see him like that, because he seemed to be a completely different person just waiting for an order so he could release the devil within him.

Liam closed the metal box and pushed it back under the bed, and only when it was out of sight, did JAC break the silence.

"Okay," he said, "I want some fucking answers as to what the hell is going on? And we can start with you?" He pointed towards Kafka, "Who the hell are you?"

Kafka did not answer, but continued to examine the various items on the table.

"He's okay, JAC. Kafka and I know each other from my time in Central America," I interjected, thinking that it would be explanation enough but no

… it wasn't. Liam's eyes wandered from JAC to Kafka to me and then back to JAC. He must have thought I had told JAC about Kafka, but JAC knew very little about my time in Belize.

"That's as may be, but there aren't many people who would know what the contents of that metal box are and even fewer would have known where it came from. And I know pretty much everyone in my line of business, so who the hell are you?"

Kafka, who was standing with his back to JAC holding a detonator in his hand, responded coldly,

"I'm Ex, Ex-marine, Ex-Mossad, Ex pretty much everything."

"We're all exes," an unimpressed Aussie replied.

"It does not answer my question of how you know what the contents of that metal box are?" JAC's voice was harsh and his eyes were cold and suspicious.

Kafka turned to him, and it amazed me that he could radiate such a calm and laid-back attitude when he was surrounded by as much distrust as he was right now.

"I know what that is …" he said alluding to the contents of the metal box, "because I have worked with it – although in a somewhat different form."

"Are we talking about nuclear weapons or chemical warfare?" JAC asked wrinkling his eyebrows so that they almost became one.

"Primarily chemical." Kafka replied while narrowing his lips, which didn't suit his face.

"Holy shit." Aussie proclaimed spontaneously and took a step back from the table with all the bomb equipment.

From the semi-darkness Wizard's voice was heard, "How did you end up as a merc?"

"You are a merc?" JAC asked and his eyes narrowed again and glanced over to me and then Liam, "What the hell is going on here, Liam?"

Liam got up from the bed where he had been sitting and walked over to JAC.

"Calm down, JAC," he said, patting him on the shoulder, "Come on, let's go for a walk."

As he passed Kafka, JAC stopped briefly. Then he looked over at Wizard and they exchanged glances before JAC and Liam disappeared out the door and then the silence returned to the barrack.

"You did not answer my question," Wizard said, "How did you end up as a merc?"

Kafka turned to him.

"It's not just chemistry I'm good at," he replied and he could have finished with a 'And it is none of your fucking business', but he didn't. There was no need to throw petrol on the bonfire called Wizard.

I bent down and picked up one of the boxes from the floor. It somehow seemed like a good idea to get all our merchandise out of the way, so I slowly started to pack up all the equipment. Kafka went to the kitchen counter, took the bottle of JD and unscrewed its top.

"Anyone?" he asked, looking at us.

"Yeah, bloody hell." Aussie replied and I signalled that I was up for it too, so Kafka began pouring into the glasses. We took one each and Kafka handed one to Wizard, who hesitated but ended up taking it, and then we all emptied our glasses.

* * *

Liam and JAC were gone most of the night, and while they were away, I took the time to look in the black metal box that Liam had given me earlier.

As I suspected, it was a new rifle and to my surprise, it was made of titanium and weighed only one thousand six hundred and fifty grams – without bullets.

Wizard, Aussie and Kafka had gone to bed, so for a change I had pretty much the whole barrack to myself and it was nice. I made a cup of coffee and sat down at the table just enjoying the silence. The heavy and monotonous bass rhythms of techno music had stopped an hour ago, so I could close my eyes undisturbed and let my mind run freely. However, my flow of thoughts was interrupted when Liam and JAC returned. They both shivered because the desert nights often offered freezing temperatures and they had been out for several hours, so ...

"Is the coffee hot?" Liam asked, smiling and rubbing his hands.

"Mmmm," I replied, nodding.

"Do you want a cup?" he asked, turning to JAC, who had walked down to his bed to put on a sweater.

"Yes, please."

Liam put two cups on the table and poured steaming hot coffee into them. When he was finished, he looked at me and signalled with the coffee jug if I wanted more. I pushed my cup towards him in response and he filled it.

JAC came over, took his cup and drank a mouthful of it. It was really incredible that he did not burn himself on the scalding coffee, or if he had, he certainly didn't let us know. Instead, he looked at me and took a deep breath.

"What a mess, huh?" he then said as he raised his eyebrows.

"Yep," I replied shortly, "it ..."

My sentence was interrupted by a faint buzzing sound from Liam's phone, and as expected, he went outside before answering it.

The barrack was quiet again and it was as if both JAC and I needed to gather our thoughts before we could resume the conversation.

JAC suddenly put his cup down violently and with rather determined steps he walked to his bed. He rummaged briefly in his bag and then slipped into the toilet. I was not quite sure if it was 'smack' or pills he took with him and to be honest it did not really matter to me as I had chosen not to interfere so I returned to my inner thoughts.

A moment later Liam came back and he went straight to the table, pulled out a chair and placed it next to me before sitting down. He then leaned towards me so that there was no more than ten centimetres between us and took a deep breath.

"Two things," he said seriously, looking me straight in the eyes, "You have to tell JAC about what happened in Belize because otherwise he's going to kill Kafka and right now I need them both." Liam spoke slowly and softly in a voice that almost bordered on a whisper, "Because as the situation is now, Kafka will not survive the next twenty-four hours if JAC doesn't start to trust him." Liam took another deep breath, "And I need that trust to be established immediately. They have to be able to work together. I know that you and Kafka have a link between you, and that you would protect him at all times, just as he would you but I cannot risk JAC eliminating Kafka for you then to eliminate JAC. I need at least one of them and preferably both, so ..." He raised his eyebrows and waited for me to answer him.

I nodded, but really he had nothing to worry about because I would never have eliminated JAC. Incidentally, it was his expression 'I need ...' that lodged in my brain, because he should have said 'we need ...' For a second I considered whether I should correct him, but on the other hand ... It would just show him, that I had heard his words and that could lead him to start thinking if it would be better to get rid of me. Had I at any time been in doubt as to whether he had a hidden agenda, I was now sure that he had.

I therefore chose to pretend that I had not noticed his mistake and nodded in agreement.

"Okay ... And the other thing?" I asked.

JAC came out from the toilet and walked towards us.

"The FSB has chosen to terminate you." Liam said and got up. I took a deep breath. I looked over to JAC, who stood a few metres from me running one hand through his hair. He really needed a serious haircut, I thought, "Not a dream scenario, but now we know who we are dealing with, so we have something to work with. Even though it doesn't seem that way, it is actually good." Liam concluded and I think he meant it.

I probably would not have used the word 'good' myself, but I understood what he meant.

Liam's phone hummed again and this time he did not go out but down to his bed. He sat on it and answered the call with a text message.

"JAC, I have something to tell you," I said quietly, turning my total attention to him. He looked at me a little sceptically, for usually such a sentence meant something ominous, but what thoughts went through his head in that second, and whether they concerned us, didn't really interest me. The main thing was that I had him one to one.

"Okay?" he answered questioningly and without further explanation I got up, took my jacket and went outside. I could hear JAC putting his coffee cup down on the table and picking up his jacket before following me.

Once outside, I turned to him and, straight away, began telling him about Belize, Kafka, the torture, the hospital treatments and my return to the industry.

Halfway through my story, we sat down with our backs up against the barrack and it was as if we both needed this backrest. That JAC didn't interrupt me, actually made it easier for me to talk about Belize, and when I was done, we both sat quietly for a good while.

"I understand if you cannot comprehend it. It was hard enough for me but this is what happened."

JAC took out a pack of cigarettes, removed two, lit them and handed one to me. He took a deep breath and exhaled the smoke slowly.

Then he said quietly, "I was well aware that you had been tortured when you were in Central America. I could see that on your body, but I did not know why and that it had been so bad. I'm also well aware that you cannot tell me what the cargo was. I just wish ..." He was silent and looked down at the cold desert sand.

"What?" I asked and must have sounded a little surprised at his comment, for it made him raise his head. He took a puff from the cigarette.

"That I had been there. Not that I could have made much of a difference, I think, but then ..." He was silent and exhaled the smoke.

"You were there, JAC," I said quietly, "When the pain came, after they had broken my fingers ... when their fists rained down on me ... when my body was about to give up after hours of beatings, chaining and burns, you were there. When I lay night after night on the cold concrete floor, beaten and abused, you kept me alive, JAC. Alive."

JAC looked at me and I could see that there were tears in his eyes.

"Thank you," he said quietly, "Thank you for letting me be there." I leaned towards his ear and whispered,

"No, JAC. It is me who thanks you." He put his arms around me and hugged me. It was an unbelievably nice feeling and just what I needed at that moment in the cold night in Afghanistan. I felt so unspeakably safe and right there I knew that no matter how many layers of skin they had peeled off me in Belize, they would never have been able to reach the layer where he was.

We sat like this for a very long time and, when we finally loosened our grip, we smiled at each other and we both had to wipe our eyes.

"JAC, I have to ask you something."

"I know … work with Kafka."

"Yes, it's important."

"I know."

"If you do, I promise you that when the time comes, I'll kill Kafka myself."

JAC looked at me in surprise and I couldn't really blame him. Kafka was my friend and I was talking about killing him. But the truth was that I had no idea who Kafka was. That he should turn up in the camp now seemed to me just a bit too coincidental and the fact that he was a merc just made me trusting his motives so much harder. Anybody could have hired him and all the bullshit about zeros on the cheque … yes, that could just be that: Bullshit.

"Okay," he said then, nodding, "But …?" His question was legitimate enough but I left it hanging in the air, for what could I really say? That I only said it to make sure he did not touch Kafka? That would have been the truth. But right now, I needed him to believe that I did not trust Kafka, which was a lie. Because I did …

"And if it turns out you can't, I will do it," he replied in a voice that was both harsh and without empathy.

I nodded knowing that he would do it in the blink of an eye.

"Okay. And Liam?" I whispered.

"Don't worry about him," JAC whispered in my ear, "He is being taken care of."

His words made me smile, because I clearly sensed that Wizard was part of that plan, and then it could only end fatally for Liam. Because even though Liam was tough Wizard was worse.

I was wildly turned on by thinking about it, and JAC and I started kissing each other – first gently then more aggressively.

"Come," I said quietly and a few minutes later we were standing by the outdoor showers located further down the camp.

In one of the cabins a soldier was bathing and I could just see a glimpse of the top of his head as he was soaping. Aggressively, I pushed JAC into one of the vacant cabins and turned on the hot water. Immediately, JAC grabbed me and pushed me up against one of the cabin walls, and as we ripped the clothes off each other and kissed violently and passionately, the cabin filled with steam from the hot water cascading down over JAC's neck and back. Naked, I pushed JAC a few steps backwards so that he ended up standing with his head directly under the hot jets of water. I could feel his wet body against mine, and feel how his hands wandered down my back and buttocks which he parted slightly. It was extremely erotic, and as we got more and more aroused, our kisses and touches became harder without losing their sensuality. Suddenly he turned me around so I was standing with my back to him. As I leaned my head backwards, he kissed my neck and my shoulders and I could feel his hands caressing me. I leaned forward until my palms hit the cabin wall and as I did so, I could feel his hands slide down my ribs eventually to end up on my hips. A second later he was inside me and from that moment on he took me hard from behind while the almost scorching sprays of water fell like tropical rain on my back and washed away all my thoughts so that only pure and raw desire was left. It was liberating in every single way and just what I needed that night in Afghanistan.

Chapter 12

Every new weapon requires some getting used to, and when it comes to precision-firearms, like the ones I primarily use, it's extra important.

The following morning I therefore took my new rifle and with a few tools and a shit load of bullets in my bag I went down to the camp's outdoor shooting range. Aussie agreed to come with me and it was not really because he needed the training, but because Liam thought it was safest that both Wizard and I were 'under protection'. As it turned out Aussie had a pretty solid knowledge of using specially designed weapons, and in fact, I could not have got a better partner than him, for this very task.

While we were away from the barrack, Liam had started JAC and Kafka on a somewhat different explosives project, and it was clear that the first stage of it, namely rigging our barrack with booby traps, was only to check if the two of them actually could work together. Each of them could easily have done the task alone, so it was their ability to co-operate that Liam was testing. From the start, it was clear that neither JAC nor Kafka wanted to be in each other's company but, as the soldiers they were, they followed orders and it seemed that their collaboration worked flawlessly. In fact, it appeared that as the hours progressed, they gained a new-found respect for each other's skills, and slowly they began to exchange professional information.

For my own part, it was several years since I had last been on a firing range, and I must admit that I was looking forward to it. It is always interesting to test a new rifle and especially the one I had got from Liam yesterday. I had previously worked with titanium rifles, but with varying success, for what they had in lightness, they usually lacked in capacity and precision, but this rifle was not a model I had seen before so it would be interesting to see if it was like the others. I had disassembled it the night before and it clearly had some improvements over the ones I had previously encountered.

It was nice to spend some time with Aussie. Of the entire team, he was the one I had talked to the least. It was actually a little weird, because he was the most extrovert of us, if you can call it that. At least he was the one who was most willing to talk about his missions, when we asked him about them, except his trip to Ukraine, which he had hardly mentioned.

As we walked through the camp, our talk naturally fell on the pending test and, as it turned out, Aussie knew a lot about titanium weapons. Currently he had a specially designed gun in half titanium, half plastic. I was quite impressed when he showed it to me because such a gun was very rare and difficult to come by.

As we entered the shooting range it became clear that finding a practise lane was not going to be easy. All the lanes were taken and the soldiers using them seemed too occupied with their practice to even notice us. I was not really in the mood to wait around for a lane to be open and I think Aussie sensed that because he told me to stay put while he went to speak to one of the officers. While I waited for Aussie to come back I glanced at the soldiers in the lanes in front of me and I must admit that they were pretty good at hitting the targets.

"Do you want to have a go at it?" The question came from a private at the lane to my right. I stared at him and the two soldiers standing next to him as they waited for my answer.

"Thanks for the offer but I need to do a little more than just a few shots. But thank you." I sent him a little smile to show that I appreciated his gesture and to be honest I had thought it would be enough to make the three soldiers go back to their exercise. But I was wrong.

"Listen ...why don't you take this lane and do whatever you have to do. We are pretty much finished here anyway." I frowned in scepticism but the offer actually seemed genuine enough. One of the soldiers next to him started to protest but the private just told him to find another lane, if he needed to fire more shots. It was obvious that the comment made the soldier a bit irritated but instead of standing his ground he and the third soldier left without further complaints.

When the two soldiers had left the private stepped out of my way and let me have the lane. I was quite surprised by the way he just told his fellow grunts to buzz off but as it gave me a free lane and therefore a chance for me and Aussie to get started I decided not to comment on it. So I just went to the lane and started to get ready to shoot.

"Well, well, well ... you found a lane. Fucking brilliant." Aussie's voice reached my ears loud and clear as I took the safety off OPUS.

"Couldn't wait for you all day. Could I?" Aussie laughed at my comment as he walked towards me.

"Let's get the fucking show on the road, shall we Princess?"

"Whenever you are ready. I'm all locked and loaded."

Aussie and I started by determining the wind direction, and already we had the attention of the other soldiers. The interest did not diminish when a few of them caught sight of my rifle, and when I informed Aussie that we were going to start with a target distance of seven hundred and fifty metres and work our way up by fifty metres at a time, some of the soldiers stopped their training just to watch us. Aussie and I were aware of it and we thought it was amusing, but we just kept on working. Aussie finished assembling his tripod mounted telescope and focused on that target.

A lot of the soldiers who are in the international forces are excellent marksmen and very passionate about their jobs, but it was still only a job to them. For us, it was a lifestyle. We did not go home after six or twelve months to our families and friends. Many of us did not even have a home. We had an overseas bank account that grew with each mission. But that should not stop us from learning from each other – although the learning primarily went from us to them – when we talk about shooting skills.

I started by shooting in a standing position. The first shots were an actual weapons test and I was pleasantly surprised by the rifle. Aussie and I constantly moved the distance to the target and I assumed both sitting and prone shooting positions each time. Then we moved on to the slightly more fun part, namely adjusting the rifle. The same approach was used and we now added sequence shooting. By this point a lot of soldiers had come to watch us and they were standing behind us along the firing range.

Then we came to the part of the test I liked the most – the fine-tuning. I fired a shot, then adjusted the rifle and scope, then shot again, more adjusting and I would keep doing that until the rifle was perfectly attuned to me.

A few times a hiss went through the crowd, for example when I hit the bullseye on a target at twelve hundred metres. For me, it was a given – for them, it was a rare chance to see a professional sniper in action up close without risking their own lives.

We kept going for two hours. I was pretty impressed with the rifle.

"Fucking brilliant," I told Aussie smiling, "Now I just need to test it on moving targets."

One of the officers in the crowd behind us stepped forward.

"My team is going on a reconnaissance tomorrow morning and you are welcome to join us," he said with hope and an eagerness in his voice that both Aussie and I picked up on. Despite the fact that the offer was intended to be a friendly gesture Aussie and I looked at each other, and then I looked over at the officer.

"I do not need reconnaissance. I need real moving targets," I said with an artificial kindness in my voice that hopefully hid the irritation I had over his lack of insight into what I really needed.

The crowd went silent and since I had got what I came for, I gathered my stuff and swung the rifle over my shoulder. We were done here.

"The show's over, guys." Aussie shouted and as the soldiers began to split up, Aussie and I slowly walked down through the barracks.

"What do you say that we visit the mess tent?" I asked Aussie, "We kind of skipped lunch."

"You read my mind," he replied and sixty metres later we disappeared into the mess tent.

There was hardly anybody in there and, judging by the clean empty metal trays where the food would normally be, we were obviously an hour too early for dinner. We therefore took a few bottles of water each and sat down at one of the back tables that by definition belonged to us.

Aussie sat up against the wall, leaning his head back as he poured the water from one of the bottles over his face. It actually looked really nice so for a moment I considered following his example, but then changed my mind.

"Aussie," I said after taking a sip of my water, "What happened in Ukraine – besides 'a shit load of bodies'?"

"Nothing. Just a shit load of bodies," he replied still with his head leaning backwards.

"Okay," I replied, taking another sip of my water.

"Why?"

"You just seem different after returning from it. Who is Frank?"

Aussie returned his head to a normal position and then he stared in front of him with an empty look.

"He's a fucking asshole, that's who he is," he replied aggressively, leaving no room for further dialogue.

With a sudden movement that surprised me, he got up and glared at the food counter.

"When the fuck is that food coming?" he shouted across the mess and it was clear that my question had provoked a violent reaction in him.

"Aussie," I said and was about to continue, but stopped when he put both his hands down hard on the table in front of me and leaned towards me.

"Don't," he said and in his eyes was a clear admonition that this subject was closed.

I raised both my hands to indicate that the message was understood and that everything was back to normal. Or so I thought. Aussie was still standing and frowning in the direction of the counters where the food would be put when ready to serve, but then suddenly he turned his attention to me again.

"Ukraine was ... it reminded me of ... fuck ... later," he said then, "Later."

I nodded to him because I knew very well, that some things are just too hard to talk about. For me, it was not what I did or had done that left a mark. It was the atrocities I saw when I was in the field. Because it was often insane scenarios, we bear witness to and yes it leaves mental traces. For me, the traces were in the form of thoughts and it was here that I used my knowledge from the world of philosophy and anthropology to get a little closer to the answers. For there are a multitude of questions when you see maltreated corpses hanging from lampposts, while children are playing football just a few metres away. I don't remember all the images from the different wars but the few that stay, when the day is over, are the ones I seek answers to. These are the ones I interpret and process, because otherwise they never disappear. It feels like the horrible images have to exceed themselves each time to have an effect on me. As if the atrocities have to surpass themselves to get a place in my inner gallery. Some of them have come back to me in my dreams and maybe that is why I have stopped having any dreams at all. Some soldiers need to talk about what they are experiencing, but I am not one of them. I need answers and once I have found them I can let go. It may be, that the answers are not equally logical, but for me they make sense, and that is what matters. Because if I have the answers, then I can let go and if I let go, the images disappear into the big black hole of oblivion. It is as if they are splintering there and becoming nothing. Maybe it's that nothing, that makes me survive ... and made Aussie survive Ukraine.

"Okay," I replied to Aussie and in more sense than one, we both welcomed the sound of heavy metal trays being put down on the counters and clinking tableware being placed in stacks next to them. Quietly we got up and a few minutes later we were back at the table, each with a portion of food.

* * *

The mess began slowly to fill up with soldiers, but it did not really bother us.

The rear tables had always belonged to the mercenaries and no soldiers dared to sit at them. Not even if they were the only tables available in the mess. If it happened that a new division, out of ignorance, took our tables they quickly moved when they were told that they belonged to the 'mercs'.

Therefore, Aussie and I were somewhat surprised when a young soldier suddenly sat down next to us at our table. I immediately recognized him as the one who had offered me his practice lane at the shooting range, and, after a few glances and overbearing smiles between Aussie and me, I signalled to Aussie that we should just let him be.

At several of the other tables the soldiers were whispering as they looked down towards ours, and it was clear, that they were both uneasy and a little envious of the young soldier that was allowed to sit with us.

To my surprise Aussie suddenly broke the silence.

"Have you ever been to Sudan?" he asked, turning to me and I shook my head.

"No."

"Too bad. Down there we would have had lots of moving targets to practice on." I looked at him and the combination of his crooked smile and the winking of his right eye made me smile as I shook my head.

'You are a son of a bitch.' I mouthed back to him because the soldier at our table had obviously heard Aussie's comment. I had no intention of going into a deeper conversation with him, if he should be so foolish as to start one. Hopefully he would be like most of the soldiers we met in the camps who shut up when they were in our presence but as it turned out, that was just a hope.

"How long have you been mercenaries?" The question came rather suddenly and unexpectedly from the soldier.

I stopped in the middle of a mouthful and Aussie completely stopped chewing.

We looked briefly at each other and then looked at the soldier, and it was as if we both wondered for a moment if we had heard right. Had the knucklehead really spoken to us?

Whether he sensed that we had stopped eating or whether he was really just so simple that he thought that interrupting a conversation between us was completely normal and acceptable, I do not know, but he continued eating as if nothing had happened. At one point he looked straight at us and with his mouth full of food he smiled at us. It was clear that he expected an answer, but not the one he got.

"You're new here, aren't you?" I asked quietly, laying my fork down on the plate. I could feel Aussie staring at me because even though we were colleagues, he knew nothing of my reaction pattern in such a situation, and it could potentially be dangerous for the soldier if I became aggressive. Now, I'm not exactly the type to explode uncontrollably and without warning, but there are some of us who are, and to some degree I can understand them. We often operate under the radar and when we finally have time off, we want to relax and not answer questions that often can discredit us.

But this young soldier seemed quite harmless and I therefore decided, to teach him a lesson in table manners.

"Yes," he answered and the expectation in his eyes of being enlightened about our experiences shone through.

"What's your name?"

"Private Jansson."

"Is this your first trip?"

"Yes."

"Okay, Private Jansson," I said, taking a deep breath before looking at him. "Let me give you some advice. When you sit down at a table where 'mercs' are sitting and when you are lucky enough to be allowed to stay seated, you keep your mouth shut, unless your opinion is requested."

Aussie started eating again but out of the corner of my eye I could see that the whole scenario amused him. In fact he was about to burst into laughter. Private Jansson on the other hand was so dazed that he sat completely still and had stopped chewing.

"Eat," I said to him harshly and commandingly while returning to my own dinner. Without having eye contact with Aussie, I could hear him chuckling with laughter and it was so contagious that I had a hard time holding my own laughter back.

"Who the hell do you think you are?" The words came from Private Jansson's mouth and they made Aussie hiccup in a combination of his food and a cough.

Quietly I drew my hunting knife and with a loud bang I stabbed it so forcefully in the table next to Jansson's tray that it startled the boy. Another three soldiers had come to our table, each with a tray on which their respective dinners were placed. They mistakenly thought they could have a seat at our table.

"Get the fuck out of here." Aussie said arrogantly and his words were accompanied by a single dismissive wave of his hand. As expected they disappeared with the speed of lightning.

"You're damn funny, Private Jansson – an idiot, but damn funny." Aussie laughed while putting his fork down. I got up, took my tray and with a firm grip on the handle of the hunting knife, I pulled it out of the table top.

"I'm the one who could have cut your throat in the middle of your fucking dinner and then finished my own," I replied as I put my knife back in its holster. The silence that descended over the mess due to this small incident began to seem a little oppressive, so Aussie and I left the establishment quietly. However, only after placing our trays in the stand that stood right at the end of the tent. There was no reason not to clean up after ourselves. We did have manners.

It was quite nice to get out into the fresh air and after one deep breath we started walking back to the barrack.

"Fucking priceless." Aussie said followed by a slightly squeaky laugh.

"Yes. Now the rookie can say, that he has had dinner with the 'mercs'. Do you think it will buy him some goodwill and Kabul pussy next time he goes to town?" I asked rhetorically while putting my hand in my pocket to get my cigarettes.

Aussie stopped and leaned forward and then guffawed with genuine laughter.

"Come on ..." I said grinning and lit the cigarette, "before Private Jansson catches up with us and thinks we are his 'BFFs' (Best Friend Forever)."

Aussie kept laughing but as we approached our quarters his laughter faded to a chuckle.

Back at the barrack, Liam, JAC and Kafka had moved a few chairs outside and with their respective beer and cigarettes they were sitting in the incipient dusk chilling. Wizard appeared in the doorway when he heard us coming and the silence that had surrounded them quickly disappeared when they caught sight of Aussie's big smiling face.

"I'm telling you, guys. If none of you are marrying her, I am. She is fucking amazing." Aussie's words surprised everyone including me but before I could respond to them, he had disappeared into the barrack still giggling. I smiled and shook my head as I exhaled smoke through my mouth.

"What the hell have you done to Aussie?" Wizard wondered frowning.

I took a puff of the cigarette.

"Oh, you know," I said blinking while wiping the corners of my mouth and immediately they all laughed. Except for Liam. He just shook his head a little and snorted.

Aussie reappeared in the doorway with a couple of chairs. He came straight out and placed them next to the others. A bit tired I collapsed into the one closest to Kafka.

"Ten minutes and there is an installation review of the barrack." Liam said. He was sitting on the chair closest to the door and was slightly bent forward, with one arm on each knee, looking down at the sandy ground as he exhaled smoke through his nose. I was curious to see what JAC and Kafka had done to the barrack but right now I just needed to sit for a while. I would have meditated but since it was neither the time nor place, I let myself disappear into my thoughts for a few minutes. I just needed a break.

"How is it?" Though it was soft, Kafka's voice hit me like a brick, and his words tore me abruptly from my reverie, which had been a welcome pause after a long day of training. I glanced at him and could see that he was looking down at my new rifle that was lying across my knees.

"Amazingly accurate," I replied bluntly. My response made Kafka raise his eyebrows a little while nodding in acceptance of my conclusion. It was clear that there would be no more questions from his side and it suited me just fine.

In the distance we saw two soldiers. They walked amazingly fast and aimed directly for us, which could only mean one thing. They wanted to give us a message and the message probably came from Command OP. Usually the soldiers in the camps stayed away from us and they only approached us if they had something concrete or important to inform us about.

"Bloody Hell." Aussie burst out before turning the cap he was wearing backwards so the shadow of it hit his neck. The two soldiers were now standing in front us and judging from the stripes on one of them, he was a sergeant. The other one we knew only too well.

"If I did not know better, Private Jansson I would think you were stalking us." Aussie said sarcastically but Jansson was too nervous to respond. He just stood there looking at us with uncertainty in his gaze.

"Are you, Liam?" the sergeant asked looking at Aussie.

"Who the fuck wants to know?" Aussie replied, agitated.

The sergeant was about to say more when Liam's voice silenced him.

"I'm Liam. What do you want?" His voice was full of irritation as was the look he gave the sergeant.

"Lieutenant Svensson wants to talk to you," the sergeant said and despite the fact that he was trying to hide his insecurity, I clearly sensed a slight tremor in his voice.

"What tent is he in?"

"He's in Command OP, that's ..."

Liam raised his hand as a signal for him to stop and it seemed as if there was nothing the sergeant would rather do right now, for he promptly kept his mouth shut.

"I know where it is."

A strange silence fell and it was like time stood still for a minute. Liam made no effort to get up from his chair, which clearly made the sergeant even more insecure, judging from his anxious eyes.

"Just go. I'll be there." Liam finally replied coolly and slightly annoyed because the two soldiers were still there. Why the sergeant stayed I have no idea but suddenly it was as if it dawned on him what had been said. He took a few steps backwards and turned away. Then at a slightly faster pace than they had arrived, both he and Jansson retreated. Liam took a puff of his cigarette, got up and exhaled the smoke as he put out the cigarette in the sand with his boot.

"Well, let's go through the barrack," he said firmly and one by one, we followed. After a quarter of an hour's review, it was clear to us that the barrack had been turned into one big bomb. Kafka walked us through the overall 'installations' such as explosive charges on doors, walls, transverse rafters and corner pillars. JAC explained the more subtle things, such as separate devices in sockets, light switches, door panels and so forth.

"It can all be operated manually or via a remote control, but in each case this switch needs to be turned on." JAC pointed to a switch near the door. Then he held up a small remote control that was the detonator.

“And who is going to have that?” Wizard asked with the usual distrust in his voice.

“Liam.” Kafka replied without displaying any emotions. I looked briefly at JAC but he did not reciprocate and when no objections came from anyone, JAC gave the detonator to Liam, who put it in his breast pocket. And that was the end of the tour.

“Well,” Liam said seriously, “I’m in Command OP if there is anything.” And in response, Wizard gave him a friendly pat on the back. Liam did not acknowledge his gesture, but instead promptly turned and disappeared out the door. It left the rest of us standing in the middle of a bomb.

“Fuck,” Aussie said, “I hardly dare to take a shit in fear that I will be blown all the way to Adelaide.”

“Look on the bright side ...” JAC said, putting his arm around Aussie’s shoulders, “you don’t have to stand in a line to check in.”

We laughed quietly because there was actually some truth to it.

“Hell,” said Aussie, “It will only be a question of checking out if this thing goes off. Fuck.”

Our laughter increased before dying out as we each continued our daily routines. As of now mine was to make some coffee. I was desperately in need of a cup but as I stood there measuring the spoonfulls my phone beeped. It was a message from Liam telling me to get to Command OP. So despite my longing for mocha it had to wait a bit. Resolutely I took my new OPUS and laid it on my bed, and then I checked if the magazine in my Glock was full. It was, so I put the gun in my waistband and slipped on my jacket so the Glock wasn’t visible. I caught JAC gazing at me wondering what I was doing.

“I’m going down to Liam,” I said calmly smiling at him.

“Good luck.” Wizard replied without looking at me, but his tone of voice still made me look at him for a moment. As he sat there on his bed checking his phone, one would immediately think that everything was okay, but in fact it was far from it. There was a restlessness in his body language. His clenched lips and shallow breathing confirmed the smouldering desperation that lay just below the surface. It was obvious that he was ill at ease and for the first time it worried me. I approached JAC who was standing in the doorway.

“Is he okay?” I asked JAC, quietly alluding to Wizard’s mental state, as I scowled at him.

JAC’s mouth narrowed and frowning, he shook his head slightly.

“Go to Liam,” he replied just as quietly and for a brief moment we looked directly into each other’s eyes. I winked at him and he retaliated with a crooked smile. Then I disappeared out the door heading for Command OP and Liam.

* * *

I had seen him disappear into Command OP several times so I knew very well where it was, but one thing I wasn't prepared for was the sight that met me inside the tent. Because in stark contrast to how quiet it was in the camp outside, in here there was an astonishing amount of activity.

Liam waved at me from the back of the tent asking me to join him and a couple of officers, as well as the sergeant who previously had been down to our barrack. I went and stood next to Liam. They were looking at a large touch screen on which several pictures and seismic maps were displayed.

The officers looked at me and we nodded briefly to one another. No doubt they recognized me which was certainly more than I did them.

Liam stood calmly with his hands in his pockets while looking at the screen.

"What do you say to a trip to northern Afghanistan tomorrow morning?"

I looked at the pictures on the screen and judging by them it immediately seemed interesting.

"Maybe. What's the mission?"

"Destroy a Taliban unit." I studied the pictures and without further comment I nodded, "Number of presumed targets?" I asked.

"Forty, possibly more."

One of the officers looked at me with slightly raised eyebrows as if to say 'that's something?' but I did not comment on his hidden statement. So far there was nothing in this assignment that I hadn't seen before so I was not impressed. And forty targets? That meant max five to six kills for me.

"I saw you on the shooting range today and when my sergeant later told me, that you needed to practice on moving targets; I thought you might want to join this special mission." I zoomed in on the pictures.

"There's just something we need to agree," I said still studying the pictures. "If I say yes to doing this, I am operating alone and do not have to verify my locations during the mission. I will not be part of your team and I will be briefed separately. No hidden agendas."

The officers looked at Liam and then they looked at me. I turned my attention to them awaiting their answer.

"You have to verify each kill you make," said one of the officers seriously but, to be honest, this comment seemed superfluous to me. It was natural for me to verify, for how else would my team know the status of the situation?

"Of course," I replied.

"And you must fight for us."

I stared at the officer. He had obviously never worked with a contractor before otherwise he would never have said that.

"I am not fighting for you. I will fight with you because I will be on your side tomorrow, but don't forget that to me this is an exercise as my rifle needs to be fine-tuned." One of the officers narrowed his eyes.

"And you do that by using living people as targets?" he said.

"For the lack of better," I replied coolly looking at him.

"Better what?"

"Training facilities."

There was a pause in which the officer measured me from head to toe and when he was finished, he turned to one of the others.

"This is not going to work," he said firmly, "I don't want to have a trigger-happy 'merc' sniper on a mission with my team." My eyes found the officer, who had said this and I began to shake my head.

"This is a waste of my time," I said snorting, "See you down at the barrack, Liam." I turned and walked towards the exit of the tent. I couldn't take any more of this conversation.

"Clear the tent," I heard Liam say commandingly and at the same time one of the officers addressed me.

"Wait," he shouted. I stopped and turned to face him.

One minute later, only Liam, the sergeant, the officers and I remained in the tent. The rest of the soldiers had left.

Liam looked at the officer and signalled that the sergeant should also leave, which he did reluctantly.

And then we were alone.

Liam looked seriously at the officer who had made the inappropriate comment about me.

"I would not stand here and demean you in front of the other ranks, but this is one of the best snipers in the world." He nodded towards me and it made all the officers look at me, "You will most likely never get the opportunity to work with her again as she usually doesn't take on assignments like this without being on the payroll. That she even considers going on your mission is something you should be happy about. We all know very well, that she will not appear anywhere in your report and, if something goes wrong, you are exempt from any knowledge and thus responsibility regarding her. Also all registered kills will be credited to you without anyone wanting to know who actually performed them. You know as well as I do, that it is not you who is doing her a favour by taking her on your mission tomorrow – even though it has to seem like that. It is the opposite. Therefore ..." Liam continued cold and determinedly looking at the officer who had given the unfortunate statement, "you owe her an apology for the comment you made before we continue."

"Do we have your word that we can count on her?"

"It's not my word you need. It's hers." Liam replied in a slightly arrogant tone as he nodded towards me once more.

All the officers looked at me and I returned their gaze with a measured nod.

The officer, who had made the inappropriate remark, was the only one not to reciprocate. Instead he squinted his eyes for a fraction of a second, so they became nothing more than two small slits. In his view I had obviously 'won' this round and at his expense. I noted this small change in him but kept it to myself.

"Sorry for the unfortunate comment," he said without the slightest remorse in his voice and I answered him by nodding a single time. I had come across countless of his kind and the only thing to do was to ignore them.

"The others can come back now." Liam said with a conviction in his voice that reflected that he didn't doubt that they would obey his command. It was clear that Liam had taken over the entire meeting and that the officers were now his puppets. It was amusing to be a spectator and observe how they danced to Liam's pipe without even knowing it. By the time the meeting was over, I had been briefed and the officers could breathe a sigh of relief. Their otherwise difficult mission had just become a whole lot easier.

It had become completely dark, when Liam and I finally left the tent. The night was cold, which was probably one of the reasons, why we saw very few soldiers on our way back to our quarters.

"Take Aussie with you tomorrow." Liam said firmly as we walked back to the barrack.

"I don't need him. I have a whole division to take care of me."

"None of them are going to take care of you. Besides, he needs to get out of the camp for a while."

"What about Wizard? Don't you think he needs it more? He behaves more and more like a lion in a cage."

"And that's exactly why he's not going tomorrow. He may snap and that would be inappropriate. At least right now."

The fact that Liam was aware of Wizard's state of mind I somehow found very reassuring, but it did not solve the problem, that we had a ticking bomb walking around in a barrack that was rigged with explosives. That Liam had used words like 'inappropriate' and 'right now' caused my alarm bells to ring, but at the moment there was nothing I could do about it. Asking him what he had meant, would only have brought a resounding silence, so I let it go.

We went into the barrack and found Kafka and JAC sitting playing cards while Wizard had isolated himself behind his screen. Aussie was about to unscrew the top of a bottle of JD and, as we stepped in the door, he turned his head towards us.

“Perfect timing,” he said taking down two extra glasses from the shelf above the kitchen counter. It was nice seeing JAC and Kafka not only getting along but having a good time together as well, because it honestly looked like they were. Liam took one of the glasses with whiskey and drained it. Then he immediately handed it to Aussie again to get a refill which, need I say, came promptly. I walked over to JAC and stood next to him and I could feel Liam’s eyes on my back.

“OPUS and Aussie are going on a mission to northern Afghanistan tomorrow.” Liam announced in his usual informative voice, which could just as well have announced a train departure between Paris and Lyon. As if it had been a starting signal, Wizard quickly got up from his bed and appeared from behind the screen.

“Can’t I go instead of Aussie?” he said frowning, “I really need to get out of here. I am going crazy from just waiting. I have to get out and feel that I am accomplishing something.”

“Not this time. Aussie is going to help OPUS fine-tune the new rifle, and he has a special knowledge of titanium weapons, but I promise I’ll get you on a mission soon. I promise it, Wizard.” Liam replied and by the look in his eyes there was no doubt that he meant it.

“You’d better.” Wizard grabbed his jacket and left.

As the barrack went silent again, I went to my bed, where my rifle was lying on top of the cover, and as usual I started getting it ready for tomorrow’s mission. JAC finished the card game and as I had expected he came over to me.

He looked at me and out of the corner of my eye I could see Liam leaving the barrack.

I sat down on the bed, grabbed JAC’s belt buckle and pulled him to me. I rested my forehead against his stomach which, due to his well-trained six-pack, was rock hard. He started gently stroking my hair. Aussie stood leaning up against the kitchen counter watching us. It was as if he was analysing the situation to decide what his next move should be. I guess he came to a conclusion because he suddenly put his glass down.

“Come on, Kafka. Let’s go to Luc’s,” he said and smiled crookedly at us.

Kafka looked down at us and then he raised his eyebrows at Aussie.

“I’ll explain later.” Aussie said and, in a few seconds, they too had left the barrack.

JAC waited until they were gone. Then with two fingers under my chin he gently lifted my head so we ended up looking at each other. Slowly he bent down and kissed me. At first gently but it soon became harder. We rolled over on my bed and I tore his jacket off. I do not know what I was expecting, but certainly not the sight, that met me, when his bare arms came into view. They looked awful with their red, yellow and all shades of violet from the needle marks.

"JAC?" I whispered into his ear.

"Yes," he replied, still kissing me.

"I do not want to lose you." He stopped abruptly and stared at me wondering.

"Not to that," I said looking at the puncture marks, "To a mission, yes, but not that." He sent me a little smile.

"You're not going to," he replied and I could see that he meant it. Then he continued to kiss me and we ended up having sex that was rougher than usual.

Chapter 13

It was five forty-five a.m. when Aussie and I walked through the camp in full gear. The team we were to join had already had their morning briefing regarding today's mission, and there they had been informed that I was to accompany them. They had been told that I would operate independently and alone, and that my mission was classified, so the likelihood that some would ask me questions was therefore minimal.

Aussie and I went straight to Command OP where we were handed our headsets and co-ordinates. The officer's surprise and irritation that he had not been informed about Aussie participating in the mission as well was understandable. However, we ignored his protests and, after Aussie informed him that without him joining I would not be part of today's mission either, the case was dropped. Five minutes later we were both sitting in one of the helicopters that was to take us to northern Afghanistan.

It was the first time Aussie and I had been on a mission together, but we had each been on so many missions and worked with so many different soldiers during our time, that it did not matter. We sat opposite each other and our professionalism in relation to the rest of the team was clear from the start. Unlike them, we spent most of the flight checking our communication equipment, as well as studying the terrain we flew over. The observations we made here could benefit us later and better to be prepared rather than be taken by surprise.

It was really quite pleasant to be in Aussie's company and I think he felt the same way about me. We knew exactly what awaited us down there – a regular desert war with an enemy who knew the area like the back of his hand and who fought on the basis of religious ideology. This was pretty much the worst scenario one could get in a combat situation, but we were not there to fight for either side. We were there to fine-tune OPUS – and as a benefit, we would get some combat training, which we both looked forward to.

Half an hour into the helicopter ride, Aussie communicated to me, that we had a guest and when I looked down along the row of benched soldiers my eyes stopped at the last one: Private Jansson was sat looking out of the helicopter. A faint crooked smile crossed my lips and it was accompanied by a slight shake of the head. Looking back at Aussie a few seconds later, I could see that he shared my enthusiasm. I leaned back, closed my eyes and as my combat mode took over my smile disappeared.

The helicopters touched down five kilometres from the target, and you did not have to be a soldier to be able to ascertain, that the terrain around us was virtually impassable. Luckily both Aussie and I had been in similar surroundings before, so we knew conditions like this and how to work with them to complete our task. We quickly put distance between us and the rest of the group, and right from the start we went to high ground. One and a half kilometres before the target, we encountered the first marks. There were seven guards occupying three lookout posts. The posts were strategically placed on some rock outcrops and were exceptionally well camouflaged. It actually took a highly trained eye to see them, but that was not what worried us. It was the number of the posts.

I signalled to Aussie and then we crouched down behind a small rock formation. And with our backs resting against it we caught our breaths.

"Do you think the same as me?" I asked him before turning around and looking over the rough terrain. I studied the individual posts closely through my binoculars. Luckily there seemed to be very little activity in and around them and it appeared that neither us nor the team had been spotted yet.

"Yep," Aussie replied, "Too many lookouts to protect a single division."

"All three are equipped with heavy artillery," I announced but my information brought anything but calm to us.

I turned around so I was sitting next to Aussie again and our thoughts revolved around potential solutions to this somewhat unexpected problem.

"I think we should check it out." Aussie said suddenly and it was as if he had read my mind.

"Agreed," I replied and without further discussion we sneaked along the ridge.

A few minutes later the ridge turned sharply to the left and we got a clear view beyond the gorge of the city that was our target and there, our suspicions were confirmed: The city was besieged by three or four companies all of which had heavy artillery.

"It's a setup," Aussie whispered through the headset, "or just unbelievably bad intelligence. The team will be slaughtered when they arrive. Do we have any way of contacting them?"

"No. We are not on their frequency."

"How long do we have, before they arrive?" Aussie asked.

"Seven, maybe eight minutes," I replied, noting where the piles of artillery, weapons, the depot, the armoured personnel carriers, and the camp tents with soldiers were located in relation to the city buildings and access roads.

"Fall back." Aussie said and moments after we were on our way back to warn the team.

It took almost four minutes before we were back with the team again and we quickly found the officer in charge. With accurate and sufficiently detailed information Aussie informed him of our observations and after just five seconds of deliberation on it, the officer confirmed that we would go on as planned. Aussie and I exchanged some rather surprised glances after which Aussie turned to the officer.

"You are fucking insane. It's suicide," he said sharply to him, but it seemed to bounce off the mission commander.

"You wanted to practice on moving targets, here's your chance," the officer said rather patronizing to me raising his eyebrows, as if to emphasize that we should just shut up and accept it. I shook my head.

"This is a suicide mission and that's not what we signed up for."

"Isn't every day that, for you guys?" the officer snorted condescendingly and then continued walking. I was used to such comments, so I ignored it, because in my eyes it merely reflected an unimaginable ignorance and disrespect for the work we were doing. We had never been and would never become kamikaze soldiers. Or at least I would not.

Aussie and I let ourselves fall back into the steady stream of soldiers who, on the officer's order, kept walking towards the city.

"This is real shit, Aussie. We are stranded here."

"I know."

We had slowed down a bit, because there was no reason to keep up with the rest of the team, as we were not sure about this and were not under his command.

"I hope damn well he's smart enough to contact Command OP so they can either call off the mission or send reinforcements – preferably airborne – and bloody quick." Aussie said. He was still annoyed with the apparent total incompetence of the officer.

"We cannot come up with a plan based on orders we do not know and believe me, we will not be informed about their plans," I said in a tone that made it sound very definite, which it was.

"We have to go back," snarled Aussie.

"For fuck's sake, Aussie ... Our extraction point is in that city, so no matter what, they have to give us a new location if we are going to get out of here."

This whole scenario was too uncertain and there was no doubt that

Aussie and I wanted the mission stopped until air support was provided, but it didn't seem to be happening. Since we could not get out of there, we made a drastic decision. We started to speed up and caught up with the officer fifty metres further ahead and pulled him aside. The team had almost reached where the lookout posts were, so action had to be taken now.

"Stop your team." Aussie said in a firm tone of voice, grabbing the officer by his shoulder. The officer looked aggressively at him as he wriggled himself free of Aussie's grip. The grip Aussie had had on him couldn't have been very firm otherwise he would not have been able to do that.

"The first lookout post is hidden around the next formation of rocks." Aussie continued unaffected by what had just happened. I was convinced that he would be reluctant to do anything, but it appeared that this time we had got him to listen to us.

The officer signalled and the team stopped but it was clearly not because of Aussie's recommendation. He looked like a man intending to set an example, but if it was Aussie that he targeted, he had miscalculated. Aussie continued to speak without giving the officer a chance to interrupt.

"We have a proposal. Let us take out the three lookouts."

The officer looked at him suspiciously but the dressing down that I could see he was preparing, remained unsaid. It was a good sign because then he had at least listened to us.

"Then you have a tiny advantage." The words came a little too cheekily from Aussie, but the remark was solely to hide his growing irritation with the officer, who turned around, took a deep breath and then he just stood there – thinking. Why he needed to do that, seemed to me quite ridiculous because in my opinion there was nothing to think about. Any other team officer would have reacted with an 'execute' and then we would have been up and running. But not him. On the contrary. He just stood there with his hands on his hips, looking up into the sky then suddenly turned towards us.

"Okay, but it's going to be on my orders," he replied sharply and it was clear that it annoyed him that he felt compelled to agree with us.

"Yes, but we need your frequency," I said.

"I have yours so don't worry. You'll be notified."

"It was not part of the agreement that you should have our frequency."

"Tough luck, baby," he replied arrogantly, smiling mockingly at me. Then it happened. Like a rattlesnake striking its victim, Aussie grabbed his throat and squeezed. In fact, I too had reached a point with the officer, that I might have done the same thing. Sadly, his attitude just reflected that he was 'an ignorant little man with too much authority'.

"I ought to fucking kill you." Aussie snarled as his eyes flashed with rage and his grip gradually tightened.

"Fuck's sake Aussie," I said harshly, "He'll be dead in ten minutes anyway."

The eyes of the officer and Aussie were locked on each other as Aussie slowly released his grip. Immediately the officer reached for his throat and coughed.

"We are going into position and awaiting your orders," I told him as I turned round and started to walk away.

"Oh, by the way," I turned to him again, "You might want to contact Command OP and tell them about your findings and then wait for their orders before ..."

I smiled artificially at him, noting that Aussie, still facing him, was taking a few steps back towards me. When he had reached me, he turned around and together we left the team with various oaths from the still-coughing officer.

We went to high ground again and quickly found a good position from where we could see all three posts.

"After eliminating post number one, we'll change position," I told Aussie through the headset and he replied with a nod. Then it was just a matter of waiting. And wait ... we did.

The sun had now really gained power and the desert sand had begun to heat up, but it didn't bother us. The longer the wait, the greater the probability that the officer had contacted Command OP and that they were making the decision whether to send reinforcements or cancel the mission altogether. As time passed our temperatures increased rapidly under the baking sun and it therefore came as a relief when the order from the officer came: A green light to eliminate the lookout posts.

Aussie and I looked at each other.

"I have an idea," Aussie said in an almost cheerful tone, "We eliminate the lookouts, slip into town and snatch one of the enemy's cars and then we head for the camp."

I chuckled a little because the idea had been cooking in my mind for a while.

"I'm in, Aussie," I replied, preparing for the first kill, "Let's rock and roll."

* * *

The elimination of the three guards in the first lookout post went quickly and easily.

The lookout post was the most prominent of the three and the first one that would have spotted the team once they had passed the last rock formation.

"The silencer is perfect," I told Aussie after the first kills. He smiled at me and it was clear that he was very pleased – and a little proud of himself – about my comment.

"Shot number two was not clean, however, and it was not due to the wind. Think it was speed-determined." Aussie took OPUS and made a small adjustment. Then we moved position to a rock outcrop, where there was actually a little bit of shade. A few minutes later, lookout post number two was eliminated.

"Better," I stated as I looked through OPUS's sight. There were three hundred and fifty-two metres to the last post, and from where we were now, I could get a clean shot, but only one of the two soldiers, was clearly visible.

"Do you want some close combat training?" I asked Aussie and could see out of the corner of my eye that he was smiling crookedly.

"Always," he replied glancing fleetingly in the direction of the last lookout post.

"Then the guard partially hidden by the rock wall is all yours."

"See you," he said cheekily before slipping away. I lay down and watched the post through my binoculars. Aussie was out of sight, but a few minutes later I saw one person in the lookout post disappear and as soon as that happened I eliminated the other.

I could not see Aussie so I let my binoculars wander between the two posts that we had just eliminated while I waited for him to come back. And then, just as suddenly as he had slipped away, he was back again. I smiled to myself. He was damned experienced, dear Aussie, and a pleasure to work with.

"All clear, over," I informed the officer and the response came promptly.

"Affirmative. Stand by," he replied.

In silence we waited for the next order, but none came. Aussie signalled to me that I should 'mute' the headset and the seriousness in his eyes reflected that what he wanted to say was not for the officer's ear nor up for discussion.

"We have to move," he said calmly and he was right. We had waited far too long and for every minute that passed, our odds got worse and worse, "In a few minutes, there will be bogies everywhere, and then ..."

"Yes," I replied, "Also if anything should happen, then ..." Our odds were so bad that I had to say this to him.

Aussie looked at me.

"I'll tell him," he said referring to JAC and I couldn't help smiling at him.

"It is not necessary. No, if anything happens, take my phone. There is a set of co-ordinates of a safe house in Islamabad on it. Try to get there."

My words triggered a little smile on Aussie's face and then he suddenly grabbed my neck and leaned in towards me.

"Let's agree to go there together, shall we?" He now smiled broadly as our eyes met.

"Deal," I replied and Aussie let go of me.

"Come on then," he said switching to the 'rapid fire' setting on his AK 47.

* * *

We sneaked down and into the city and just as we had passed the first house, we could hear shouts and the first soldiers came running. Presumably they had now found out, that there was no radio contact with the guards in the lookout posts, so in a few minutes, when they found them eliminated, the whole town would be on alert.

We had to find some clothes so we didn't stand out, so we slipped into a low-rise building to get them. In one of the rooms, two elderly men were arguing, but their voices fell silent as we entered. Aussie signalled to them that they should be quiet and strangely enough, they listened. He hit one man on the head with his rifle and before the other had as much as opened his mouth, he too lay unconscious on the floor.

As if out of thin air, Private Jansson suddenly stood in the doorway. I was a little surprised to see him, because he should really be with his team. Aussie, on the other hand, did not seem to have any problems with his presence, providing he kept his mouth shut, which Aussie signalled to him and Jansson nodded his agreement, so I put my scepticism aside for a moment. Aussie waved Jansson over so he stood next to us and then he commanded him to undress the man who lay closest to me and while the clothes slowly began to come off him, Aussie stripped the other man while he and I exchanged some short commands before I patted him on the shoulder.

"Checking the exit," I said to him and he nodded to me. Then he turned his attention to Private Jansson, who had almost finished his task and silently I left the room. But I hadn't got very far before I heard in my headset the sound of a shot from a gun with a silencer. For a moment I stood still. Then I quietly called Aussie's name on the headset, but there was no answer. Quickly and quietly I ran back to the room and I arrived just in time to see Aussie kneeling in front of Jansson before being shot twice in the heart. Aussie fell backwards on the floor and Jansson's gaze, which was icy cold, turned towards me. In pure reflex I had already pulled my Glock and I shot him first in his right shoulder and then in the left as I moved towards him. The jerk it gave in his right shoulder when the bullet hit was like a wake-up call to him. He blinked quickly a few times and then he looked down at his hand with the gun, a hand that now hung limply down by his right side. Then he looked at me as if surprised that having been shot he was still alive. He had probably thought that if I shot him, it was to kill, but no.

Despite the fact that I was both shaken and furious, my inner voice told me that I needed him alive. The innocent boyish look on his face, that for a brief moment had been replaced by that of an assassin, suddenly returned, but he could not dazzle me with it any more. I had seen the emptiness in his eyes after he had eliminated Aussie and therefore I knew what I was dealing with. He was not a 'private'. Such do not possess that kind of gaze. He was trained and trained well, otherwise he would not have been able to fool us as he had done.

I took one last step towards him and hit him with the butt of my rifle first in his head and then with full force into his shoulder right on top of the bullet wound. His facial expression switched to pure pain but it did not affect me. I kicked the gun out of his hand and it flew to the other side of the room and then put my Glock against his forehead.

"Raise your fucking hands," I commanded in a calm and very quiet voice and, when his eyes caught mine, the assassin was back.

Slowly he raised his hands and when they had reached the height of his chest, I grabbed his right wrist and shot him twice in the hand. I did the same with his left hand. Despite the fact that his facial expressions told me that it hurt, no sound came out of his mouth.

I could hear two voices. They came from the hallway and got louder and louder.

I moved so I was standing next to Jansson with my Glock hard against his right temple and as the voices were just about outside the room, I pressed even harder against his skin.

The two men turned away from the hallway and left the house without having seen or heard us. When they were gone, I pushed Jansson to the other side of the room and kicked him so that he ended up on the floor on his knees. I tied his wrists with zip ties from my kit and gagged him so he couldn't scream. I crossed his ankles and also tied them together so he didn't have a chance to get up.

Then I looked him straight in the eyes and there was no doubt that the hatred I had in mine frightened him, for behind his outwardly cold attitude, which he had no doubt developed throughout his training, there was a small glimpse of fear – an intense fear. It was not a fear I knew, but I had seen it countless times in the eyes of my enemies, so it was no stranger to me.

I left Jansson alone with his fear about what I was going to do to him and went over to Aussie. The asshole had eliminated him with a shot right in the forehead and then the two in the chest, which was a typical signature of a trained assassin. As I stood there looking at Aussie my hatred towards Private Jansson increased. Normally I would have made sure I brought Aussie home, but it was clear to me that I did not have the opportunity in the current situation.

Systematically, I emptied his pockets, took his headset, mobile, ammunition, and his custom-made Glock, as well as one half of his dog tag, before quietly closing his eyes.

"Bye, Aussie," I whispered, "I will miss you, you lovely crazy Aussie." For a moment I just sat next to him and looked at him, but then I bent all the way down to his ear, because there was just something that I had to tell him, and they say that the hearing is the last thing to disappear when you die, so ...

"I promise you, that I will reach Islamabad for the both of us. And Aussie ... Don't you doubt for a second that I wouldn't have married you. Bye." I kissed him gently on the cheek by his ear.

My eyes watered and I had to bite my lower lip to prevent the faint quiver in the corners of my mouth from becoming more pronounced. Slowly I got up and looked up at the ceiling while wiping my eyes with my sleeve. I looked across at Jansson, who was staring at us while he slowly bled and had I not hated him before I certainly did now. That son of a bitch, I thought, wiping my eyes once more. The fucking son of a bitch.

The total chaos that reigned outside the building caught my attention and suddenly I was back in the real world. I could hear shouts, screams and lots of gunshots, so it was definitely time to move on.

I bent down and picked up the robe that Aussie had taken from one of the two men, both of whom were still lying unconscious on the floor. Calmly I put on the robe and, to complete the disguise, I removed one man's headscarf and wrapped it around my own head so only my eyes were visible. Before I stepped over Aussie, I looked at him one last time and to my relief he looked very calm and peaceful. Somehow it was now okay to leave him as it was only his shell that lay on the sandy floor. Aussie himself had moved on to a better place – I could see that by the look on his face – or rather I thought I could.

My eyes turned to Private Jansson again. For every step I took toward him, I could feel the hatred for him growing. As I cut the zip tie around his ankles with my hunting knife and raised him up, I told myself that I had to get control of this hatred. Because if it took over, then my chances of getting out of this hellhole alive could diminish and damned if I would give Private Jansson that satisfaction too.

"Move," I said coldly as I jammed Aussie's Glock into his shoulder again. It gave Jansson another jerk of pain but again no sound came from him. As the situation was now, his only chance of survival was to obey, so he did. With a firm grip on one arm, I led him out of the building and into the chaotic inferno of war.

* * *

Outside the deafening noise of soldiers firing rifles, of grenades exploding and the endless hail from automatic weapons, suggested a quick exit in a direction away from the cacophony. Everyone had their attention elsewhere so we could walk relatively unnoticed beside the walls of the houses.

After a few minutes we passed a dead enemy soldier lying in the gutter and in one smooth motion, I picked up the Kalashnikov rifle next to him. If someone were to look at us it would be better, if it was that and not Aussie's Glock, which was in Jansson's back. So I exchanged the guns and discreetly put Aussie's pistol in my waistband under my robe.

We continued through a couple of short narrow streets until we were out of town. On the way we had been passed by some Arab soldiers who had fleetingly asked if I needed help with the prisoner but I had refused and they had hurried on. Mentally, I concluded that my Arabic must have become pretty good, since the soldiers had not noticed anything. If they had, the situation would have been very ugly very quickly.

As Jansson and I turned a corner my eyes caught the sight of an abandoned Jeep and, miraculously, it had a full tank. I pushed Jansson into it and before I pressed the starter button, I knocked him unconscious with the AK 47 rifle butt. As I raced across the desert sands and away from the war zone, I couldn't help but look up into the sky.

"Thanks for the car, Aussie," I thought smiling a bit, "Thank you, you crazy Australian. Now I'll reach Islamabad – for the both of us."

I had driven for about half an hour, when I stopped the Jeep. You could still hear the sound of mortar shells and the planes above us testified, that fighter jets now had arrived. I did not really care who the planes belonged to, because my full attention was on Jansson. I shook him and gave him a few slaps on his cheeks to make sure he was awake, and when he was, I got him out of the car.

I had deliberately sought out a hilly rocky area and even though the small narrow path in front of us seemed impassable, the place was just perfect for what I had in mind. I shoved Jansson in front of me and at a fast pace we started moving up along the path. In some places it was so narrow that it was only possible to put one foot right in front of the other and here my small shoe size benefited me. Jansson had a hard time gaining a foothold between the sharp rocks, but I didn't care as for me it was no problem. I scrambled nimbly through the terrain and it was only when we came to a small flat area I ordered Jansson to stop and kneel.

I wanted so much to put a few bullets in his body and then leave him to die in the afternoon sun but I knew that I needed information from him before doing that, and since he evidently not was going to give it to me out of free will I chose a different approach.

"You know as well as I do that you won't leave this place alive," I began my interrogation of him, "so the likelihood that you will give me the information I want is minimal. Therefore, I will instead tell you what I know. You work for the FSB and have been told to eliminate me ... And credit where it's due you almost succeeded. But you were not as close as you think."

Jansson stared at me furiously. It did not suit him to have the truth slapped right in his face.

"I could have shot you back in the camp when we were sitting in the mess," he replied confidently and without the slightest emotion in his voice.

"No," I replied, "because your cover would have been blown and you would have been shot. It was a smart thought, to try to do it in the field. Unfortunately, my friend got in the way so you had to get rid of him first."

"Yes, it was a bit of a nuisance." Jansson commented sounding slightly annoyed. "But ... for what it's worth, you're probably the best sniper I've ever come across. I have been studying you and your kills for several years. I bet you have no idea that the FSB has you in their standard teaching material and then again at the advanced level for shooting techniques."

He was right. I had no idea and in fact I didn't care. It was easy enough to learn the techniques, but when you were in the field and had to put the theories into practice, you quickly discovered that the actual skill was not just in the execution of them. Of course, my survival depended on how skilled I was, and not only on the shooting level. No, it was often determined by how good I was at improvising. For no two situations are alike and therefore neither are the shots.

A random thought ran through my head and raised doubts in my mind.

"You are FSB, Jansson, but are they also who you work for?" There was a long pause and for every second that passed, my doubts were confirmed. The stony look Jansson had had slowly disappeared and after taking a deep breath he replied,

"No."

"Who are you working for then?" A crocked smile appeared on his lips as he raised both eyebrows and tilted his head slightly to one side.

"You know better than to ask me that," he replied slightly arrogantly, but his attitude disappeared the very moment I aimed at his forehead with my Glock.

"Will you let me go if I tell you?" he asked but his voice hid a faint shiver that revealed that not even he believed it was a real possibility.

Now it was my turn to put on a smiley face. If that was the price for finding out who his employer was, I could easily live without being enriched on that front. There was no chance he would leave this place alive. None.

It seemed that Jansson knew it and he therefore shrugged.

"Hmmm ... let's get it over with," he said and now the arrogant tone was back.

But if he had thought I would just pull the trigger he was horribly wrong. I secured the Glock and put it back in my waistband and for a brief moment there was hope to be seen in Jansson's eyes. A hope of me changing my mind. Hope that death had been put on hold and that I would let him live. Therefore, the disappointment was also traceable when I took the Kalashnikov and unlocked it.

"Listen up ..." He said with a slight desperation in his voice. "I have respect for you and I wish I had never said yes to the assignment, but I could not say no. You are the ultimate target for me and the temptation to get you on my kill résumé was just too big. Your death would have opened up possibilities for me that no one else would have been able to. Do you understand?"

I stared at him and inwardly smiled. He had just made it so much simpler for me.

Without answering his question, I shot him like a partisan would have shot him, which is to say randomly. However, it was not entirely coincidental how I let the bullets penetrate his body. He needed to suffer.

Afterwards I went back to the car, checked my GPS on the phone, disassembled OPUS which I had hidden under the cover of my robe, stowing its various parts in my kit and then drove towards the Pakistani border – knowing that the few minutes Jansson had left of his life that he would be in more pain than he had ever known before.

Chapter 14

Early that same evening I reached a small village. I managed to swap the car for a horse and some food after which I hurried towards the mountains.

After two hours of both riding and walking on the sandy and stony paths I reached high ground. It didn't take me long to find a cave in which I tied the horse up before I went outside and turned Aussie's phone on. Luckily there was a full signal so I sent a message to Liam with my co-ordinates so he knew my location. Then I picked up my own phone and sent a message to JAC. The message was short and also accompanied by co-ordinates, for the safe house in Islamabad, which he had previously posted on my phone.

I sat for a moment just waiting for the phones to beep and it was my own phone that sounded first. It was JAC repeating the co-ordinates and I smiled. It gave me peace of mind to know that JAC knew I was alive. Hopefully the others would figure out that it was me who had sent the details of my current position via Aussie's phone once they found out that Aussie was dead.

But there was no response to the message I had sent from Aussie's phone. I was okay with it because it just meant that I was alone and had to find the way to Islamabad without any help from the team. When there was no response after five minutes I took the SIM card out of Aussie's phone, destroyed it and stuck the remains of it in the sand. Then I went into the cave to rest.

The night passed quietly. I was awake most of the time thinking about ways I could disappear from the face of the earth while still being alive and reviewed all sorts of scenarios and possibilities. The FSB would no doubt be informed that their agent – or whatever Jansson really was to them – had been killed by partisans, and therefore it would be best if the same partisans had killed me. That way, I ensured that whoever had sent Jansson stopped hunting me. So, to make this happen I decided to go hunting for a human the next day.

If my plan was to succeed, I had to find a woman of my own height and stature. I knew it could never be a perfect match, since it was a little difficult to judge what the individual women looked like under their burkas, but after a few days searching I had found someone who met the requirements fairly well.

The woman lived in a small nearby village and it was easy enough to lure her into the mountains. I used the excuse that I desperately needed help getting my sick children down to the village for medical attention and she took the bait. I had been preparing everything since I first spotted her so I only had to carry out my plan, but it amazed me how easy the trip up into the mountains was. For a brief moment it made me a little suspicious that we didn't encounter anyone on the way but whatever doubts I might have had disappeared with each step we took away from the village.

After an hour of walking, which was mainly up steep sandy paths between rocks, we reached the cave. Here I had already made a bonfire ready to be lit before I left for the village so I now only had to knock the woman unconscious to get everything rolling. A blow to her temple with the handle of my Glock did the trick and she fell to the ground right next to the awaiting bonfire. I lit the fire and while the flames took hold, I got out my emergency kit. The kit contained a syringe and I filled it with one of the two ampoules of morphine that were in it.

It may well be that in many areas I had lost my humanity but there was no reason for the woman to suffer unnecessarily. After all, I am not that inhuman.

So while she was still lying unconscious on the floor, I simply injected her in her right arm and whispered "Allahu Akbar." It was not a mockery of either her or her faith, rather the opposite. It was actually to honour her and the ultimate sacrifice she would be making by giving me a life in exchange for her own.

I waited for two minutes before checking if she still had a pulse.

It was there, but it was very weak, so while I was waiting for it to disappear completely, I threw some more wood on the fire. The fire was almost ready, so I took off my coat and scarf before I bent down and laced up my boots extra tight. They had to be fit for what I had to do. Then I went to the woman and tried to find her pulse but only to confirm that she was dead. I carefully took off her burka and in addition to wearing a traditional tunic with matching trousers underneath, she had to my surprise a small flimsy gold cross hanging around her neck. For a moment it struck me. Was she a Christian? Just in case and, for the same reason as I said "Allahu Akbar" before, I made the sign of the cross in front of her.

"May God be with you," I said quietly, and began to take off the rest of her clothes so I could put mine on her instead. And it was then I noticed that she was pregnant. I had not been able to see it. She was probably five or six months along, I guessed.

It was as if a huge force weighed me down and I instantly felt nauseous. I checked again if she had a pulse but she didn't. If she had had I would have done everything to resurrect her but she had flat lined. There was nothing I could do. She was gone and so was her baby. As I starred wide eyed at her and her baby bump my mind became blank. I had killed an innocent. Not her, not the woman because at some stage in her life she had probably committed a sin but her baby hadn't. Her unborn baby had not had a chance to sin yet and therefore it was innocent. Totally innocent.

I stumbled as I got to my feet. I had killed an innocent. I had killed an innocent. Like a broken record the words kept repeating in my head. Over and over again. Once on my unsteady feet I started pacing around the cave. I folded my hands behind my neck as I frantically tried to get my thoughts under control. My mouth was as dry as the sand under my feet and I felt like throwing up. I had to get my thoughts 'boxed' because as of now they were making me unable to proceed with the things I had to do. But it was so difficult. I had killed an innocent.

A sound that resembled a scream resonated in my head and as it became louder and louder I put both my palms to my ears to try to cover it. It had to stop and stop now. Otherwise it would drive me insane. My face contorted into an expression that made it look like a creature from out of this world and as snot and tears poured out of me, I heard a voice. At first I couldn't tell where it was coming from but then I recognized it. It came from me. It was my voice. And it screamed.

Screamed, "STOP".

Still holding my palms to my ears my knees hit the sandy ground next to the fire. Gasping for air, I leaned forward and as drool and saliva hung from my mouth, I felt violently sick. I moved my hands to my stomach and before I knew of it vomit moved up through my throat. I opened my mouth wide and spewed out a cascade of vomit. Where it hit it turned the sand thick and dark and the more I vomited the darker the spot got. For minutes I spewed my guts out and when I had no more inside me to puke out I sat back on my heels starring numbly into a great big nothing in front of me.

I don't know for how long I sat there but I suddenly felt a power rise inside of me and a voice that kept growing stronger in my mind said: 'Enough. Get back to the task at hand.' Empty and hollow I slowly began to rise and then my survival instincts kicked in. My thoughts became rational again. In fact so rational that I could look at the woman although I avoided any glance towards her pregnant belly.

I started pacing a bit. There were so many psychological issues in this scenario that it just seemed to tear me apart, but I managed to concentrate on the physical ones and it was almost as if doing so brought me into a daze.

As if I had hit an invisible brick wall, I suddenly stopped pacing. I had to get started. There was no need to delay it any more. For the last time I checked if the woman was dead and when confirmed that she was I rolled up the sleeves on my jacket. It was imperative that her charred remains weren't identifiable when they found her and at the same time it had to look like it had been done by a non-professional. That she was pregnant was a serious problem because she had to appear to be me or rather the remains of me; I had to smash her pelvis so much that even an autopsy would not reveal the pregnancy. But before I did all this, I had to remove the foetus from her body first. What I was going to do with it, I had no idea but I had to figure that out at a later stage. For now I had to act.

Calmly – almost too calmly – I looked at the woman again. I kind of wished JAC had been here. He would be so much better at this than me. Slowly I bent down and took off the woman's necklace with the gold cross and hung it around my own neck. It was by no means a trophy from my kill, rather the opposite. If there was anything or anyone, I sincerely wished they would help me now: That they would let me keep my focus and at the same time show mercy when my deed was done. That they would somehow say that what I had done was okay and that they would forgive me. That she, the woman, would forgive me.

I touched the cross around my neck. It felt smooth and a sense of purity and innocence flowed through me. For a moment I stood just wondering if forgiveness was coming but it did not. The cross was just golden metal. Nothing else.

Suddenly it was as if I woke up from this monumental feeling of guilt. I had never sought answers before and if there were any, the voice that carried them was silent right now. In fact, the silence suited the situation very well for what was there to say.

I let go of the cross and, with firm and determined steps, I went to the opposite side of the cave. I had to get the right speed for what I was about to do. I took the stand as if I was about to start a race and I set off with such a power in my legs that I think I could have broken the world record for a sixty-metre sprint. As I reached the woman, I kicked and stamped on her face. I could hear the cracking of her facial bones and I kept going until the sound of breaking stopped. I then bent down to her smashed face and ripped her fractured jaws apart. With the butt of my knife I crushed her teeth to the state where they were just white powder. Next, I broke her arms by taking aikido grips on them and they snapped as if they were twigs. I then crushed her kneecaps with my AK 47 and shot her – one shot in each ankle, one shot in the right shoulder and one in her right hand. This is what a bunch of partisans would have done if they wanted to neutralize me and that was exactly the situation I wanted to stage. Eventually I cut her hair off so that the length corresponded to mine because even though she had to be burned I could never be absolutely sure that there were no remnants left when the embers cooled and the forensics took over.

Not once during all this had I looked at her belly, but now I had to. I sat down next to her and closed my eyes.

"Sorry," I said in a low voice, "I'm so sorry. I did not know you were pregnant. I could not see it. I would never have chosen you if I had known. Believe me. And I am so, so sorry for what I have to do now. I will try to do it as honourably as possible."

But the truth was, that there was nothing honourable about what I was about to do and when I took my hunting knife to cut her open across her abdomen I was filled with sorrow. There wasn't really as much blood as I had imagined so maybe it wasn't that bad anyway I thought as I put the knife down. Gently I put my hand through the deep slit that I had made and to my surprise her guts still felt warm.

I had previously been in contact with a dead person's anatomy, through the lessons I had had – both theoretical and practical – when I learned interrogation techniques, but the corpses had always been cold and in the early stages of rigor mortis. To cut up such a corpse was completely different from sitting – as I did now – with a warm corpse's smooth and bloody intestines in my hands. There were certain similarities but in the present moment I had to mutilate the woman and not just take her apart. I had mutilated people before but what I was doing now – and which in my wildest dreams I had NEVER imagined having to do – was in so many ways totally repulsive and so far from what I stood for as a human being.

As I sat there by the dead woman, with one hand inside her abdomen looking for her unborn child, I changed my mind. It was not JAC I needed here – it was Wizard. He would be better in this situation.

Why I thought I would only have to use one hand to get the baby out, I don't know, but in fact I had to use both hands to get it out of the womb. It was very small and thankfully dead, so I wrapped it in the woman's burka and put the bundle aside at the far end of the cave. Then I went back to the woman and crushed her pelvis by jumping on top of it and when it was broken into pieces, I crushed the last parts of it with the butt of my knife, just as I had done with her teeth.

The fire was now burning wildly so I threw the woman's body on it along with my clothes. The flames quickly enveloped both and the familiar smell of burnt human flesh spread in the cave. I looked down at my hands and my forearms. They were smeared in the blood from her womb.

Empty and silent I went to the entrance of the cave and sat down. As

I stared out into the totally black starless night, the hollow feeling sneaked up on me again. I couldn't stop it and to be honest I didn't really want to. I deserved it. Deserved the numbness that I for so many years had tried to explain without any success and that now seemed to slowly devour me. The smell from the fire hit my nostrils again and it reminded me of Belize. However, back then it had been burns from my own flesh that had filled my nose and not the woman burning in the fire behind me. But smell is not discriminatory. Roasted human flesh smells the same no matter where or what human it comes from. The smell does not distinguish whether it is a man or woman, or what ethnic origin or religious or political belief the person has. The smell of burnt human flesh is the same everywhere.

As I sat there at the cave entrance with the woman's corpse crackling and smoking in the background, a single thought consumed me. Had I now lost my last remnant of humanity?

Before this I had never taken an innocent civilian's life to secure my own survival. I had of course killed to survive, but not in this way. Here I had selected a human being who was to die instead of me. Who was I to do this? If it had just been the woman, I would not have had the anguish because according to my philosophy, no human being is innocent – not even a child. Everyone has committed a sin at one time or another – to a greater or lesser degree – and it was precisely this philosophy that had always justified my kills.

But an unborn child had not sinned. An unborn child was innocent and I did not kill innocent people, only sinners.

So this really was my first deliberate kill of an innocent.

The nausea came back and I just managed to get up and lean against the cave wall before I threw up again. Afterwards I collapsed, empty and dehumanized by my action and I didn't move until the fire had gone out and the first rays of the sun appeared over the rocks opposite the cave.

As if in a kind of trance I slowly got up and put on the woman's clothes. I then deleted all the traces of me in the cave and then I took the bundle and the rest of my gear. I broke my dog tag and threw half of it on the floor so it was just hidden enough by the sand to not be immediately noticeable but just visible enough that it could be found. Then I disappeared – empty and mechanically – into the dawn.

* * *

The terrain was pretty impassable, so I led the horse most of the way.

I walked over a ridge and then began to climb down into the gorge on the other side. To this day I do not know why I did it this way, for it was unbelievably risky. I was totally exposed as I walked there along the rock walls with my horse and I would have been the perfect target for partisans, soldiers and of course a sniper.

And maybe that's just why nothing happened to me because in no way did I resemble someone who posed a threat. Because who would just trudge through a hostile mountain range in a country at war without doing the slightest thing to hide or protect themselves? No one – other than a simple innocent woman with her horse.

However, if anyone had been near me they would have noticed that I periodically kicked the ground in front of me. In most places it was rock hard and only covered with a few millimetres of sandy dust but there were places where it was a little looser.

After a few hours I spotted a spring in the rock formation where there was some shade and after pulling the horse there and attaching its reins to a boulder, I walked around a bit kicking the ground. It was, as I had expected, relatively loose, so I sat down and began carefully to dig. Approximately ten centimetres down, the ground became extremely hard but just the fact that I was able to go that deep, was probably the best odds I would get in this barren terrain. So I used the AK 47 both to loosen soil and sand and afterwards as a shovel to remove the dirt.

The ground was so insanely hard that before long both my biceps were completely acidic, but I did not give up. That's how it must feel to be a mason I thought as the hole slowly deepened. I had to take several breaks, but I kept going until the hole was big enough to bury a baby. How long it took me to dig, I have no idea, but when it was finally done, I sat for a while looking at it. Without conscious thought, my gaze began to wander slowly to the surrounding cliffs, but there was nothing to worry about. There was, as before, complete silence around me and only the horse's random lashing with its tail interrupted now and again. It seemed like the perfect place I thought as I walked to the horse to get the bundle containing the foetus. There was an incredible peace and quietness over this secluded spot and the stark contrast to what I had done just a few hours ago was almost unreal.

With the bundle in my arms, I walked apathetically back to the hole and carefully and with the deepest respect I put it down in it. Then I took the gold cross I had had around my neck, and placed it gently on the bundle.

"Sorry," I whispered, "I'm sorry you never got the chance to live. Sorry I took your life before you were born. Sorry you never got a chance."

I sat for a moment looking at the bundle and the cross and slowly my vision became blurred and the corners of my mouth began to tremble. My whole body suddenly turned into one big knot and it was as if someone was just tightening the knot more and more. I could not swallow, could not breathe and the tears began to run down my cheeks.

I got up and started to walk around while looking in all directions.

Then I collapsed and screamed. Screamed like I had never screamed before.

Screamed and screamed and screamed.

* * *

The scream died out slowly, ending in a gasping sob, while tears, saliva and snot poured out of me uncontrollably.

I leaned forward and put my hands on my stomach. All my muscles were like hard knots. I gasped. This was too violent. Too painful. Completely out of control. I had to regain control and as fast as possible. I spotted all the clotted blood on my arms and I began feverishly rubbing them with sand. I took more and more sand and rubbed faster and faster. It had to go away. Away ... now ... immediately. Everything. As abruptly as my movements had started they suddenly stopped and again I became completely numb. And there I sat. I could not feel anything either physically or mentally. All energy had left me. I had neither the courage, the will, nor the desire to continue.

I looked at the small hole that now seemed to me like a bottomless pit ready to engulf me. And that was okay. Okay to disappear into it. Then I would be gone. Away from the pain and this inexplicable indifference that had filled me all these years. It was so strange and at the same time liberating, because for a brief moment, my inhuman action actually made me unbelievably human.

How long I sat there, I have no idea. It was as if I had disappeared into a big nothing. As if I was in a trance.

In the distance I detected a faint sound and it took me – what felt like an eternity – to return to reality. The sound came from my phone in my pocket and for each beep, I became more and more present. I took the phone out of my pocket and looked at it. The message was from JAC. I smiled, tired and relieved, as I read it. It was his co-ordinates in Islamabad. That meant he would meet me there. Without answering him I sat for a while holding the phone. I just needed to gather myself before replying. I took a while but when I finally did I gave him the co-ordinates of my current position. Then at least he knew how far I had come. I put the phone back in my pocket and sat for a moment. Thanks, JAC, I thought and smiled. Thanks for bringing me back to reality – once again.

It was as if the message from JAC gave me energy because I managed to crawl to the hole and cover it. It was important that no one could see that I had been digging in the sand, so I spent a relatively long time getting the place completely level. Why I subsequently scratched a small cross in the rock wall above the place, I do not really know, but it was probably just to mark the place somehow. I ran my fingers over the little cross in the stone, because I wanted to be sure that even though it was almost invisible, you should be able to feel it. I took a small rock and laid it on top of the sand where the hole had been. Now it was a real grave, I thought, as I mounted up and disappeared – leaving the place to its original peace.

Chapter 15

The trip into Pakistan went amazingly well. On my way I only encountered a few 'travellers' and we kept a proper distance from each other, so there were no major problems.

The nights were bad though. I could hardly sleep. My thoughts were like soap bubbles. They were of all sizes and I was constantly bombarded with them. As soon as one cascade had disappeared, the next appeared and it was as if someone was standing blowing them straight at me all the time. It was unbearable, but I could not stop the flow. All the mindfulness and meditation techniques that, under normal circumstances, I would have used to regain mental balance were being shot down by the constant blitz of thoughts.

It was as if my body and my brain were working separately from each other. Where my body was running on autopilot and my actions sprang from routines and repetitions, my brain raged in an almost inhuman haste and exaggeration, leaving me mentally exhausted. As if I only had the ability to channel my energy to one source at a time; you could literally divide my actions into either being physical or mental. It was as if my body took over during the day and transported me towards Islamabad while at the same time my brain was on standby. As soon as my body rested in the evening and at night, my thoughts took over and they galloped away at what felt like the speed of light. I was in a constant phase of exhaustion and on the fifth day I was close to succumbing.

It is therefore no surprise that throughout this period I have huge gaps in my recollections of my behaviour and whereabouts and it is probably best that they never see the light of day either.

When I finally emerged from this misty blur of reality, I found myself sitting in the back of a car and we had just passed a road sign reading a hundred and thirty-seven miles to Islamabad. My horse was gone – so apparently I had swapped it or sold it – but I couldn't remember. Everything was hazy.

It was a double-lane paved road that we were driving on, and next to me sat a couple of young men looking silently at the traffic. In their paint stained grey and sandy coloured tunics with black harem trousers underneath they looked like men on their way to work. Not that I really cared. It was more of an observation than an actual interest in them.

The traffic around us increased and two hours later we drove into Islamabad.

By request I was dropped at a square next to one of the many bazaars in the city. It was getting late and the city was buzzing with sounds from cars, buses, motorbikes, people hurrying from A to B, vendors shouting out prices of the various items they had for sale, food stands handing street food over their counters to hungry customers, women shouting and kids crying. It was as if I was experiencing everything for the first time: The scents, the sounds, the colours. It all seemed so clear and clean.

I followed the co-ordinates on my phone, and half an hour later, in a back street to one of the main roads, I was standing in front of a staircase leading down into a basement. Slightly hesitant, I walked down to the black door at the bottom of it. It was unlocked and as I slowly opened it a long corridor unfolded. It looked like a typical basement with a lot of closed doors on each side of the corridor leading, I presumed, into small individual rooms.

It was as if I suddenly woke up because as I began moving slowly down the hallway, I pulled my Glock. I felt like I was back in my own rational state of mind again and it was a nice familiar feeling.

The GPS on my phone suddenly indicated that I had arrived at my final destination and not surprisingly I found myself standing in front of a rusty metal door. As there seemed to be no immediate danger around me I gently grasped the door handle. The door was unlocked and with my usual precaution I slowly opened it. I fumbled a bit but I finally managed to find the light switch inside the room next to the door frame. As I turned on the light a bare room was in front of me. It had no windows and a fluorescent tube light in the ceiling and a mattress on the floor, were the only things that implied that there had once been people here. On the inside was a key which I gently turned locking the door. This was a room with no escape, but despite that, an unspeakable calm spread within me. Here I could hide and forget the outside world. This was truly my own personal coffin.

I took my robe off and put all my gear over by the wall. Then I moved the mattress over alongside it so I would be hidden by the door if it were to open. Then I picked up my phone. It was time to let JAC know I had arrived. When the message was sent I sat down on the mattress. Now it was just a matter of waiting – waiting for JAC.

I woke up to a soft knocking on the door and automatically I reached for my Glock. It had only been twenty minutes since I had sent the message to JAC so, whether it could be him on the other side of the door, I had no idea.

As I got up I felt a little dazed and it took a couple of seconds for my eyes to focus. As I unlocked the door the knocking stopped. I took a few steps back and raised my gun. Slowly the door opened and to my relief, it was JAC followed by Kafka on the other side. I immediately lowered my gun and started sobbing uncontrollably. JAC took me in his arms and we stood there for a very long time hugging each other. Once in a while he kissed me on my head and even though I felt him loosening his grip a bit I did not let go of him. I needed so badly to just feel him – feel his calmness and his strength. After a few minutes he signalled to Kafka to take my things and I could feel his arms around me starting to let go and this time he meant it.

"We have to go now." I heard JAC say but then everything went black.

* * *

When I woke up again, I was lying on the mattress. JAC was sitting next to me with his back to the wall gently stroking my hair.

"Hey," he said quietly smiling at me as I began to move.

"Hey," I replied looking at him a little disorientated as one does when waking in a strange place. I shivered a little and immediately he took off his jacket and put it over my shoulders. We were alone in the room and all my gear was gone. Normally I would have reacted to that, but I was too mentally and physically exhausted to do anything about it.

"What's going to happen now, JAC?" My eyelids felt so heavy and since there was no force left in my body to keep them open, I let them close.

"Shhh," he said, "Just lie down and sleep. You are safe here."

I did as he said. I crawled into him and his calm heartbeat seemed very soothing – almost meditative – to me.

"Don't let go of me, JAC, you hear? Don't let go of me," I whispered.

"Never," he replied holding me tight, "Never."

Tears began to roll down my cheeks. I had never felt so weak but I literally had no more strength in me and I wanted so bad just to disappear. My mind went blank and lying in JAC's arms I fell asleep crying.

How long I slept I have no idea, but I woke up when Kafka touched me gently on one shin. He had squatted down at the end of the mattress and was now looking at me.

"Good morning, sleepy head," I heard JAC say and I could tell that I was still lying next to him. I sat up and blinked a couple of times. The light in the room seemed very strong. Too strong I thought.

"What's the time?" I asked slightly absently while wiping some drool from my mouth. My mouth and throat were so unbelievably dry that they almost burned and the dried saliva in the corner of my mouth was no help.

"It's nine p.m. You have slept for fifteen hours." Kafka replied quietly.

"Fifteen hours?" I repeated in surprise. "And you've been sitting here all along?" I looked at JAC but he just smiled.

"Yes," he replied.

I touched my arm. It was hurting.

"We had to put a drip of fluid into you while you slept. You were very dehydrated." Kafka said calmly still with one hand lying on my shin.

I nodded.

"Yes of course."

"We have to move now," he said and I saw a hint of concern in his face.

"Yes, yes of course," I replied, and began to stand up but the room spun and Kafka just managed to grab me otherwise I would have collapsed on the floor. JAC jumped up.

"I'm okay," I said holding out both hands as a signal that I did not need help and quietly Kafka let go of me.

"No, you're far from okay," JAC replied, "When was the last time you ate?"

I shrugged. I couldn't remember. My memories from the previous days were blurred and full of holes.

Kafka opened the door and silently we all left the room. It was very reassuring to walk between JAC and Kafka through the basement corridor. They were like two reinforced broad-shouldered pieces of rock protecting me and it gave me a safe feeling, something I hadn't felt for a long time. As we came out the basement door an overcast sky revealed itself. Kafka almost jumped up the stairs to the street but if I had thought that I would follow him, I was wrong. JAC took a firm grip on my arm which brought me to a halt. He then pushed me aside before walking up the stairs. As he took a sneak peek down the street to see if the coast was clear I heard the squealing sound of a car braking right next to the staircase. JAC turned to me and he waved me up and five seconds later we sat in the car and drove at high speed through the narrow streets of Islamabad.

It was clear that Kafka, who was behind the wheel, knew the city well because the detours he took were definitely not on any tourist map.

Half an hour later we arrived at a large villa outside Islamabad. It was surrounded by an eight-foot-high white concrete wall with barbed wire at the top and there were security cameras everywhere. The large solid iron gates opened and as we drove in they started to close slowly behind us.

"Who lives here?" I asked rather surprised because usually I only saw this kind of security at embassies, industrial estates and residences of powerful people who needed maximum protection.

"At the moment, a professor." Kafka replied and the tone of his voice did not encourage questions. As we approached the house, I couldn't help but stare wide-eyed at it. It was huge. And then we disappeared down into the underground garage, where another set of massive iron gates automatically closed after us.

There was something very magnificent and grandiose about all this, but without it being exaggerated and staged. Almost the opposite. It was stylish without being minimalist and it was clear that nothing had been left to chance. Everything about the house was designed to make it seem as anonymous as possible.

Once we had parked the car, we went up a narrow staircase and then entered a large auditorium that most of all resembled the entrance to a museum. There were white marble floors, Persian carpets, green plants and paintings everywhere. It all seemed a little strange to me, so I pulled my Glock – just to be on the safe side.

"You don't need it here. We are alone." JAC said, laying his hand on my gun. I slowly lowered it still a bit wary. Kafka had gone into the kitchen and when I followed, I had a pretty hard time hiding my astonishment. It was approximately a hundred square metres and any Michelin chef would have been envious of it. Here was everything and more, so much so that the chef could have won another star.

Kafka put his Glock on the kitchen counter and went to the fridge where he filled a jug with ice-cold water. Together with three glasses he put it on the oval dining table that stood at the end of the kitchen, poured and then he gestured that I should drink some of it. I stood in the doorway looking towards Kafka and the table which was so big that eighteen to twenty people could have easily sat around it. Calmly I walked over to him and took one of the glasses that he had poured and it was only when the water hit my lips that it dawned on me, how thirsty I really was. I immediately emptied the glass and handed it to JAC, who had come to the table. He filled it up, and I emptied that too. This happened four to five times until Kafka put a dish of finely chopped fruit in front of me.

"Eat," he commanded, "You'll get 'real' food later. We just need to get your blood sugar up, but ..."

"But not too fast. I know," I replied, taking a handful of melon and eating it greedily.

That I had completed the sentence was a great relief to JAC and even Kafka. As I chewed the fruit JAC put his arm around my shoulders and he could not hide his excitement.

"Welcome back," he said with joy in his voice as he chuckled. I took another handful of fruit and this time I washed it down with water.

The sound of Kafka closing the fridge door made me turn my head and I saw him standing with some fresh bloody steaks on a plate. That was the evening menu I guessed. Heavy on proteins. I ate three or four more handfuls of fruit and then looked at JAC, who was just standing there and smiling.

"You eat worse than a monkey," he said alluding to all the fruit I had managed to smear around my mouth.

"Fuck you, JAC," I replied, smearing a piece of kiwi on his face.

He laughed and wrapped his arms around me.

"My monkey woman," he said hugging me, "Fuck, it's good that you're here." I wrapped my arms around him. It was so wonderfully liberating to be able to do that and, with Kafka's indifference to it, made it even more amazing and yes, almost completely normal.

"We'll meet in the lounge in thirty minutes." Kafka said after deactivating the alarm to the first floor on the electronic display next to the kitchen door and then he disappeared upstairs.

"Lounge?" I queried looking very curiously at JAC but he just smiled at me.

"Come," he said and together we went out of the kitchen, into the hall, and up a large wide staircase, which in the middle split into two stairways – one going to the right and the other to the left. We went right and along a long hallway.

"Kafka sleeps in there." JAC said pointing to the first door on his right.

"Next door is your room and I'm in the next one. All three rooms are connected by interior doors." He opened the door to my room and I entered a huge suite with a king size double bed, sofa set, desk, walk-in closet, fireplace and a master bathroom with jacuzzi and infrared sauna. I stood for a while just taking it all in.

"JAC," I said quietly and a little sceptically, "Who owns this house?"

"A professor," he replied in his own sober way, "Take a shower and I'll see you downstairs in twenty-five minutes." He kissed me on the forehead and disappeared through the door into his own room. Speculatively and with my senses on alert, I walked around the room just taking it all in, but since everything seemed okay, I undressed.

The last thing I noticed before I went into the bathroom was that Kafka had put my gear on one of the sofas. The sight of it made me smile. Although the place seemed safe, it was nice to have it within reach. Just in case.

* * *

After a twenty-minute-long bath that if nothing else rinsed all the physical remnants of the trip off me, I was back in the auditorium. Since I had no clean clothes, I had put on a white terry dressing gown and even though JAC had said that I did not have to walk around with my Glock, I had put it in one of the gown's large pockets. This whole setup still seemed pretty unreal to me and until I got some answers the gun stayed.

I glanced around the beautiful room, and then I saw JAC coming out of one of the living rooms.

"We're sitting in there," he said smiling and then disappeared in the direction of the kitchen.

I don't know what I expected when I entered the living room, but it was definitely not the sight that met me. The living room was just one of four interconnected rooms and, if you didn't know any better, you would think that an interior designer had been employed.

Everything was kept in earth tones only interrupted by a few individual colourful paintings on the walls. The fire was catching and its faint crackle combined with the dim warm light coming from the individual lamps gave the room a very soft glow. My eyes fell on Kafka, who was reclining in one of the two Chesterfield sofas that were in front of the fireplace. He was staring at his iPad. It did not take many seconds before he caught sight of me and immediately he put down the iPad.

"JAC is getting the coffee," he said, smiling, "There is water, whiskey, spirits and ... yes whatever you want. Just let me know." He nodded towards the table where all the choices were lined up just waiting for me to pick one of them.

Quietly I sat on the Chesterfield sofa opposite him and curled up my legs. Right now I did not really want to do anything other than just sit for a while in peace and enjoy being here. I don't know whether Kafka understood this, but at least he let me be and that was all I needed. A few minutes later, JAC came back with a pot of coffee and three mugs. With an almost deafening clatter, he put them down on the wooden living room table between the two sofas and then sat down next to me on the couch.

"Kafka, who does this house belong to? And don't just say a professor." I asked because to ease my mind I had to have answers.

"The house belongs to a professor. A very dead professor. In fact, he has been dead for ten years without the world noticing." I couldn't help detecting the tone of voice with which Kafka said this. It revealed that this was something very personal to him.

I looked at Kafka quizzically and, out of the corner of my eye, I could see that the news of the dead professor was also news to JAC.

"The professor was a loner, a weirdo, who had virtually no contact with the outside world. He never went out. Got everything delivered first via phone orders and later by the Internet. He never made any appearances –

neither privately nor publicly. Not even the guy who kept his garden and those who cleaned the house, saw him. He preferred to live in isolation, so no one knows that he is actually dead."

"What about his family?" I asked.

"No family."

"And how do you know him? Was it you who terminated him?" I asked, but Kafka just smiled.

"No I didn't. Not that I sometimes didn't feel like it, but no. He was my stepfather." There was a moment of silence between us and there was no doubt that we were each sitting with our own thoughts about what we had just heard.

"So this is actually your house?" said JAC quietly, looking around.

"No, because officially my stepfather is still alive, so ... but we are safe here. Nobody will look for us here and if they do, then I have made the 'alarm system' myself," he said and smiled crookedly. JAC took his Glock off his waistband and laid it on the table. Then he leaned back and put one arm along the back of the sofa and the other on the armrest.

"When I'm here, I rarely walk around with my gun." Kafka said glancing at JAC's Glock, "No one comes here except for the two cleaners and the gardener. By the way, speaking of cleaning, when they clean our rooms on the first floor we move to the other side of the house. The rooms are identical on both sides of the staircases. So once a week we shift rooms."

"Of course." JAC replied, still a little stunned about all the news.

"But now I want to know what the hell happened in Afghanistan?" Kafka asked leaning forward on the couch while looking at me with serious eyes.

I could not blame him for wanting to hear what had been going on, but I was not sure how much of the truth I should tell them. There was a short pause that seemed like forever. But then I decided I might as well put all the cards on the table.

I poured myself a cup of coffee, leaned back and told them everything. About Aussie, the ambush, the attack, Jansson's assassination of Aussie, the escape from the village and later my elimination of Jansson, about sending my co-ordinates from Aussie's phone to Liam without getting an answer, the killing of the woman and the unborn child, and how I subsequently lost myself in the desert, when I buried it and finally about the trip to Islamabad of which I only remembered fragments.

Yes, I told them everything.

When I was finished, there was a complete silence in the room, and it was a silence that I did not like. While I was talking, Kafka and JAC had exchanged worried, shocked, and horrified glances with each other depending on where I was in my story, and now they were both just sitting and staring at me. As if they were paralyzed in shock. Suddenly JAC broke the silence.

"I have no idea what to say," he said staring into the air as he shook his head.

I looked into the flames of the fire.

"I find it difficult to accept what I have done and the fact that I could not protect Aussie. I had no idea that it was Jansson, who had been given the assignment to kill me. Aussie and I had dinner with him in the mess the day before." I closed my eyes and put one hand up in front of my mouth.

"You did what?" JAC said wrinkling his nose in disgust.

"Yes," I replied, "and we had no idea. In fact, he was standing in front of all of us that night the sergeant came to the barrack and wanted to talk to Liam. None of us suspected him. Therefore, I staged the elimination of him as being a murder committed by partisans, as I did with the woman. She had to take my place, so whoever was after me would think I was dead."

"That was fucking smart though." The words came from Kafka as he scowled at me, "If the FSB thinks you died in the mountains, everyone in the industry will think you are dead. That means you can disappear right now. Because it is probably the FSB that is behind this or ...?"

I had no idea what to answer because Jansson had not confirmed that he was FSB.

What he had done was to confirm, that he did not work for them. That is if he was telling the truth.

"Yes, I can disappear but where? I cannot move around freely and carelessly because of fear that someone suddenly will recognize me. I cannot have any more plastic surgeries performed due to all the ones I received after Belize. All new soldiers will get to know me and my face because I'm apparently on the military academy training syllabus. I will have to live the rest of my life in fear of being recognized. To survive, I would have to live like your stepfather – isolated from the outside world. Is that a life? Trapped and alone? For a while maybe, but then what? I do not want to go down the same path as Wizard – I do not want to end up like a caged lion and be forced to just pace from side to side. I'd rather have a bullet in my forehead before that happens." I paused as Kafka and JAC sat silently. I think they actually understood me because who would be able to live like that? None of us – that was for sure. "And as for the FSB, I do not know if they were the ones behind it. Maybe indirectly. Jansson did not seem to work for them. Maybe they had hired an outside company to do it. Maybe Jansson was someone who had gone solo and just wanted me on his kill summary, as he said. I don't know. But it is not so important now, as everyone hopefully thinks I am dead. By the way, where is Wizard?" My question was addressed to both of them. "I'm more worried about him."

"He has teamed up with Luc and participates in missions with him. Liam is crazy about it, but can't do anything." JAC replied and opened one of the cola cans that stood on a tray on the table.

"What about the contract on Wizard? Has it been given?" My words made Kafka look up questioningly.

"Yes, indeed it has. Wizard is worth fifteen million dollars. Dead or alive." JAC replied.

"And he doesn't care?" I asked.

"Stop," Kafka said resolutely, "Is there a contract out on Wizard?"

"Yes," JAC replied, "It was he who actually carried out the assassination on the political leader for the FSB." Judging by Kafka's facial expression, he obviously had no idea what he was going to use that information for because he seemed completely indifferent to it.

"Where is Liam now?" I asked, and both JAC and Kafka shrugged slightly.

"In camp I suppose," Kafka replied, "He was, in his own controlled way, furious when he was told about the ambush on you and Aussie. Wizard, JAC and I were ready to go up there to get you out, but we were not sure if you were alive. When we heard that Aussie's body had been found and that you were gone, we knew that something had gone horribly wrong. At no point did we have Jansson in mind, almost the opposite. The whole division except one was either killed or is MIA – Missing In Action."

"Liam and I got into a fight in the barracks," JAC continued after a short break that was much needed for all of us, "I knew you were alive, but Liam was not so sure, so we ended up in a regular fist fight. Kafka, Wizard, Luc plus two other legionnaires had to separate us." I looked at JAC and then at Kafka who nodded.

"A few hours later, the message from Aussie's phone showed on Liam's, but by that time we already knew that Aussie was dead. I was sure that it was you who sent the message but Liam doubted. Liam told us nothing about it being co-ordinates that you sent. Had he done that, we would have left immediately."

"Maybe that's why," I said quietly, looking blankly into the air, "I was expendable. You were not." For a moment the room went silent. What went through the minds of the other two, I don't know, but for my own part it was the fact that Liam had been willing to sacrifice me. I'd never doubted that he would do it one day, but I had thought he would check the facts and not just assume I was dead. The thought that I, as a person, had not meant more to him than an unknown soldier would have done, actually hit me. It was not because I expected him to have feelings for me, but a little empathy would somehow have been nice.

JAC's voice tore me out of the slightly melancholy state of mind that I was heading into and the whirlwind of justification that I was building up.

"When I received the message from you with the co-ordinates of Islamabad, I knew for sure that you were alive and where you were going. So Kafka and I immediately left without Wizard because he was nowhere to be found."

JAC emptied the cola and squashed the empty can with one hand. Then he laid it on the table.

"Does Liam know about Islamabad and that I'm alive?" I asked hoping that the answer would be no.

JAC shook his head. "He doesn't. The safe house is mine and mine alone. No one but the two of you know about it." JAC looked at Kafka and me as he smiled crookedly.

"Good," I said relieved and took a deep breath, "What do we do about Wizard?"

"Nothing," Kafka replied coldly, "We leave him in happy ignorance of where we are and that you're alive." Kafka got up and went over and threw another log on the fire. He stood for a moment in front of it with both his hands on the mantelpiece and his back to us while he stared into the flames.

"I'm not going to leave Wizard in the lurch." JAC said softly but very, very definitely.

"He would come for us if the shoe were on the other foot," I stated.

Kafka turned around.

"I did not say that we should not help him. We just have to do it the right way. Otherwise, we all end up being hunted like wild animals, and for the moment we have a huge advantage. We have a hiding place where no one can get near us. We have time to make a flawless plan. We know where Wizard is and ..." Kafka pointed at me, "We have the best dead sniper in the world. But then we have Liam too," he said looking at us.

"Liam? Don't worry about him." JAC replied calmly while staring at Kafka, who immediately got the message.

"I hope you are right, because he is a very, very dangerous man. He is a pure sociopath. He lures people in and uses them, and when he no longer needs them, they get a neck shot. Liam does not kill for the sake of money or because he likes it. Liam kills because he can, and because that's what works for him. Liam does nothing if it does not benefit him and his ideology on some level. Therefore, the combination of Liam and the contents of the metal box is something that sends cold shivers down my spine and can give me sleepless nights."

Kafka looked at JAC then me and then something happened.

Quietly, JAC took something out of his jacket pocket, leaned forward and put it on the table in front of Kafka.

"He can't use the contents of the metal box without this." JAC leaned back on the couch and smiled smugly. Kafka took the small metal ampoule and looked at it. Then a huge smile spread across his lips.

"You're brilliant, JAC," he said quietly, "Fucking brilliant."

"No. It was Wizard. I got him to eavesdrop on Liam's code on the metal box and then it was a done deal."

Kafka looked at us and smiled even wider if that's possible.

"Well, that settles it. Let's go and get Wizard." He lifted his glass and we toasted in water, coffee and a crumpled cola can.

"But before we go to bed, we have a few steaks that must be eaten." Kafka said sharply, while he looked at me.

I almost felt I was back in boarding school and that it was the strict Frau Wilkes, who stood in front of me. However, Kafka's sharpness was quickly accompanied by a small wink and Frau Wilkes returned to my box that was named 'The Past'.

While the sound of Kafka rattling plates in the kitchen hit my ears, my gaze and my thoughts disappeared quietly into the flames of the fire, which had now taken hold of the log Kafka had put on it a while ago.

"JAC," I said but regretted straight away that I had opened my mouth, "I do not know if you can ..." I could not bring myself to ask because I was not sure I would like the answer.

"Can what? Understand you? Forgive you? Love you?"

We sat in silence for a moment.

"I understand if your answer is no to all of the questions. It is okay by me."

The leather of the Chesterfield sofa gave way a little as he got up and it became strangely empty as his weight disappeared from the seat.

"I do not know what the hell to answer other than ... I would have done the same. Or ... I do not know if I could have done it. Wizard could without even blinking."

I snorted, because that was at least something we could agree on, in the midst of all these acts of brutality and murder.

"We are not just taking lives. We also give others a chance to live theirs. Think of all the people we have killed so that others could have their freedom, be it economic, political or ideological. Yes, the woman and the child were unfortunate. What you did you have to live with. Let their lost lives give life to others."

He paused and to this day I'm not sure, that he knew how much his words burned into my grieving mind.

"What I'm trying to say is, do not let their deaths be in vain, but give them meaning." He looked at me seriously, "Do not be a hypocrite. Take your time and get it into the right boxes. Do you understand?" He looked down.

For a moment I thought I had heard wrong. Had he called me a hypocrite? A hypocrite? What the hell was he saying? A hypocrite was probably the last thing I was. Melancholy and guilty yes ... but not hypocrite. Had he not understood one word I'd said? I had killed someone who had never done any harm. Had never made a mistake. I had deprived a human being of life before the person had the opportunity to live it. Before even the first breath before I ...

"It's true that I cannot see how the death of an unborn child can make sense."

JAC walked around the couch and looked me directly in the face.

"It was not their time to live, babe," he whispered referring to the mother and the child. At the same time Kafka came into the living room with three steak-laden plates.

* * *

It was late before the plates were empty and we broke up.

Kafka and JAC cleaned up and then disappeared upstairs. I sat for a while and let my thoughts disappear into the alluring flames of the fire before finally retiring as well.

There was silence throughout the house and it was a lovely safe and reassuring silence. I really felt that I had nothing to fear. Only two people knew I was alive and they were both here in this house and both were colleagues that I trusted. For a moment I stopped in front of my own door, but then I continued to JAC's and went inside.

The light from one simple lamp in the room was just enough for me to see JAC lying in his bed sleeping. His Glock lay on the bedside table next to him and it was, as always, secured. I opened my bathrobe and let it fall to the ground. It gave a bump as it hit the floor due to my Glock that was still in the pocket and it surprised me.

It was the first time that I had ever forgotten where it was.

I looked at JAC to see if the sound had woken him, but he was not moving. My heart stood still. He lay completely still.

Carefully, I sneaked over to him to see if anything was wrong. My heart rate was a hundred and eighty and rising, but as I got closer, I saw the reason why he did not respond. He had just had his fix and was far away in intoxication.

It was as if the weight of a boulder disappeared from my shoulders and I drew a sigh of relief. Then I removed the leather cord and needle he had used for his fix from the bed and lay down next to him. His body was warm and his breathing was calm and regular. I slid my hand over his bare chest and stomach. On its path I let my fingertips wander around all the scars they encountered on their way and I could not help but think that our bodies were like diaries.

If you wanted to know something about us, you could read it directly on us. Our deeds were cut into our skin and what one could not see with the naked eye, was probably not worth knowing.

'Please read my body but not my mind,' I thought, 'That is reserved for Him who will hold me accountable one day. If there was such an inventory when the time came.' Maybe in reality there was just nothing. A flash of light and then everything was black. Then you were gone. Like when I pressed the trigger. A glimpse and then you fell.

I had never really taken a stand on such issues and had no intention of doing so now. I just wanted to lie here with JAC and enjoy that I was alive. I once again sent a thank you to the woman I had killed in Afghanistan, and immediately the pain and nausea of what I had done returned. Maybe JAC had the right idea. Maybe that was the way to get away from all this hopeless pain and guilt. Maybe it was our only way to lift this curse – to disappear into it. I laid my head on JAC's chest and fell asleep.

Chapter 16

The next day started with the three of us going on an on-line shopping trip. JAC shopped for weapons and electronic equipment, Kafka shopped for information and I ... I shopped for clothes, for Kafka, JAC and myself. The only clothes I had had were the ones from the dead woman, and for safety reasons we had to get rid of them. Therefore I had temporarily borrowed a pair of trousers and a t-shirt from Kafka. He was only a little bit taller than me, so they almost fit.

We had breakfast in the kitchen and, as a thanks to the guys for having cleaned up from the night before, I volunteered to clean up now. While JAC and Kafka discussed security and storage capacity in terms of our weapons, especially the ones JAC had just ordered, I went on a tour of the house.

The house was seven hundred square metres and contained a basement, two upper floors and an attic. The security of not only the house but the entire estate was admirable and the more I saw of it, the safer I felt. There were bulletproof doors and windows everywhere and they were all equipped with electronic locks and sensors. All of the rooms were fireproofed and connected to each other by doors. In fact, all rooms including the living rooms had two exits. There was special one-way glass in the windows so that from inside you could look out but from the outside you could not see in, neither during the day nor at night, which gave us incredible security when we walked around in the house.

The garage in the basement had not only room for two cars, a Nissan Patrol GR Turbo and a Mitsubishi Pajero, but also housed two Ducati motorcycles, a Hummer and a fully equipped car workshop with a separate area specially designed for welding and repainting. In addition there was a one hundred square metre utility room, a fitness room and a temperate wine cellar. On the ground floor there were, in addition to the auditorium and kitchen, four linked living rooms, one of which was a library in Old English country style. The first floor was exclusively bedrooms and bathrooms with four rooms on each side of the grand staircase. They were all exclusively decorated in a mixture of southern Europe meets the Middle-East and although you would think these two styles would clash it somehow worked. My trip ended with a look at the outdoor areas of the house and as inside here nothing had been left to chance. The house was surrounded by a large marble terrace, where a few individual Greek statues emphasized its grandeur. The garden itself contained mostly small bushes spread across a lawn that would have made any green keeper envious.

When I had finished my inspection of the surroundings I went to the lounge where as expected I found JAC on the phone and from his conversation I noted that his Arabic had become fluent. Kafka sat in the library and surfed information on the Internet and so as to not disturb JAC I went to join Kafka. I sat down in one of the high backed dark wooden chairs opposite the massive Empire-style desk and looked at him.

"Have you considered what Liam will do when he finds out that the ampoule is missing from the metal box?" Kafka asked.

"If he finds out that it was Wizard who snatched it, he is going to kill him." I smiled at Kafka and winked.

"Then we have to hope that he doesn't ... find out I mean. I honestly believe that he will suspect JAC of being the traitor."

"Or you!" I answered.

Kafka looked up.

"Or me!" he replied.

I looked around the library.

"How did you get out of the camp without Liam following?"

"It was damn simple. After the fight between JAC and him, it was kind of written on the wall. JAC packed his things and left – but he only did it after your message had arrived on his phone. Liam didn't really care, because he had me so, when I split too, he must have been furious. I didn't see it though. I kind of slipped out when he briefly left the barracks."

"I can imagine that he wasn't pleased to have found out that you were gone. He's told me he needed at least one of you, so he must have been fuming when you both disappeared. Do you think he suspected you of teaming up with JAC?"

Kafka looked at me.

"Doubt it," he said smiling slyly, "JAC went to Kabul and caught an unauthorized transport from there. I went to Kandahar and then took the train – without a ticket."

"Good boys," I said a little teasingly. It was section one in the military manual for how to 'slip away' so Liam had probably figured it out by now, but we had to wait and see.

"Let's meet at four p.m. and brainstorm," I said to Kafka as I got up, "We have to figure out where to go from here."

"Sixteen-hundred it is," he replied nodding while still engrossed in whatever was on the laptop screen.

JAC was still on the phone when I entered the living room. We exchanged just a few brief glances before I disappeared upstairs again.

The professor's house was truly a great place to be. It was surrounded by tranquillity mixed with an underlying melancholy and for the first time in years I felt totally protected. As I stood there in my room, not having to fear who stepped in, I felt the kind of security that only a child can feel washing over me. It was a feeling I had long forgotten and even though it made me feel a bit concerned, there was also a nice recognition about it. A recognition I welcomed so that I, at least for now, could put my job aside and just be 'completely ordinary' without mistrust and fear.

In the midst of my own joy of recognition, I suddenly felt JAC's arms around me and I automatically leaned back. His chest felt like a concrete wall when I hit it and it made me smile. I closed my eyes and let my head tilt to one side. He kissed me gently on the neck and the feeling of his soft lips against my skin immediately brought the longing in me for him.

"We may have a problem." The voice came from Kafka who stood in the doorway with a very serious look on his face. Immediately JAC let go of me and like two robots we simultaneously turned towards Kafka. To our surprise he had a scanner in his hand. It was one of those scanners that we used to sweep rooms to check for electronic equipment, such as microphones, detonators, etc., but they could also be used to sweep people.

Without further explanation Kafka walked over to me and, while he swept me, JAC stepped aside. It went pretty well until he reached my right armpit and the scanner started beeping like crazy. Kafka and I looked briefly at each other and it was clear that whatever it was, the scanner had found, it was not to our advantage. He then turned around and scanned JAC and luckily the scanner gave no result.

"You are clear," he said to JAC before he turned to me again, "Then it's just you and me."

"What the hell is going on?" JAC's question was completely legitimate and weird enough, so was the answer.

"Mossad." Kafka said briskly as he and I kept eye contact.

"Mossad?" JAC frowned and scowled at us.

"It's the only thing we have in common," I replied, shifting my gaze to JAC.

"I have been affiliated with a special unit under Mossad and it was through that, I was in Belize." Kafka replied without any kind of suggestion in his voice that JAC should pursue the matter.

"And it was Mossad that paid for my operations in the US after Belize," I said quietly.

"They must have put the chip in during one of the operations." Kafka stated and sighed.

"There were plenty of them," I replied as I walked over and looked out the window, "Why? And why you?" I turned and looked at Kafka who in response raised his eyebrows and shook his head slightly.

"Tracking?" He snorted once and then returned to the impending problem, "I guess in principle it doesn't fucking matter 'Why'. What matters now is how we get the chips removed."

Under normal circumstances I would have been on the same wavelength as Kafka regarding what we should do, but it was as if all my focus had gone and I was left with an incipient rage, that did not immediately let itself be tamed.

"Fuck, I've been walking around with that thing in me for years. They have been able to follow me all the time. They've been able to kill me whenever they felt like it without me knowing. I've been like a fucking animal on the savannah, sending out a beacon so they could track me. Get that shit out of me now, Kafka. NOW." I had wound myself up in such a way that the last sentences were shouted aggressively and with such a volume that it even stunned JAC.

"I don't dare to take it out," Kafka replied bitterly, "We do not know exactly how deep inside you they placed it. They have been damn smart to put it in your right armpit – your 'trigger arm'. The bloody idiots made sure that it would take a skilled surgeon to remove it. Otherwise you will risk getting muscle and nerve damage possibly permanently."

"Great. Not only have they made me into a fucking monitored animal, they have also made sure that I would be wounded if I managed to get rid of their 'collar'. They had me all along in their telescopic sight. Following me like you would follow a game animal you want to kill. Like trophy hunters and me with no chance of defending myself." Slowly I felt my control being taken away from me by their action and as it dissipated, my rage converted into desperation. In my heart I was ready to take revenge for this violation of me.

"I ... am ... not ... and ... will ... never ... be ... their ... trophy. NEVER." I was boiling with anger but then my eyes fell on JAC.

"We need to get a doctor who can operate to remove these microchips," he said with a voice that displayed an astonishing calmness and authority. It brought me instantly back to reality and put my private revenge on hold.

"And how the hell do you propose we do that? OPUS cannot be seen out there ..." Kafka snarled and pointed towards the city, "And a surgeon who makes 'house calls'? Good luck with that." Kafka's rather condescending tone of voice did not affect JAC in the least.

"Relax. If I get the surgeon can you raise the money to pay him?" JAC replied and it suddenly dawned on me, that he actually was the only one of us, who right now was trying to solve the problem rather than seeing all the obstacles that prevented us from doing so.

"Yes, I can." Kafka said with a little less suspicion in his voice than before.

JAC took his phone out of his pocket and dialled.

"Hey, it's JAC. I am calling in a favour," he said briefly and then there was a short pause. "Get me a surgeon in neurology in Islamabad." Another break, "ASAP ... Deal." And then he hung up.

Kafka and I were in shock to say the least.

"Hell, JAC," Kafka shook his head and smiled, "I don't even want to know."

"Don't worry," JAC replied as he smiled crookedly, "You don't get to know but the surgeon has to be picked up at the Hilton Hotel in thirty minutes, so you better start counting to $50,000. That is what it is going to cost."

I was positively stunned at what had just happened. I thought I knew JAC but this was a side of him that I had never seen and it made me curious.

As he went into his room to pick up his Glock, I couldn't help wondering how the hell he could do what he had just done. What kind of person can make just ONE phone call and then have a neuro-surgeon making a house call? Obviously a well-connected one or ... I suddenly realized that it was not only JAC that was connected but indeed the person he called: The person who owed him a favour.

"Let's get those things out of you," JAC said as he walked back into the room, "and then we'll go and get some fucking answers to all of this shit." His voice was harsh and determined and clearly showed that he had had enough. We had to find answers which usually meant corpses in our industry. I smiled. How I loved to see him like this.

We went downstairs and into the library. From one of the wooden desk drawers Kafka got a set of car keys. He threw them to JAC and then explained to him about the alarm system in the basement, the garage, the driveway and the front gate. When JAC left, Kafka typed in a code on his cell phone. Suddenly all the security cameras appeared on the big flat screen that hung on the wall opposite the desk. I stood and watched as the Pajero, with JAC behind the wheel, came into view, but then shifted my focus to Kafka. He had moved to the other side of the library and stood in front of a picture. As he pushed it aside a built-in safe was revealed and after a few taps on an electronic lock, Kafka opened it. My gaze slid back to the flat screen and while the iron gate closed behind JAC, Kafka took out a stack of money, as well as a metal box. He then closed the safe again.

"Come. We'll set it up in the kitchen," he said and without looking at me, he disappeared into the hall. I stood for a moment staring at the flat screen and the closed gate. 'Damn all this' were the only words that went through my head.

In the kitchen Kafka and I sterilized the lacquered surface of the dining table, got some cotton pads and gauze from a first aid kit as well as some freshly washed towels from one of the bathrooms. Metal trays for instruments were prepared and disinfectant was placed next to them. If you didn't know better you would think we had worked together all our lives because of how smoothly everything went. At least until Kafka opened the small metal box that contained a kit ready to use if you needed a fix. With a mixture of wonder and disbelief I looked at him and he must have registered it because he addressed my concern.

"Don't worry," he said as he used the syringe to suck up the contents of one of the ampoules of morphine that were in the box, "I know what I'm doing."

"I can see that. Should I ask?"

"Let me put it this way," he replied putting the filled syringe into the metal tray. "A year ago I was like JAC and Wizard, but today I'm clean ... pretty much." I snorted and glared at him.

"Pretty much? What the hell does that mean? That you only junk at parties? That you fix to celebrate your kills? What the hell does that say about you? Of all the mercs, I never thought you would be one of THEM. What the hell went wrong, Kafka? The Kafka I know is ice cold and without scruples and ..."

"Yes," It came wearily from Kafka, "And that is precisely why. Have you ever considered that I was that because of that?" He nodded down towards some ampoules in the metal box, "We make a living by killing people and we do it in every way possible, and from every conceivable and imaginable position and angle. Through the temples, the ears, the eyes, under the chin, through the mouth or the nose and let's not forget the frontal lobe. If we are 'gracious' we do it with a simple head shot or a shot to the heart. We strangle marks, cut their throats, cut them open with knives, so OPUS, if I choose to go to a place once in a while where these things don't happen and where everything is okay, I damn well will."

For a moment I stood still because basically he was right. Who the hell was I to judge him? Did he judge me?

And yet ...

"We – ourselves – have chosen this lifestyle no matter how fucking tough it is and if you need a 'picnic' once in a while then peace be with you, but if I ever have any reason to doubt that you are not here when I need you I'll ..." I pointed with two fingers at his forehead as if I were about to shoot him.

I turned around and walked to the dining table.

"If you believe ..." he began but I interrupted him.

"Believe? I believe nothing. And if you need to explain or confess your sins go to a fucking priest or psych, not to me. Because to be honest, Kafka. I don't give a shit."

I had no doubt that Kafka was both disappointed and hurt, but honestly, I did not care. It had just dawned on me, that the ones I was fighting alongside were junkies – JAC, Wizard and Kafka. What the hell was I doing? What had become of the mercs that could handle it? Those who could do the work and live with it? Was I completely wrong when it came to all this? Wasn't it really mercs like Liam and legionnaires like Luc, who had a future in this business? My thoughts were all over the place. I went over to the kitchen sink, turned on the cold tap and sprayed water on my face. I had to have control over my thoughts, because as difficult as it might be, I had to accept, that the only ones I trusted were two junkies and a third one, who was on the run and needed us. And funnily enough I had to admit that I had never doubted their loyalty. NEVER.

I could understand if they needed to escape once in a while. After what happened to me in Afghanistan, I had thought about doing it too but if the price of my humanity was to become a junkie just to be able to endure being human, then I would rather objectify my actions. Even if that meant I would become an unempathetic individual. Fuck it. I could not comprehend this – not right now.

And that's when I came to the frightening conclusion that I actually needed JAC, junkie or not. I needed him so that things made just a little bit of sense.

As I stood there by the kitchen sink, I could feel Kafka's piercing eyes on my back and even though it was highly uncomfortable, I did not let it get to me.

"Kafka," I said wiping my face dry on one of the towels that was meant for the operation, "I am so sorry." I lowered the towel, "I have no right to judge you. It's just that we tackle our demons very differently and ..."

Out of the corner of my eye I saw Kafka walking towards me and he only stopped when he stood right next to me. His piercing eyes had softened and beside me stood a calm and relaxed man. How the hell he could switch from one extreme to the other in just a few seconds, I couldn't grasp, but apparently he could.

"Let bygones be bygones," he said looking me up and down, "What do you weigh – a hundred and twenty-four? A hundred and thirty pounds?"

"Maybe. Have no idea."

"Let's say a hundred and twenty-six pounds." His voice was neutral and factual, a bit like a surgeon explaining a pending procedure to a patient. Then he went to the metal tray and picked up the syringe containing the morphine, "I can always give you a little more if you need it," he said as he flicked at the needle measuring the correct amount of morphine.

One question that had been nagging me for the last quarter of an hour was how Kafka had got the idea, that we could be chipped? Oddly enough, it did not seem to come as a surprise to him when asked. I think he expected it because the answer came promptly and without hesitation or any display of emotion.

"Last time I was here I ordered a new scanning system for the whole house, one which would be able to detect infrared and heat-seeking objects. Then last night when I couldn't sleep, I started to put it up and when I finished this morning, I switched it on to see if it was working and *voilà* ... Since we haven't got any heat-seeking missiles here ... well you get the picture. I have to admit that I hadn't imagined this, but what the fuck. When I think about it, I do know that Mossad 'marks' the people they have a special interest in."

"It's shit, Kafka. Who says Mossad isn't going to sell my whereabouts to the FSB or others for that matter?"

"No-one. But I'll find out more later. For now, we just have to get the chips out of us."

The door to the cellar opened and a blindfolded man appeared. JAC was right behind him, carrying the man's bag. He escorted him into the kitchen and only when they were standing in the middle of the floor did he remove the blindfold.

Judging by the man's appearance he was in his mid-forties, of Arab descent and average build, with hints of grey in his otherwise black hair. He seemed pretty nervous but he relaxed a bit when he caught sight of me. JAC, seemingly, had no intention of introducing him to us because in his eyes the doctor was just there for a couple of hours to do a job so no names were therefore required. However, Kafka obviously had a different idea so, after a few greetings, we learned that the doctor's name was Pawseena.

"You start with her." JAC instructed as he pointed to me.

Nervously Dr. Pawseena began to ramble about anaesthesia and drips but was interrupted by Kafka who, in a very relaxed and almost mesmerizing tone of voice, made it clear to him that he should not worry about all that. His only task was to perform the surgery, nothing else. After some exchange of views Dr. Pawseena finally agreed to it and I was called over to the table.

I had been waiting by the kitchen sink with JAC so while Dr. Pawseena was occupied finding something in his medical kit I went over to Kafka who stood behind the table. It was as if Dr. Pawseena didn't see me at all, as he passed me on his way to the sink to scrub his hands and arms.

I will never forget the way JAC watched him. There was no doubt that he would kill him if he suspected the slightest mischief or if the doctor fumbled during the operation. His ice-cold eyes had a soothing effect on me and they somehow seemed to calm me down. Kafka on the other hand was tranquillity itself. Had it been anyone else I would have said it was a good thing, but not when it came to Kafka. Quite the contrary. It screamed vigilance and distrust and that was not a good combination.

"The doctor and I have agreed that he will operate on you first. You'll be given just enough morphine to numb the area but should you feel something, knock on the table top and I will give you a little more. But I would rather you felt a little than being completely gone. Okay?"

"Okay," I replied pretty indifferently because no matter what they did to me it would most certainly not be more painful than what had been done to me in Belize.

I took off my t-shirt and lay down on the table and I could see Kafka looking stunned at my chest and my stomach. Very few had seen my naked torso – or for that matter my whole body – after all the surgeries in the US – and even though the doctors over there had done a fantastic job, I would be scarred for life.

JAC must also have been shaken when he first saw me after Belize. It was in the bath in Liam's suite, but what he and I had was so much more than just the physical. However, I understood why some would have a hard time looking at all the scars.

The most beautiful aspect of my torso was my breasts. They had been totally reconstructed and therefore sat perfectly and were largely without scars, but of course they are also artificial.

"Kafka," I said as I grabbed his chin and made eye contact with him, "Give me the morphine." He nodded and walked round to my right side.

The doctor came over and, as I expected, he stopped abruptly when he saw my body.

"Wow," he exclaimed startled, taking a step back.

JAC straightened up and took a few steps towards him, and his reaction immediately caused the doctor to raise his hands defensively while looking at JAC. His spontaneous outburst had by no means pleased JAC, but he accepted the doctor's gesture and held back.

"It's okay," the doctor said nervously with a slight tremor in his voice before turning his attention to me again.

I stopped Kafka from preparing the area for the injection and got up on my elbows so I had eye contact with the doctor and no wonder he looked scared.

"Doc, it's okay. As you can see, I am used to surgery – so don't worry. Everything is going to be fine." Whether my words reassured the doctor, I am not sure but I lay down again and looked at Kafka. We nodded to each other and he disinfected where he wanted to stab me with the needle. Shortly after, I disappeared into the darkness.

For the next twenty minutes, I found myself in the borderland between being conscious and then being far away. I could occasionally feel a pain, but it was by no means unbearable, and when my shoulder and chest were taped up, I began to return to reality. JAC came over and helped me down from the table, but my legs failed, so he ended up lifting me up and carrying me onto one of the sofas in the lounge.

Here I lay while slowly returning to the land of the living. I was in no pain but that was probably because of the morphine. I could have just stayed there, but for some unknown reason I got up and staggered slightly dazed towards the kitchen.

There I saw JAC standing at the dining table while the doctor was taping Kafka's arm. Kafka was sitting upright on the edge of the table while JAC held his arm out to the side so the doctor could complete his work. It was clear that Kafka was in the same condition as I had been a short while ago, and as I stood there, leaning against the door frame trying to focus, I made eye contact with JAC. He had already registered my presence but had maintained his focus on Kafka and the doctor. When Kafka was taped up, JAC looked in my direction and nodded indicating that everything was okay.

I walked slowly and unsteadily towards them while JAC lifted Kafka up so he was standing. Like me, he did not have full control of his legs and therefore JAC supported him all the way into the lounge. When he passed me, he gave me his Glock and without further contact between us, I went to the dining table. I was still not quite sure about my legs, so I thought, it was safest to have something to lean against as I watched the doctor. He was at the kitchen sink washing the remnants of blood off his hands. Suddenly I felt JAC standing behind me.

"Are you okay?" he asked. I nodded, a little dazed.

"I just have to say something to the doctor before you take him back," I said to him and it was only now that I heard my voice. It was so blurred and so was my speech. The doctor turned to me and as he wiped his hands, we found each other's eyes.

"Thank you," I said quietly to him, "Thank you." I could feel my legs about to give way beneath me, but I stayed upright.

"You are welcome," he replied, smiling at me. In vain I tried to smile back, but my body screamed to lie down, so it just turned into a slightly awkward grimace.

Quietly, the doctor packed his things together and JAC handed him an envelope with what I presumed was the money. The doctor glanced shortly at the content before placing it in his bag. When he'd finished JAC blindfolded him before escorting him to the basement.

I stood for a while just to gather some energy so I could go over to the kitchen sink, and when I finally mustered it, it was only to throw up. I had never been good with anaesthesia and pure morphine was not my brand either.

* * *

Towards the end of the evening, Kafka and I had slowly regained our composure, and after eating a light dinner inside the lounge, Kafka went into the library and put the morphine kit and our chips in the safe. Mossad knew where we were, so whether the chips were in our armpits or locked in the safe, was irrelevant. What mattered was that they emitted a signal if they tried to track us.

JAC and I sat on different sofas in the lounge, and it was strangely liberating to have the knowledge that from now on no one would be tracking me without my consent. I leaned my head back and let it rest on the back of the sofa. Then I closed my eyes and took in the relaxation my body felt and so desperately needed.

As I was dozing, Kafka suddenly came in and sat down on the couch next to JAC.

"I will contact Mossad tonight and set up a meeting with them. When do you think you will be able to use your arm?" Kafka asked as his dark eyes focused on my right arm. I raised my head and started moving my shoulder around a few times.

Kafka's and JAC's facial expressions reflected the pain I felt but there was no trace of agony to read on my face.

"Tomorrow," I replied leaning back on the couch again. There was no reason to make a song and dance of it. The pain would probably have lessened by tomorrow, as it had so often before.

"Well. I'm arranging a meeting." Kafka said dryly, leaning back on the soft leather as well.

"How much do you have to do with Mossad?" I asked Kafka because, in my mind, it was possible that we could use them going forward.

"Mossad is my only client," he replied stretching his back.

There was an almost Wizard-like distrust in JAC's voice as he asked,

"What the hell were you doing with Luc?"

"I was looking for Liam's metal box. Luc was just a way in to the camp ... and Liam. I have known Luc since I bumped into him in Libya many years ago."

"Does Luc know about the metal box?" JAC asked.

"No, thank God. He would have sold its contents to the highest bidder."

"But without the isotope, it's pretty much worthless." JAC smiled, and the crooked smile Kafka replied with confirmed how important JAC's and Wizard's actions had been.

"It was fucking brilliant, what you and Wizard did there. Fucking brilliant."

"And with those words we will bid you good night." JAC signalled to me that we were leaving.

"Watch your shoulder." Kafka said, winking at me.

"Always," I replied smiling back, and then JAC and I left the lounge heading for my room.

When we got there, we did not turn on the light. The moonlight was so bright that it almost illuminated the whole room, and there was a lovely, almost romantic glow about it. Very gently JAC pulled me to him and wrapped in his arms he kissed me on the neck. Slowly I walked him backwards to the bed and we lay down. I could feel my shoulder now and I must have shown it somehow, because JAC stopped suddenly.

"Do you want some painkillers?" he asked thoughtfully, touching the tape gently.

"No. It makes me sick. I'd rather have the pain."

He looked at me questioningly.

"You'd rather be in pain than be pain-free?"

"Yes. There comes a time when the pain is no longer painful, where it just disappears and turns into physical numbness. You can then choose whether you want to stay in numbness or transform it into a mental ecstasy."

JAC was just lying and staring wide-eyed at me. I don't think he really believed me.

"Are you telling me you're getting a mental orgasm from pain?"

"Why do you think they couldn't break me in Belize, JAC?" JAC rolled over on his back and stared up at the ceiling.

"Like you, I have been trained to endure pain but, for me, pain has never been a problem like it is for you. I'm fine with the pain as long as I can control it. In Belize, I was in so much pain that I didn't know what to do with it, and it dawned on me that the only way I could control it, was by letting it take over my mind. I couldn't be in it physically, so I transformed it into a state of mind. And the easy way to do that was to transform it into you. And by mixing you and it, I could endure it and so keep myself alive."

JAC was completely silent and, in fact, his silence made me a little worried about his reaction.

"You could say," I continued, "that I imagined that you inflicted the pain on me because you loved me and that made me endure it."

"You survived by imagining I tortured you?" JAC's voice was filled with horror.

"No. I survived knowing that every pain I endured was you loving me. You loved me every day and at night you comforted me and told me that I just had to trust you. That you were there. And that I was strong enough to absorb your love a little more – a little longer. You didn't hurt me. You saved me, JAC." JAC rolled on to his side so we looked directly into each other's eyes.

"I'm so fucking scared of you right now and at the same time I never wanted you more," he said and I could hear that he was a little short of breath. I put my hand on his chest and could feel his heart pounding rapidly.

"Get it under control," I said gently, "Then the pleasure will be so much greater when you finally let go. Close your eyes and feel your heartbeat." He closed his eyes and tried to control his breathing, "Take a deep breath and hold it. Exhale slowly. Do it again until you feel your heart rate slowing."

And after a minute or so, I could feel his heart rate dropping. He was still lying on his side with his eyes closed so I gently pushed him in the chest so that he rolled onto his back. Then I leaned over him and whispered softly, "Keep the rhythm of your breathing as it is now. No matter what happens, keep the rhythm there. Control it. If possible, make it even slower. When I say, you let go and let it run free."

I could see that he was in unfamiliar territory and I knew that the kind of self-control I was demanding of him right now was not his strong suit. On the contrary. Fortunately he did not have to learn to love the pain as I did but, if I could teach him to enjoy it, he would be close to being the perfect soldier.

That night I guided him through pain and he took his first baby steps into my universe. Hopefully he would then never again be in doubt that he truly saved me in Belize.

Chapter 17

At seven o'clock Kafka woke us up. He had arranged a meeting with Mossad in the afternoon and since he had been up all night, he was now going to bed. Without expecting any reaction from us, he disappeared into his room and closed the door. Whatever questions we may have had were shelved for later.

I slipped into the shower and a few minutes later JAC stepped in as well. He stood facing me, placing his hands on my hips.

"It was fucking unbelievable last night," he said, looking me straight in the eyes with a wry smile, "You have to teach me more. I need to have more of what you did last night."

The hot jets from the shower hit my neck and I leaned back, closed my eyes and opened my mouth so I could feel the water on my face and in my mouth. JAC started kissing me on the neck and I wrapped my arms and legs around his wet body. He lifted me up and we made love wildly and intensely against the white tile wall of the shower stall while the water poured down on us.

When we were back in the bedroom later on, dressed in only white towels, he suddenly grabbed me from behind and threw me down on the bed.

"Well, what's your answer? Do you want to teach me?" he asked before lying down next to me.

I rolled over so I sat on top of him letting my wet hair drip down on his bare stomach. The contours of his abdominal muscles were clear, and as the drops from my hair hit them, he began to tighten them. I put both my hands on his chest and leaned down to his face with our gaze locked while I could feel his hands move up my thighs.

"There's nothing I would like more," I whispered smiling and kissing him.

He grabbed my neck and we kissed – first gently and then more greedily. Slowly he loosened my towel and let one hand wander up to my breasts.

As he cupped and squeezed my right breast, his left hand moved to my ass. To grant him fully access I lifted my pelvis a little and seconds later he had two fingers inside me. I was ready for him but at no point did my heart rate exceed 140. It wasn't because I didn't enjoy him pinching my nipple and finger fucking me but it would take a lot more to get me off than just a bit of petting. I leaned forward and stopped his fingers from entering me. Then I grasped his stiff cock and guided it to my entrance.

"Now JAC ..." I whispered in his ear, "Control your breathing. If in doubt put your hand to my chest and feel my heartbeats. Keep the rhythm of them. Don't let it take you over. Control the urge. Don't let it take over." He nodded at my words and then and only then did I let his cock penetrate. As I raised my body, I felt how his dick went all the way inside me until it could get no further. He closed his eyes as he groaned and I could feel how his entire body tensed as I started riding him. I was kind enough to start at a very slow pace and where I normally would be doing this for my own physical pleasure this time was different. I did it to give JAC a chance to control his rising pulse; to keep it as low for as long as possible. His breathing was getting faster and as much as I loved the sound of it, it was not the purpose of this exercise.

"Control it, JAC. Control it or I stop." My threat was real but I don't think he cared. He was obviously struggling and instead of putting his hand to my heart as I had instructed him to do he simply just squeezed my breast tighter and tighter. I liked the pain it produced but this was not about me. This was about him so I yanked away his hand from my breast and put his palm to my heart.

"Feel the rhythm, JAC. Feel it and copy it," I demanded in a low voice and even though he tried he didn't succeed, "If you want this ..." I said and started to ride him faster and harder, "then get your fucking heart rate under control." His narrowed eyes found mine and I could see how desperately he tried but without luck. I had by now slowed my pace down again but it didn't matter. He had absolutely no control and the frustration in him for not having it was building by the second. I was about to stop and get off him when he placed both his hands on my hips and flipped me over so now he was on top.

"I'm sorry ..." he said but there was no sorry in his voice, "I can't control it and I need you so fucking much so ..." He thrust deep into me as he groaned from pleasure but it was anything but pleasure for me. I managed to bend my legs and knees so far up that they touched my stomach and as he pulled himself back to thrust once more I used all my leg muscles to push him back.

The force with which my knees hit his stomach made JAC instantly fall back and tumble out of the bed. He landed heavily on the floor and before he could get up, I was standing over him.

"What the fuck, JAC? Are you crazy? This is not how it goes. You fucking do as you are told or we are done. Do you understand? Done!" I yelled the words into his face and I meant every single one of them. If he wanted to continue being a good soldier that was fine with me. But if he wanted to be an excellent one, an unbreakable one .... Well, then he had to learn how to tame the pain so it was of no consequence to him. And the easiest way to do that was learn to love it, so when his body was racked, his mind would welcome it like an old friend.

Angry with his fucking impatient nature I went to my room slamming the door behind me. I was so frustrated that I was almost shaking all over. I had been trying to teach him and he had completely disregarded it and just given in to his own desire and needs. I knew that our relationship was not built on love but mutual respect. But there was nothing mutual about what he had done ... or tried to do. It was pure selfish satisfaction and from now on he could take that and fuck himself with it.

A faint knock sounded at my door and I knew it was him.

"Fuck off, JAC. I'm in no mood for your pathetic excuse." I was so furious with him that it was best it he stayed the hell away from me right now. Best for both of us.

"I'm sorry," he said from outside the door, "So sorry. I was an ass. Please, OPUS. Please forgive me." I was startled and blinked a few times. In all the years I had known JAC I had never heard him apologize to anyone. Least of all me. He was always so cocky and self-assured. Slowly I opened the door and outside a pleading JAC was standing with guilt written all over his face.

"I am so sorry," he repeated sincerely, "I don't know what happened."

"You happened JAC. YOU. You are the most selfish bastard I've ever known. Thinking you can take whatever the fuck you want."

"I wouldn't have taken it if you hadn't threatened me."

"Threatened you?"

"Yes. Threatened to stop if I couldn't preform."

"Are you fucking crazy? It had nothing to do with you not performing. It had a lot to do with you not concentrating. Not wanting to. It has something to do with you camouflaging your defeat. You were about to lose and you couldn't deal with that. So instead of admitting your defeat you decided to turn it around and make it a win for you. You didn't give a shit about me or what I was trying to teach you. It was all about you and you getting off. All about you getting gratification."

"I know. I don't know what is happening to me. Lately I haven't been thinking straight." He combed his hair with one hand as he looked down, "I don't know what is wrong with me." He seemed so frustrated and bewildered that I almost felt sorry for him. Almost.

"May I come in?" he asked graciously and I stepped aside so he could enter. He went to the middle of the room before he turned to me and spoke.

"I hope you understand that I would never hurt you. NEVER. I just didn't think in there and I don't know why. Normally I would never do such a thing. I just .... I just snapped." I could see that he was hurting and that every word coming from him was truth.

I knew that JAC would never hurt me. Not intentionally anyway and although he was extremely self-centred, he wasn't a prick. An idiot at times maybe but not someone who would harm the people he cared about.

JAC scowled at me while rubbing his chin with two fingers.

"Can you forgive me?" he asked in probably the most sincere voice I had ever heard coming from him.

"Yes," I replied letting out a sigh, "But don't let me regret doing it."

"I won't," he promised, "And I will do anything to make it up to you."

"Dangerous words, JAC," I replied and gave him a wry smile that didn't reach my eyes.

"I know. But I mean them. Anything ... if you teach me to be a perfect soldier." There was a long pause between us and it was only now I registered that I was still naked. JAC had his jeans on but that was all. No t-shirt or shoes. I think he noticed me looking up and down at him and then myself because he shrugged and smiled.

"Get some clothes on and we will have some breakfast," he said still with a smile on his face.

"Yeah. I don't want to scare Kafka," I said and snorted. As JAC passed me he stopped and whispered in my ear.

"You don't scare anybody off. You are beautiful," And then he kissed me on my forehead and walked into his room.

I stood for a while pondering on his words. Beautiful. No, JAC was definitely not himself. The JAC I knew would never have said that. I smiled and closed the door. He was right about one thing though .... It was time for breakfast.

* * *

Since Kafka was asleep and JAC had gone into his room to disappear into the day's first smack intoxication, I ended up having breakfast alone in the kitchen. It was pretty nice and for once I let my brain be on standby while the slightly burned sausages were rinsed down with black coffee.

Suddenly, while I was sitting there and enjoying the silence, the alarm to the front gate sounded. I rushed into the library and still chewing on my slice of toast, I looked at the monitors of the surveillance cameras on the flat screen. I could hear Kafka leaping down the stairs and with his Glock in hand he entered the library.

"It's just a courier with the items we ordered yesterday," I said, still chewing.

Kafka pressed the intercom system that was on the wall and a slightly scratchy sound came from it.

"Just put the goods within the white-marked area," he commanded. "Next to the bell is a scanner. There you can scan your receipt."

The courier put the items in the white square area. It measured two square metres and was next to the wall opposite where the intercom system was located. When he had placed the packages, he scanned the order form and got a receipt before going back to his van to drive off. Kafka waited until he was gone, after which he activated another scanner that swept and x-rayed the boxes. The result appeared on the flat screen and, as expected, it was clothing and weapon parts.

"They are cleared so JAC can go and get them," Kafka said, saving the scans in a file on the laptop.

"JAC is unavailable at the moment," I replied. Kafka looked at me briefly. There was no doubt that he understood what 'available' meant, but he clearly did not care.

"Wake him up," he said firmly. "Neither of us can bring it in. If we are monitored by Mossad – or others for that matter – we risk being scanned if we go out there and if we are, they find out that we are not chipped anymore and then we lose our advantage. So JAC will have to bring the stuff in." There was no reason to argue with Kafka for he was absolutely right, but whether or not I could get JAC out of his morning high was a whole other ball game.

Luckily for me, JAC was already on his way out of it, so five minutes later, Kafka and I were standing in the auditorium looking as he picked up the packages from the front gate. After checking the contents Kafka went back to bed while JAC and I went into the kitchen, where I went straight over and poured two cups of coffee. Without words I handed one to JAC but instead of taking a sip from it he put it down on the kitchen table. Quietly he pulled me to him and as we stood there, wrapped around each other I closed my eyes and disappeared for a moment into him and into the security of him. He might be an ass but he was my ass – so to speak. We stood like that for a few minutes, but nothing lasts forever, and eventually he let his arms drop and took his coffee cup from the table.

"We must change your bandage," he said, nodding towards it. He then took a sip of his coffee. I looked at the somewhat loose-fitting gauze. Wearing it in the shower had probably not been a good idea. Luckily there was no sign that the wound had bled and therefore it only took ten minutes before I was re-bandaged. It was a little tighter than the previous one, but it should also be able to withstand one or more possible recoils from OPUS, so that was okay. I swung my arm around to check that everything was in order and, happily I had full movement and mobility. Then I took my newly purchased clothes and went upstairs. It would be nice to get into something other than Kafka's khaki pants and t-shirt.

When I came downstairs again, JAC was sitting at the dining table sampling the new weapons. I poured myself a fresh cup of coffee and sat down opposite him. He smiled briefly at me and then continued what he was doing.

"JAC. What is in the little metal ampoule you stole from Liam?" The question had been bugging me and I just had to have an answer – if not for any other reasons than it now lived under the same roof as me.

"A radioactive isotope." JAC replied shortly without raising his head and continued preparing an M16 rifle.

"And?" I asked.

"No, you can't build a big atomic bomb with the substance." JAC said.

"But you can build a small one or use it as a catalyst for hydrogen bombs and certain gases." The voice came from the door. I turned my head and there leaning up against the frame stood Kafka yawning.

"What the hell was Liam going to do with it?" My question was quite legitimate and presumably also one that JAC and Kafka had asked themselves many times, although it did not seem to trigger great panic in either of them.

Kafka went and poured himself a cup of coffee and then sat on the kitchen counter next to the coffee machine.

"We have no idea," he replied, sipping his coffee, "and since it is Liam we are talking about, the possibilities are endless. But one thing is for sure. No matter how and for what it was to be used, it would not be a happy outcome for anyone. Fortunately, Liam cannot construct such a bomb himself. He does not know enough about that kind of technology, so that was probably what JAC and I were to be used for," continued Kafka and took a proper sip of the coffee.

"But who says he has not got hold of a new isotope and has brought a new explosives expert in? Honestly, you know as well as I do that he does not let himself be stopped by the fact that you ..." I was watching JAC. "have stolen the main ingredient to complete whatever he is doing."

"Isotopes are not exactly something you order on-line." Kafka responded giving me a crooked smile.

"Ahhh ..." It came from JAC, who at the same time put a full magazine in the M16 rifle, "The Russians have boxes of it, and depending on who controls the boxes that week, everything is for sale."

"But there are still not that many who dare to work with them. Most of the qualified people sit behind bars in laboratories belonging to various unnamed military units around the world." Kafka replied, pointing with his coffee cup toward JAC to emphasize his point.

"So how come the two of you know about these isotopes and are NOT 'locked up'?" I asked.

"They tried but they could not keep us behind bars," JAC replied, winking at me. With hint of a smile, he laid the assembled M16 rifle on the table, "I worked with them in Iraq," he said dryly, " ... and believe me, they are no joke."

"Were you one of those who 'sprinkled' them down on the Kurds?" Kafka asked teasingly, but judging by JAC's quick glance at him, he certainly did not think it was funny, "Don't worry, JAC. Without me at the other end, you would never have made any bombs explode," Kafka said coolly and took another sip of his now lukewarm coffee, "At the time I was one of those under lock and key and yes ... When the day came when they were to be tested in real life, it became BOOOOM over the Kurds." Kafka raised his eyebrows and smiled mutely.

"Stop!" JAC looked harshly at Kafka. We all knew what had happened to the poor Kurds, and I understood if JAC would not want to recall it.

"Well, it's nice to know that what you make is what you blow up," I concluded dryly, getting up, "It's like being with two eight-year-old boys who have grabbed a packet of bang snaps. Except in this case I would appreciate if you would let me know before you start 'playing' with the isotope that is in the safe. Just so I can get a head start and slip away."

Kafka smiled.

"I promise you that you will have a five-minute lead before we start." He winked at JAC and as he made a smiley face, he said ... "So, when you hear me say 'run, babe, run', you grab everything you can and run."

JAC and Kafka burst out laughing and what could I say to them other than,

"Idiots."

Maybe that was just what we needed, because the mood after this little exchange of words was quite relaxed, and when Kafka was subsequently told that my shoulder was fine, it was another problem gone.

JAC handed out ammunition to us. For the Glocks, the AK 47s and OPUS and he left the two loaded M16 rifles he had assembled on the dining table so they were ready for use.

Kafka jumped down from the counter and went into the library, and when JAC and I entered a few minutes later, he was standing looking at a large city map that he had displayed on the flat screen.

"The plan for the meeting today is as follows ..." he said pointing at the screen, "OPUS and I are driving to the Belgian Embassy ..." He pointed to a building in West Islamabad, "where the meeting will take place. JAC, you stay here and wait. As you can see, there are a number of low-rise buildings surrounding it, but they are all swept and unofficially they belong to the Embassy. The four large residential properties located there ..." Kafka pointed to four three-storey properties located approximately half a kilometre down the same street as the Embassy, "they also belong to the Embassy and house their Pakistani administrative staff."

"Okay, but tell me, why is the meeting with Mossad at the Belgian Embassy?" Actually, I expected Kafka would answer, but JAC beat him to it.

"Pakistan is one of the countries that does not recognize Israel as an independent state and therefore Israel has no embassy in Pakistan. In fact, not many countries have embassies here. They consider it too dangerous."

My eyes were fixed on him as he spoke, but when he was done, I quickly returned to the screen.

Kafka turned to JAC.

"We will take the isotope and ..." Kafka was about to continue his explanation but JAC interrupted him.

"Why the fuck do you want to give them our advantage?" it came sceptically from him, as he folded his arms in front of his chest and weighed up Kafka.

"My job was to get the metal box from Liam. But you stole what was valuable in it. When they get our chips thrown in their faces at the same time as the isotope, then we are free of them and can take care of Wizard and Liam." Kafka said confidently.

"You hope," I replied dryly knowing that my statement would make both JAC and Kafka stare at me, "Be realistic. They will not let us go, Kafka. They need you and apparently me too. I've been expensive for them and, let's face it, I'm an asset to them now." I took my eyes off the map and looked at them, "What if we offered to work for them. But chip-free?"

"You want to work for Mossad?" JAC asked and his surprise was obvious.

"Evidently I have already been a part of them for years, so the difference would just be that I would be official."

"I'm not going to work for Mossad," JAC said harshly and I could understand him. Why commit to one client when the price of the same piece of work could be twice as high with another, "I will not work for an agency again. Not even as a freelancer," he said defiantly.

"JAC, we are frequently hired by them so the difference would not be that great," I replied but even though it was true I knew my voice did not sound convincing. It was one thing to work as a contractor for them; another was to work exclusively for them.

"There is no such thing as freelance when it comes to Mossad. Are you crazy?" Kafka said and it was clear that he was annoyed with JAC and his attitude, "It's all or nothing with them."

"What if we formed our own merc group? You, JAC, Wizard and me?" I asked.

"And gave Mossad the 'green light' to use us?" Kafka's facial expression was serious, but the small nods he made at the same time were not to be mistaken. The idea was not impossible, but required a lot of consideration.

"Yes, we are practically doing it anyway. But this time we would be the ones in charge," I stated.

"A merc group working primarily for Mossad?" Kafka clearly continued his inner whirlwind of thoughts and I was not quite sure if the sentence should have been said out loud or he was just thinking aloud.

"Yes, but without working directly for them," I said.

"Mossad has their own 'hit squads'." Kafka said dryly, but he was still not totally dismissive of the idea.

"Mossad already has all the services, and despite that, they still use us ... We know that." I raised my eyebrows when I said this and did not really expect to be contradicted.

"True enough." Kafka replied while looking thoughtfully down at the carpet.

"And let's be honest. You already work for them so by doing this we would just legitimise us doing the same." I looked at JAC to see his reaction to my idea, but there was none. He just stood still, watching us.

"They would insist on knowing everything about the jobs you would take," Kafka said with a slight question in his voice, turning his gaze to JAC and me, "All missions – even those that did not concern Mossad. It would be an information transfer – one way. Ultimately your independence would be non-existent. You would unofficially 'belong' to Mossad and officially you would be subject to counter-espionage. It will be an insane move. A rock-solid suicide operation." I sighed a single time and nodded gently. Kafka was right. My idea was okay, but not an option if we wanted to live as independent contractors.

"How about we give them the isotope and let them believe that we're staying here. Then we can go to Afghanistan and get Wizard?" JAC suggested. It was his first contribution to the discussion in a long time. Kafka and I looked at him because it was actually not a bad idea. JAC continued, "When they find out that you are no longer chipped, they will probably come for you anyway and then we can offer them our services on equal terms with other agencies."

"It will work, but only – and only – if Mossad are the only ones who know where we are. If the FSB has been told then ..." I said with a crooked smile and slightly snorting, "Then we remain targets yes, but we are that anyway, because it's just a matter of time before Mossad find out. What if they believe I'm dead? Then they will stop searching for me?" JAC looked at me scowling slightly.

"At some point they will find out that you are alive and then hunting season will begin all over again," he snorted.

"Unless they get their shooter." Kafka said, raising his eyebrows to camouflage the hidden question that lay within his statement.

There was silence in the room and it was as if we were just sitting and waiting for the answer to fall into our laps. Personally, I hate such situations, because the longer it took before the solution materialized, the more we exposed ourselves to each other and, honestly, I felt vulnerable enough as it was.

"Give them the isotope and then find out as much as you can about my and Liam's situation," I said impatiently. For me this conversation had lasted long enough.

"Liam's situation? What the hell do we want with him?" JAC asked sceptically.

"If Mossad has a hit out on Liam, take it," I said resolutely to Kafka.

"You are crazy. How will you get close to him without the FSB finding out you're alive? Liam has obviously got connections to them, so do you not think he would 'sell' you at the first given opportunity?"

Kafka's answer made me a little irritable, because of course I knew that, but if anyone could get close to Liam without him being suspicious, it would probably be me.

"No, because Liam does not know I'm here. And besides, Liam can't stand the FSB."

"Liam took assignments for the FSB," it came calmly and thoughtfully from Kafka, "He knew it was the FSB who ordered the hit in Moscow and despite the risk for Wizard, he sent him anyway."

"Wizard took the mission himself. He bid on it. He knew the risks," I said stubbornly, scowling over at Kafka.

"Wizard should NEVER have been allowed to do that. Liam should have taken care of it, but he did not. He knew full well that Wizard would be hunted for the murder, and in Liam's eyes that was okay. The FSB would have got their hit, Wizard would have been chased and killed, and Liam would have been the one delivering everything. And he would most likely have had a bonus for it. The Hague and various agencies including Greg would look positively upon him and he would have put 'one in the bank' regarding his own situation as former IRA. You were never in the game, OPUS. And yes ... I know all this from my sources in Mossad."

"Did you know I would be in camp when you got there?" I asked Kafka. He shook his head.

"Not for sure. I knew you worked for Liam, so you were likely to be, but I was surprised to see you there that night in Luc's tent."

"And?" I asked.

"And yes ... Mossad had asked me to find out your affiliation with and loyalty to Liam, if you were there." Kafka replied.

"Is Mossad happy with your feedback?" I said sarcastically.

"I have not reported back to them yet."

"Why? Not sure what to report?" Kafka did not answer, but raised his eyebrows and gave me a crooked smile. It was clear that he was still not sure about my relationship with Liam.

"Fuck you, Kafka. I just said I want to eliminate Liam for you and you still doubt me. Idiot."

"OPUS, there were all sorts of rumours about your group. Among other things that Liam and you had something going on. That's why I was positively surprised when I found out it was you and JAC. Mossad would have liked it to be Liam, because then they would have recruited you to kill him, but personally I would have preferred you not joining Mossad."

"Why? That would only be to your advantage."

Kafka took a deep breath and for a brief moment it was as if he did not know what to answer.

"Because you don't want to work for Mossad. You are too 'unstable' and would end up being an internal elimination assignment and I would be the obvious candidate to perform that task, and I will not, but I would have no choice unless I went AWOL."

"Have you gone AWOL now?" I asked.

Kafka looked at me seriously without answering.

"Your lack of an answer says it all," I replied and I really regretted asking. The thought that Kafka could be given such an order made me rather uncomfortable and therefore JAC's question came almost as a relief to me.

"If you got the job now, would you go AWOL?" JAC's tone of voice was hard and knowing him, right now he was regretting not having his Glock in his waistband.

"Yes." Kafka replied and it came promptly and from the heart. Some of my malaise disappeared after his answer, but I could not hide the fact that some distrust had been awakened in me, though it was very small. There was a moment of silence in the library and once again it was JAC who broke it.

"Contact Mossad and say that you are bringing someone to the meeting

– and that someone is OPUS. If they refuse, we disappear immediately. If they accept you have to establish: if there still is a contract on OPUS, if Wizard is alive and whether they want Liam eliminated. If they do, you make an agreement that OPUS is 'free' from them when Liam is dead. And if Wizard is still alive, include him in the OPUS deal. To seal the deal, you give them the isotope and then you leave. We attach the chips to both of you so they have no idea that we have removed them. When we have taken care of Liam and all the pieces have fallen into place, we dump the chips and Mossad is out of the picture." JAC pointed to Kafka, "It is up to you whether you want to go AWOL with us, because we will disappear when this is over."

Silence fell. JAC's plan was actually not that bad and we all knew it.

Kafka was the one to break the silence. He walked to the desk, where he picked up his phone. The conversation that followed was relatively short and in Yiddish, so what I understood of it was limited. Kafka ended the conversation and informed us that Mossad would return with an answer, so now it was just a matter of waiting. He then sat down behind the desk while JAC settled himself in the chair that stood on the opposite side. I went to the window, and as I stood there in the midst of the all-too-noisy silence, it slowly dawned on me that it was paramount that the answer be a 'yes'. If it was not, Mossad would have signed my death sentence, and I had no doubt that Kafka was right when he had said that he would be the one to execute it.

To my annoyance, my Glock was upstairs, but ... I turned around.

"Do you want something from the kitchen?" I asked a bit perky, looking at the both of them. JAC, who was reclining thoughtfully in front of Kafka, shook his head in response to my question, and despite the fact that I had hoped he would look at me, his gaze remained blank and staring into the air.

"No thank you." Kafka replied leaning forward in the soft leather chair. He let his arms rest on the desk as he sighed.

Silently, I went to the kitchen and took a bottle of water from the fridge. I stood over the kitchen sink and unscrewed the top, and while I was drinking, I looked over at the two M16 rifles that were locked and loaded on the dining table. I shut all my thoughts out and focused on finding the justification in what I might have to do in a little while, because if it came to it, then I had no doubt that I could do it. I just hoped that JAC had thought the same, because sitting across from Kafka, he would be first in line, and Kafka would not hesitate to eliminate him on the spot. My thoughts were interrupted by Kafka's phone ringing and, gently, I put the water bottle down next to the kitchen sink.

On the way over to the dining table, my thoughts were divided: On one hand, I sincerely hoped that the answer would be a yes, so that we would all stay alive – and on the other, I was ready to use one of the M16 rifles to send Kafka to his eternal hunting ground.

Quietly, I walked towards the library. My senses were sharpened, as when approaching a kill, and even though I moved closer and closer to Kafka's voice, it seemed to fade further and further away, with each step I took.

From the chair where JAC was sitting, he had a full view of the auditorium and he straightened up when he saw me with the M16 rifle. Kafka had got up and stood behind the desk with his face turned away from the door and continued talking on the phone. I stopped when I reached the door frame into the library so the rifle was hidden from his view and at that moment Kafka ended the call and turned to me.

"We have to meet them at seven p.m.," he said looking at his watch, "It gives us just under five hours."

"Perfect," I said and as the word left my lips, I immediately regretted that I had been so careless as to voice it. Kafka looked at me and I think he caught that bit of relief that I had mistakenly expressed. Little things like emitting a sigh of relief at the wrong time can, in our business, be enough to trigger a true *Ragnarök*, so that's why it was so insanely careless of me to have opened my mouth without having my emotions under total control first. It was also a bit grotesque that even in a situation like this, where I was surrounded by friends, I could not allow myself to show what I felt. Had we been in the normal world, then it would probably have been perfectly okay, but we were not in the normal world, we were in ours – the real world – and here things looked very different, even when it came to showing emotions.

JAC had also noticed my mistake, but he did not react. I think that it was very deliberate when he got up and turned towards the flat screen. I hoped it was enough to divert Kafka's attention from it.

"Throw an area plan on the 'overhead' and let's get started," he said very determinedly to Kafka. While Kafka was busy with that, JAC came over to me. "Give me that," he whispered calmly taking the M16 rifle out of my hand. Then he continued into the kitchen while Kafka, who had found a map, made it come to life on the flat screen. When JAC returned, Kafka blew up several photos of the area surrounding the Embassy and with the electronic pointer in his hand, we began planning.

* * *

It took three hours, by which time we had four possible scenarios planned. The last details such as departure times, execution dates etc. had to wait until after the meeting at the Embassy later that evening, but otherwise everything was organized.

This gave us a couple of hours to kill before leaving, and JAC and I chose to spend them together in his room on his sofa. We started by running through a few details regarding the forthcoming meeting and, when we were finished, he leaned back on the couch, folded his hands behind his head, and stretched his neck back. Quietly, but also very expectantly, I got up and went and stood behind him. I began to calmly massage his broad shoulders. It was intended to be a stress relieving touch but it soon became more sensual. He bent his neck forward and from his faint grunting sounds, he seemed to be enjoying it.

"Are we okay?" he asked alluding to what happened between us earlier that morning.

"Yes," I replied and meant it. JAC was not a rapist. He had not pinned me down but simply flipped me around to have sex with me and even if his timing had sucked, he had not done it to hurt me. Our sex had always been about self-gratification and to please one another had always come as a bonus not a goal in itself. We would make sure we got our own pleasure first and then we would attend to each other's needs – if necessary.

"Good," he replied but his tone of voice soon turned serious, "Would you have killed Kafka if Mossad had said NO?" he asked while I continued massaging him.

"Yes," I replied. For that was the truth. I would without hesitation have shot him on the spot.

JAC grabbed one of my hands and I stopped massaging him.

"Before you decide on something like that again run it by me first, okay?" His voice was determined but without any undertones of what unpleasant things might happen if his order was not followed. I removed my hands and came round and sat on his lap straddling his thighs.

"I cannot promise you that," I whispered into his ear and then kissed him on the neck.

Immediately I felt a hard grip on my neck and he pulled me backwards.

"You do not eliminate Kafka without talking to me first. Do you understand?" He enunciated. His grip on my neck seemed violently arousing to me and combined with his eyes being completely black and cold, as before a kill, I wished he would continue. I raised both my hands, in surrender, but I could feel that he was slowly releasing his grip, which had not really been my intention. When he had completely let go of my neck, I got up and lit a cigarette.

"You have to trust me, JAC."

"I have always trusted you, but it would have been unspeakably stupid if you had got rid of him. The whole house is a big bomb and only Kafka has the codes to lock us in and out of this bulletproof castle. It would have taken me weeks to get it dismantled to a stage where we could have opened the front doors. From there we'd have to go to the gate. The area in between is mined and there are sensors everywhere. And this is just the things I know. There are no doubt traps and booby traps besides that. And not only that – if we did not have it before, we would most certainly have Mossad breathing down our necks. Personally, I don't think we should give them a reason to chase us." He looked at me and basically I could see that killing Kafka might not have been the smartest move, but rather him than me – or JAC.

"You're right. It would not have been the wisest move, but I might not have had a choice. He would have shot us, JAC."

"No, because I would have shot him first," he said dryly.

"I was sure you did not have your Glock on you," I said softly and rather puzzled because I would have sworn he didn't have it. JAC smiled.

"One of us had to and yours was up here." His smile became crooked and his eyes were back to normal again, "Come here," he said, holding out his hand to me. Smiling, I went to him and he took the cigarette from me and took a puff before putting it out in the ashtray on the table. Then he pulled me down so I sat on his lap again.

It was a strange feeling, but also nice to know that although I was not myself having left my gun in my bedroom, JAC had complete control over the situation, and even though I had never been in doubt that he was there for me, this somehow cemented our trust in each other.

"Promise me that when it comes down to it, you'll take care of Liam." It was obvious that JAC was genuinely concerned, but when it came to Liam, I was not so concerned. Liam loved – just like me – control and by giving it to him, I would have him exactly where I wanted him.

"You do not have to worry," I said half-whispering, "I know how to get him."

"That's exactly what I'm afraid of and then all of a sudden it's him who gets you."

"Stop, JAC," I said quietly putting one hand in front of his mouth. He was silent and then we kissed each other gently and then more aggressively. I sat thighs wrapped round him and this time he did not stop me. Our hands wandered on each other's bodies and within minutes we had ripped off our clothes.

"No control," he whispered in my ear.

"No control," I replied and then I rode him hard. I could see that it hurt him at times, but this was as good an occasion as any to teach him the pleasure of this pain. "This is as much as I love to make love to you," I whispered and I could see the singular expression of pain on his face. As I rode him it gradually increased and I could see that he was reaching the maximum of what he could endure. When I noticed that the pain was taking the lust away from him, I automatically slowed down until his lust came back. As expected he quickly became rock hard again, so, I started riding him hard again. We kept weaving back and forth between pain and pleasure, and it was only when the pain was at its height and he was still hard as concrete that I let him explode. The sight of his body shaking in ecstasy and excruciating pain, also made me explode, and for a while we disappeared into our sweaty bodies while gasping for breath.

"Jesus, OPUS ... what the hell are you doing to me?" It came breathlessly from him.

"I'm turning you into the perfect soldier," I whispered, breathless, putting my head to his sweaty throat. Because apart from achieving satisfaction myself, this was actually my intention.

How long we sat like that, I do not know, but to my surprise I suddenly felt him getting hard again. With a mixture of a commanding and praying voice, he whispered, "Continue" to me, and slowly I began to ride him again.

It was clear that it hurt him insanely, but he remained fierce. Seeing how he enjoyed this intense pain turned me on wildly and, even though I wanted to set the pace and just indulge, I kept the slow movements so he stayed in the pain.

"Place the pain," I said quietly to him, "Place it in a box with me. Let the pain be me."

He was short of breath and his moans got louder and louder until it was almost screams. He drilled his nails into my back and I could feel how the blood quietly ran down, but there was no pain associated with it – only pleasure. I knew exactly where he was. A place where the extreme pain, becomes the ultimate enjoyment.

"Let the pain be me," I repeated again and again and he started screaming in pain and pleasure. Eventually he leaned forward towards me and bit me so hard in my shoulder that I thought I was going to faint and then we exploded at the same time.

Trembling, breathless, drenched in sweat, the silence enveloped us. There were no words to describe this. None.

* * *

An hour later I was standing in the kitchen lacing up my newly purchased black boots while Kafka was about to open the safe to take out the isotope and our chips. On the kitchen table were patches, cotton pads, superglue, a roll of plaster, a bottle of demineralized water and a scalpel. Then JAC walked in with a bottle of Vodka.

"That's mine and that's OPUS's." Kafka told JAC as he laid the chips on the table.

"Okay. Get rid of the sweater." JAC commanded and poured the alcohol on one of the cotton pads to sterilize the chip, while Kafka unbuttoned his white shirt. JAC sprinkled an area on the right side of his chest with alcohol and then, with the scalpel, he made fine small surface cuts in the shape of three sides of a square. Next, lifting the flap he placed the sterile chip in the middle of the square, closed it, glued the edges together, and finally put a small patch over it so that no blood would get on his shirt if it unexpectedly bled.

"Done." JAC said then, turning around and starting to rinse the scalpel with the demineralized water. Kafka secured the patch with a strip of plaster before buttoning up his shirt. Then he moved away from the 'operating site'.

"It's your turn." JAC said still with his back to me. I took off my t-shirt and JAC came over and performed the same procedure on me as he had just done with Kafka. As he stood there working totally focused, we had no eye contact, but I could not help myself and put my hands on either side of his hips running them slowly down the outside of his thighs. If he felt the pain like me, then the slightest touch would awaken all the nerves and thus the pain. His face clearly showed pain.

"Don't," it came quietly from him as he concentrated. For a brief moment we had eye contact, but he did not smile. Instead, he put the patch on and turned away and began demineralizing the scalpel. Had I expected him to smile at me? To be honest – what was there to smile about other than the pain and we obviously felt it very differently. For me it was more than just enjoyment, but for JAC ... yes, there was a long way to go before he saw it like me – if he ever would. Quietly, calmly and thoughtfully, I put my t-shirt back on.

As if he had done it all of his life, Kafka stood, tucked his white shirt into his light-coloured trousers, then he put on the linen jacket that had been hanging over the back of one of the chairs. It was strange to see him in civilian clothes and in no way did he resemble a merc.

Kafka stared at me and I think he shared the same opinion about me because he looked me up and down and smiled. It was quite nice for once to be out of combats, because even though I occasionally wore normal clothes, it was very rare that I went out into the normal world wearing them. Usually I wore military clothes and despite the fact that I loved the colour green, it could sometimes be a little tedious to co-ordinate colours with it. I took my newly purchased dark long-sleeved cardigan in addition to the t-shirt and brushed my dark trousers off with my hands, so that any fluff from the internet shop's white paper, that had lain between the legs of the trousers in the shipping bag, fell to the floor.

"If you have not heard from us in two hours, then you disappear," Kafka said seriously to JAC, swinging his car keys, "I'm turning off the alarms now so you can get out, and the code for the gate is 2086QZ."

"Okay," he replied and began to clear all the stuff from the table.

"The keys to the cars are located in the bottom desk drawer in the library. Just take one."

JAC looked at us seriously.

"I certainly expect to see you again," he said firmly, and the sincerity he had in his voice, which was only expressed when there was something he really meant, was clear. It was precisely this that I had initially fallen for in JAC, and I loved him for still expressing it, despite all that he had been through both as a human and as a soldier.

"It's just in case," Kafka said, with a little smile, "see you," he said then and disappeared down the stairs to the basement.

In fact, I think it was on purpose that he left us alone, but it had not been necessary, because even though JAC grabbed my left upper arm and looked me straight in the eyes as I walked past him, this would be our only physical contact before parting. I could see he was just about to say something, but I stopped him.

"I know," I just said, "But nothing will happen."

Nodding, he released my arm and then I followed Kafka down the stairs.

Chapter 18

We took the Mitsubishi, which was the smallest of the cars and the most agile – if you can call a car agile.

The embassy was half an hour's drive from the house. There was a lot of traffic but Kafka managed to avoid the worst jams.

At the gate to the Embassy, Kafka showed his ID card to the soldiers and we were immediately waved through. He parked the car in a bay to the right of the front door, where a small sign indicated that it was for GUESTS. I was surprised at the lack of security on the premises and it undoubtedly contributed to me being on high alert. It was therefore almost a relief to see two big metal detectors just inside the door of the Embassy building. However I could not have been more wrong regarding the security, because as we approached the detectors, three soldiers with machine guns appeared, and when we had passed the two large scanners, they each checked us with a hand scanner. When we had been cleared, we were handed over to two men in dark suits. They greeted us briefly and then led us to the first floor and into a conference room where three men and one woman were sitting on one side of a big white table. In front of them lay folders and judging from scattered papers and half-filled water bottles they had been there for a while. We all greeted each other; introductions were made and Kafka and I were asked to sit down across from them. We had our backs turned to a big window and a quick glance revealed that, unlike the other two windows in the room, this one was not bulletproof. Also the blind in front of it was a little open. Not much but just enough to offer a sniper an opportunity.

"Sorry," I said calmly, "We came here in good faith, but we are not idiots." I turned around and closed the blind quietly, "And now we swap places," I continued. Kafka stood quietly and watched the four people at the table looking at each other. Without any objections, they got up and swapped seats with us. As they did one of the security guards at the door said "Stand by" into his headset. I snapped my fingers at the guards so I got their attention.

"Throw the two headsets to me," I commanded and after having exchanged a few glances with one of the men at the table, they did so. I immediately switched them off.

There was silence in the room.

"Was that all?" asked one of the men slightly indulgently; the question was undoubtedly addressed to me.

"I can live with the rest," I replied and sent him a false smile, which indicated that I was aware that we were being monitored and recorded.

Shrirov, one of the men at the table, leaned forward with a grave face and said.

"Let's get the formalities over with. Hand over the isotope."

Kafka smiled,

"Yes, once you have answered some questions." Shrirov looked at Kafka in astonishment, but this look was quickly replaced by a thoughtful expression.

"Do you refuse to complete your mission? If so, it would not be the first time." The words came from one of the others at the table – a Dr. Mirza. Kafka ignored him.

"Is Liam O'Dawning eliminated?" he asked, completely unaffected by what had been said.

"No," Shrirov replied, "We have not been able to get close enough. He is surrounded by former IRA people who work for him."

"Do you know where he is right now?" Kafka continued.

"Yes. In Zagreb. He went there today. We expect him to pick up a new isotope."

"Can you prevent him from doing that?"

"No, we do not know who the seller is. Possibly one from the Ukrainian army."

"Could it be Frank?" I asked putting my arms on the table as I leaned forward. Everyone at the table – including Kafka – stared at me. I noticed that Shrirov and Dr. Mirza exchanged a few brief glances.

"How do you know Frank?" Shrirov asked, folding his hands in front of him on the table.

"It's not relevant," I replied, "but what is, is that you cut out the bullshit and tell us something concrete." Kafka put his hand on my forearm. It was clearly a signal to me to take it easy which I did.

"You have received my report, I assume?" They all nodded at Kafka, "If you want to take Liam O'Dawning out, here's your chance. OPUS can do it."

"And if we don't want to?" Dr. Mirza said arrogantly and a bit patronizingly.

"Then you're lying." Kafka replied with the utmost sincerity.

Shrirov turned his attention to me and asked,

"And how exactly are you going to do that?" His question was clearly to get information about the method, and not out of scepticism whether I could handle the job.

"That's my business," I replied, continuing, "The question is, does Liam know I'm alive?"

"If he does the information has not come from us. As far as we are aware, only the people in this room know that you exist." If that was true, and I had no idea if it was, the situation suddenly looked different. Because if only seven people knew I was alive, then ...

"My suggestion is ...," Kafka said calmly, "when OPUS takes care of Liam, I will get the metal box and hopefully the other isotope, if he has it."

"And what's the price?" Shrirov asked, looking at me angrily, "Because there's a price, isn't there? What is your going rate? Still one million per kill?" It hadn't occurred to me that he would know what I charged for a kill, but of course he would. Everyone, both inside and outside the agencies, knew a skilled contractor's tariff. I knew what other snipers were charging, so ...

"Call it a payback for patching me up after Belize. And then we are quits."

"If you get us Liam O'Dawning ..." said the third of the men, pointing alternately at Kafka and me "and you get us the metal box plus the isotope, then we're quits. But only when it comes to you."

The speaker who until now had remained silent stared directly at me, saying the last part of the sentence harshly and firmly. His name was Jacoby, and there was something about him that just radiated ex-military. Out of the corner of my eye, I could see on Kafka's face that what Jacoby had asked was okay by him.

"It's a deal," I said calmly.

"We will need intelligence from you regarding the planning and an anonymous transport to the mark's whereabouts." Kafka said as he leaned forward in his chair. It was strange that Liam in less than two minutes had got a last name and had become my mark, but it was also very predictable and not something that bothered me greatly.

"We will give you all the information you need." Jacoby said in a flat tone that seemed completely out of place in this situation.

"No," it came resolutely from me, "We must be given ALL the information we ASK for."

Jacoby and I stared each other straight in the eye and it was a complete relief for me to see that he, unlike the others in the room, was icy cold and not in the least affected by our presence or the situation in general. I preferred people like him because then I knew what I was dealing with. Facts and not bullshit.

"Okay." Jacoby replied, taking his eyes off me.

"What about Oleg Manikoff? Is there still a hit on him?" Kafka raised his eyebrows and looked pointedly across the table as he asked the questions. I tried to look like I knew who he was referring to, but the truth was, I had no idea who Oleg Manikoff was.

"Yes, but he has apparently disappeared. He might have been killed in the Khandahar province, but this still has to be confirmed. Why?" Shrirov shrugged at Kafka.

"I would like intelligence on that." Kafka replied as his gaze wandered between Shrirov and Jacoby.

"He is not to be eliminated," Jacoby said harshly, "And that's a direct order."

"I guarantee that he will not be terminated by any of us and we will not conspire to have him killed. On the contrary," I said.

"Oleg Manikoff, you leave. He is not a part of this agreement." Jacoby said so loudly that his voice almost seemed trembling. Had I at any time been in doubt as to whether he came from a military background or not, it was now clear to me. Any soldier would have carried out the order which he had just given just by the sheer commanding tone of his voice.

"He is," Kafka said taking the isotope out of his inside pocket and putting it on the table, "Because without him, this would not be here."

Suddenly the penny dropped for me. Oleg Manikoff was Wizard and immediately all my antennae were on high alert. There was complete silence in the room.

"All we need is for you to verify his eventual death." Kafka continued.

"We will come back to that." Shrirov said trying to move on. But it was no use.

"No," Kafka said harshly, "Manikoff is in the agreement otherwise no deal." There was a long and rather oppressive pause and it was almost as if everyone was holding their breath.

"Okay," it came from Jacoby, "but then you owe us three kills." He pointed at me with two fingers and the icy look under the wrinkled eyebrows was even more intense than before.

"No," said Kafka, "No kills."

"No kills. No deal." Jacoby replied and I had no doubt he meant it. Kafka was about to say something, but I interrupted him.

"Two kills," I said, staring straight into Jacoby's eyes, "and I want the opportunity to say no to a task based on the identity of the mark." There was silence again.

"Okay." Jacoby replied at last and with a touch of satisfaction in his voice – a touch that irritated me. Quietly Kafka handed over the isotope and then we got up to leave the room. The meeting was over. At least for now.

Jacoby, who had placed himself at the door, stopped me as I was about to pass him. There was no doubt that he had sensed my irritation regarding having to compromise about the two kills in return for Wizard.

"Don't fuck with me," he said in a low threatening voice as he narrowed his dark eyes until they were just two fine lines in his face.

"Likewise," I replied narrowing mine as well just to emphasize that I too meant every word I said. No doubt it would be very ugly if the agreement was broken from either side and we had to meet again.

Outside the door the two guards from before were waiting to escort us out of the Embassy and as we sat in the car driving – at a somewhat more moderate pace – back to the house, I couldn't help but feeling a little bit pissed off. We might have got what we came for but we also had to pay a price for it. And in my case the price had been two kills.

On the way home, Kafka sent a message to JAC saying that we were okay. Even though this was a small thing to me it indicated that we were a team and I liked that feeling.

"A lot can be said about you, OPUS, but you'll probably have to work on your diplomatic skills a bit." Kafka suddenly said and he began to laugh.

"You can laugh," I replied coolly, "but they assumed we were naive. Anyway, we got what we came for so ...."

"The two kills were not in the plan," Kafka stated.

"No, but Wizard is worth it," I said quietly, "Do you know who Wizard really is?"

"Yes." Kafka replied and then the silence returned to the car.

Neither he nor I felt the urge to elaborate on it and especially not considering, that if it was truth we had in fact just helped a war criminal to 'disappear' – if he was not already dead. Basically, it was morally reprehensible, but that was pretty much most of what we did, so the boundaries of what was ethically acceptable and morally reprehensible were repeatedly moved and – in this case – they were completely blurred. After all, it was about whether we could vouch for our agreement and – yes, we could. Whether I personally thought Wizard should escape punishment for his war crimes, was less relevant. Wizard was probably going to be held accountable for his deeds at some point and it was not going to be by me.

On some kind of level Wizard's – and for that matter Liam's – deeds were noble, as they arose from a patriotism and thus had been carried out for a cause. I had never fought for my own ideological or political beliefs, because I had never had such an agenda. Not until now. So did it really not make my deeds more vicious and bestial than theirs? After all, they could excuse themselves by thinking they were doing the right thing. I, on the other hand, knew that what I was doing was not right on any level and yet I was doing it – and worst of all – I was totally okay with it.

"Do you really think the FSB has stopped looking for me?" I asked Kafka in an attempt to stop all this soul searching.

"Jacoby would have had no reason to lie about it, so yes."

"And while we're at it ... who is Jacoby?" Out of the corner of my eye, I could see Kafka's face becoming expressionless.

"He's a merc who you do not want to fuck with," he replied, turning the car towards the gate of the house. As Kafka entered the gate code, I couldn't help thinking about what he had just said. Maybe I just needed to do exactly that. Fuck Jacoby. He was certainly my style but as the gate opened and we drove in and down to the garage I closed the subject of Jacoby. If it was meant to be we would meet again. If not ... who the fuck cared.

* * *

On the way up the basement stairs, Kafka checked the alarms and it was so unbelievable comforting to know that no one could touch us here. Of course, this did not mean that we were untouchable. In reality a mortar shell or a missile could take us out, but to be realistic that would not be the case. Such means were hardly ever used against mercs so we could feel safe in the house.

Kafka went straight into the lounge, where JAC had lit the fire, and put a bottle of JD and three glasses on the table ready for us. I slipped up to my room and tossed the cardigan in the bin. I would not be needing that anymore and besides it was not really my cup of tea. 'Too much of the normal world', I thought as I shrugged.

I threw some cold water on my face. I really needed just five minutes to myself. It had been a long time since I had that.

The five minutes turned into a quarter of an hour before I entered the lounge. I had put a pair of sandy-coloured khaki trousers on and a white t-shirt and I had to admit that this was much more me than the clothes I had thrown in the bin.

In the lounge I saw that JAC and Kafka had already opened the JD. Kafka had just finished telling JAC about the meeting and its outcome, as I sat down next to JAC.

Kafka filled a glass three fingers up with JD and pushed it towards me and I took it and took a sip. As the heat from the whiskey warmed my throat, I could feel JAC's hand caressing my back. It was nice, soothing and for some reason just what I needed as it made me relax even more then I already was.

"So, now we just have to decide which way to approach Liam." Kafka said in his usual logical and neutral voice, as if we were going to the supermarket and had just to make a shopping list.

"It's simple," I said, looking down into my glass of JD, "It will be method number two that we discussed earlier today – but it will have a twist." I was fully aware that JAC's and Kafka's eyes were on me as I emptied the contents of the glass.

"And the twist is?" JAC clearly expected the worst.

"That I must appear to have been interrogated by the FSB. And their reason for it ... to obtain information about Wizard's whereabouts."

JAC leaned towards me and the scowl from his dark brows and eyes made his face seem like he was wearing a Zorro-mask. He looked at me so seriously that his expression alone had me doubt my decision for a split second.

"Do you mean that?" he asked.

"Yeah, JAC," I said with a bit of a dead pan look on my face, "I must appear to have been in the FSB's interrogation machine for at least seven days."

"And who do you think is going to do that to you?" Kafka's voice reflected that he in no way wanted to hear his own name mentioned now. There was silence in the living room and it was, as usual, JAC who broke it.

"I am." JAC said quietly. Then he took a deep breath that could be mistaken for a heart-breaking deep sigh. I took the JD bottle and filled my glass half up.

"Can you do that?" Kafka asked sceptically, staring at JAC with slight disgust on his face. JAC took the JD bottle.

"Yes," he replied, pouring JD into his glass.

Kafka's eyes wandered back and forth between JAC and me – and it was intentional that I did not have eye contact with either of them, because I really did not want to elaborate on what I was asking them to do.

"I have a demand to add to it," I said and they both looked at me, "That it is done in full view of Mossad's people and, preferably, with some of their special forces as spectators and ... that there have to be women amongst them."

JAC and Kafka both sat with mouths open staring at me.

"Why is that?" Kafka asked, slightly shocked, which was really quite understandable. Seven days in the FSB's interrogation machine would be able to break most soldiers and I was willing to do it without coercion.

"For several reasons. Mossad – and especially Jacoby – must know what we are 'sacrificing for him', and the women in the special forces have usually only tried 'superficial' interrogation techniques during their training. They need to see what the real deal is all about. They need to know what they are risking out there. They need to be so close to me that they almost get blood splatter on them." I took a sip of my glass, "That is my demand. Do you think you can do it, JAC? Do a counter-espionage interrogation of me in front of spectators?"

JAC was silent and looked into his glass.

"If that's what you want, then ... yes," JAC replied softly but firmly, "But you have to be present, Kafka." He looked up at Kafka, who was sitting perfectly still with his hands around his glass.

"Okay," Kafka replied, "but why?"

"Because it has to be videotaped and there are always two conducting an interrogation – preferably more when the rapes take place," I said coolly and emptied my glass of JD. JAC closed his eyes and bowed his head.

"Do you want to post it on-line?" Kafka asked while the wrinkles of concern on his forehead deepened. JAC raised his head again and opened his eyes.

"Yes, but only a few hours before the two of you contact Liam. It will provide credibility. With a little luck, he'll get so mad at the FSB that it will create a rift between them."

"That is if he sees me as a friend," I replied. None of us said anything until I finally got up.

"That's what we'll do," I said as I took my glass and the ice bucket with the remnants of melted ice cubes in it, "Mossad must also be informed about this."

My eyes caught Kafka's gaze and a small nod from him indicated he would take care of that. There was nothing more to say, so I left JAC and Kafka. I went to the kitchen and after putting my glass and the bucket in the dishwasher, I went upstairs.

* * *

As the full moon shone through the window, the clock passed midnight. The powerful white light from the sphere illuminated my entire bedroom so amazingly that I did not have to turn the ceiling light on. I took my clothes off and crawled into bed. I wondered about all that lay ahead and then there was a knock on the door. It was JAC.

"I'm not sleeping," I said calmly, turning on the lamp on the bedside table next to me. In his usual casual way, and with his hands in his pockets, he strolled to the bed and sat down next to me. He took his hands out of his pockets and rubbed his face. Then he bent down and kissed me very, very gently.

"I'm going cold turkey tonight," he said almost whispering, "The abstinences are slowly increasing, so ... not tonight." We looked at each other and I immediately felt like crawling into him and just taking all the pain that I assumed was waiting for him. Just for a moment it would be nice to be able to enjoy it and him at the same time.

"Is there anything I can do?" I asked, a little worried about what JAC was about to do.

"Listen to Kafka," he said, "And only to Kafka. He knows what to do. He has been there himself. I'll be locked inside a room in the basement. It is best and safest – for everyone."

He looked worried and I could see that he did not exactly expect it to be a walk in the park.

"Actually," he said quietly, brushing a couple of stray hairs from my forehead, "I got the safe house so I had a place where I could go and get 'detoxed' when that time came. But now it's going to be here." He smiled as a small groan came from him. I looked at him and stroked my fingers through his hair.

"How long have you had the safe house?"

"For six months. It's just never been the right time."

"And it is now?" I asked. He groaned again.

"I do not know. I do not know if there will ever be a time that is right. My logic says yes, but when it is time for the next fix ... the urge ... is stronger than all my arguments and my reasons not to do it. Not to take it. I don't know if I will succeed. I do not know if I can handle it and what then? When I have come out on the other side? Can I handle what's there? What lies ahead?" I had sat up on my elbows and looked directly into his eyes.

"You can, JAC. If I could survive what happened to me in both Belize and in Afghanistan, then you can survive too. And you have us – me and Kafka – to help you through." His body trembled.

"Kiss me," he said and without any hesitation I kissed him. Why I had expected his kiss to be tender and gentle, I do not really know, but there is no doubt that it came as a surprise to me how hard and aggressive it was.

"Got to go," he said suddenly, getting up, " ... and remember it's not me you see down there, okay?"

"Okay."

"See you in a few days," he said, forcing a smile before closing the door behind him. Silently, and a little sad, I lay back on my bed. I could not really do anything to help him, but equally I could not just lie there in the bed either. It was impossible for me to sleep now, so I got up, dressed and went downstairs.

It was completely quiet, and since neither JAC nor Kafka were to be found anywhere, I went into the kitchen. The M16 rifles were gone from the table and replaced by a bowl of peaches and, as strange as it may sound, it suddenly dawned on me that I was extremely hungry.

The peach I sank my teeth into was juicy and sweet and the juice ran down my chin, totally surprising me. I took a piece of paper towel to wipe my mouth and chin and I was just about finished when Kafka came up from the basement.

I do not know whether he saw me, because he went directly and very purposefully into the library. For a moment I considered whether I should follow him, but after throwing the wet and slightly sticky piece of paper towel away, I went after him.

As expected, I found him standing behind the desk with the remote in his hand. On the flat screen JAC's face faded out. Kafka struggled a bit to fine-tune the picture and ended up sitting down in the chair behind the desk while constantly adjusting the settings to the monitor. For a while I stood in the doorway looking at the picture, whose sharpness varied as Kafka cursed at the function buttons on the multi-controller. You could clearly see JAC and see the mattress that was the only thing that was in the room, and then suddenly the picture was razor sharp.

"Perfect," Kafka said while staring at the screen, "Now we can follow him twenty-four-seven." He laid the remote on the desk and smiled in visible satisfaction at the result of the picture quality on the flat screen.

"In three hours it's serious, so if you want to see him before and say something to him, it's now." I shook my head.

"We've already talked," I said with my eyes glued to the screen and JAC.

As he stood there up against one of the walls with his eyes closed and scratching at his visible needle marks on his arms, there was something insanely raw and untamed about him.

In many ways, he looked like someone who was just waiting to be sentenced – a sentence that he always had known would come, but which he had just postponed and postponed. But now the time was here – and what the sentence was to be he would know in a few hours.

"We must sweep his room for substances, weapons and sharp objects."

Kafka looked at me and I was well aware, that I had just 'won' that job. It was probably also for the best that it was me who went through his stuff.

"We'll put him in my bed. Then the problem is solved," I said without moving my eyes from the screen and without expecting a reaction from Kafka. In my mind, it was the right thing to do because I knew how much JAC hated anyone touching his belongings even if the person was me. In a way, I could not blame him, because many of us had very few personal possessions, so those we had, we not only cherished but we often perceived as a part of us. Therefore it was a violation of our personal integrity if others interfered or touched them. In spite of this, his room still needed to be thoroughly cleaned, which I would do.

Like a jack popping out of its box, Kafka suddenly got up from his chair and walked into the lounge, to retrieve the bottle of JD. When he came back, he almost threw himself in the chair again and unscrewed the top of the bottle. He took a sip, leaned back and then turned up the volume on the screen. It was not because it made much difference as there was complete silence in the room where JAC now sat against the back wall. Sat and waited. I turned one of the chairs opposite Kafka and sat down. From here I had a full view of the screen.

"This is exactly the kind of room we need for the 'interrogation'," I said softly to Kafka as I studied the room on the flat screen.

Kafka did not answer, but I could hear him taking a sip of the JD. As I leaned back on the chair it surprised me how hard it was. Immediately it brought back memories of the spartanly decorated dining room at the boarding school and just like then there was now only one thing I could do, and that was to wait ... wait for the 'party' to begin.

Chapter 19

The next seventy-two hours were absolutely horrible.

Not so much for Kafka and me, but for JAC: He shouted and screamed, cursed us all to hell, banged his head and fists against the walls, knelt on the floor and shook, lay on the mattress in the foetal position while shaking all over, his body convulsing. He threw up over the walls and the mattress, scratched his arms and legs till they bled, and tore tufts of hair out of his head.

After twenty-seven hours, he went into such violent cramps that Kafka decided to go down and give him an injection that would make him relax a bit. And while he was doing that, we took the opportunity to flush the room, flip the mattress so he didn't have so lay in his own vomit and – last but not least – to put a bucket of water in there for him to drink from. It might seem cruel, as if we were treating him like an animal, but it was for his own safety. A plastic bottle could easily be turned into a weapon to do self-harm. It was a bit more difficult with a bucket.

As we came up to the thirty-sixth hour, JAC had a severe fit of rage that ended with him collapsing and Kafka went once more down to him to check his heart rate and blood pressure. I stayed in the library watching the screen as Kafka entered the room. I saw him picking JAC up from the floor and helping him on to the mattress. JAC suddenly started crying, and as it escalated into an almost frantic childish screaming he clung desperately to Kafka, like a small child. It moved me and I think it did Kafka too because he stroked his hair gently before he gave him a piece of paper towel so he could wipe his eyes.

But then ... out of nowhere JAC's mood changed and he became violently aggressive and attacked Kafka.

I jumped up and a few seconds later, I tore the door to JAC's room open. I entered just in time to see JAC knock Kafka's head into the wall. Without hesitation I kicked JAC in his face and he hit the floor with a bang.

I quickly grabbed Kafka by his heels and dragged him out. He was unconscious but with JAC slowly coming to his senses, there was no time to waste. Out of the room I slammed the door and locked it. It was just in time, for a few seconds later I heard JAC shouting and screaming and banging on it.

To be honest, I really did not care about him because all my focus was on Kafka. I could not wake him by slapping his cheeks, so I picked up the water hose we used to fill the bucket for JAC and aimed the jet at him. After a few seconds with a cascade of water against his face, he woke up. I turned off the hose and kneeled beside him.

"You have to lie still," I said softly, "I have no idea if you have internal bleeding in your head. How is your vision?"

"Okay," he replied, following my index finger, which I moved in front of first his right eye and then his left.

"Are you dizzy?"

"No, but fuck my head hurts." I felt his head carefully and it hurt him a lot when I reached a huge swelling between his skull and neck. We looked at each other because we both knew the size and location of the bulge was not good. I took my t-shirt off and placed it carefully under his head.

"Get some ice cubes," he said softly and I think his tone of voice was more to calm himself down than me.

I hurried up to the kitchen, and the first thing that caught my eye, when I opened the freezer, was a bag of frozen peas. Like a frog snatching a fly with its tongue, I grabbed the bag and ran back to Kafka. Carefully I placed the bag under his neck and directly on the bulge and then it was just a matter of waiting.

I sat down next to him and for the twenty minutes that passed before he removed the bag, we did not exchange a single word.

"How are you feeling?" I finally asked as Kafka gently touched the bulge. It was only half the size it had been before, so the probability that it had caused damage was minimal, or so we hoped.

"Okay. I'm a little dizzy, but otherwise okay. Fuck, it was good that you turned up. He could have killed me. He is insanely strong. The withdrawal process has doubled his normal strength, but that ... it's utterly grotesque ... Like a fucking Hercules on steroids. It was like I was a fucking fly he had to crush."

Kafka was clearly shaken, something I had never seen before, but I fully understood him. JAC's strength was unbelievable. I had seen him carry incredibly heavy weapons and once he ran a mile and a half with our old teammate, Washington, who weighed over a hundred and sixty pounds, on one shoulder.

"How did you get me out?" Kafka asked obviously curious.

"I kicked him in the head which sent him to the floor. I knew it was only a matter of seconds before he would be up on his feet again, but it gave me just enough time to get you out and yes ... I know he is frighteningly strong."

"I don't even want to think about how strong he will be, when all the toxins are out of his body and he regains all his strength." Kafka replied still slightly shaken. Slowly he got up and even though I offered him my support he refused it. As we started walking up the stairs I glanced over my shoulder to the door JAC was behind. He had apparently calmed down because all was quiet from inside the room. However, when I reached the top of the stairs I did not only close the door behind us but double locked it as well.

For the next couple of hours, Kafka lay on one of the sofas in the lounge resting, while I sat in the library, looking at the screen showing JAC sleeping on the floor in the room downstairs. Had it not been for the fact that his body trembled once in a while, it could have been the perfect screen shot on the flat screen.

We passed the forty-hour mark and everything was still relatively calm.

JAC sat quietly up against one of the walls and Kafka's head had got better as the headache was gone but fearing a concussion, which under the circumstances was a possibility, he did not dare to go to sleep, so he just lay and relaxed on one of the Chesterfields.

My eyelids started to feel a bit heavy so I got up and went into the lounge and lay down on the couch opposite Kafka. I must have fallen asleep, because when I woke up a few hours later, Kafka was sitting inside the library eating fruit while watching JAC on the flat screen.

"He's almost detoxed," he said grinning at me as I entered the room. I looked at the clock and saw to my surprise I had slept for six hours.

"Has he drunk any of the water?" I asked and Kafka nodded as he chewed on a piece of orange. The sweet scent from the fruit made me ravenously hungry, so I took a piece from the plate where all the orange segments lay. "When will he be safe to approach?" I asked while eating the piece of orange.

"In twelve to fourteen hours. Not before, but he will probably tell you himself. You will not be in doubt when you hear his voice that he is ready." And Kafka was right.

After sixty-one hours, JAC called to us in a calm, tired and detoxed voice.

Kafka had taken his Glock with him because of JAC's earlier attack. Understandably he did not want to take any chances, even though the man was clean now. Carefully Kafka opened the door to JAC and I entered the lion's den before him. With cautious steps I went to JAC and I could immediately see that there was no danger. He sat on the mattress with his head buried in his hands and without looking up at me, he grabbed my legs and leaned his forehead against my shins. I let my fingers run through his dark hair, which was greasy and sticky from perspiration.

"Now the worst is over," I said quietly stroking his hair, "Come on," I whispered and he let go of my legs. Slowly he leaned his head back and looked up at me, and it was only then that I saw, how awful he really looked. His eyes were bloodshot and surrounded by black grooves that made his eye area look sunken and skeletal. And his facial skin was ruddy and sticky with sweat and blood from small cuts and bruises. Clotted blood lay like dark crusts in the corners of his mouth evidently originating from the hole he had bitten in his otherwise smooth lower lip, which now looked dry and cracked.

"Come," I repeated softly and smiled at him, and despite the fact that he was trying to reciprocate, it was clear that he simply did not have the energy to do so.

Slightly dazed, he got up and looked over at Kafka, who in recognition nodded silently to him.

"You need to have a bath," I said quietly and with no objections from JAC, we all three went upstairs and into my bathroom. Kafka stayed with JAC in the bathroom as he washed the last couple of days of hell off, and the length of his bath gave me exactly enough time to sweep his room.

When I got back, JAC was lying in my bed sleeping while Kafka was walking around gathering his clothes.

Without a word, he disappeared out of the room with them and I was finally alone with JAC. I went to the edge of the bed and sat down next to him. He was fast asleep and even though I gently touched one of his upper arms and kissed him, he did not move – but it was okay. He had done it. He was clean. A moment later, Kafka came back with a dish of fruit and some water bottles which he placed on the table between the two sofas at the other end of the room.

"He is going to sleep for the next twenty-four hours, so let's take turns watching him. If you take the first four hours, then ..." Without looking at Kafka, I nodded expressively.

"My door is open if there is anything." It was clear that Kafka did not expect me to answer him, because as the words were said he turned and went into his room.

I felt the silence descend upon the house, and as before, it made me feel safe. I crawled into the bed next to JAC and I just sat there letting my thoughts fly. When all the thoughts had flown away, I started meditating. It was nice and something that I had needed for a long time, but only now did I have enough peace around me to do it.

* * *

For the next twenty-four hours, I did not leave JAC.

When it was my watch, I sat next to him in bed meditating, listening to audio books on my iPod, or zapping TV.

When Kafka came and relieved me, I lay down next to JAC and slept.

After twenty hours, I woke up and felt JAC's arm around me. He was still asleep, but just this small sign of life from him, made me happy and I smiled while kissing his hand gently.

Kafka was sitting over by the window reading emails on his tablet, and I do not think he noticed anything. It was an incredibly safe feeling to have both JAC and Kafka within reach, even though JAC was by no means at his best.

I lay for a while just looking at Kafka. He was a really good-looking guy. I would think him to be in his late thirties, but he could be younger. He was not that tall, but he was muscular and his dark curly hair on the top of his slightly round face made his eyes appear even more marked than I had noticed before. There was something Middle Eastern about his appearance, but he was very light in complexion, so I had a hard time placing him nationality-wise.

"Where do you come from?" I asked suddenly and Kafka looked up from his iPad.

"Egypt," he replied and looked at me.

"I would not have guessed that."

"I am half Syrian with a quarter Moroccan and a quarter Lebanese, but I was born and raised in Egypt." He returned to the tablet without further comment.

"Why the name Kafka?" I continued, hoping that he did not mind that I asked him all these personal questions.

"Because I hate inefficiency and bureaucracy. Why complicate things when the answers are most often very simple? Why drag out the process? That only leads to doubt and confusion, which in turn, can lead to wrong conclusions and thus catastrophic decisions; decisions that often end with the murder of the individual and ultimately also the truth." He looked at me and smiled wryly, "Therefore Kafka – after Franz Kafka."

I smiled. There were so many questions in this that I hardly knew where to begin. So I did not.

"You're fucking amazing, Kafka. Do you know that?" I said still smiling.

"Yes, I know," he replied slightly teasingly, smiling, "What about you?" He put down his iPad.

"What about me?" I repeated teasingly.

"What is your background?"

"Grew up in Italy with Swiss / Italian parents. At six years old I was sent to boarding school in Lucerne and then ... yes now I am in Islamabad."

"And the name OPUS?" It was rare that I was asked this question, and the few times it had happened, I had avoided answering. Not because I minded, but I usually found it unnecessary for whoever asked the question to know. But this time it was different. Kafka and I had a past together and somehow it entitled him to be told.

"Every time I perform a kill, it's like I'm adding a note to my life's symphony. You could say that I end another person's life song in order to compose my own. If you want to be really theatrical, then you can probably call me a composer of death."

"Poetic ..." he said with a devious smile on his lips, "Did you ever tell JAC about us?" The smile was gone from his face as he scowled at me but I think he already knew the answer.

"There wasn't really anything to tell, was there? We fucked once in Belize and that was it." To be honest I had never given it much thought. It happened the night before I let myself get caught. I don't really know why I did it. Maybe because I knew what was awaiting me and just wanted to make sure that my last night was going to be good. One where I would feel close to another person for a couple of hours before going into the devil's dungeon. Why Kafka did it I had no idea. Maybe he wanted to say thank you to me for the sacrifice I was about to make and to give me a memory to take with me that not everybody wanted to hurt me.

Kafka turned his attention to his iPad and just as he had known the answer to his question I knew the answer to the one I was about to ask him.

"Did you tell your wife?" Without as much as blinking he kept staring at the iPad.

"Nope ..." he finally replied, "And she is my ex-wife."

"Sorry to hear that," I said and I truly was. Married life in this business was hard and seldom lasted.

"Don't be .... I can't really blame her. I was a bastard. Couldn't keep my dick in my pants." He looked up from the iPad and into the garden. Then he snorted, "Anyway ...," he finally said letting out a sigh, "She was better off without me and ... she is married now to a twat of an accountant but she seems happy so .... Who the fuck am I to judge her?" His reflection in the window revealed a bit of sadness in his eyes and I don't know if it was for losing her or because he still loved her. Whatever it was I truly felt for him. He had told me about her after we had fucked and were lying in his bed sharing a cigarette. Had I known about her before I'm not sure we would have had sex ... but who knows. I was no angel ... and as he said 'he was a bastard' so we might have done it anyway even if I had known about her existence. But one thing was sure: I wasn't interested in him now and I think the feeling was mutual.

A movement from JAC ended our conversation. As I turned my attention to him, I could hear Kafka jump from the window sill and walk over to us. With two fingers on JAC's throat, he took his pulse while looking at him.

"He's okay." Kafka said when finished, looking briefly at me. Then he left the room.

Whether it was Kafka's announcement or whether it was the sound of JAC's calm breathing, I do not know – maybe it was a combination – but for a moment I felt an inner joy that I usually only felt when I was completely alone in my own little universe.

* * *

The news feed from CNN was rolling across the screen when I suddenly heard JAC's voice.

"Hey," he said very quietly with his voice rasping. I immediately turned off the TV and looked at him.

He lay with his head up against my chest and one arm lying across my thighs.

"Hey," I replied, kissing him on the head, "welcome back."

Without raising his head from my chest, he looked up at me with a grin on his lips.

"Have you been here all along?"

"Yes. Where else would I be?" He sat up on one elbow and ran the hand that had been resting on my thighs over his face and through his hair while blinking his eyes. Then he sighed.

"This," he said hesitantly, "I will NEVER do this again. NEVER."

I looked at him and smiled. Our eyes met and, for the first time since I left camp to go to Central America, I saw the depth and humanity that I loved so much about him. But there was also a trace of vulnerability and I had not seen that before. I kissed him gently and he kissed me back. One kiss turned into several and we let them fall like raindrops on each other's faces and necks.

"What the hell would I do without you?" he suddenly whispered in my ear.

"You should never wonder about that. I'm not going anywhere." We found each other's lips again and kissed sensually.

"I wish I had more strength, but I'm so exhausted ..." he said but continued kissing me.

"There's no rush," I whispered as I held his face in my hands, "We have all the time in the world." For a moment I regretted the words for, not only were they a cliché, but at the same time we both knew that it was wishful thinking and that reality could quickly change everything. But for now, we had all the time in the world and that was what was important.

* * *

The next few days were all about getting JAC back on track.

I spent hours in the kitchen making protein-rich meals for him. He devoured everything from health smoothies to big juicy steaks.

Kafka had placed electrodes on him so he could monitor his heart rhythm, for such a form of detox could well result in cardiac arrhythmia, so rather be safe than sorry.

The whole house had been cleared of everything that could be perceived to have a euphoric effect, even our cigarettes were gone, and even though both Kafka and I had sworn that we were in no way dependent on them, we both had to admit that we actually missed smoking.

The room we had used in the basement to detox JAC, had been returned to its original purpose, a fitness room and when JAC was not eating or sleeping, he was there with Kafka training. Exercise was important not only to maintain his physique but also to stabilize him mentally. According to what I had read on-line, depression and discouragement were often dark companions to detoxing, and exercise was a healthy and healing way to counteract them.

At night, JAC and I had hard and borderline violent sex, and as the days went by, a pattern began to emerge.

JAC was no longer hooked on smack – he was getting hooked on pain.

The satisfaction he could get through climaxing in pain was apparently his new fix and, to achieve it, he needed me. I had become his new addiction. His pusher. Because I gave him the pain he so desperately needed to function optimally.

It began to dawn on me how essential it was to teach him to control his desire and craving for the pain, because if he could he would have power over himself and his lusts. However, the process was not so straightforward because in order to achieve full control of the pain, it had to be given in different doses, and it did not suit JAC, who by nature was not the most patient person in the world.

Some nights when I only gave him a 'small dose' of pain he became so angry and frustrated that he inflicted it on himself in order to try to achieve climax, and it was so hard to watch, but it was necessary.

Kafka avoided asking questions about what was going on because he had to admit, that combined with the hard physical training, what he and I did worked. And worked well.

Soon JAC was back being the person he had been before the heroin and it was great to have him back.

Chapter 20

After two weeks, JAC was sufficiently recovered for us to launch our plan. Kafka had contacted Mossad and they were more than willing to make an interrogation room available. As I thought, they agreed it would be a good 'training' for their elite units to see a 'real' interrogation of a woman, and the fact that it would be recorded on video made them even more excited. They wanted to use the recording for future training of their agents. Personally, I did not think they could imagine what was about to happen, because, if they had, they probably would not have been so keen to participate.

The only thing we were waiting for was confirmation that Liam was back in camp again, and while we waited, we trained.

Then came the day we had been preparing for: Liam was back and he had evidently reinforced his team with four other mercs. From what we were told they did not immediately pose any threat. They were apparently from the IRA's internal ranks and we did not consider them to be a problem.

JAC and Kafka had put all the weapons we needed for the mission on the kitchen counter, as the dining table had been given the honourable task of hosting all our accessories; two complete bomb kits, detonators, grenades, grenade launchers, tripwires and ammunition for our various pistols and rifles. Many of these accessories Kafka and JAC had designed and fabricated themselves during the wait.

Unfortunately, we had not received any new intelligence about Wizard, so we had no idea if he was alive, and if so, where he was. So we had to rely on getting more information once we were back in camp but even that depended on us being accepted by the alpha male Liam and his pack.

I went to my room and picked up my hunting knife along with my Glock and Aussie's specially made gun as well as OPUS. It was kind of reassuring, to feel its titanium between my fingers again and it brought a little smile to my face. We were finally going back into the real world. Not that I hadn't enjoyed being in the house, where I had been given a much-needed break from marks and kills, but I could feel in my bones that it was time to get back to work.

It is strange that you can be looking forward to going to war, but for me that was not the entire reason for my obvious delight. It was more the fact that before long we would all be free. Free from FSB, Mossad and Liam.

Free to disappear – if that was what we wanted. Free!

When I was finally downstairs again, the others were getting ready for departure too. Kafka had already gone down into the garage with the first load of bags and I found JAC standing in the kitchen about to zip the last one. As the most natural thing in the world, I went over and hugged him from behind. My spontaneous little emotional outburst immediately made him spin around and wrap his arms around me and we kissed.

"Are you ready?" he asked, moving some strands of my hair away from my eyes with his fingers.

"Yes," I replied, smiling, "And this time you will be there, physically and mentally. It will be absolutely fantastic."

JAC wrinkled his nose as if saying 'wrong word'.

"There is nothing fantastic about beating the living crap out of the one you love."

I do not really know why I was so surprised to hear him say those words, for I had no doubt that he loved me, but it was somehow different when it suddenly came out of his mouth. It was actually the first time he had said it and maybe that's why I reacted like I did. I looked at him with my eyebrows raised in surprise but he just smiled at me telling me how very conscious he was of what he had just said.

"Because I do," he said quietly and we kissed again. With my eyes closed and my lips glued to JAC's, I heard Kafka come into the kitchen and take the last two bags. With a cheeky remark from him that we better detach ourselves from each other, our lips parted, and we turned our attention to the handguns lying on the kitchen table.

"Here" I said, giving JAC Aussie's Glock knowing that in all its decadence it would impress him.

He looked at it and he whistled.

"It is partly made of plastic and therefore we can smuggle it into the 'embassy'."

"It's rare to see one like this," he said, turning it over a few times, "Aussie must have paid a fortune for it." He nodded approvingly as he said it and then he stuck it in the back of his waistband. He covered it with his t-shirt and finally his jacket. It was as if he had read my mind when he took two single bullets that matched the Glock and inserted them into two of the metal links on the wristband of his watch. One had to have a trained eye to spot them there and, as he would normally take off his watch when being scanned, it was unlikely that they would be revealed by that either. We gathered our weapons and went to the basement door, which Kafka immediately opened.

"That's the last of it," I heard JAC say to him before opening the garage door and disappearing in the direction of the cars.

A minute later, Kafka was in the driver's seat next to me in the Hummer and funnily enough we slammed the doors at the same time.

Kafka turned on the ignition and with a tap on the phone, the garage door began to open. We left the safe haven, sharply followed by JAC on one of the Ducatis. I could see the front gate opening and it was perfectly timed, fully open as we drove through. We turned sharply to the right and Kafka pressed the phone again and the gate began to close behind us. I got a strange melancholic feeling, because I really did not want to leave the house and the trinity we had built up the last month living there, but I knew that if we wanted our freedom this was necessary. Neither of us said anything. There was somehow nothing left to say.

On the short drive, I looked several times in the wing mirror and every time I could see JAC riding right behind us. It gave me a sense of satisfaction that repeatedly brought out my inner smile. JAC had a way to do that and I think he secretly knew it.

* * *

The meeting – if you could call it that – was to take place in an empty, flat-roofed office building down by the river. As we rolled past the temporary guards into the parking lot in front of it, it was clear that we were the last to arrive, for several cars and a small truck were already parked along the side of the building. We parked the car and JAC put the Ducati a little further away. Almost simultaneously, Kafka and I jumped out of the Hummer and while Kafka locked it, JAC put his helmet on the seat of the Ducati.

"Are you ready?" Kafka asked me, as he threw the keys to the car to JAC, who came walking towards us. I looked up at the building and in two of the windows I could see some curious faces looking out.

"Let's do it," I said quietly and, like the three musketeers, we walked across the parking lot and into the building.

* * *

The entire session was to take place on the first floor in an open plan office, that for the occasion had had a fifteen square metre room built in it. One wall was of Plexiglas, the other three were plasterboard, so the photo editing afterwards would be easier. It had been agreed that all voices would be muted and JAC's and Kafka's faces would be blurred before the video was released.

Inside the room was a chair, one large and one smaller table. The smaller table held a stun gun, knuckleduster, blindfold, leather straps, several different metal chains, knives and various scalpels. Before our meeting, Kafka had emailed a list of tools that might be needed and judging from the display on the table, it seemed that everything on the list had been complied with. In addition, cameras had been set up on the long side where all the spectators stood behind the Plexiglas.

When we entered the large room, the eyes of all thirty spectators were not surprisingly on us.

There were a number of senior officers, a couple of interrogation specialists, a couple of doctors and a nurse and approximately fifteen women of different rank and from different units present.

We walked calmly to them and as we did Jacoby stepped forward. We shook hands and he seemed unaffected by the situation, which I could not say about Shrirov, who was thrilled, almost completely euphoric in his movements. As agreed, we laid our weapons on a table and then we were scanned with a hand scanner and cleared.

"All those present have been security-cleared and briefed." Shrirov said in a voice that was ecstatic and trembling with anticipation of what he was about to witness. JAC frowned at his behaviour, but I did not care.

If this was all it took to get the idiot up and running, he would probably get off several times during what was about to happen inside the 'glass cage'.

I took off my sunglasses and looked at everyone present.

"Before we start I need to say something: Everything you are about to see and hear in the next few hours is consensual. I do this of my own free will and I've been through something similar before – but then it was just ten times worse – so I know what I'm getting into. None of you must interrupt the process and that also applies to the doctors." I pointed at them and they nodded in acceptance. "The three of us standing here are friends and JAC ..." I turned and looked at him and suddenly froze. Because what should I call him? My partner, my lover, my best friend?

JAC could see the panic in my eyes and completed the sentence for me.

"I'm the one who is to do the 'interrogation'." I was incredibly grateful for his intervention and there was no doubt that he could see the relief in my eyes.

"Does anyone have any questions, because now would be the time to ask them. I will not be able to answer them afterwards."

As expected, no one had any questions and thus the 'party' could begin.

"Okay," Kafka said in a loud, penetrating voice, "Let's get started."

I went to JAC and whispered in his ear, "The password for you to stop is 'Yemen', if I faint without saying the password, you wake me up with water ask me for it, okay? If I don't answer you continue. Understood?"

"Okay," he replied, brushing a few strands of hair from my forehead.

"Give me the bullets," I said firmly touching him discreetly on his wrist where his watch was.

"Why?"

"Just do it," I said and he clicked both bullets out and gave them to me. Then he kissed me fleetingly on the forehead and went to Kafka, who was standing by the door into the artificially constructed room and he was annoyed.

"They have forgotten the bucket of water," he snarled and it was clear that his irritation was escalating.

"Calm down," JAC said casually opening the door, "We'll get there." Then they both entered the room.

"Remove the glass!" JAC's voice was that of a commander but even so no one reacted to it. A strange silence fell upon the spectators instead.

"You must have the opportunity to get really close, because next time it may be one of you who is the main character and then you must have felt and smelled the fear, anger, hatred and powerlessness – so remove that fucking glass now."

Jacoby quickly mobilized some of the assembled people and, during the time it took to procure a ten-litre bucket of water, they had removed the glass wall.

* * *

As I stood outside the door to the interrogation room my body began to shake. But it was due to the pressure of anticipation and not fear. I took a deep breath, went in and closed the door behind me. Shrirov shouted that they should start the cameras and the order was obeyed.

I stood for a while, looking blankly into the air, but then I made eye contact with JAC, who was leaning against the large table with his arms folded across his chest. I looked at Kafka standing up against the wall nearest to me. Then I nodded to Kafka and the show began.

Kafka walked over to me and with a firm grip on my upper arm he led me to the chair in the middle of the room. When he reached the chair, he planted his fist in my face so I tilted back and landed in the chair. While I was gathering myself after the punch I could feel Kafka tying my ankles together with plastic zip ties. After he had done that, he went behind my chair and tied my wrists together before fixing them to the back of the chair. I could feel the plastic cutting into my wrists but it didn't bother me as it was a pain I was all too familiar with from Belize. When Kafka was done he returned to where he had stood before but this time, he leaned against the wall with his arms folded across his chest.

Now it was JAC's turn. I could hear his footsteps as he approached me from behind. He walked around the chair so we faced each other but he did not look me in the eyes. He just stood there quietly as if he was waiting for something to happen. Nobody in the room said or did anything.

I remember thinking that it was incredible how so many people could simultaneously hold their breath for so long.

Then suddenly Kafka blindfolded me from behind and it baffled me as I hadn't noticed him leaving his post at the wall.

For a brief moment I tried to sense where JAC and Kafka were in the room but then a fist hit my face. It was undoubtedly coming from JAC because it hit me so hard that the chair tipped to one side and sent me to the floor with it. As I was lying there JAC kicked me hard four or five times in the stomach with his military boots before grabbing my hair. He pulled it so hard that it lifted me and the chair back to the upright position.

And then the interrogation began for real.

JAC tipped the chair backwards and at the same time I could hear the bucket of water being pushed along the floor. When the sound stopped the bucket was right in front of me and that was when JAC let go of the chair. As it returned to the upright position my feet went in the bucket. The cold water in it made me instantly shiver but then he put the stun gun to one of my thighs.

As the power went through my body I started to scream and suddenly I was no longer in an empty office building in Islamabad with an audience watching my torment; I was back in Belize.

I screamed and screamed and screamed to such an extent that I didn't even realize that JAC had put the stun gun down.

"Shut the fuck up." JAC's voice pierced my ears and brought me back just in time to receive a massive beating from his rock-hard fists.

When he stopped, I tried to re-orientate myself, I could hear him walking over to the little table where all the different torture tools were laid out.

He returned and the beatings continued with first a wide leather belt and afterwards with a massive metal chain. And then he kicked the chair to pieces so I ended up on the floor where I instinctively curled up in a foetal position to protect my body. As the chain continued to strike it felt like heavy raindrops as it had done so many times in Belize and, just as in Belize, I cried out for JAC.

"JAC help me. Save me, JAC. Make it stop. Stop it, JAC." I begged but I didn't mean it. He was not to stop. He had to carry on. Carry on until ...

Suddenly JAC stopped torturing me and before I could react he had cut the zip ties and as he pulled me up from the floor he removed the blindfold. One of my eye brows had split open as a result of one of JAC's punches and as the blood from it reached my eye I wiped it off with my hand. Then I stared at JAC.

"Why the fuck did you stop? Why? Do you want to take the pleasure away from me?" I yelled into his face. "Give it back to me, do you hear? Give it back to me." But nothing happened. He just stood there and stared at me. Then I launched at him and to my surprise he didn't do anything to avoid the blow to his chin. He took a step back and continued looking at me. But then it was as if it suddenly dawned on him what had happened and a second later his fist hit my face and sent me directly to the floor.

"That's more like it," I said while spitting blood as I tried to get up. But before I was up I felt JAC's arm around my neck and as he lifted me he choked me. I twisted and turned as I desperately tried to loosen his grip but he was too strong for me. I gasped violently. I couldn't breathe but just as I was on the brink of passing out he let go of his grip and threw me across the room and into the white plastered wall on the other side. The wall was made of wooden boards so it bounced a bit but remained standing leaving my bloody silhouette as a calling card on it.

Slowly I started to crawl across the floor away from the wall. Fuck, it was fantastic. The numbness I was feeling in my body combined with the rising rush of sexual euphoria.

"Where the fuck do you think you are going?" JAC's cold voice boomed as he grabbed me by my collar and dragged me across the floor. When we reached the big table that stood in the middle of the room he took a firm grip of my hair and slammed my forehead into the edge of it. He then threw me on the table and as I lay there face down he spread my legs. With one hand he then pressed my head hard into the table top while with the other he tore off my t-shirt. Then Kafka picked up the bucket of water and suddenly I felt the icy cold water on my back and my thighs. Kafka then grabbed both my arms by my wrists and stretched them over my head holding them tight.

For the next ten minutes JAC beat me with the leather belt on my back and thighs, only pausing to use the stun gun to send shocks of electricity through my body. I didn't really feel the pain as my body had gone more or less numb by now but when he put the stun gun to my inner thigh and groin I screamed.

Screamed. Screamed. Screamed.

"Stay with me, JAC. Don't go. Please stay with me," I screamed but much to my surprise the words did not come out in English but in Italian – the language we spoke in my childhood home. "Stay and make love to me. Make love to me. Love me ...." My voice got weaker as the beating continued and the stun gun sent its ray of pleasure through me. "Love me ... Make love to me ... Please JAC ... Please." And then I passed out.

I was woken up by a cascade of cold water hitting the back of my head.

"I'm not done with you yet," I heard JAC's voice say, "You want pain? I'll give you so much fucking pain that you wish you were never born." I could hear in his voice that he definitely was in character and that he meant it but it didn't scare me. Quite the opposite. It aroused me. He was going to take me to the level of ecstasy that I wanted and for that I needed him to inflict the pain that took me there.

There was so much blood on the table where I was lying that it made my body slippery so when JAC turned me over his grip on me was extra firm, otherwise I would have slid right off.

"I'll give you pain but only because I love you," he said in a low voice as he turned me over.

"Please, JAC ... Love me ... Love me now." My words were English again and came out weak as I gasped them in a mental state of euphoria tinged with fear of what was going to happen.

Suddenly I felt the cold steel knife blade cutting through my skin. I couldn't really feel any pain but I could sense the blood running over my ribs and down across my stomach. I don't know if I screamed but if I did it was in pure pleasure. JAC had put his hand across my mouth and although I bit it hard, he did not move it. If there had been any feeling left in my body it was now gone and replaced with pure sexual ecstasy. And the best thing was that JAC was there with me making it happen by making love to me. It was as if he lifted me out of the pain and into a universe of love. A universe where only he and I existed. A universe I had been so craving for. It was amazing.

A couple of slaps on my cheeks brought me back to reality.

"Now I'm warmed up so let's fucking party." JAC's voice was fierce but I could see warmth shining in his eyes as he briefly looked at me. He loved this. Loved it as much as I did. I could see it in the way he looked at me and somehow it was both terrifying and total arousing. Suddenly I became aware of JAC walking over to the little table.

* * *

While he was gone, I turned my head and looked at the spectators in the room. Expressions of shock, contempt and disgust were written all over their faces and some women were even throwing up. As my eyes wandered along the rows of people, I suddenly caught sight of a woman standing with her mouth wide open and tears running down her cheeks: For some reason that affected me. I made eye contact with her and it was obvious that she was going into shock but apparently none of the people around her had noticed.

'Stop' she mouthed to me but I just closed my eyes in the hope that her tormented face would disappear from my memory.

"Stop." Her loud frantic high-pitched voice cutting through the air in the room made me open my eyes. JAC was standing over me with two metal hooks in his hands but as we made eye contact he stopped. My eyes wandered from hook to hook. Then I nodded to him letting him know that I consented but just as he was about to proceed a painful and heartbreaking scream filled with despair rang out. I immediately gave the safe word "Yemen" and JAC put the metal hooks down. Slowly I tried to get up but my hands kept slipping on the blood on the table so JAC helped me. Carefully and unsteadily I stood on the floor and with wobbling steps I walked over to the woman who stood trembling and tearful.

"Get that bitch out of here," I hissed to the officer standing next to her, "Can't you see she is on the verge of collapsing? Where is your fucking humanity?" The officer stood petrified and in the background I could hear JAC laughing. I realize that saying these words must have sounded grotesque as I was currently being seduced by the somewhat inhuman treatment from JAC. Or so it seemed. But I guess it highlighted the absurd paradox many of the spectators were experiencing in the room. And really .... I could not blame them.

"Get her out of here," I screamed to the officer as the blood from my cuts started dripping on the floor.

"Why do you let him continue to do this to you? You have endured enough torment to make it believable, so why?" The words came from an officer further along the line of spectators and the comment infuriated me although it was understandable why he felt this way. But he didn't know when enough is enough and for his sake I hoped he never would.

I staggered towards him and only stopped when I was right in front of him.

"I decide when I have had enough. Nobody else. Do you understand? And if he ..." I pointed at JAC, "if he shouldn't inflict the pain on me I don't know who should. He loves me."

The room went silent.

"He loves you?" The question came from the woman who had uttered the heartbreaking scream before.

"Is she still here?" I snarled, "You think this is painful?" I said pointing at myself, "Look at her. I will guarantee you that she will collapse when she sees what is going to happen next. So get her out of here."

I turned to JAC who stood very calm and relaxed over by the table seemingly enjoying the show. Slowly I started to walk towards him but my legs failed me and as I started to fall JAC caught me in his arms.

"Put me on the table, JAC. It's time for you to rape me."

As the words left my lips it occurred to me how grotesque they sounded. Here I was in the arms of the man who had tortured me asking him to rape me. The contrast became even clearer in the way he laid me gently on the table and stroked my blood-stained hair. The quietness in the room somehow emphasized the intimacy between us and for a few seconds it seemed to be only JAC and me.

"Did she say rape?" one of the officers asked and his voice brought me back to reality.

* * *

The last hours had been primarily to convince Liam and to educate the spectators, but for me they had been so much more. They had been amazing and pure enjoyment of pleasure through pain with the only one I could imagine taking me to those heights – my saviour, JAC.

Since it was JAC who was in charge of the rape, it was not a real rape, and I perceived it as a game of hard sex, but for outsiders it was so gross and extreme that it could easily be confused with a real assault. However, it took some time to get him to do it, as he initially refused. According to him, he could not do it, but it was then that Aussie's gun got him thinking differently. I managed to snatch it from his waistband and load it with the two bullets from his bracelet and under threat of shooting him if he did not rape me, he completed his task. It was obvious that he did not enjoy it but he did it and, in the process, he was so hard on me that I fainted several times, but it just made the whole scene more real, so it didn't matter.

When he was done, he collapsed on top of me. I could feel him shivering in what I perceived was awareness of what he had just done.

"I love you so much," he whispered, "so much, so much."

"I know," I replied quietly as he lifted his head and we found each other's eyes. There was no doubt that we both meant those words, and just as gently we stole a kiss from each other. We should not have done so, but we needed to, to underline the authenticity that the events of the last few hours were done in the name of love.

As I lay there on the table the pain began to wash over me. Happy that nobody could read my mind I succumbed to it and every single wave that gushed through my body.

Reality returned, however, when JAC got up and silently buttoned his pants and I felt Kafka's hands around me as he, in the best nursing style, helped me up from the table. It was as if I was in a daze where the mists of ecstasy were about to evaporate; suddenly the fog lifted and the waves of pain were now closer to a Tsunami washing over me. My eyes found JAC, who was a metre away from me, fastening his belt. He approached and Kafka benevolently stepped aside just as my legs failed me. JAC grabbed me before I hit the floor. He gently lifted me up, and while Kafka opened the door, he marched across the room and left the arena.

"Start the helicopter," he said in a harsh and commanding voice, as he moved towards the exit with me in his arms, and it seemed like this time people listened to him. A couple of officers and one of the doctors ran in front of us and I could hear Kafka gathering our weapons. The pain was now so exquisite that despite the fact that I was fighting back, I lost consciousness.

* * *

When the sound of the helicopter's massive rotors brought me back to reality, I was lying on a stretcher inside it, and a doctor was attaching a drip to my left arm. I could see that JAC was standing right outside handing bags and weapons to Kafka and, despite the fact that I didn't move, he must have registered that I was awake, because immediately he jumped into the helicopter. He squatted on his haunches and took my right hand and kissed it.

The doctor had finished inserting the drip and I caressed JAC's cheek with my left hand. He bowed his head down to me but, despite only being a few centimetres from my ear, he still had to shout to drown out the noise from the helicopter.

"Are you okay?" I winked at him and we kissed each other gently and for a long time. In fact, it was Kafka who interrupted us as he patted JAC on the shoulder and made signs that we should take off.

"See you later." JAC shouted into my ear and then he disappeared out of the helicopter. My eyes flickered for a moment, but as Kafka sat down where JAC had been sitting, I calmed down and suddenly everything went black.

Chapter 21

The flight from Islamabad to Kabul took approximately two and a half hours. I was periodically conscious, but I only really woke up a quarter of an hour before we touched down.

During the flight, the pain in my body had been nasty but not unbearable, and in fact, at one point, I panicked a little and wondered why I was not in more pain.

"Have you given me any painkillers?" I shouted and the sound of my voice startled everyone close to me. The doctor shook his head.

"No. Nothing," he shouted back, but the suspicion in my eyes must have been so strong that it prompted Kafka to reassure me that the doctor was right as he leaned towards me.

"You're clean." Kafka shouted, "Why?"

"I can't feel any pain," I shouted back and judging by Kafka's facial expression, my distrust was contagious. After exchanging a few glances, the doctor immediately set about examining whether my nerves and reflexes were normal.

"You're okay." Kafka shouted after getting a thumbs-up from the doctor, and with those words in mind, I put my head back on JAC's shirt. At first, I could not recall him putting it there, but it was his, because it smelled of him. It was nice to have him there, so I closed my eyes and smilingly thought of how he had made me feel a few hours ago.

* * *

We landed thirty-five kilometres west of Kabul on the bare and dusty sand.

The two officers who had accompanied us immediately jumped out, and while one ran to pick up a jeep parked some distance away, the other began to unload weapons and kit from the helicopter.

Once the doctor had removed my drip Kafka helped me up and, supported by him, I once again put my feet on Afghan soil. I was a little dizzy and my body was bruised but I still had no excruciating pain which seemed very strange. It was as if the body was back in Belize and, just like then, it was now trying to protect me because it expected more torture to come.

Stumbling, I reached the jeep which the officer had left with the engine running and, with Kafka's help, I sat down in the passenger seat. Once I had positioned myself, he put OPUS in my lap and it was quite nice to feel the familiar weight across my thighs. While the officers threw our luggage in, Kafka sat in the driver's seat. It all happened without exchanging a single word, and in fact the only communication we had was a few seconds later when one of the officers banged on a panel indicating that we could drive now. As we heard the helicopter take off, we left the place without looking back.

* * *

As we raced through the desert to the sound of the jeep's straining engine, I took a firm grip on OPUS. The surface we drove on was very uneven and the bumps cut through my body like sharp spears every time the jeep hit one of them. I smiled to myself, because even though the pain was severe it confirmed that I was not completely dead.

Ten kilometres from Kabul, we drove into a small bombed village. In principle, we could have been anywhere in the Middle East, because when it came to small villages that were pretty much levelled to the ground, they were everywhere in this part of the world. Obviously the place had been abandoned and only five or six houses had something that resembled walls. The rest of the houses had either been blown up or collapsed due to bombing.

Kafka stopped and left the engine running while he unloaded most of our luggage and threw it into one of the ruins. The plan was for JAC to pick up the bags and equipment and then wait for the co-ordinates to the pick-up location.

"Take off your t-shirt." Kafka said when he was back in the jeep again, but my arms were so sore that I could barely lift them. He therefore helped me get it over my head and then he used his hunting knife to remove the chip that we had put back in me earlier. He put it in his boot and then helped me put my t-shirt back on again. In fact, I could not remember at all when someone had put the t-shirt on me in the first place. Maybe when they changed the drip, because it was completely covered in half-dried blood.

* * *

It was early afternoon and the sun's rays were baking down on us, but I could not really feel any heat from them. It was as if my body had anaesthetized itself and shut down vital senses to protect itself, and in the Afghan heat it was very nice that it did not really record the temperatures. We raced through the streets of Kabul and, a little over half an hour later, we turned sharply on to Main Street in the camp. With the horn blaring Kafka drove like the devil to our old barrack and along the way, several soldiers had to jump for their lives to avoid being hit. He braked so hard outside Liam's barrack that for a brief moment I thought I was going to fly through the windshield of the jeep. It was as if my body woke up at the recoil in the seat because suddenly, I felt a cutting pain in my ribs and I screamed out in pain.

A couple of Liam's new people came rushing out of the barrack with their guns raised towards us, but neither Kafka nor I paid any attention. On the contrary. Although Kafka was under gun-point he jumped out of the car and ran round to my side to help me out. To make me totally immobile, he gave me a hidden fist blow in the diaphragm. In fact it was unnecessary, because the pain from my ribs was so massive that I was on the verge of fainting.

"Where's Liam?" he shouted aggressively, "Get Liam ... Now Goddamn it."

Liam's soldiers did nothing. They just stood and watched us and they made absolutely no attempt to either answer or help us. I could feel by Kafka's quiver that the irritation over their lack of response was about to make him explode but I didn't do anything to calm him down.

"Find Liam," he shouted, "Say Kafka is back with OPUS ... NOW." But it was in vain. The soldiers did not move an inch.

The door to Luc's barrack suddenly opened and he with another legionnaire came running out.

"Where's Liam, Luc?" Kafka screamed at him as I almost collapsed in pain in Kafka's arms.

"How the fuck should I know," Luc replied frowning in astonishment, "Is that OPUS?" His expression showing he could not believe his eyes.

"Yes, for fuck's sake. We have to get her in now." Kafka tightened his grip on me and I screamed in pain.

"Get the hell out of the way," Luc shouted to Liam's men, who were blocking the door to Liam's barrack, but they still did not move.

"Fuck them. Get her into our barrack and get a fucking doctor." Luc shouted without addressing a direct order to anyone. However, one of the legionnaires immediately set off in the direction of the infirmary while another helped Kafka carry me into Luc's barrack. The two Asian girls at the back of the barrack screamed in terror when they saw me and fled behind their beds.

"Get those bitches out." Luc shouted, and while one of the legionnaires chased them out, Luc pointed to a bed in the middle of the room, "Put her there," he commanded. The pain in my body moved around and made it virtually impossible for me to pinpoint so, even though they put me down gently, I screamed fiercely. Ironically, it actually helped to scream. It was as if for a short time the pain disappeared along with my screams into the barrack.

The legionnaire who had run to the hospital reappeared, this time with a doctor.

"What do you need?" it came in a definite and not debatable tone from Luc glaring at him.

"Space," replied the doctor, and judging by his gaze and tone of voice, he was already pre-occupied. Three legionnaires promptly removed the surrounding beds so that there was nothing around me and the bed I was lying on. The doctor examined me superficially, and as the pain returned, I screamed no matter where on my body he touched me.

"I want her down at the infirmary now," the doctor said as he continued to examine me.

Kafka and Luc exchanged a quick glance in agreement.

"She stays here, Doc. Sorry." Luc replied, but it seemed that his comment bounced off the doctor.

"I can't treat her here. I need my equipment."

"You just say what you need and it will be brought to you." Luc replied again, signalling to one of the legionnaires who took his phone out and was ready to write.

"I want her down ..."

"Not happening." Luc said harshly, and his eyes clearly showed that his patience was running out. If the doctor was to treat me, it would be here and he had to come to terms with that. The doctor sighed resignedly and, while shaking his head, he began to list what he needed. The legionnaire's fingers danced across the keys, so there was no doubt that he was used to text messages with the speed at which he managed to note down the doctor's requirements. With a nod from Luc, he left with the list and there was a brief moment of silence in the barrack.

I made eye contact with Kafka and held out my hand to him. Immediately, he hurried over and took it. Now the play could begin.

"Liam?" I mumbled faintly.

"I do not know where Liam is," Kafka replied, turning his head towards the others, "Who the hell can tell me where Liam is?" he shouted, but no one answered. He looked back at me and smiled.

"He's probably coming soon."

"And JAC?"

"Shh ... Try to relax," he said quietly and although his voice seemed very reassuring to me there was an underlying tone that made me a bit unease.

"We have to take her clothes off." The doctor's voice was neutral but pleasant and, without looking at him, Kafka gave him his hunting knife. The doctor took the knife and cut up my t-shirt, and as it was ripped, several of the legionnaires looked shocked as they saw my torn body. Some of them even turned away completely.

"Hmmm," was the only sound from the doctor, pausing for a moment to look at my torso. Then he opened my pants but when he tried to take them off, I screamed so loud that he stopped immediately. It was clear that he was confused about what to do, but he was saved by Luc.

"Let me." Luc said, coming over and taking the knife out of his hand.

With a few quick cuts he had my pants off and the only thought that went through my mind was that he had definitely done that before. A strange silence descended over the barrack.

"Where is OPUS?" I asked, looking at Kafka.

"Safe," he replied, giving my hand a little squeeze while smiling and winking at me. But even though he tried to disguise it his smile didn't reach his eyes.

The legionnaire came back loaded with equipment and then I was swiftly linked up to a heart monitor, had a drip applied and my heart rate and blood pressure taken.

"No morphine," I whispered to Kafka and he looked up at the doctor.

"No painkillers," he said, turning his head back towards me.

"No painkillers? Why? Is she a masochist?" I don't think it was the doctor's intent to ask the last question out loud but he did and he immediately regretted it.

One of the legionnaires who had been present the night I told them about Belize, went over and grabbed the doctor's neck and pressed him down towards me.

"Look at her," he said in broken English, "Such a person is honoured. Fix her." He let go of the doctor and stepped back.

The sound of a vehicle outside drowned the beep of the heart monitor, and then the door to the barrack was ripped open by Liam. As he came rushing in the sight of me and my abused body made him stop abruptly and it was as if his entire body froze.

"Jesus Christ," he said with a mixture of distrust and surprise in his voice, "You are alive!" I looked at him.

"Barely," I said quietly, grimacing at the rush of pain from my ribs that ran through my body.

"Kafka?" I searched his face and fluttered my eyes a little.

"I'm here," Kafka replied quietly, squeezing my hand again, "I'm not going anywhere. Nowhere."

"I did not say anything to the FSB," I said, "I kept quiet." I nervously swallowed a few times and hoped that Liam would buy into my lie.

"I have no doubt about that. Not at all." Kafka replied smiling but there was something about his smile. It was not genuine.

"Liam?" I was looking at him as he moved quietly towards me, "Aussie is dead," I continued, and it took all my strength to muster a look that would reflect that I was not aware that he already knew.

Liam nodded and without any emotion in his voice asked,

"Who shot him?"

I could have smashed him in the face. To stand there and pretend he didn't already know, because if he really worked with the FSB, then he was complicit in Aussie's death. Or ...? Maybe Liam didn't work for the FSB? Maybe ... Kafka? My eyes flickered between Liam and Kafka. What the fuck was happening? Why was I suddenly having these thoughts? To shake off whatever tricks my mind was playing on me made both of my hands into fists and squeezed them so tight that I could feel my nails almost piercing my palms. I quickly regained my rationality and for safety I went back to our 'script'.

"Jansson did," I replied, trying to read him, but he was expressionless. Then he looked at the doctor.

"Once you have stabilized her, she will be moved into the barrack next door," he said firmly, implying that it was not a topic for debate.

He put his hands on his hips as he turned to Luc.

"Two of my people will come in here and guard her till that happens."

"Hell no. We guard her ourselves. You will get her when she's feeling better and has slept – and that is NOT up for discussion."

Luc's voice thundered and I am sure his eyes flashed, but from where I lay, I could not see them. Liam stood for a moment before leaving the barrack, but less than three seconds later, he burst back in.

"You're in charge of her in here and I'll personally kill you if anything happens to her." Liam snarled, pointing at Luc.

"Piss off." Luc replied and Liam slammed the door so hard behind him that the frame almost broke.

"Idiot." I heard Luc mumble, but then my pain increased again.

The doctor had started cleaning my wounds and it cut through my whole body every time he touched a new place.

"I rarely see something like this," he said seriously, "And I do not understand why you do not want anything for the pain." Silently, he continued to clean my torso from all the clotted and fresh blood that was oozing from my wounds.

"Because I want to know what's going on," I replied lifting my head slightly and scowling at him. He briefly returned my gaze before I laid my head down again.

"Can I get help to turn her over?" the doctor asked and the legionnaire from before stepped in.

"Fuck," the legionnaire exclaimed when he saw my back and his outburst was very understandable. My back was one big bloody mess of stripes of flesh cut open broken blood vessels and veins clearly visible. I could feel the doctor's hands touching my thighs and calf muscles, which bore marks after JAC's treatment of them with both the leather belt and stun gun. After a while the doctor signalled to the legionnaire that he could roll me back. It was a little weird, because at that moment I could not feel any pain from my back and thighs, but it was probably because there are limits to how much pain a person can feel and – as I lay there on the mattress – I had crossed that line long ago.

Now that I was lying on my back again, the doctor continued to examine my legs and my groin and then he asked for a sheet. It came immediately and I was covered from the chest down with it. The doctor wiped his hands on a towel brought along with the rest of the equipment and then he turned around.

"A broken nose, two fractured eyebrows, possibly a broken jaw – I think – two fractured collarbones, an injured left shoulder and shoulder blade that may be fractured – deep cuts on the main torso, broken ribs, damaged back muscles, possible nerve damage and possibly raped." The doctor took a deep breath and looked down at me.

"Possible rape?" I repeated, raising my head slightly, "There was definitely rape!" I shouted at him and at the same time Kafka squeezed my hand.

"He's doing his best, OPUS," he said calmly.

"It's not good enough! Give me your fucking gun!" I shouted at Kafka as I let go of his hand. The doctor took a few steps back.

"Calm down," Kafka countered, smiling, "You can kill him when you feel better. Right now, you need to be bandaged and then rest."

He signalled to the doctor that he should continue and that I did not pose a threat to his life – nor would I ever. But he did not know that. Quietly and obviously on guard for what reaction might come from me, the doctor removed the sheet from my body and continued where he left off cleaning my wounds.

"What the hell happened, Kafka?" Luc asked and it suddenly struck me that it had taken him a long time to ask this question. He should really have asked it when he first saw me and not now when I was in the process of being patched up. I became a little insecure and cursed that I did not have OPUS or my Glock with me.

"Where did you find her?" he continued and luckily, I just managed to see the look in his eyes before my vision was briefly overshadowed by the doctor standing in front of me. Luc seemed sincere and truthful and it made me draw a little sigh of relief. No danger there then.

"It's a long story." Kafka said, and I could hear his voice changing, which in a split second made me very uneasy. However, I did not have to speculate about it for long, because their conversation continued – and more importantly – the doctor moved, so I had a full view of them.

"I have plenty of time," Luc replied, "and she's not going anywhere yet, so ... grab a chair." A legionnaire kicked a chair towards Kafka and he sat down on it with his back to me.

"You better open a bottle of JD and then get Liam. He deserves to hear this."

Luc looked sceptically at Kafka, then signalled to one of the legionnaires that he should bring a bottle of JD.

"What if we start without Liam and then see if it becomes necessary to give him a shout?"

Luc stood in front of Kafka, leaning against a table with his arms folded. It dawned on me that, despite the fact that he could hardly wait to hear what had happened, he was not so sure whether Kafka would tell him the truth.

The legionnaire put a JD bottle next to Luc, but he made no effort to take it.

There was silence in the barrack and only the sounds of the doctor's persistent attempts to wrap me in gauze and my random small outbursts when he hit a sore spot could be heard.

"Before we begin," Kafka said calmly, "I have to know where Wizard is"

"Wizard?" Luc repeated, frowning. "Why? What the hell has he to do with all this?"

"Do you know where he is, Luc?"

Luc was silent and stared at Kafka. It was clear that he was trying to figure out what Kafka was going to use this information for, but he obviously decided to answer so they could move on.

"Yes," he said then.

"Where?"

"He was killed in Kandahar two weeks ago."

"Are you sure?"

"Yes. I'm fucking sure. I was there myself." His voice was annoyed as it was clear that he was beginning to lose his patience. Kafka leaned back on his chair.

"Sorry, Luc. But your word is not good enough. I need something more concrete."

"What the hell do you want? His body? It's going to be difficult. It is spread out over a gorge, but you are welcome to go there yourself and see if you can find the pieces."

I looked intensely at Luc and judging by his facial expression, it appeared that he was telling the truth. Kafka had come to the same conclusion, for he got up and went over to the table.

"Okay," he said then, and I sensed a kind of relief in his voice as he took the bottle of JD and opened it. Luc, who up until now had followed him with his eyes, made no move to drink with him. In fact he just stood there with his arms crossed in front of his broad muscular chest. Kafka took a sip of the JD and then stood for a while looking blankly into the air. Then he took another sip. He and Luc stood so close together that their biceps almost touched, and it seemed quite strange that the mood between them had not improved.

"To answer your last question first, I found her in Islamabad and it is JAC who has done that to her." He nodded towards me.

I was stunned. Had I heard correctly? What the hell was he saying? Was he about to expose us? Had he gone insane?

"JAC?" Luc was very surprised, "JAC has tortured OPUS? I don't believe it. He would never dare to touch her. Liam would kill him."

"Why would he? Because OPUS is Liam's?" Kafka snorted and took another sip of the JD, "Wake up Luc. OPUS has never been Liam's. It has been JAC all along."

Luc looked at him sceptically. Then he looked over at me and back at Kafka.

"You're full of shit," he said harshly, walking out into the middle of the floor so he stood between Kafka and the bed where I was lying. "But let's say you're right, so what's that?" He looked over at me, "The result of a lover's quarrel?" He snorted and pulled a face, "It's absurd ... can't you hear yourself? That there, Kafka, in case you should be so fucked up and have forgotten ... that is torture and not just a little chatter to the bitch because she does not want to suck his dick. And even though JAC is on smack and therefore can be totally erratic, that ..." Luc pointed to me, "is planned and systematic torture and not a random act. It was done for a purpose." He turned towards Kafka, "So you have to come up with something better."

I was speechless. Fuck all that shit that Luc had said ... it did not matter, but Kafka had to be stopped. He could cost me my life. And what about the plan? And Liam? And JAC? Did Mossad know this? Was there an alternative plan that included me and JAC being disposed of? What the hell was going on? No matter what, Kafka had to be stopped before he told Luc anything else.

Kafka looked calmly at Luc and took another sip from the bottle. "That has been done on purpose." He pointed at me with the bottle, "And under full control and in front of a crowd of thirty people from Mossad."

Luc turned and with his eyes wide open he stared at me. Then with quiet, calm steps he walked over and looked me up and down and there was no doubt that he did not know what to believe. Actually, I could not blame him, because if I had been in his place, I would have felt the same way, because yes ... it was an incredible story. The doctor was putting the finishing touches to the bandages and for an instant Luc and I made eye contact.

"He's lying," I whispered very quietly to Luc, "Do not trust him. Get Liam."

Luc looked away for a moment, but then he leaned over me and looked me directly in the eyes again. I nodded very weakly and slowly he stood up.

"You can go," he said to the doctor as he nodded towards the door and without any objection the doctor disappeared out of the barrack. Luc looked over at a legionnaire standing a few metres away.

"Get her some clothes," he commanded, and the legionnaire went and found a t-shirt and a pair of trousers. Luc held out his hand to me and I took it and he pulled me up to a sitting position. It hurt my entire body, and it did not get any better when the legionnaire helped me to get dressed. As I sat on the edge of the bed with the pain chasing around my whole body, I tried to gather my thoughts. Every time I tried to move it felt as if I was being stabbed from all sides and it made me scream.

"Give her a shot of morphine," Luc said to the legionnaire.

"No," I shouted, "No, Luc," I repeated somewhat calmer, "Please, Luc. Don't. Please."

Luc looked up at the ceiling and took a deep breath. Then he looked at the legionnaire who had returned with an ampoule of morphine and a syringe.

"She only needs to be pain free so don't knock her out," he said, and the legionnaire drained morphine from the ampoule, looked at the syringe, flicked it, and sprayed some of the morphine out. Then he took my arm and, despite the fact that I was trying to resist, he held on tight and gave me the injection. I bent my arm and Luc looked at me. His face was so serious and then suddenly he turned towards Kafka.

"Where's JAC?" he asked.

"He's on his way from Islamabad, but don't worry ..." Kafka smiled crookedly and raised the bottle to his mouth, "He's not going to make it to here."

A smile spread across his lips before he took another sip from the bottle.

"And all this, dear Luc, is in honour of Liam." Kafka lifted the bottle as a salute.

But no one said anything.

My inner rage was at boiling point for never had I felt such a betrayal. Kafka had sold us out. I did not know why, and his morals and ethics for doing so, shook me. He had used us. Used me. He had literally stripped me bare and made me vulnerable. But that was not the worst because in Belize they did the same to me. But this time I had trusted him and in such a way that I had let my guard down and thereby let go of my control. I needed to take it back and I needed to do it right now.

"Get Liam." Luc said coldly and the legionnaire standing by the door left.

I looked over at Kafka, who was staring emotionlessly at me. What the hell was he up to? Where was our friendship? Had he forgotten all that we had been through? Was he so selfish that ...?

Luc stood a few metres away with his back to me and I could see his Glock in the back of his waistband. I looked down at my knees and ached. Luckily the pain was disappearing now that the morphine was kicking in and that was when I, out of the corner of my eye, noticed Kafka's hunting knife. It lay on the bed, a few centimetres away, hidden by a towel that the doctor had used to clean my wounds. Luc continued to stand with his back to me, but had put his hands on his hips, giving me exactly the chance I needed, as Kafka's view of me was limited.

After that, everything was a blur. I grabbed the knife and threw it at Kafka. Then I jumped up and tore the Glock from Luc's waistband and aimed at Kafka. And that is when I saw that the knife I had thrown was embedded deeply in Kafka's left side just below his ribs. All legionnaires in the barrack – except Kafka and Luc – had drawn their weapons and aimed at me, but it didn't surprise me. I had already calculated that they would but I did not consider them a threat to me. Kafka was still standing with the bottle in his hand, looking down at the knife and there was no doubt that he was totally surprised.

"I have no quarrel with you – only with Kafka, so lower your weapons," I said to the legionnaires as I stepped forward to stand next to Luc. I could feel him looking at me, but my eyes did not waver from Kafka.

The barrack was quiet, and somehow it fitted Kafka's expression of astonishment.

Then the door opened and a legionnaire and Liam entered. The legionnaire immediately drew his gun and Liam stopped abruptly at the sight of all the weapons drawn. Nobody said anything.

"Luc?" I said calmly, "Will you order your men to lower their weapons?"

"No," he replied firmly and his answer did not really surprise me. I would not have accepted such an order either.

"Suit yourself," I said unemotionally and then I walked slowly towards Kafka, whispering, "You fucking coward," to him. As we stood face to face, I could see that he had opened his mouth a little and gasped for breath. There was no doubt that the knife had punctured his left lung, which I had intended, and we both knew it was only a matter of time before it collapsed. I reached behind his back and took Aussie's Glock from his waistband. Then I threw it to Liam, who caught it.

"Here you go," I said, "It's Aussie's."

Out of the corner of my eye I could see that he was looking at it and then he walked quickly towards us. For a brief moment I was unsure of his next move, but I was relieved when he released the safety on his own Glock and held the gun against the back of Kafka's head.

"Talk," he said coldly to Kafka.

"You should aim at her. She's here to kill you." Kafka gasped in a faint quavering voice.

Liam did not move his stiff and cold eyes from Kafka, and strangely enough he seemed completely unaffected by the information he had just received.

"Carry him down to the infirmary," it came from Luc, "We will not get any answers if he dies."

There was a short pause where no one said anything. Deep down, we all knew that if Kafka did not get some sort of medical treatment soon, then his lung would collapse and he would bleed to death, so Luc was right when he ordered Kafka away.

While a couple of the legionnaires grabbed Kafka and dragged him out the door, Liam secured his Glock and put it in his waistband. His gesture automatically made me lower mine and as if my pain had been holding its breath while all this happened it was now back – and tenfold.

"Give me my fucking gun." Luc whispered, taking it out of my hand with such ferocity that I was actually quite surprised. When Luc put his gun behind his back again, I noticed that the legionnaires were slowly lowering their weapons and securing them. Liam shook his head.

"Do you call this having things under control?" Liam's comment was aimed at Luc, and somehow it was very understandable, because if there was anything this situation had not been, it was under Luc's control.

"How the hell can this happen? She is totally shattered and yet she manages to seriously hurt Kafka, and she could have shot you at any time."

Liam started walking around in small circles, scratching his head, but suddenly he stormed over to Luc.

"Are you fucking insane?" he screamed into Luc's face and then he turned to me.

"And you ... you have obviously recovered enough to be able to kill people, so you are coming with me." With a lightning-fast motion, he grabbed my upper arm and pushed me out of the barrack. I screamed in pain, but he took no notice of it. Instead, he pulled me by my broken shoulder through the door to our old barrack. He threw me onto the floor in front of the four IRA soldiers who all sat on their respective beds. My somewhat unusual entrance made them all look at me, but they did not do more than that.

"Guys, meet OPUS." Liam said dryly, at which point in stark contrast to his previously violent treatment of me, he calmly walked over and poured a cup of coffee. I crawled over to one of the beds and used it as a support to get up. Then I turned around. I had to have Liam in my field of vision so I could be just a little prepared for what he would do, but I did not have to look far. He stood right behind me, holding out the steaming cup of coffee to me. I looked at him, looked at it and looked back at him.

"Here you go. Take it," he said softly and in a voice that at any other time would have been interpreted as being kind. In this situation, however, it made me so very uneasy, for who the hell offers his executioner coffee? Even though the executioner is as badly wounded as me and therefore not an immediate threat. Although every idiot knows that even a wounded merc is a threat, so ...

"I know you like it," he said a little sarcastically referring to the coffee.

I took the cup and while standing with it in my hand, Liam walked over and sat down at the table. With a gallant gesture of his hand he offered me the chair in front of him and despite the fact that I did not really have a great desire to sit so close to him, I did not feel that I had any choice. With slow and gentle steps, as if I were a cat approaching its prey, I went over and sat down in front of him, still with my steaming cup of coffee in my hand. Liam sat relaxed with slightly spread legs and scowled at me while I took a sip of the coffee.

"Have you come to kill me?" he then asked with an astonishingly calm voice that almost frightened me. His eyes were hard but not cold, as when he was about to press the trigger, but as always this could change rapidly.

"Yes," I replied, putting the cup down.

He raised his eyebrows, smiled crookedly and nodded a little.

"Okay. May I know why?"

"The truth is, right now I have no idea why."

"Since when do you need a reason to kill?" We looked at each other and actually he was so right. When exactly was it that I had become so morally and ethically correct that I let my conscience play into why I killed a person?

And the only answer I could give was:

"Since I killed a civilian woman and cut her unborn baby from her womb."

Liam looked down at the table top and bit his lower lip a little. Then he leaned forward on the chair and stared directly into my eyes.

"How far should I go? Should I kill you? Should I extradite you to the FSB? Or to Mossad, perhaps? Tell me ... how far do I have to go, OPUS?" he asked in an almost whispering voice.

His gaze and voice were so emotionally cold that I do not remember ever witnessing it in others. For the first time I had no doubt as to what Kafka had meant when he had said that Liam killed because he could. What Kafka had forgotten to say was that Liam could beat whoever preferably to death – and his gaze and voice revealed that it also applied to the people he loved – for he had no honour, no stop button, no sense of what was right or wrong. Liam was a product of cynicism and vengeance, and recognizing this I began to shake.

"You decide. I have no control any more. I am so tired." He sat for a while looking at me.

"You have control. You even have full control. What you did in there ..." He alluded to the scene in Luc's barrack "it could only be done by one in control. The only reason you did not kill Kafka was because you lacked an answer – otherwise you would have blown his brains out." Liam got up and walked around a bit. "Do you realize how incredibly stupid it is of you to come back here? We all thought ... everyone ... CIA, FSB and MI6 that you were dead. Christ ... We thought you had been captured, tortured and burned to death by local rebels here in Afghanistan. You were home free. Nobody was looking for you. No-one. Why come back? Why?"

"Because Mossad knew I was alive and as long as they knew it, the whole idea of disappearing didn't matter."

"How did they know?"

"They paid for my operations in the US and there they had a tracking chip implanted in me. They have been able to follow me for years. Kafka also has one. They know where we are right now."

"And you thought you could 'buy yourself free' by making a deal with them?" He shook his head, "You never make deals with agencies that include words like freedom. No one will ever let you go. You damn well know that."

Deep down, I knew he was right. It had been naive of me to believe that I would ever be free, but truthfully, it was never really the ultimate freedom that I had sought – that is, the freedom to be able to disappear and never reappear. Because I liked what I was doing. It was just a job that I was good at, and to me, it was not inhuman. On one level or another, I loved the inner validation that it gave me – to be successful. I was well aware that I was hated by all those who had lost a person to my telescopic sight, but it didn't really matter that much. My endless indifference prevented me from taking an interest in it.

The freedom I wanted was the freedom over my own life. To not be a pawn in anyone's game. To just do my job and then disappear. That was what I wanted, and I would have had it if all this had not happened and if Mossad had not 'chipped' me. Liam interrupted my train of thought.

"Go to bed," he said suddenly, and I had a hard time hiding my amazement at his words, which he could clearly see, "Don't worry, I'll not kill you." He put his hands in his pockets and snorted.

"Liam, I know JAC did shit when he took the isotope," I said.

"The isotope?" Liam stopped and turned towards me.

"The isotope, but ..."

"But what?" Liam's smile was gone and he had become very serious again.

"He may be being slaughtered right now."

"And?"

"Let me help him. At best, we both come back here and then you have us both. In the worst case, you will get rid of us permanently."

"You have to stop. Do you want me to help JAC, who stole from me and nearly cost me my life? Fuck JAC. He has to fend for himself."

"You are not going to help him. I am."

"You?" He raised his eyebrows, "You are not gonna last a minute out there."

"Yes, if you pump me with morphine and give me a car."

"You ... you're insane."

"Liam ... I'm not leaving him alone. He came after me, even though you thought I was dead. You did not even want to confirm when I sent you the co-ordinates from Aussie's phone."

"I did not believe it was you."

"You never gave me the benefit of the doubt. You wrote me off too quickly. I will not do that with JAC. Let me go, Liam."

Liam put his hands on his hips and looked up at the ceiling. He thought for a minute and in my mind, I hoped he would let me go. It was unrealistic, but I could not just let JAC drive directly into Kafka's orchestrated ambush without ...

"I can't," he then said, looking at me, "Go to bed ... and make sure she stays here," he commanded, looking around at the IRA soldiers before turning around and disappearing from the barrack.

I sat for a while looking with empty eyes into the air. Deep down, I knew he was right. I was by no means physically able to help JAC, and in a mixture of rage and powerlessness, I threw the coffee cup in the direction of the barrack door. When it hit the edge of the door, it smashed into a thousand pieces. I got up and went over and sat down on one of the beds. I could not leave JAC in the lurch, but at the moment. I had no choice. I could not help him – no matter how much I wanted to.

"Fuck it," I said loudly and lay down on the bed. This was shit. Kafka had sold us – why, I was far from sure, but maybe he had made a deal with the FSB, maybe with Mossad, maybe with Liam. He had at least got JAC out of the way and maybe he had hoped that Liam would do the same with me.

Why Liam chose not to do so was actually a mystery to me. If I had been Liam, I would have killed me without hesitation. He would not get a better chance. Wounded and unarmed – that was what I was. On the other hand – if he changed his mind, I was lying right here waiting for him to execute the sentence. Somehow I had to get out of the barrack and down to the infirmary. Kafka had to be eliminated as soon as possible. Why the hell had I not shot him in Luc's barrack? It was completely incomprehensible to me now. I got up from the bed and one of the soldiers straightened up on his chair.

"Calm down," I said, raising one hand, "I'm just going to the bathroom." He relaxed again and I walked with slow steps down through the barrack and out to the toilet.

Had this been in Luc's barrack, there would have been weapons and ammunition on the beds, but here everything was almost clinically ordered. Not so much as a bullet case anywhere. I took my time in the toilet because I needed to think. On my return Liam was standing at the small kitchen counter and the four soldiers were sitting at the dining table eating.

"Are you hungry?" he asked with his back to me. I went with small short steps up to him, for my pains did not allow me to walk any faster.

"Yes," I replied, at which he pushed his plate of food over to me. It was half full of rice and some kind of stew.

"Thank you," I whispered as he chewed.

"Tell me if you need more painkillers." If I did not know better, I would have sworn I could sense a little care in his voice, but it seemed so absurd that there should be. On the other hand – this whole situation was absurd, so ...

"I'm okay, right now," I replied, eating the food very carefully. My jaw was damaged, so I could hardly chew, but luckily the food was sufficiently soft that I was able to eat some.

"Where the hell have you been the last month?" Liam asked looking at me.

"In Afghanistan and Pakistan. The first two weeks I only remember in fragments. The last couple of weeks ..."

I was doubtful what I should say. That they had been lovely? That I had been with JAC and Kafka and for the first time in years had felt safe, so safe that I did not constantly walk around with the Glock? I was silent and the long pause that followed seemed strange.

"Is it true that it was JAC who tortured you?"

"Yes." I swallowed a little more of the food and took another mouthful. There was no reason to lie now.

Liam stood with arms folded, looking down at the four soldiers.

"He has been thorough. Was it voluntary or ...?"

"Voluntary." I knew it sounded crazy, but it was the truth, and in a few hours Kafka would confirm it, so ...

Liam went over and took his jacket and walked towards the door, but stopped abruptly when he reached it turning towards me.

"Do you even know what this is all about?" His voice was patronizing and annoying, and no matter how much I wanted to hear his side of the story, I just could not bear it right now.

"Among other things. a metal box with an isotope," I replied, looking coldly at him.

"No," he said, walking back towards me, "It's about stability. And nothing else. Everyone wants stability and I am just one of many who deliver it in the best possible way and with the least possible risk – no matter how fragile it is. And whether the stability costs a few casualties or thousands, it doesn't matter as long as in the end it is upheld."

"You tell yourself that but this has nothing to do with stability. You are nothing but a tool – just like the rest of us. You are set a task to complete, and your terms are the same as ours, namely, to accomplish the mission and return to get the next one. You don't give a shit about who or what you're doing this for. I thought you were an idealist, and I could understand that to some degree – maybe even have respect for it – but no. Your ideology is drowning in political statements and paragraphs. Your fight is dead and instead of accepting it, you are contributing to the struggles of others to justify that your own failed crusade has come to an end. You're a hypocrite, Liam. A hypocrite with a metal box full of mass death and that ... that makes you dangerous."

Liam smiled before he took a few steps forward and said quietly, calmly and eerily.

"It takes one to know one." His smile was stiff and almost porcelain-like, and as he walked out of the barrack, I earnestly wished he would take me with him. Maybe he really had found a promised land somewhere out there. If so, that was a hell of a lot more than I had. And who would not want that?

Chapter 22

The evening progressed and so did my pain, so much so that against my will I had to resort to more morphine. However I was not the only one in the barrack who had to compromise, because after some persuasion I managed to get Liam to agree to having the legionnaire from Luc's barrack who had given me morphine last time to give it to me again – under his supervision, of course. He could probably have administered it himself, but I felt more confidence in the legionnaire, so luckily it turned out that way.

I had been in the camp for eight hours, living precariously from hour to hour. Apparently, Kafka had been on the operating table twice and was unable to talk, which had bought me some time and since Liam was hardly ever in the barrack, no great danger there either. I had no idea where he was, and finding him would be impossible because of my physical condition and my prison guards. There were constantly two soldiers near me and at Liam's order they had to make sure I did not leave the barrack.

It was past midnight and everything was quiet when Liam suddenly burst into the barrack with his laptop under one arm. We had all gone to bed except one of the soldiers who was sitting at the table eating an apple but Liam's entrance made us all react and he immediately had our full attention.

"We're leaving camp at five a.m. and not returning, so pack everything." He did not look at any of us as he said it but went straight to the table and laid the laptop on it. The soldier who was already sitting there calmly finished his apple, while the others just as quietly began getting up. I sat on the edge of the bed fully clothed, because I had not been able to undress when I lay down – it had simply required too much effort.

My attention was on Liam who by now had opened his laptop and stood bent over it with his eyes glued to the screen in his usual focused and deeply concentrated way. One of the soldiers put some big bags on the bed next to mine and in a matter of seconds, the other three had placed bags on their mattresses as well. All of the bags were unzipped and ready to be filled. As on count, they began to flip the mattresses on the other beds near to them which revealed a whole arsenal of weapons and equipment hidden underneath them. There was something mechanical in the way they slid different items from under the metal bed frames and filled the bags – a place for everything and everything in its place. Once a bag was full, it was zipped and set down on the floor, and with the speed and efficiency at which they worked, they would be finished in ten minutes, I guessed.

I was speechless, to say the least, because there was enough weaponry to start a minor war. Not only was there ammunition, handguns and grenades, but under almost all the beds were large black metal boxes, which were just lifted up on the beds without being subsequently opened. I guessed they contained weapons like mortar shells and rocket equipment, but in principle there could have been any explosive charges in them. One of the boxes was marked with a biohazard sign and when it was pulled out, Liam said that he would take care of that and then no one touched it.

I bent down and started putting on my boots but stopped when I heard Liam say calmly and coldly ...

"Not you, you're not going anywhere."

I froze and my heart started pounding. It was as if my whole body was on alert and without getting up, I looked over at him, but he was still standing with his eyes fixed on the screen and typing on the keyboard. I released the laces and slowly straightened up. It was as if my brain was split in two. One part desperately wanted to fight for my life, while the other part was resigned to the situation and ready to face its finale: This inner struggle between wanting to fight or accepting my fate which, to my surprise, created an emptiness within me.

"May I ask you to do it?" I said with a relaxed tone of voice that in no way advertised the chaos that reigned within me. Liam did not answer but, no doubt, he had heard what I had said.

I wanted to jump up and scream 'Then do it and let's get it over with', but I resisted because my survival instincts were winning. For every second was a second alive. Everything suddenly became very present, and I could hear, see and feel with an intensity that I had only experienced a few times before – at my first kill and when I had been thrown into the ditch in Belize. My body and my mind were hypersensitive and I was approaching a state of euphoria. It was so fucking weird and grotesque, and at the same time so fucking amazing. Liam suddenly closed the laptop and took out the USB key. As always, he put it in his left breast pocket and then he put his phone in his back pocket. Without looking at me, he pulled his Glock from his waistband and unsecured it. Calmly he walked around the table and, as he approached me, his eyes locked onto mine. While my inner self screamed 'Stop, let me live', my logical sense knew that this was not what was going to happen. And right there in that second I envied all my marks. None of them had known when the bullet – and thus their end – would come. They had been able to be relatively indifferent and continue their lives carefree until everything ended abruptly and without warning. Not this wait for the inevitable.

Liam was now standing in front of me and his gaze was that of a real killer – cold, stiff and without empathy.

"Because it's you, you can decide how you want it done," he said, and it occurred to me that he was giving me a choice. It was something I had never considered – how I wanted to be eliminated. Probably because I had never even given my marks the choice, so why should anyone give me one? Somehow I always knew I would die 'at work' which you have to accept when you are in this type of job, but like this? – No, it had never been one of the scenarios.

Slowly and deliberately I got up so we stood quite close together and for a moment we just looked into each other's eyes. Neither one of us blinked or averted our gaze, which just made the situation even more definitive.

"One frontal and three chest shots," I said whispering, but in my ears, it seemed as if I was shouting the words. Liam took a step back and raised his gun, "May I ask something of you, Liam?" His eyes were icy cold and without feeling, as he waited to shoot, which meant he was willing to hear what I had to say. "When you have shot me, stay with me a little while and speak quietly to me. It is said that the hearing is the last thing that disappears."

I had no idea if he had heard what I had asked and I could not read anything emotional in his face but I hoped he would grant me my final wish so I closed my eyes. I focused on my heartbeat because maybe it was the next beat that would be the last. Or maybe the one after? I began to breathe deeply and a wave of gratitude for every breath I managed to experience washed over me. In fact, the beats were amazingly calm which considering the situation was unreal.

There was a shot and my face felt wet but I did not fall. My heart stood still for a brief moment, but then it was as if it was jumpstarted by the thud that followed. I opened my eyes and there approximately five metres in front of me, stood Wizard with raised Beretta. Luc was standing just behind him inside the door with a couple of his legionnaires who were keeping the IRA soldiers covered. I looked down at the floor and there in front of me lay Liam – killed by Wizard.

What were the odds for what had just happened? I should have been dead, and a man I thought was dead was the one who had saved me. To think that it would be Wizard who would be the one to give me a 'second chance'.

I looked at him and then down at Liam. For a few moments I was stunned but then I stepped over his body to get to Wizard. The corners of his mouth indicated a little smile, but you had to get very close to see the twitches. I don't know what I had expected but when I stood in front of him he just handed me a Glock.

"Okay?" he asked, and for once I was speechless, for what to say when someone has just brought you back from the dead? Thank you? No that seems inadequate.

"Yes," I said, as I took the Glock and put it in my waist band, "Fuck, am I glad to see you," I continued quietly as a smile that reflected real relief spread across my face.

Luc stepped forward and signalled to the IRA soldiers to put their hands behind their heads, after which the two legionnaires searched them for weapons and then escorted them out of the barrack, quietly and efficiently. Out of sheer gratitude for still being alive, I wrapped my arms around Wizard and gave him a big hug, and no doubt it took him by surprise. He did hug me back though it took him a few seconds to do so.

"I thought you were dead," Wizard whispered in my ear, "Had I known you were still alive, then ..."

I could feel him squeezing me extra hard and it made the pain from my broken ribs reappear. I must have given a gasp of pain, for he immediately let go of me.

"I know, Wizard. I know," I said, coughing a little.

"What the hell is all this?" The words came from Luc, who had opened one of the metal boxes on the beds. With a mortar shell in one hand, he turned to us. Wizard and I looked at him.

"I do not know," I replied, "but Liam had arranged a transport out of the camp at five a.m. today. They were packing up and not planning on returning."

* * *

Wizard went across to Luc and they both stood discussing what to do. I turned and looked at Liam's dead body. Then I squatted next to it. The floor under his head was red with blood, and a strange peace rested upon him, which made his face look quite mild and calm. I stroked a couple of strands of his dark hair to one side and then I whispered to him:

"Sorry. I know if you were here, you would say it was part of the game, but it should never have got this far. If I find your promised land, I will take good care of it. See you – sooner or later."

I closed his eyes, took one dog tag from his chain around his neck and kissed him. It seemed so right to do and yet so wrong. He would have been my executioner, but he was also the person with whom I had the most similarities and for whom I, after all, had a great deal of respect. He had been a front-runner all his life – and not just ideologically. As one of the few, he had enrolled in Irish history's darkest war chapters and he had – at least according to rumours – been a beacon for many soldiers and civilians, showing the way in an otherwise very foggy conflict – although the fog was primarily created by smoke from assassinations, car bombs and bombed buildings. Whether he was a legend, I do not know, but the shot Wizard had put in Liam's head would at least mark the end of an era for many Irishmen, certainly, when they discovered he was dead.

I took the USB key and remote control to the detonation of the barrack out of his chest pocket. Then I removed his cell phone from his back pocket and put all three things in my own pocket along with the dog tag and then I got up and went over to Wizard and Luc, who, after opening several of the metal boxes, had become louder in their discussion of the contents.

"What the hell are we doing about all this?" Luc scratched his cropped scalp.

"Blow the shit up," I replied patting them both on their shoulders. We all three stood for a while and looked at the collection of hand grenades, missile heads, C4, mortar shells, landmines and various kinds of ammunition, which lay neatly in rows in the individual black boxes.

"It's damn dangerous," Luc replied, "The whole camp could go up in smoke."

"That was not what I meant," I said. Luc looked at me, but my gaze was still on the arsenal of war. "We remove all this and then we blow up the barrack."

"Do you know where the transport was going?" I could feel that there was something much deeper underlying Wizard's question than just a general interest.

"No," I replied, "but we have three hours before it arrives."

"We're checking out at six a.m. this morning," Luc said suddenly and I looked at him. "We have been given a new mission and will not return either."

There was complete silence in the barrack, but had our thoughts been audible, there would have been a hell of a noise. Wizard suddenly took a deep breath, breaking the silence.

"Okay, here's a plan. We get a truck and then we load all the shit on it, blow up the barrack and disappear. We blow the barrack up at five past five, so make sure everyone is out."

The last message was addressed to Luc with regard to his team.

It was a plan and the only one we had, so Wizard left to commandeer a truck while Luc went to organize his legionnaires and I ... yes, I went to the infirmary to tie up a loose end!

* * *

As I could feel the pain from my shoulder and my broken ribs, I used it as an excuse to gain access to the tent. So while the nurse was fetching some morphine for me, I located Kafka and quietly sneaked to his bed. On the way, I released the Glock's safety and, as I stood there by Kafka's bed, it was clear that he was not conscious.

I leaned over the bed and put the gun to his heart. It really shouldn't be so hard especially not considering he would make no resistance and I had eliminated hundreds of marks before but this was different. We had a story together and ... it just did not feel right. Even though he had sold me and JAC, this felt wrong. I removed the gun and stood and looked at him. Then, I noticed that the nurse was hurrying towards me.

"You shouldn't be here," she said desperately and a little agitated, but she didn't have to worry. The danger had passed, "You must come with me – now."

I looked at her and sent her a wry smile.

"Do not worry. He's still breathing," I said, taking the morphine from her. I was hurting, but I was not in so much pain that I needed it. If nothing else, I could always give it to Wizard. He would probably appreciate it. Quietly I left the infirmary again.

Outside in the cool night I took a deep breath. The wind took hold of my hair and reminded me that it was time to go back, but then it hit me. What the hell was wrong with me? It was the second time I failed to kill Kafka.

"Fuck it," I said loudly as I turned to walk back into the infirmary to finish him off, but the headlights from Wizard's truck hit me and, like a deer caught in a car's light cone, I stopped. He braked so a dust cloud surrounded the truck, and I dropped my venture with Kafka and jumped in. Fortunately Wizard did not ask if I had done the job. I guess he just assumed. And why would he not? I did not usually hesitate so ...

Without exchanging a single word, we parked in front of Liam's barrack. Wizard jumped out but as it took me a bit longer to get out of the truck, the legionnaires were already loading boxes and bags before my boots touched the desert sand. I went into the barrack and saw Luc standing with the box with the biohazard sign.

"Put it in the cab," I said resolutely, because even though I had no idea what it contained, it was probably not confetti. But it had to wait until later. Luc was going to say something but I had already passed him. I needed to find the box with the isotope. Neither Luc nor any of his legionnaires had seen it so, with a little luck, one of the four IRA soldiers that Luc had led into his barrack would know where it was.

So, I went to find Wizard.

No matter how much I wanted to, I had already reconciled that I was physically unable to interrogate anyone. My shoulder and my ribs hurt insanely, and that combined with the pain from my jaw and my fractured collarbones made me need Wizard to do my dirty work. I found him out by the truck loading it and it did not take many words to persuade him to come with me.

As I had never been to one of Wizard's interrogations before I decided to stay and as expected his interrogation methods proved to be quite effective. When we entered Luc's barrack, the first sight that caught our attention was the four fully clothed IRA soldiers sitting in a row on the bare floor. They had zip ties on their hands and feet, but were not gagged. Wizard started the interrogation by going straight to the nearest one and punching him in the face so his nose broke. Well ...that was certainly a way to start, I thought as he moved to the next one and beat him unconscious. When Wizard made eye contact with the third soldier, there was no doubt the guy was more than willing to talk. He spoke rather quickly and feverishly, hoping to avoid a further escalation of Wizard's violence but unfortunately for the soldier his rambling could not help us. The only thing he knew about the metal box was that Liam had taken it out of the barrack the day before and it had not been seen since. Soldier number four confirmed this, but despite that, Wizard knocked him out.

There was not much help either to be had when it came to finding out where and to whom the weapons were intended to go as Liam had chosen to keep this knowledge to himself. I had expected that, but it just made our work a lot more difficult. I knew the USB key, that was in my pocket, was likely contain all the information we were looking for, but I also knew that it would be lost the moment I plugged it into a PC.

That information could only be retrieved by an expert, so it had to wait.

I walked out of the barrack while Wizard stayed. Why, I did not really want to know, but judging by his dissatisfied expression I think he intended to 'force' other information out of Liam's soldiers. Basically, I did not care what he did. If he became really aggressive, then the legionnaires were there to stop him.

Outside the other legionnaires had finished loading the truck and they were now standing in small groups talking and smoking. I went into Liam's barrack and found Luc standing by Liam's body. Crouching with his back to me, was a figure and the sight of it, made me freeze. The figure turned his head and – it was JAC – without so much as a scratch.

"Hey, are you okay?" he said smiling.

"Am I okay? I thought you were dead."

I could hear my voice trembling, but it was simply with joy to see him alive. Somehow, I had thought I was going to find him lying shot on the road between Islamabad and Kabul, so to see him here was an immense relief.

Without much haste he got up and walked to me. As we stood directly opposite each other, he put a few fingers under my chin and, while smiling, he lifted it slowly so that my head tilted slightly backwards.

"You do not get rid of me so easily," he said quietly, winking at me. Then he kissed me.

"But ..."

"Where's Kafka?" His voice remained the same but the smile had disappeared as did his fingers from under my chin, "Did you kill him?" I shook my head, "Good," he replied, "Mossad wants him back. I was seriously afraid that you would have killed him when you found out that he had 'sold' me to the FSB."

"I almost did. How did you know he was going to have you killed?" And I was so confused. Had JAC known that Kafka was working for the FSB?

"After you left Islamabad, I had a chat with Jacoby. They had suspected Kafka of collaborating with the FSB and their intelligence pointed to the both of us getting killed ..." He looked over at Liam's body "because the FSB needed Liam."

"Do you think Liam knew that?"

As my question hung there in the air, it seemed irrelevant, for Liam was a contractor and thus did not care who he worked for – or almost did not care. JAC nodded at the same time as a 'Yes' came from his lips.

"Where's Kafka?" he asked.

"At the infirmary."

JAC smiled a little crookedly.

"We'll take him with us when we leave."

JAC leaned towards me and grabbed my neck so that his mouth was close to my ear. "Do you have the chip – the one from Mossad?"

"No, it's in one of Kafka's boots – at the infirmary. I have not been able to get it. JAC, I simply do not think Kafka worked for the FSB. If he did, then he could have killed us much earlier. After all, we just spent a month with him in Islamabad."

"Kafka probably had a double contract on you and Wizard." JAC said calmly.

"But Kafka believed that Wizard died in Kandahar and especially after Luc confirmed it." There was a pause, "And therefore he sold me. I was the only one left, and when I was gone, he had fulfilled the contract."

I looked at JAC. It made sense and still I doubted.

JAC smiled at me but then let go and turned to Luc.

"We're going to make a deal, Luc."

There was a snort from Luc.

"No deal, JAC."

"Shut the fuck up, Luc." JAC turned to him.

"You get the weapons – we get the box in the cab." Luc looked sceptically at JAC.

"You know there's a small fortune here, don't you?" he said but JAC just smiled and nodded.

"Yes, but we're not interested in the weapons, only the box and I know you can 'move' them quickly." He nodded at the weapon boxes.

"With Wizard's help, yes ... they can disappear ASAP."

JAC stared at us.

"Wizard? Is he here?"

"Yes," I replied, "He's at Luc's."

JAC smiled as he turned towards the door and was just about to leave when I grabbed his upper arm and our eyes meet briefly.

"He shot Liam." The smile did not waver on JAC's face and just as suddenly as I had grabbed his upper arm, I released it and he left the barrack without commenting.

For a moment, Luc and I stood looking at each other. Then Luc glanced at his watch.

"Seventy-five minutes to go," he said coolly and walked to the door.

"Luc?" He turned towards me looking slightly irritated, "Thank you, for your ..." I smiled briefly and corrected myself, "for all your help. You did not have to step in."

"I know. Whatever they say about us legionnaires, we work from the concept of honour and we ... my team ... have great respect for you ... and when they ... we ... saw you today we could not stand by and just watch."

I went to him and said in a low voice, almost whispering:

"There are very few people I would ever say this to, but if there comes a time when I can be of any help to you, let me know. But the offer stands for you, and only you. Nobody else."

I was very serious when I said it and Luc was well aware that I had just given him a voucher, which in our industry is extremely rare. One should not owe anything to anyone, because it could lead to mistrust, strife and unnecessary murder, but in this case, it was the only thing I could offer him to show my appreciation. The only thing that had a real value to me and that showed him how grateful I was. Luc nodded quietly and words were unnecessary. We both walked out of the barrack just in time to see Wizard coming out of the other barrack briskly followed by JAC. Wizard was furious and he was cursing loudly in his native Croatian. To vent his frustrations, he suddenly slammed a clenched fist into the truck's front wing denting it.

"What the hell is wrong?" I asked, because we simply did not have time for Wizard and JAC getting in each other's face right now.

"How the hell was I supposed to know ..." Wizard pointed to the barrack, "that they are Black Water? Fuck." As he kept cursing, this time in English, he dropped his hands to his sides and turned around so he had his back to us.

"What the hell? Are they ...?" Luc frowned so hard that the wrinkles on his forehead made him look like an angry ram just before it attacks. JAC nodded.

"They are Black Water." He raised his eyebrows indicating the truth in his words, and it immediately triggered a deep breath from Luc, which could be confused with a huge sigh. Black Water was an American Company that was known for their mercenaries and rumours had it that they were quite good.

"That's it," he said turning to the legionnaires still standing by the truck, "We're moving out now." And without further explanation on his part, the legionnaires immediately disappeared into their barrack to inform their team mates and retrieve their belongings. Luc looked at JAC.

"This is your mess. You fix this," he said pointing at him, "I do not have and do not want any trouble with Black Water. This is on your shoulders." He looked briefly at us and then he went into his barrack.

"Are they alive?" I asked in a low voice.

"Yes, but only just."

"How the hell do you know they're Black Water?"

"I've worked with two of them in Iraq and they are okay, but what the hell they are doing with Liam ...?"

"Maybe he hired them to complete his task? Whatever that might have been."

* * *

The idea was legitimate enough, but the scenario was wrong. Black Water would NEVER co-operate with the FSB, but on the other hand, this was, after all, the perfect setup for them if they wanted to get into that market. Liam was the middleman and Black Water would only indirectly have had something to do with the FSB – if things went wrong. And if it went well, then they would be able to credit the success to themselves and thereby ... I don't know. I had always perceived Black Water as one of the more legitimate private companies in the business so for them to get involved in FSB! But what the hell? I did not see Kafka selling us out either so I guess everything was possible. I looked at all the weapons and decided to change the subject.

"Are we convinced that all this is for the FSB? The FSB has enough weapons. Maybe it's for the Taliban?" I was gradually doubting everything and was looking forward to leaving this desert hole.

"Maybe. I have no idea." JAC went to the truck's bonnet and sat up on it. He lit a cigarette and, while Wizard was still cursing, I went to JAC and leaned up against the front grille.

"Shut the fuck up now." The words were meant for Wizard and his fiery temper that had made him hiss like a pressure cooker. Wizard responded by turning the volume down a tad, but still paced around.

"We have to get rid of the four Black Water soldiers. They have seen us and can confirm that we are alive. I had thought that ..." JAC scowled at me, but words were unnecessary because we both thought the same thing.

"Let Wizard do it," he said quietly, "then he can complete what he was doing and maybe we can have some peace." JAC blew smoke through his nose and threw the cigarette on the ground, which I then stepped on to extinguish the glow. He then jumped down from the bonnet and signalled to Wizard, who was slowly cooling off.

"Get the four Black Water guys and bring them into Liam's barrack," JAC said, "I'm rigging the place now. What did you do with Sweeper?" JAC alluded to the bomb dog, which had attached itself to Wizard.

"He's back with the bomb boys. Do you want to use him?"

"No, not if he's not here. We sweep the place ourselves." JAC was calm, almost too calm, for my taste.

"And Wizard? ... the guys have to be alive, okay?" Referring to the Black Water soldiers while sending Wizard a crooked smile.

Wizard, ignoring the gesture, snorted before announcing loudly that JAC was an idiot, and then he went to get the four Black Water guys.

As Wizard disappeared, JAC and I went to Liam's barrack and swept it.

The reason we did that was so we could find out if everything that Kafka and he had installed, in the early days, was still there, and more importantly, if more had been added. To our relief, it was all intact and the small adjustments that had been made were easy to incorporate into the blast. I gave Liam's remote control to JAC, and before I got it back, he had programmed the entire barrack into it again. How long it took before Wizard came back with the four Black Water soldiers, I'm not quite sure, but JAC was not quite finished getting the barrack ready for blasting, so Wizard and I kept the guys under gun-point.

When JAC was done, there was half an hour before the transport departed.

Luc suddenly appeared and exchanged a few quiet words with JAC and when they were done, JAC signalled to me to come along. Wizard had the four Black Waters under control, so there was no danger leaving them alone.

Outside it was clear that Luc and the legionnaires were ready to depart. They had procured another truck and had loaded their own equipment into it and behind the wheel of each truck sat a legionnaire awaiting the order to drive.

JAC and Luc had a fierce disagreement over the weapons. Apparently JAC was not so sure that it was the right thing to sell them when the destination for them had not been clarified, but Luc did not care. As for me, I was not bothered, as long as we got the metal box on the front seat. I looked in through one of the windows and discovered that the box with the biohazard sign was still in there and, without thinking further about the reaction from the legionnaire behind the wheel, I opened the door and grabbed the metal handle of the box. Luckily, he didn't react but the pain from my damaged collarbones prevented me from lifting it.

A random passing legionnaire came to my rescue and lifted it out and put it on the ground then, he jumped into the back of the truck. Luc and JAC were done talking for as I stood there, next to the metal box, Luc passed me and climbed into the first truck. The few legionnaires still standing around the trucks got on board and both vehicles departed.

When the cloud of dust from the trucks had settled, JAC threw the keys for Kafka's Hummer at me.

"It's behind Luc's barrack," he said briefly and without waiting for a response, he went back to see Wizard again. For a moment I stood and looked at the metal box with the biohazard sign, but since I could not move it, I might as well get the Hummer – so I did.

The sky was slowly changing colour, and in the wing mirror I could see the first rays of the sun appearing over the distant rocks. It was as if the rays crept along the ridge of the cliff to finally make themselves known by rising completely and proclaiming that a new day had arrived. And so had I, as I swung the Hummer sharply to the left. JAC was standing just around the corner waiting for me.

"What the hell took you so long?" he snorted and lifted the metal box into the back seat and then he jumped into the front seat himself.

"We're going to the infirmary," he proclaimed, and less than a minute later I stood on the brakes in front of the tent with the red cross on the white background indicating 'hospital'.

"JAC," I said, turning to him but he just sat and looked out the side window of the car, "Are we okay?"

A moment passed before he turned his head towards me, but when he finally did, he leaned forward and kissed me gently. It came as a total surprise to me and I must have shown it because when our lips finally parted, he smiled at my expression.

"We are perfectly okay," he said, "Perfectly okay. Now we just have to take Kafka with us and then ..." We jumped out of the Hummer, sentence unfinished and went into the tent. Our roles were a given: while JAC was having a brief discussion with a couple of nurses standing inside the door, I went straight down to Kafka and woke him up. As expected he resisted when I grabbed him, but it was an act of desperation as I was armed so he might as well have saved his strength.

"Stop," I said resolutely. "Nothing is going to happen to you. You are going with us to Islamabad, so relax." Kafka stared at me with an expression that was a mixture of wonder, distrust and question, which from his point of view was very understandable. The person whom he had betrayed in every possible way, now stood in front of him assuring him that he would not be killed. If it had been me, I would have wondered too.

"I do not have time to explain now," I said, and he must have believed me, for he stopped resisting. I got him out of the bed and took his clothes from a box underneath it. Before I gave it to him, I took my chip out of his boot. Quietly he dressed and then we left the infirmary. But JAC had disappeared, so I ordered Kafka into the front of the Hummer and then we drove to the landing site, where JAC was waiting.

"Where's Liam?" he asked, but I did not answer him, "Have you killed him?" I wanted to kill Kafka just to shut him up but it was not worth it. In a few minutes he would be gone anyway, so why waste time and the little physical energy I had left on him.

As we arrived at the landing pad, the helicopter touched down and Kafka got out of the Hummer assuming I was going to join him, but when he spotted JAC, he froze. JAC walked over to us, nodded to Kafka, took the metal box from the back seat and went to the helicopter with it. I had pulled my Glock just to make sure Kafka followed. Kafka was not particularly willing to walk, but did, and, as we reached the helicopter, JAC turned around from conferring with the pilot, signalled for Kafka to jump in. Kafka did and sat down.

"See you." JAC shouted to me trying to shout over the noise of the rotors and I nodded and signalled 'take off', and they left – Kafka and JAC. I watched them go and wondered why it felt so weird to me. It was as if there was something final about it. I couldn't clarify it, but I just had a feeling and became a little sick in my stomach. But then reality hit me and I hurried back to the barrack.

Wizard stood outside awaiting my arrival, and with the car idling, I jumped out and walked over to him.

"Are they ...?" I alluded to whether the four Black Water soldiers were dead and he nodded before getting into the driver's seat. Carefully I fished the chip out of my pocket, opened the door to the barrack and threw it in. There was no need to look in there, so I returned to the car, climbed in and we drove off. A couple of the Scandinavian soldiers were on their way across Main Street with their towels over their shoulders when we whizzed by. They looked after us, but continued without pausing in the direction of the outdoor showers.

We disappeared out of the camp and shortly after our exit I took out the remote control and pressed it. We saw the glow and heard the roar as the barrack blew up. Neither of us said anything. We both knew we had just said goodbye to our lives, so what was there to say?

* * *

After a half hour drive, we were at the ruins where Kafka and I had stored our equipment the day before.

Wizard got out of the car and picked up the bags, and with JAC's two large bags of special equipment on the back seat, we now had a significant arsenal of weapons. When Wizard was back in the driver's seat, he leaned back and looked into the air.

"Where to?" I asked, assuming he had made a deal with JAC.

Wizard shrugged.

"Karachi? Mashhad? Tehran?" He left the question to be answered by me, so why not just go with the first and best?

"Karachi," I replied.

"There are more mercs in Mashhad."

"Exactly," I replied, fastening my seat belt. Wizard started the engine and then we were on our way to Karachi.

Chapter 23

The trip to Karachi took nineteen and a half hours. We drove through desert-like landscapes with barren cliffs and flat sandy steppes that stretched as far as the eye could see, and it was very serene in its own gruesome way. We did not see many other vehicles which was quite nice, probably because we had taken one of the less travelled roads just to avoid the possibilities of encountering roadside bombs and partisans.

Time went fast. Wizard and I had a lot of catching up to do so maybe that was why. We started out by him telling me what had happened to him while I was in Islamabad and it came as no surprise that he and Liam had been at each other's throats pretty much the entire time, after I left. After a while, he had therefore decided to move into Luc's barrack and Luc had welcomed him with open arms.

And who would not? Getting a highly-trained and unscrupulous mercenary for free was not exactly something you said 'no thank you' to. On the contrary. Subsequently, he had therefore been on assignments with Luc's team, but it became problematic when a bounty of fifteen million dollars was put on his head. Some in Luc's division might feel tempted to collect it, and since it had not been possible for neither Luc nor Wizard to control that, they had instead agreed that it was best for him to 'disappear'. So they had made sure that happened in Kandahar.

Subsequently he went to Mashhad in Iran, and there he had easily been able to hide because not only did he speak fluent Arabic he also had connections in these parts. The only one who had known he was still alive was Luc and it actually seemed rather strange to me that Wizard would trust him like this. On the other hand, Luc had shown loyalty to us, so why not? However, as it turned out the loyalty was bought with a transfer of three million dollars to Luc, which only gave Wizard three months 'rent free'.

"So when the three months expire you are hunted again?"

"I have been hunted for many years, so there is nothing unusual about it. The only difference is that now it is the FSB who offers the bounty and not the CIA or Interpol," he said calmly.

"Does Interpol do bounties?" I asked perhaps a little naively for why would they not?

"Oh, yeah ..." Wizard replied, "The goal justifies the means and fifteen million dollars can quickly be camouflaged in a budget like Interpol's. But fuck it ... that's how it is."

And Wizard was right. You have to learn to live with the fact that there is a price on your head.

I had completely forgotten that I also had an amount on mine, and what the hell did that really mean other than that I could not trust anyone? But I couldn't before either so ... Everyone wanted something from us. A kill, a collaboration, an edge or victory so a promise of loyalty was only valid until a mission was completed.

So yes, he was right. What did a zero more or less on the 'wanted poster' mean? Behind the scenes agencies added or subtracted us from their contract lists according to their mission requirements anyway. In some cases, it was even the same agencies who put the bounties on our heads to start with.

"Do you want to switch?" I asked as I stretched.

"In an hour. Then I'll have to have a break and ..."

I knew what he was going to say. It would be 'medicine time'.

"JAC is clean," I said quietly. I don't know what kind of reaction I had expected from him, but the one I got was the most obvious.

"Good for him." Wizard stated without any sign of wanting to hear more about it or start a discussion about his drug use. To be honest I did not intend to go any further with this, because it was his problem just as it had been JAC's – and if Wizard wanted my help to get clean, so yeah ... but until then I was pretty indifferent.

Many years ago, I had decided that I could only help those who wanted to be helped and above all, those who could and would help me. It was not some kind of charity, but a simple *quid pro quo*. So if Wizard wasn't asking then I wasn't volunteering.

During the next hour I told him about what I had been doing while he had played 'hide and seek' in Mashhad and it was actually quite cathartic, but also a little thought provoking because he did not react at all, when told about the killing of the pregnant woman in Afghanistan.

I was well aware that Wizard was the toughest of us and, although much was due to training and experience, the apparent 'indifference' he had developed towards the bestial was somewhat commendable. Scary but commendable. But Wizard was also a wonderful human being. It may sound hollow, but he was caring, loyal and always ready to fight for the ones he loved although his temperament could take over sometimes which made him somewhat unpredictable. However, I had never and will never doubt that he would be there for me.

An hour later I took the wheel. The rest had been good for my arms and my shoulder, and while Wizard took his 'medicine' and 'disappeared' for a while, it was quite nice just to drive this comfortable, civilian Hummer. Yes, it was almost meditative.

* * *

We refuelled in Khost and at Tirazayi we drove across the border into Pakistan.

At Alizai we drove south and after sixteen hours and three full tanks of fuel, we arrived in Karachi.

It had been many years ago since I had last been there. So much had changed, but not the slightly spicy scent mixed with metal and car-fumes. That was the same.

We stayed in a small hotel in a narrow side street close to the harbour, and our room, which was a double, was actually very cozy despite its spartan decor. The young man at the front desk was incredibly helpful –bordering on irritating – so I took over so that Wizard's annoyance would not turn into something catastrophic, and we got our room. Wizard carried our luggage up, because even though the pain in my shoulder was less, it had only allowed pain from elsewhere in my body to surface.

I went to the bathroom and after looking in the mirror it was obvious that I looked like a victim of a vicious assault. It was not far from the truth although in reality I had been complicit in the attack.

When Wizard came into the room with the last bags, he slammed the door and I could hear him locking it. After a few minutes he was standing at the bathroom door way looking at me.

"Do you need any help?" he asked as I stood in front of the mirror, examining my jaw. It was not broken – not even partially, as the doctor in the camp had said – but maybe it was cracked. I was not even sure that was the case.

"I need the bandages off, if you could help," I replied still examining my face for injuries and swellings.

Wizard came over and together we took off my t-shirt. Judging from the blood on the white gauze bandages wrapped around my torso, several of the wounds had opened. Wizard removed the gauze, looked at me from the front and then he turned me around and studied my back.

"JAC has done a good job."

Wizard's voice was strangely expressionless and his eyes continued to survey my body.

I could feel his fingers wandering over the injuries on my back, as if they were equipped with sensors to assess the damage of my wounds. I turned around and looked at him, but he did not notice and just continued his inspection of my chest and ribs.

"Did he use a stun gun?" he asked calmly.

"Yes," I replied quietly. His question reassured me. I have no idea why, but maybe it was because it went hand in hand with his touch, which was so strangely light – almost tantric. A crooked smile spread across his face.

"You son of a bitch, JAC. Clubs in the kidney region." Wizard looked at me still smiling, "Either he is unbelievably good at 'interrogating' or he has been extremely lucky. He could have smashed your kidneys."

"He did not use clubs," I replied coolly, "He did it with his bare hands." Wizard's facial expression changed to scepticism.

"He beat you with his bare fists? It's not something we usually do. Yes, a few pacing slaps maybe, but ..." He seemed very puzzled, "We usually wear half-gloves."

"Wizard, he was going to harm me, not interrogate me."

Wizard raised his eyebrows, tilted his head and without saying anything, he continued examining my injuries.

"At least he has done a 'nice' job."

And with those words hanging in the air, he left the bathroom and I took a shower.

As I stood enjoying the hot shower my thoughts drifted back to the last time I had felt the water from a shower head on my body. It had been with JAC. I smiled to myself, and as the images of us crossed my mind, Afghanistan's desert sands disappeared down the drain. We had to figure out how to get a hold of JAC, because he had no idea where we were.

When I came out of the bathroom, Wizard was sitting up against the headboard in the bed and next to him lay a field kit for emergency operations.

"Come here," he said firmly and I sat down on the edge of the bed. He took some cotton wool and alcohol and neatly cleaned one of the deep cuts that JAC had made with the knife and then he stitched it.

In total, there were eight cuts that needed stitches and it did not seem to affect Wizard in the least as he sat and embroidered me. I could just have been a piece of fabric or leather to him, for it did not seem to interest him as to whether it hurt me when he stuck the needle in my skin and pulled it and I doubt he would have noticed had I spoken out, for he was totally engrossed in his work. He never asked if I wanted anything for the pain and I don't know if it was because he assumed I could take the suffering or he simply forgot but it didn't matter. I couldn't feel anything anyway.

After these successful procedures, I was wrapped in gauze again. My legs were not that bad in terms of colour and since I had full mobility in them and nothing was broken or sprained, I was not that worried.

I put my clothes back on and lay down on the bed to relax and just enjoyed being there. Wizard had gone for a shower. In fact the water hitting the plastic floor of the shower and the acceleration of a couple of cars down on the street were the only sounds in the room so I tried to gather my thoughts. Annoyingly, I had to admit that I was too tired to keep track of them, so I let them fly and they mingled with the call from a nearby minaret that had started to sound. Shortly after, Wizard came out of the bathroom with a towel wrapped around his waist and for some reason I found myself checking him out.

As he sat squatted on the floor with his back to me roaming through one of the bags after some clean clothes, I had to admit that he was not half bad looking. He had an insanely well-toned body – muscular and marked all over – and the proportion of it was astonishing. He was literally square. His broad shoulders and back ended in what looked to be a perfectly shaped ass and his thighs and calf muscles were in perfect alignment with the rest of the body shape. But there was one big difference from his body to other male bodies I had seen: Wizard's features were NOT created from lifting weights and doing squats. No ... his body was the result of years of natural mending. And to me that made it even more impressive. I think he read my mind, for without looking at me he said,

"Yeah, it's nice, isn't it? Not exactly what you associate with a drug addict." I laughed a little, but it ended in a cough and subsequent pain from my ribs.

Wizard did not pay any attention to me as he went back into the bathroom again, and the next time I saw him, he was fully clothed. He sat down on the edge of the bed and opened one of the bags full of weapons and then he began to lay them neatly out on the bed.

"Can I ask you something, Wizard?" I said in a quite curious tone, not that it was important but it just puzzled me.

"Mmmm ...," he replied and I took that as a yes.

"Why don't you have any tattoos on your body?" Wizard didn't even look at me as he answered.

"Do I look like a fucking sailor?"

I couldn't help but laugh but it ended even before it really began due to my pain in my rips. No. Wizard did definitely NOT look like a sailor. Not even close. I switched my gaze to the weapons on the bed.

"How do we get hold of JAC?" I asked optimistically as Wizard continued.

"We don't. We go solo from now on. Didn't he tell you that?" I gasped and stared at Wizard.

"No. Not a word." Wizard stopped what he was doing and looked at me.

"Babe, we're officially dead. You died in the blast – I was blown up in Kandahar – and those who know I'm alive have been paid off. And you ... no one knows you exist except for me and JAC – and I'm dead and JAC ... he won't talk." He paused, "And if he does, he knows he will never be able to feel safe again." There was no doubt that he meant it, and he had presumably said it to JAC as well.

I suddenly became strangely empty inside. My life – as I knew it – was over. No more missions, no more marks, no more kills. An intense nausea appeared. What the hell was I supposed to do now? I rushed into the bathroom and threw up in the toilet, and while kneeling in front of it, I sensed that Wizard was standing right behind me looking at me. I got up, went to the sink and rinsed my mouth with water. My whole body was shaking and I could barely breathe. Gently, Wizard touched my healthy shoulder and I spun around to grab his sweater.

He put his arms around me and held me tight and even when I began hitting his chest with my fists, he did not let go. I was shaking so violently it was as if shock waves were going through my body. We stood like this for a long time ... a very long time. Whether Wizard had foreseen that this was the way I would react, I do not know, and only when the tremors stopped did he let go of me. He looked at me and smiled indulgently.

"Okay?" he asked raising his eyebrows.

"Yeah, okay," I replied, turning around and looking in the mirror. Wizard walked out of the bathroom and I splashed some water on my face. When I had dried myself with one of the white towels hanging on the side of the sink, I went back to the bedroom and as I stared at Wizard I felt like it was *déjà-vu*. Wizard was sitting in the exact same spot as before examining the weapons and ammunition as well as all the other equipment we had. I was so empty inside and felt like I needed air, so I went to the window and opened it. The heat hit my face like a warm slap and made me gasp a few times.

"Wizard, what now?"

"What now? You're free. Retire. Get lost. Buy an island in Thailand, get yourself a husband and live there until you die of old age. What the hell do I know? It's your life."

He was clearly annoyed with my question and it was understandable. Most people would have accepted this with great relief – to be free – so of course he could not know that his words cut me like knives. I did not want an island in Thailand and the man ... he was in Islamabad and had said goodbye to me ... yes, to both of us. Now I could understand his kiss at the infirmary and it suddenly struck me that I was never going to see JAC again. Buy an island in Thailand? What the hell was that all about? I turned to Wizard and considered for a split second saying something to him, but on the other hand ... starting a discussion with him would only trigger him, and I was not in the mood for that.

"Only if you're the man," I said dryly, thinking for a moment that it would lighten the mood, but I could not have been more wrong. Wizard looked at me without giving an inch, and when I smiled at him and winked, there was no reaction. On the contrary, he just stared at me momentarily and then continued the weapons inventory. I walked over to him and put my hand on his left forearm.

"Wizard, stop. Please." He stopped without looking at me and remained seated, completely motionless, "You know very well that people like us do not retire. We love what we do and we are good at it." Now he looked at me and his gaze revealed that he was waiting for me to continue but I was silent. Then he shook his head quietly.

"OPUS, take the chance. I would if I could." The last sentence he almost whispered and it seemed completely unreal to me that I should hear those words from him. He was – to me – the epitome of a contractor: A real contractor. One who lived for his job and who knew the risks and loved them. One where indifference and inhumanity went hand in hand, and weren't we all like that when it came down to it? He just knew it. Knew what humans are capable of doing when the conditions are right. He had seen it, and for that matter had condoned it. I removed my hand from his arm.

"You would not," I said calmly, "You had the chance, but you came back when you heard I was alive. You could just have disappeared."

"Yes, I could, but I made a choice. We are 'family' – remember?"

"Yes. So let's start one together. You and I."

He looked at me quizzically and then a smile appeared on his face.

"I'm assuming you're referring to a 'security company'," he said.

I nodded as an indication that it was exactly my thought and at that very moment, Wizard's facial expression changed from questioning to deeply serious.

"Do you know what such a setup requires? First, we would need to go on-line then the contacts and then we need to negotiate, but we're dead. There are contracts, accounts, transfers ... all the administrative side of it and not forgetting we would both have the FSB on our backs and then there is Kafka ... And finally do not forget Greg and his 'terminators'. We would become two wandering targets – two marks. Do you want that?"

I was pretty well aware of all of it but, if the alternative was an island in Thailand, then I would rather be chased by the FSB and anyone else who would have me on their kill list.

"Get me a hacker and you've got the set up here," I said calmly, taking

Liam's USB key out of my pocket. A smile spread on Wizard's lips as he reached for the USB, but I put it back in my pocket again. There was no reason for him to have it – at least not yet.

"You're fucking brilliant," he said, "Do you happen to have his phone as well?" With a crooked smile on my face, I took it out and threw it on the bed. Wizard laughed out loud.

"Fuck, you're good. Let's do it. Let's fucking do it." He picked up the phone and put it in his trouser pocket.

"Come. Let's go eat," he said and, with Wizard in a buoyant mood, we locked the door behind us and went down the stairs.

It was nice to see him like this, but as nice as it was, I was also aware of how suddenly a change of mood could occur and that would not be constructive ... not in the long run at least. Wizard was to be kept on a very tight rein, but for now everything was okay.

We quickly found a nice little restaurant down by the harbour. It was the first time we had sat like this, just the two of us, and we had, instinctively, placed ourselves at the back of the room. This was primarily to avoid our, sometimes macabre, conversation being overheard because we never knew who might be sitting at the table next to us listening in. However tonight there was no danger. We pretty much had the back of the restaurant to ourselves and combined with a clear view of the whole room this resulted in us both having fun in a relaxed atmosphere. In fact, we laughed a lot and it was wonderfully liberating.

When we got back to the hotel we went to bed and here we lay talking about the details of how we should do all this, as we had now agreed to start our own agency. The first thing that had to happen was that Wizard had to find a hacker and I had to acquire a laptop so that we could access the information on the USB key. We talked for a long time and slowly I could feel the fatigue wash over me. Wizard obviously noticed it, so shortly after, we said goodnight and turned off the light.

Around three a.m. I woke up to Wizard cursing loudly. I sat up in bed to see him sitting on the floor with the contents of the bags scattered all over the room.

"What's wrong?" I asked sleepily.

"No morphine," he replied in a feverish voice bordering on hysterical, all the while rummaging through his bags.

Carefully I crawled out of bed and took my jacket, that hung over one of the wooden chairs in the room. I gave him the two ampoules I had been given by the nurse in the camp. Without a sound or glance at me, he took them and went to the bathroom. I crawled back into bed and, despite the fact that I was really tired, I registered when he came back in. He lay down on his side next to me so we almost spooned and put one arm around me. His arm pressed against my ribs, which hurt and at the sound of my grunt, he immediately moved his arm.

"It's okay, Wizard," I said quietly, but he did not put his arm back.

"Thank you for ..." He hesitated when he said it. It was just one of those sentences that should remain unfinished – and we both knew it.

"*De nada*," I replied, "But I only had those two ampoules, so ..."

"Don't think about it," he replied, "It was me who fucked up and it's not going to happen again."

"And if it does it's your problem, and if you make it mine, it will have consequences," I said and closed my eyes. Family or not – I meant every single word, because I had neither the time nor mental space to accommodate his addiction problem. Wizard knew that I would not hesitate to show him what I meant by consequences – even if it was him.

I was awakened at five a.m. by the Imam calling to prayer from the nearby minaret and, despite the early hour, the temperature was already near thirty degrees. I looked over at Wizard's side of the bed, but only to find him gone.

The bathroom door was open and it was dark in there, so he had evidently left the hotel room. The pain from my ribs had returned sometime during the last few hours, but they felt sore rather than stinging – and thus they became more bearable.

I got up and enjoyed a cool shower. At the sight of Wizard's stitches, which, despite not being pretty, still held, I smiled. I was reminded of Mary Shelley's book 'Frankenstein' and my smile turned to laughter. Considering the rest of my body, they really fit in.

After showering and getting dressed, I went out and found a nearby café where I had some breakfast. It was nice to sit there all alone and just enjoy the sun and my own company. Maybe it was not so crazy an idea to go to Thailand and just disappear. The idea was there, but realistically, I would never be able to come to terms with it, even if JAC was there. The fact that I missed him tormented me and it seemed completely surreal to me that we should not see each other again. Even in Belize, when it had been the worst, I had never doubted that I would see him again, but now ...

In line with this doubt and subsequent realization, a void grew within me. It spread from my stomach and up to my chest, and luckily, I had finished breakfast because I completely lost my appetite. I felt like screaming. It could not be right that I should lose the only human being that I really trusted and who I loved: My best friend, my confidant, my lover and then it hit me. I was a damned hypocrite. I was actually worse than Liam. The way I felt now, thousands of people had done – and still did – after someone they loved had been taken from them. The choice was often not theirs but had been made for them and in some cases, it was me who had been the trigger – or at least pulled it. It was me who had taken their loved ones from them and brought them this grief.

It was as if all the consequences of my actions were slapped in my face. Somehow, the mark and his or her feelings did not matter, because it was those who remained who suffered with the desperation and deprivation and all the questions which would never be answered.

But I was in a situation where I could get answers and could get to see that person that I missed so unspeakably much again. I was in a position where I could hold him and feel his body and pulse again. The others could not.

* * *

I got up from the chair in the café and put on my sunglasses. Fuck it. Fuck it all. Why should I live in hiding and misery for the rest of my life, when I could be with JAC?

Having debated this, any doubts I might have had were definitely gone. It may well be that the relatives of my marks could never get their loved ones back, but I could and because they were unhappy, it did not mean that I had to be.

"Fuck them all," I said to myself, strolling back to the hotel and then I made a decision that started with me stopping at a phone shop where I bought two mobiles and two SIM cards.

When I entered the hotel room, Wizard had not returned and I was therefore able to pack a few of my things without him questioning me. When done, I put one of the newly purchased phones on the bed for him. I called it from the other newly purchased phone, left a message and while putting the phone in my pocket I left. Whether he would understand my decision I really did not care. I just had to find JAC. So, determined to go back and find him, I went down the stairs and it was here that I bumped into Wizard who was on his way up.

"Where the hell are you going?" he demanded looking at the bag.

"To Islamabad. I have to find JAC." Wizard looked at me seriously.

"Get back up," he said, grabbing my arm. I protested, but he led me up the stairs and pushed me so forcefully into the room that I ended up on the bed. Then he slammed the door so hard that I thought the frame was going to fall out.

"You're both crazy," he said, starting to pace around. I looked at him uncomprehendingly, but then he suddenly stopped and looked at me, "JAC is on his way here," he said and his voice reflected an astonishingly calm attitude, which was in stark contrast to his physical agitation, which was anything but. I simply could not believe my ears.

"How do you know that?" My surprise was quickly replaced by a scepticism that was fully justified and Wizard knew it as well, for of all of us, he was the one who was the most suspicious.

"I talked to him an hour ago." He shook his head, "I've been with Knox, you know." I remembered Knox from our old team. He was a quiet guy but insanely good at his job. And I remembered him as being extremely loyal.

"We were sitting in a café when JAC called him to find out if he had heard anything about us. Knox did not know anything about you, other than that you were killed in the explosion, but as I was sitting directly opposite him, I took the phone and yes ... now he's on his way. That fucking idiot." Wizard's eyes flashed, but then he caught sight of the mobile on the bed, "What is that?"

I told him about my plan, which didn't matter now and at the same time I picked up the phone. He shook his head.

"Fuck! You deserve each other. You and JAC. You are both fucking crazy," he shouted as he left, slamming the room door behind him.

I was sitting on the bed, my thoughts a mixture of shock and surprise, but in my turmoil, I could actually understand him. We had been given the opportunity to move on, but I just could not do it. It could well be that the emptiness that I felt before was gone now, but only to be replaced by this total selfishness. We did what was best for ourselves. If JAC and I had thought logically and in spite of our feelings for each other, then we would have stayed away from each other in mutual respect and understanding. We would have given each other an opportunity to move on with our 'new' lives, no matter how badly it hurt, but instead we, as true egotists, had chosen to put our own needs first – as we had done so many times before. To some extent we could excuse it by saying that we fought for our 'family', but that was only partially true. We fought for ourselves, for our lives together as individuals and as a unit.

Despite that, there was no doubt that it felt right that the three of us – Wizard, JAC and I – were reunited and it would definitely work between us. The thoughts were many and in order for them not to boil over, I filed them under 'for a rainy day'. Then I put my cap on and went out. I needed air and something cold to drink.

Chapter 24

Three hours later I was back in the room with a newly purchased laptop under my arm. Wizard had come back and from his brief look at me as I entered I could tell that his fury had been replaced by hollow indifference.

"We're moving to the Marriott Hotel," he said with a determination in his voice that did not invite any contradiction. Not that I had any so I just replied,

"Okay."

Half an hour later, after checking into one of their suites, I found myself sitting at a round glass table, that was intended as a dining table, but which I had now converted into a work station. I needed to install an anti-virus programme on the laptop before anything else and I had just finished doing so when a faint knock on the door made me look at Wizard. Much to my surprise he didn't seem too bothered about it. He just got up from the white coloured sofa he was sitting on and opened the door. A young guy I had never seen before entered the room and I could honestly not tell from the look on Wizard's face if he knew him or not but I assumed he did.

Without further introduction Wizard showed him to the table where I was sitting and judging from their very short conversation, the guy's name was Hendersson and he was a hacker. After exchanging a few nods, I explained to him that we needed him to unlock the USB key and that there was a time frame regarding doing this because if he did not manage it, all the information on it would be lost. I then pushed the laptop over to him so he could work his magic and shortly after, he pushed it back to me.

"It's open," he said dryly, got up, and went to Wizard, who gave him a stack of dollars, and then Hendersson was gone. I could not help but smile as I thought that in a way he was just like us. He went in, did his job and was gone the next minute with a pocket full of money. An IT-crusader. I snorted at my own conclusion before turning back to the laptop.

* * *

I spent the rest of the day reviewing the contents of the USB, because as it turned out there were more than a hundred folders on it. The contents of some of them were self-evident – contracts, telephone numbers, hotels, etc. – but then there were others that were not so obvious. One of these folders contained an address and a telephone number and, judging by the post code, the address was somewhere in Geneva. The telephone number however was not traceable. I transferred the data from this folder to my phone and then deleted the folder on the USB.

It may seem strange that I chose to do so, but it was almost as if my fingers were working independently from my brain when they pressed the delete button and the files vanished. Whether that was the right thing to do, time would tell. At least for now, it was done.

All Liam's contacts: clients, various contractors and bank connections were on the USB. As a precaution, I saved all the essential folders to the 'Cloud' and told Wizard where and under what password they were stored. Just in case anything happened.

Somehow Wizard seemed utterly uninterested in the information I gave him but he did write the password down on his phone so I guess it was just one of his mood swings.

The clock struck eight p.m. before I had viewed all the files. But then I was able to start on the actual setup and despite the fact that I was quite tired, it was so important, that a night without sleep was necessary if subsequently we would have the framework for our company in place.

Another sudden knock on the door distracted Wizard and me but, really, we should have realized it would be JAC because no one else knew which suite we were staying in. Why it surprised me that JAC was in civilian clothes when he stepped in, I do not know but I have to say jeans, a black leather belt, a tight white rib t-shirt that showed off his muscles underneath it and a pair of black trekking boots suited him. In addition to this he had two large blue bags with him, which he put down before he and Wizard hugged.

"I come bearing gifts," he said jokingly after the hug, referring to the contents of the bags, "I was so lucky to catch a ride with a military transport, so ..." He blinked and smiled in his usual whimsical way and I got an uncontrollable urge to throw myself at him. Quietly I got up and we went to meet and greet each other, both with an eagerness that we in no way tried to hide. As we faced each other, he gently grabbed my head with both hands and we kissed each other greedily and for a long time.

"Can't you just go to the bedroom and get it over with?" a slightly resigned Wizard said annoyingly without dignifying us with as much as a glance, "Then I can concentrate on what is really important." He alluded to the bags and their contents, which he was already in the process of inspecting. JAC and I let go of each other which made Wizard turn his attention from the bags to us.

"We need to talk, JAC." The seriousness of Wizard's voice indicated that it had to be now and even though JAC obviously would have preferred to spend some one-to-one time with me he knew it had to wait.

"Okay. About what?" he replied as he walked towards Wizard.

"After Liam was killed Opus retrieved his USB key and phone. I've had a hacker eliminate the key so now we have full access to its content. Opus has spent the day going through all the files and ..." Wizard looked at JAC as he spoke but there was no visible reaction from him, "with all the information we have retrieved we are now in a position where we can start our own company. Opus and I have already talked it through. What do you think? Do you want in on it? It would just be the three of us running it."

JAC looked at me and Wizard. He then raised his eyebrows in surprise before sending us a little smile.

"I leave you two alone for a couple of days and the next thing I know is that you are planning to conquer the world with your own private army. Well ... why not? If we've got the set-up we might as well use it. So tell me more." JAC took a cigarette from the Marlborough packet that Wizard had casually thrown on the coffee table and lit it.

I went back to the laptop and sat down and over the next few hours and several coffees I gave JAC an outline of the information that we had from Liam. I never doubted that JAC would be in on it, if not for the hell of it then, at least, for the money.

After several hours of turning back and forth between the laptop and JAC my body hurt and, though I did not want to, I probably had to find a place to get some x-rays done. It was my ribs that gave me the most pain, both when I moved and when I was breathing, but it was actually my right shoulder that worried me the most. When we had finished, JAC sat quietly for a few minutes, reflecting, then suddenly, out of the blue, asked,

"Where's Knox?" and it sounded as if he had expected him to be here with us.

Wizard took five boxes of headsets out of one of the bags.

"I don't know. Why?" he said dryly while inspecting the boxes as if he had never seen anything like them before.

"Knox? He's okay. Do you think he would be interested in working with us?" I enquired hopefully.

"Maybe." It was difficult to interpret from Wizard's voice whether he was interested in getting Knox on our team, but Knox would definitely be an advantage for us, if only for the extra manpower it would give us.

"What is the status of Kafka?" I asked, actually hoping that the answer would be that he was not alive.

"Jacoby took care of him." There was a trace of indifference in JAC's voice as he stood by the table with his phone in one hand and the *á là carte* menu in the other. He began to order dinner for us and I signalled that he should add two jugs of coffee to the list. When he had placed our order, I continued.

"And that means?" JAC threw the 'No Smoking' sign from the table into the trash can and lit a cigarette.

"It means that Jacoby took care of him," he replied.

"I hope you are right. The last thing I need is to run into him on the street."

"I do not understand why you handed him over to Mossad alive. Couldn't you just have put a noose around his neck and then hung him from the helicopter?" As Wizard stated this, his attention was still on the contents of the bags. I turned my head and looked at him.

"What?" he said obviously thinking there was nothing wrong with what he had just said. I smiled. No doubt Wizard would have done it and then flown with Kafka's dead body hanging from the helicopter through Islamabad's airspace. And when he had reached the agreed point for pick up, he would have cut the rope so that the body had fallen straight into Jacoby's lap. He was amazing, Wizard.

JAC walked over to him, put one arm around his shoulders and kissed him teasingly on the head.

"That's why I love you, Wizard. I can always count on a hanging or two when it comes to you." He laughed while Wizard, annoyed, pushed him away. I smiled quietly to myself. It was nice to see the boys together again. I returned to the laptop because I had a long night ahead of me with all the files that were on the USB.

"Wizard," I said calmly as I continued surfing the files, "I've thought about something. When was the last time you had sex?" Neither of the boys could see my mischievous facial expression when I said it and judging by the silence, all physical activity in the room had stopped.

"Why? Are you going to be my fucking pimp now? Or maybe you need to kill a few hours? I thought you had JAC for that, but you might be tired of him ... oh no, that was Liam, you got tired of it and we all know what happened to him ..." I spun the chair around and stared at him. What I had said in fun, he had clearly misunderstood.

"What the hell is that supposed to mean?" I snarled at him, "You need to do something about your 'problem' so that you are not so nasty. Fucking addict."

JAC had quietly moved towards me, and he was now standing so close that in a few steps he would be standing between Wizard and me.

Wizard was astonishingly calm, which scared me a little, for it was like looking at a volcano that could erupt at any given moment. He zipped up the bag in front of him and put it on the floor.

"Addict or not. If you had not been injured, you would have jumped me last night. And we both know that." He looked at me viciously and there was no doubt that he enjoyed saying this because if nothing else, it would trigger a reaction in JAC.

"You're sick, Wizard," I said, trying to control myself, as I had such a desire to shut him up.

"Maybe ... but healthy enough not to have sex with you."

"Wizard, what the hell is wrong with you?" JAC asked and if I thought he would be borderline aggressive I was totally wrong. Instead, there was a slight concern in his voice. For a moment images of him and Wizard in a fight went through my mind and the scenario was anything but good. I would not be able to separate them unless I shot one of them. And would I be able to? Wizard looked viciously at JAC.

"Keep your bitch on a VERY short leash, JAC. VERY short otherwise ..." His eyes flashed pure uncontrolled aggression and he had some unnatural ticks in the corners of them.

"Wizard, are you okay?" My voice reflected a sincere concern for him, but he did not respond. At the same time, there was a knock on the door and Wizard almost tore the door open only to find that it was room service with the food. With one hand, Wizard grabbed the trolley and pulled it in, then gave the waiter a fifty-dollar tip before slamming the door shut in his face. JAC and I followed every movement he made and it was like watching the countdown of a ticking bomb. Wizard took one of the plates of food, cutlery and a coke before walking over to us to sit down across from me at the glass table.

"Shouldn't you have something to eat?" he asked in a tone of voice that did not fit the situation at all.

I sat for a while looking at him as he took a few mouthfuls of couscous.

"Are you going to sit and count how many times I chew my food?" he then asked looking at me and winking. I had no idea what to answer, because he was so extremely unbalanced that one wrong word could easily trigger a disaster. And he was cold and cynical enough to eliminate both JAC and me on the spot if it pleased him.

I got up, took the laptop and walked towards the back bedroom. As I passed JAC, we exchanged a quick glance and I could see the concern for Wizard on JAC's face.

On the way into the bedroom, I stopped at the trolley and grabbed a coke and a plate of food. There was a strange oppressive atmosphere in the room so maybe it would help if I slipped away. Then JAC could talk to

Wizard – alone. I left the door ajar just in case they would get at each other's throats. I put the laptop and my Glock on the bed and that was when I heard the bang. I flew into the living room and there on the floor lay Wizard in a heap of shards of glass from the broken dining table, and he was shaking. JAC sat next to him and was about to take off his t-shirt to put it in Wizard's mouth so he would not bite his tongue off.

"Hold his legs," JAC commanded, grabbing his arms at the same time Wizard's eyes rolled up to show only the whites. His tremors were in no way violent and they could be described as similar to an epileptic seizure. They seemed to go on and on but in reality, they only lasted a few minutes. When they were over, JAC carried him into the second bedroom and laid him on the bed while I hurried into the adjoining bathroom and wet a towel. Wizard was still unconscious as I laid the towel over his forehead and JAC, who for a brief moment had been on the phone, now came back into the room.

"Knox is on his way with a doctor," he said, sounding worried as he looked at Wizard, "When he comes ..."

"Yeah, I slip into the other bedroom," I said without looking at him.

"It's best that way. At least for now."

"I know."

A few minutes passed and Wizard gained consciousness again, but he was obviously very confused and disoriented and spoke incoherently. After five minutes he fell silent again, but it was not a loss of consciousness. It was if he was in a kind of trance.

"While the doctor is here, can you try to find out where I can get some X-rays of my shoulder done?" I asked JAC as I continued to wipe sweat off Wizard's forehead and face and there ... on the right side of Wizard's neck, I suddenly noticed the blood.

I called JAC, who was on his way out of the room, but the sound of my voice slowed him down and he turned around. I grabbed the collar of Wizard's shirt and pulled it aside so he could see the source of the blood and JAC immediately ripped Wizard's shirt off exposing his chest and arm and it was obvious the blood came from his arm where all his needle marks were.

"Jesus Christ." JAC exclaimed as he saw Wizard's right arm. It was inflamed with deep wounds from needle punctures. In fact, the entire forearm was infected.

"What the hell is he on to fix himself into this state?"

"He ran out of morphine yesterday, but I had some from the infirmary in the camp – two ampoules – but I don't know if ..."

"This is something else. He's got enough money to buy the clean shit, so it's probably due to a bad supplier. But he's been taking it for a while. Christ,

Wizard." JAC seemed genuinely worried, but there was also an underlying irritation in his voice.

There was a knock on the door. JAC walked over and opened it while I slipped into the second bedroom and closed the door. It was eleven p.m. and there was not much I could do right now, so I opened the laptop and continued working.

It was not because I did not feel anything, because I did. It was not like with Snake, but then of course my relationship with Wizard was also different and closer. Compared to Wizard, I had only known Snake superficially, and although he had also been a good and loyal team mate, Wizard was invaluable to have on our side when we were on missions. But that was not all. Wizard also had a human quality that I deeply admired and at the same time felt deeply repulsed by. Not because I judged him, NO, I certainly did not. He was a product of his surroundings, a man who had grown up witnessing a lot of injustice and misery, and who, with the war in the Balkans, had found his place both career-wise and personally. I would not think that Wizard had tried to change anything ideologically or politically in his country. I think he enjoyed being part of a well-oiled war machine, and when that machine stopped, the choice was easy.

What had bothered me for a long time, though, was why he had started on the morphine. It seemed illogical. He had an eminent ability to shut out all the atrocities – perhaps because he himself had often been the prime mover in the execution of them – and he acted without conscience and without remorse. A psychologist would probably have categorized him as a psychopath, but that's not how I saw him. A psychopath would have himself as the centre and act for his own gain. Wizard did not. He worked best in a team and acted on what was best for the team. So was he a sadist? If he was, he was the purest of the kind I had ever met, and if he really got a pleasure out of the things he did, then I was sure it was a mental satisfaction and not a physical one. Or was he the purest executioner?

I believed we could all reach a point where even in the atrocities there was a certain reassuring normality, but Wizard was then just one of those who broke the boundaries of this normality, and that in itself required a certain amount of admiration, in my view.

Others would probably distance themselves and judge him, but not me. I envied his ability to take things to the next level. Yes, I could witness it, but my conscience would not let me match it. The passivity that I felt was almost worse because it legitimized the deeds and to be completely honest, I was okay with that.

* * *

After an hour, I came across a file that got my full attention. The file was named 13268 and the first documents in it were contracts – primarily on deliveries of heavy equipment and dated back to the mid-nineties.

The subsequent documents were blueprints of buildings drawn in Revit, the building information modelling software, and with accompanying MEP (mechanical / electrical / plumbing) installation drawings, so I initially skated over them until a drawing appeared that looked a lot like the isotope. The document was in Russian, but some of the words were underlined and on the side was the English translation of them. It was dated one and a half months ago. Had Wizard been himself, he would have been able to translate it right away, but now he was lying and hovering somewhere in Neverland, so the translation had to wait.

I memorized the location of the file and moved on.

The subsequent documents were unimportant, until an email to Liam caught my eye. It expressed concern about the impending transaction in relation to individual named team members, in this case Kafka and me. Liam's response to the email was that Kafka could be of use until the cargo was delivered and then he would be terminated. I however posed a real threat, and measures had been taken to eliminate me within the next twelve hours. I looked at the date on the email and it was dated the night before I arrived at the camp with Kafka, but that was not what sent a chill down my spine. It was who Liam was corresponding with: Jacoby.

So Liam had been warned about us and it was Jacoby who had sold us. Kafka had not known. He had been prepared to sacrifice me and JAC to survive himself, but why had Jacoby warned JAC? Maybe because JAC would have put an end to Liam when he found out I was dead. And if Kafka was alive, it would be safest to get him home. And that was JAC's job together with the cargo. In other words: Jacoby had made a deal with Liam and at the same time played JAC as a wild card: the elimination of Liam and, if he was alive, the 'repatriation' of Kafka. As for me, Jacoby had been sure that I would be dead, and maybe he had even asked Kafka to take care of it and therefore he – Kafka – had 'sold' me. But no matter what, Jacoby did not know that I was alive – nor that Wizard was. But he probably knew that JAC was in Karachi. I had to check my luggage for any tracking devices and then I had to screen JAC. Could JAC have made a deal with Mossad? I refused to believe it, but there was so much I would not have believed about all this.

The last of the files in the folder was the video of JAC's interrogation of me. The video was not scrambled which meant that you could clearly see both JAC and Kafka in it. Its presence proved to me that Liam had known everything before we arrived at the camp.

There was a knock on the door and as JAC stepped in, I closed the laptop, jumped down from the bed and walked towards him.

"They're gone," he said coolly, leaving the door open, "Wizard will probably make it. Long term drug use has weakened his blood vessels and a bad drug fix has created the infection, which untreated has given him blood poisoning, but he will most likely recover."

It was good news, but honestly my thoughts were somewhere else. JAC handed me a note with an address.

"You have to be here at five thirty tomorrow morning. It is a private clinic run by the doctor. The agreement is that he will take x-rays and then you can discuss what should happen."

I took the note and I started walking back to the bed engrossed in what was written on it. Maybe it was a little insensitive of me to ask JAC to close the door behind him, but knowing I was totally preoccupied with the files, it was best for us both if he just left. Undoubtedly he must have looked confused by my request, but I did not seek his gaze, and soon after, he closed the door behind him. That night I slept alone in the bed and it was my choice.

* * *

The next day, the X-rays thankfully showed that my shoulder was NOT broken and that my collarbone fractures were sitting so close together that there had been no displacements of them, so I avoided having any surgery. Four of my ribs were broken – which I already knew – but despite the doctor confirming that there was no sign of a lung infection, I still got some painkillers (codeine) and antibiotics. So with the x-rays in a sealed envelope, and a recommendation to rest for four to six weeks, I thanked the doctor and left the clinic. Of course, no medical record had been made and the doctor had been paid in cash.

Two and a half hours later Karachi had woken up completely when I turned from one of the main thoroughfares and into a narrow street. In my head I longed for peace, and for a brief moment I just considered disappearing from it all. It seemed like a real opportunity here in this busy metropolis. Just turn a corner and then never show up again. My way of thinking was in many ways very inspiring, but unfortunately I also had to admit that after all, I could not leave JAC and Wizard. We are a team, and on one level or another, we are in this together. It was not like when we were on assignments together, because we then knew who we were working for and who paid our wages. Now we are working to save ourselves and each other – and I would go a long way for them, just as they would do for me – but if we could not, there was no doubt that we would die.

I walked into a small shop selling fruit, vegetables and herbs and bought some aloe vera and tea tree oil that we could apply to Wizard's infected arm. It was supposed to help against infection and itching, so maybe it would be useful. Quietly – and undetected – I strolled back to the hotel with the X-rays in one hand and Wizard's herbal remedies in the other.

When I arrived at the hotel, I went to reception and ordered breakfast for us, and as the foyer was busy, I hurried to one of the elevators. Two minutes later, I opened the door to the suite. JAC, who was lying on the couch, sleepily noticed me, but when he did not bother to wake up completely, I went in to Wizard instead. He slept heavily, so I put the purchased items on a chair in his room and then went back into the living room. I laid the envelope with the X-rays on the coffee table, emptied my pockets of codeine and antibiotics next to it, before finally sitting down on the couch opposite JAC. Whether it was the sound of the pill bottles hitting the table that woke him up or whether he was already awake, I do not know, but he sat up and we looked at each other in a slightly compassionate manner.

"How many hours have you had?" I asked, for his limp body and dull facial expressions indicated that he was more than just plain tired.

"Five hours in two days," he replied, and the words almost disappeared in the yawn he made at the same time. With difficulty he got up and stretched.

"I ordered breakfast," I said as JAC half-sleep-walked around behind me, placing both hands on my shoulders. It was nice to feel his hands massaging my sore shoulders and neck gently, and for a brief moment, I closed my eyes and enjoyed it, "According to the X-rays, I'm okay and just need some peace and quiet to heal. The doctor said four to six weeks." My voice was whispering and when no response came from JAC, I suddenly wondered if I had said it so low that he had not heard it. I touched one of his hands with my cheek and he stopped massaging me.

"Okay. We probably all need that amount of time to recuperate," he said, nodding towards Wizard's room. I smiled indicating that he was probably right, but he did not see it.

"Are we okay?" he suddenly asked and I straightened up. The question did not come as a surprise to me as I had been thinking the same thing before I fell asleep last night.

"Yes, I certainly hope so. What did Jacoby want with Kafka?" JAC removed his hands and I could sense that the question was not one he expected.

"No idea. He just wanted Kafka and the metal box. Why?"

"I've been thinking about all this and our future, and having fallen foul of an unknown chip myself, I'm gonna have to sweep you, JAC," I said as I looked up at him. I could see his eyes slowly changing to the colour black –

and why shouldn't they? I had just given him a statement explaining my lack of trust in him but it was necessary so I could get rid of my suspicions.

"Be my fucking guest," he replied, standing defiantly in the middle of the floor, raising his arms to the sides. Quietly, I got up and went to one of the bags that Wizard and I had collected outside Kabul, and found a hand scanner. When I turned to JAC I could see that he was extremely annoyed with me because his jaw was moving a little from side to side, which was one of the things he did unconsciously when something angered him. I swept him and thankfully he was clean, but I had needed to be sure. We did not say anything to each other nor did we when I continued by sweeping the kit he had brought with him. Again, the scanner did not show anything, so I put it back in the bag.

There was a strained silence between us afterwards, and it was as if neither of us knew how to break it. The silence was suddenly broken by a knock on the door. JAC opened it and greeted the waiter with the trolley of breakfast buffet. The little guy placed it right behind the couch I had sat on. He stared at the smashed glass table, but JAC quickly escorted him and last night's dinner trolley out so no questions were asked.

We ate our breakfast in silence and afterwards JAC went into my bedroom and went to bed. I followed him to pick up the laptop and before leaving the room again, I went to the bed and we kissed each other. It was a kiss without any real emotion, and as I walked to the door, JAC turned his back on me.

Out of the corner of my eye, I glimpsed his Glock on the nightstand, its safety catch off. It was the first time he had done that. Actually, I could understand him after the mistrust I had just shown. If I had been in his place, I would have done the same.

The following hours I spent sitting on one of the sofas with the laptop. The more documents I read, the more knowledge I gained about not only Liam's entire setup but also about his complete network of contacts regarding customers, suppliers and mercs. Every time I came across information that could be relevant, such as email addresses and phone numbers, they were entered into my phone and important documents were copied, after which I stored them in the 'Cloud', before saving them on the laptop. But there was also some information that I copied over to my phone and subsequently deleted from the USB. It was information that concerned Liam as a private person and that no one knew about. When I came across the folder with his bank details, I copied Liam's account numbers and then deleted everything about them. Out of curiosity, I looked through his balances and not surprisingly, Liam had saved a lot of money. And then I made a decision.

I wanted to find Patrice and give her Liam's account numbers. Maybe she already had them – or maybe Killian had – but no matter what, it was her money now, and she might as well have them. They were all accounts in the Bahamas so not traceable. Liam probably had a will somewhere where his bank details would appear anyway, but for now, I left it at that.

Time flew by, and as I sat buried in files, a few sounds came from inside Wizard's bedroom. Despite the fact that I had tons of work ahead of me, eventually, I got up and went to check if he was okay.

To my surprise, he was awake, but not himself because of all the medication the doctor had prescribed. I shook his pillows and subsequently put one of them at his back so he could sit up. He looked at me, but it was clear that he did not see me. He was somewhere between his own world and this one, and for once I could see nothing but indifference in his eyes. They were eyes that belonged to an old war veteran – and not a forty-two-year-old man – and no doubt they had seen far too much evil. I touched his arm and it was as if, only then, did he register it was me. He looked me in the eyes and I smiled. Then he put his hand over mine without taking his eyes off me and then he drifted away into the void. I sat down on the edge of the bed and stroked him gently on the hand. His forearms had drips attached testifying that he was constantly getting antibiotics and painkillers pumped into his body.

"You are a son of a bitch, Wizard, but never doubt that deep down I love you."

It surprised me that those words came out of my mouth, but they were true ... and honestly, Wizard had been right when he said I would have jumped him that night at the hotel if I had not been in so much pain.

How long we sat like that, I have no idea, but suddenly I heard a knock on the door of the suite. I grabbed my Glock and hurried to JAC and woke him up. He immediately jumped out of bed, took his Glock and went to the door and asked who it was.

"Knox," it came quietly. JAC and I exchanged glances, whereupon I retreated into my room and closed the door. It took fifteen to twenty minutes before JAC joined me and my questioning eyes must have said it all.

"Knox is in the room with Wizard," he said, "We need to talk about him."

"About Knox?"

"Yes," JAC said seriously, sitting down on the small sofa furthest away from me, "Knox would like to work with us." He leaned forward and rested his elbows on his knees as he clasped his hands, "All of a sudden, I'm just not sure about him."

"Why? Knox has always been damned stable. Quiet and stable. Who has he worked for lately?" I asked as I walked away from the window and sat down in the chair by the coffee table that was opposite the couch where JAC sat.

"He was contracted to another team, but ended up signing a contract with a small French security company." JAC leaned back and put his hands behind his head.

"Any others?" I asked, knowing from Liam's files, he had.

JAC shook his head.

"Not according to him."

I took a cigarette out of my breast pocket and lit it.

"Then he's lying," I said coolly as I made a few smoke rings in the air. They danced towards JAC, and through them I could see that he was sitting and watching me with disbelief.

"Go out and ask him when he was going to tell you about his work at DynCorp. He protected oil pipelines in northern Iraq and it was DynCorp that had that contract."

I took a puff of the cigarette and noticed that JAC leaned his head back and looked up at the ceiling,

"I knew there was something."

"JAC, Knox is okay. To be honest, I don't think he sees helping to secure an oil pipeline as contentious or prejudicial to being able to work with us."

It seemed unlikely that Knox would pose a potential risk to us and to some extent, I think JAC was of the same opinion. He got up and walked towards the door, but then he suddenly changed his mind and turned around.

"You said that before about Kafka."

His voice was filled with cynicism, but without the underlying hatred for Kafka that I had anticipated.

"And I meant it too, and I still do."

JAC walked over to me and, by his posture, I could see that he was annoyed by what I had said. However, if I could just make him understand that even though Kafka had tried to hurt us, he was just a pawn in a game, and somehow, I had no doubt that if Kafka had known that, then he would not have participated in the plans to exterminate us. Not the Kafka I knew and who, after all, I still thought he was deep down.

"You don't mean what you just said, do you?"

JAC was visibly surprised and it was very understandable, because in his eyes Kafka was still a traitor who would have killed us.

"Yes, I mean it. I think we were all played against each other. The strategists were Liam and Jacoby – yes, your friend Jacoby. He had warned Liam that we were on our way to the camp. There is a lot of email correspondence between them so ... JAC. Get the laptop from the living room ... NOW."

My voice reflected that this was not something he should question but just do and luckily he caught on. He immediately went into the living room and one minute later he was back. The USB was still plugged in and I breathed a sigh of relief.

"There is your answer regarding Knox," I said, taking the laptop, "If he really wanted to hurt us, he would have taken the USB. But it's still here ..."

"Or he's just smart and thinks that's how we would think and therefore he left it, to win our trust."

"He does not have to win it, JAC. You and Wizard trusted him enough to contact him and you saw how he 'delivered' the doctor when you called him. Loosen up, JAC. Knox is not the enemy."

"But a short while ago, you had doubts," he replied and he was right. For a fraction of a second, I had doubted. It was more the fact that I could forget something as important as the USB than that I had actually doubted Knox, that had triggered my reaction. It must never happen again. NEVER.

"Tell Knox that when Wizard is better, the three of you will sit down and figure out something. Then you can always play me like a trump card." I smiled at him and he reciprocated with a few nods before walking back into the living room.

Ten minutes later JAC reappeared. Knox had gone and judging by the tranquillity of the suite, Wizard slept. JAC went to the mini-bar and took a bottle of cold water. He drank half of it and handed me the rest. I took the bottle and went to the coffee table and took a couple of codeine tablets and washed them down.

"Are you in pain?" he asked, but it was clear that it was more of a polite inquiry than a reflection of a sincere concern. I shook my head.

"It's a precaution for later." I got up and walked over to him, "What's wrong with you, JAC? Why are you so distant?" He looked at me, then he looked up at the ceiling and then out to one side, "JAC, answer me." I stood completely still, expecting the worst.

"What I did to you in Islamabad ..."

"It was okay, JAC. It was agreed."

"Yes, but it was not agreed that I should enjoy it." He hid his face with his hands, "I enjoyed seeing the pain in your eyes. To hear you scream when I hurt you." He paused, dropped his hands and went over and looked out of one of the windows, "I enjoyed it. I enjoyed it so fucking much."

There was no doubt that he was shaken up, and it made him no less shaken to say it out loud. Quietly I walked over to him and, as he stood there with his broad back facing me, I let my arms wrap around his waist. He put his hands on mine but continued to stare out the window as if the answer to the emotions that were going through him right now were out there.

"I know you did, and that's just one of the many reasons why you were the right one to do it."

I kissed him on his back, just to emphasize that he had in no way done anything wrong by me. The truth was, I knew very well where he was mentally right now. Nor had it been easy for me to accept that I could actually achieve satisfaction out of extreme pain, but I had had to come to terms with it and, like him, admit that the rush of it was better than anything else. JAC interrupted my flow of thoughts as he suddenly turned towards me.

"Can't you see how fucked up this is? The rush it gave me to abuse you ... it was better than any rush I've ever had ... not even when I took smack did I achieve anything that comes close. That's not normal. It was as if all my ..." He was silent for a moment, "It was as if I was beating all my sins, my frustrations, out of myself by beating you, and at the same time I achieved a mental satisfaction and forgiveness."

"JAC, why do you want to be forgiven? What is your sin? Being good at your job? We are trained for this."

"No, I'm trained as an explosives' specialist – not this. Not to enjoy this."

"See the enjoyment as an advantage – a benefit. Work with it. Use it. The only thing you do not have to do, is blame it for being there. Feel it. Love it. There is nothing wrong with that." He looked at me quizzically, but his gaze was quickly replaced by contemplation, "If you need forgiveness for what you do, take yourself out of the game," I said quietly, knowing that it was not an option for him because, just like me, he basically loved what he did and would under no circumstances trade it for anything. But I could easily follow his logic, without in any way feeling the same as him.

"Do you never need forgiveness for what you do?" His voice revealed a sincere wonder and it came as a surprise to me, that he had such thoughts.

"No, I don't contract to do anything that requires forgiveness. I do a job and, like you, I am one of the best in the industry at what I do. Why should I ask forgiveness for that? It's not me who gives orders for mass exterminations and eliminations ... yes, it's me who helps to carry them out, but does that make me a bad person? I don't think it does, but if it does, then so be it. If I am to be judged, let it be when the Day of Judgment comes, and if the judgment is not satisfactory, then there is always the option to eliminate the judge. After all, this is common practice in certain parts of the world and we have all had our share of murdered judges and magistrates. But is forgiveness really what you are looking for?"

JAC thought for a moment.

"No," he replied quietly and leaned his head back and looked up at the ceiling, "I don't know what I want. Yes, the pain. The kind of pain you showed me in Islamabad. There I felt more alive than I have done in years."

"You've also been on heroin for years, so you haven't been able to feel anything."

"The smack made me forget to be alive – the pain confirmed that I was and it made me long to be even more so. The pain was and is better than smack. It is sincere, honest and passionate and not an escape."

I went and sat down on one of the sofas and drank a sip of the half-full water bottle that stood on the table.

"The point of showing you the pain was to make you understand what happened to me in Belize. To show you that pain can be replaced with something else, in this case love, and thus make you survive when you think things cannot get any worse. It was intended as a tool, a method of converting pain to love. Not as a new kind of fix."

Of anyone, I was aware of what a rush it gave, when the pain and pleasure culminated, but it was never intended as a fix to survive in everyday life, but I could see on JAC that it was for him. He wanted to replace smack with the pain to achieve the intoxication. And I was basically indifferent to this. If that was his new fix, I would like to be his pusher – at least for now.

JAC looked at me and there was a rare gentleness in his eyes which made me pretty irritated. Why should he complicate things? Why could he not just accept them as they were?

"Don't, JAC," I said harshly, "But if you need a 'fix', say so."

We looked at each other and I could see in him that he knew what I meant. Gently, he grabbed my dog tag and pulled me to him.

"Somehow you've always been my fix," he said, kissing me. His lips were moist and soft, and even though I enjoyed them, I had had enough of all that talk and tenderness. I let my hands run up over his chest, further up over his shoulders and in one sliding motion I took his jacket off. Our kisses became more aggressive and it all ended with him taking me hard against the wall by the bedroom. After that I dragged him into the bedroom and there he got his rush – and I my satisfaction, but no rush.

* * *

The rest of the evening and night passed calmly. JAC and I took turns being near Wizard so we could change his drip and bandage every four hours. By six o'clock in the morning, Wizard was back. I woke up to hear JAC's laughter coming from Wizard's room. Immediately I got up and put on my pants and one of JAC's t-shirts. I walked through the living room and into Wizard's room. JAC was changing a drip while Wizard sat up in bed eating pancakes. He had regained his normal complexion and at the sight of me, he smiled. It was nice to see him sitting there and wiping his mouth after his 'food orgy', and when he had put his plate with the remaining pancakes aside, he asked JAC to leave.

JAC withdrew immediately, and when he had closed the door behind him, I went to the bed and gave Wizard a giant hug, which he without hesitation reciprocated. We held on to each other for a long time and when we finally let go, I sat down on the edge of the bed.

"Good to have you back," I said and couldn't stop smiling. It was a huge relief that he was getting well.

"I owe you an apology. The things I said ... that was not okay."

Wizard looked me straight in the eyes and they radiated a sincerity that somehow touched me.

"Forget it, Wizard. I have already. I'm just glad you're back." I took his hand and he squeezed mine as he looked down at it.

"I heard what you said to me when we were alone, and you must know that it is reciprocated." He turned his gaze to me and despite the fact that it was severe, there was an honesty in it that hit me.

"I know." I put my index finger in front of his lips, "Let's leave it at that." Gently I leaned over him and whispered, "But remember that if you ever talk to me like you did yesterday, I ..."

I pulled away from him and our eyes met. There was no doubt that he had got the message. It was clear that he knew I meant it. He smiled and there was a relief to be traced in his eyes. Now we did not have to be so fucking sensitive to each other anymore. It was too complicated and could easily lead to misunderstandings.

"You have my full permission. No regrets," he said coolly and I returned his smile.

"No regrets."

I went and opened the door to the living room, where JAC had settled into one of the sofas and was in the process of eating breakfast. He threw a brief glance at me, but just continued his feast. I left the door open and walked over and sat down next to him. Of course, he handed me a slice of orange, which I accepted and ate. It was unbelievably juicy and moreish.

"Is there coffee?" I asked, knowing that of course there was. He nodded with his mouth full of pineapple that was so juicy that it ran down his chin. I got up and straddled him and licked the juice away. Then I kissed him and got half of his pineapple in my mouth. He smiled at me and swallowed the pineapple he was chewing on. I wrapped my arms around his neck, and as he stood up. I swung my legs around his waist. Kissing, he carried me into the bedroom and slammed the door and the next few hours we made love – hard and intense.

Chapter 25

In the afternoon, Wizard had come around sufficiently for us to be able to have a 'bedside meeting'. JAC and I sat next to Wizard's bed and together we discussed the whole setup. Regarding Knox, we agreed that he would be welcome in the group, though without being made aware of my existence straight away. During our conversation we agreed, that I would have the role that Liam had had, which was team co-ordinator, with the exception that it would be JAC who negotiated the contracts when it came to personal meetings with clients. I could take care of the administration including selection of missions, price agreements, payments, schedules, obtaining new identities and passports, certificates, clearance at airports, flight and hotel bookings and all kinds of hardware / software issues, phones, SIM cards, headsets and so on.

Wizard would take care of weapons and ammunition, and JAC of course everything incendiary, which included detonators, grenades, explosives devices, sweeper equipment etc. We also had to consider our location. For now we could stay in Karachi, but not in the long run. We had to find a safe base, and preferably one that would eventually become permanent.

Our initial assignments would ideally be assassination oriented, as they were often the easiest and fastest, and we all three needed to get out in the field again – and if we could get some easy missions, it would be a good start.

As for potential clients, we would start with the names that were on the USB and time would tell if we needed further 'marketing'. All clients had to be legitimized and a screening of their identity was therefore essential, and this is where Wizard's hacker Hendersson came into the picture. We had to background check all the email addresses for security clearance and who better to do it than him? Wizard set up a meeting with him for the next day and we agreed to offer him a contract.

None of us were IT experts therefore he was the obvious choice. Hendersson had previously worked for a well-known whistle blower and he had been part of the team that leaked information to the public about the authorities' illegal use of surveillance and control of citizens. He detested all forms of abuse of power and control of the individual and wanted a society where information could flow freely without any kind of restrictions and censorship. But, as Wizard so beautifully put it, we must never forget that he was also an opportunistic capitalist and with an existing bounty on his head – from his involvement in the whistle blower case – therefore it would be logical to include him in the group. In short, we could protect him while he made money. However, it is one thing to buy loyalty, and another to be loyal, and it's amazing how loyal people can become when their lives depend on it.

The 'bedside meeting' had taken three hours and subsequently we literally went our separate ways. JAC went to the hotel gym, Wizard took a shower and I went to my bedroom to meditate.

During the evening, we gathered again and to our great delight Wizard was on form although he was somewhat tired but he looked better than he had done in a long time. JAC had ordered dinner for us, which consisted of meat, eggs and vegetables, and I had made sure that housekeeping had cleaned the suite and replaced the broken glass table with a new dining table – this time of solid wood. We all sat round it eating our dinner and it was incredibly cozy. We joked, laughed and the old sarcasm was, to everyone's delight, definitely back. It was nice and just what we needed.

By ten p.m. it was my turn to check out the hotel's exercise facilities which fitted nicely with Knox stopping by to talk to Wizard and JAC.

To be honest, I had imagined that I would be pretty much alone in the gym – considering the time – but there were an astonishing amount of people there when I arrived. I took it easy on the various machines, but due to the codeine I'd taken I barely felt any pain.

Afterwards, I went to the infrared sauna and it was great just to sit there being warmed up completely. Incredibly enough, I was the only one using it, but it didn't matter to me. It was wonderful just to let my mind fly, and in the end, I was – as so many times before – left with a beautiful emptiness that filled me completely and utterly. It was a nice familiar feeling that I had had countless times when I was on missions. It could probably best be described as a kind of indifference to everything and nothing that just got bigger and bigger and eventually swallowed me up completely. On the missions, it was that feeling that made me come alive, but here and now it just gave me a sense of being. Strange that emptiness can do that, but it can – under the right circumstances.

It was past midnight as I sat in the hotel bar waiting for JAC to send me a message telling me Knox had left and the coast was clear. There were not many in the bar, but at a far table sat a rather noisy group of men. At one point, one of them came up to the bar to order more drinks. I don't think he saw me because I was well hidden in the dark corner of the bar farthest from him. One of the guys at the table suddenly yelled that he should just put it on Greg's bill and then they all laughed. The guy at the bar, however, announced loudly that he dared not do that, because he wanted to live to see the next day.

In fact, I probably would not have been worried about their outburst had I not suddenly seen the tattoo on the guy's right wrist as he reached out to get the drinks. He was a Navy SEAL. Or at least trained as one. I waited until he was gone from the bar, after which I discreetly settled my bill in cash and disappeared. If Greg was in the hotel, it would be too risky to take the elevator, for in reality I could bump into him there, so I took the stairs to the suite. On my way up, JAC messaged me. Knox had left so, less than thirty seconds later, I was standing in the suite.

"Greg's boys, they are primarily SEALs and Special Forces, aren't they?" I asked and the question made both JAC and Wizard stare quizzically at me.

"Uh ... yes," JAC replied, frowning, "Why?"

"Because ... he's here at the hotel," I said clarifying.

Wizard jerked his head back and took a deep breath,

"Yes, of course he is," and then he started laughing ironically.

"It's incredible," JAC began, while Wizard was still laughing, "Now we have to fight them too." JAC got up and took a bottle of JD, out of one of our bags. Then he unscrewed the top of it and took a sip. As I walked over and closed all the curtains, JAC threw the bottle to Wizard who stopped laughing to take a slug of it.

"We don't have to fight HIM. We just have to avoid him and his gang, and what better way to do that than to isolate ourselves in here while he's in Karachi? We have a lot of things that we need to get up and running before we can move on."

I looked at Wizard who was now just sitting with the JD bottle in his hands.

"Tell me," said JAC, annoyed with the whole situation, "am I the only one who thinks this is just a little too coincidental that Greg is here at the same time as us?" We all looked at each other, for he was actually right. With Greg, there was nothing that was random – at least not that random.

"We're moving out – tonight." Wizard said firmly and an hour later everything was packed and stood in large bags at the door. We agreed to take the stairs down and I volunteered to pick up the car. Luckily no one noticed me as I calmly walked through the foyer and out through the revolving doors. I picked up the car and parked it fifty metres from the hotel waiting for the boys. Wizard was the first one to get to the car. He threw four of the bags in and then sat in the passenger seat next to me. Two minutes later, JAC came and threw the last three bags into the back. He then jumped into the back seat and I floored the accelerator and we were gone.

"I guess we have a ten-minute lead," he calculated, tightening his seatbelt.

"Did you pay with ...?" I asked.

"An alias card ... yes, of course. Not that it matters much. The receptionist was already on the phone to someone who I assume was Greg by the time I had reached the revolving doors." There was silence in the car for a few minutes while Karachi's winding streets were travelled at high speed.

"Where's the last place Greg would look for us?" I asked then.

"Amman." Wizard replied.

"It's a hell of a long way to Amman in a Hummer," I said quietly, making a sharp right turn.

"Yes," replied Wizard, placing one hand on the panel in front of him to counteract the force of the turn, "and us with a ten-minute lead." There was silence for a moment and then we all started laughing. It all seemed so grotesque. We did not even know if Greg was after us. Presumably not, because then his approach to us would probably have been different, but since Wizard and I would like to remain 'dead' a little longer, there was no reason to risk running into him and his boys at the hotel. One thing we could assume was that Greg was now informed that we had left and so it was up to him to follow us and down to us to find out if he did and how to avoid him. JAC leaned forward between the front seats, pointing at a road sign.

"Aim for the Korangi Creek Marina," he said and Wizard smiled recognizing the name. It meant nothing to me but obviously they had been there at some time in their past.

As I headed for the marina, Wizard picked up his phone and called Knox. The conversation was short and in it he asked Knox to be in Amman in forty-eight hours. Telling him that before he arrived he would have received the co-ordinates for where he was to be picked up. Then Wizard messaged Hendersson and moved the meeting with him indefinitely.

* * *

It didn't take long before we could see the silhouette of the marina buildings in the distance and when we reached them I slammed the Hummer to the side. A two-metre-high wall and some tall trees on the right side were all that separated us from the boatyard and the jetties. The harbour was lit, but the trees gave us some cover from the light. Although there were port holes for every twenty metres they were decorative so JAC used the height of the Hummer to climb over the wall.

"Give me fifteen minutes," he said before disappearing over it and then everything was quiet. I had turned off the car engine and while Wizard and I sat in darkness waiting for JAC to signal that he had found a boat with sufficient fuel and the coast was clear we didn't exchange a single word. I am sure we were both going through several scenarios of what was to come but until JAC returned there was no reason to discuss them. At one point Wizard took his phone out and sent a text. Immediately after – and without waiting for an answer – he put it back in his pocket. I knew it wasn't any of my business and, under normal circumstances, I wouldn't have thought about it but, given the situation, it seemed strange to me.

As if he had read my mind Wizard suddenly said that the text was private and I didn't need to worry. I didn't comment on it. I trusted him and I knew that he was not going to betray us.

The minutes felt like hours but finally JAC sent us a text saying that all was clear and that he had found a boat. Both Wizard and I jumped out of the car and a few minutes later we had thrown our luggage over the wall. Just as JAC had done Wizard used the Hummer to climb the wall and when he was over it, I started the car and I parked it down the road with some other luxury vehicles. Then I ran back and using one of the trees I managed to scale the wall.

Despite the pain in my shoulder, which can be best described as being impaled by an axe, I picked up the bag that Wizard and JAC had left for me and then I started to run through the boatyard. One hundred metres ahead and twenty-five metres out on one of the wooden jetties I spotted JAC and Wizard. They were aboard a speedboat and the very second I stepped onto it, JAC short-circuited it and it started with a hollow drone. Wizard and I let go of the mooring ropes and raised the fenders and with JAC at the helm we moved quietly out of the harbour. As we passed the outer pier, we saw two security guards with dogs running down towards the empty mooring, and at the same time, JAC pulled the throttle control all the way down and we disappeared rapidly into the darkness.

* * *

The concept of being lucky is not really something I, in any shape or form, count on in my profession, either you know your job, and then you survive, or you die – it's that simple. But that night we had luck on our side. We had escaped a possible confrontation with Greg and there was enough fuel on the boat for us to reach Dubai.

As I had absolutely zero experiences with boats JAC and Wizard took turns steering, using what looked like a wheel from an old Buick in the fifties. It wasn't a huge speedboat but big and fast enough to get the job done so while it cut through the sea, I made myself comfortable in the white upholstered seats in the back. For a while I just sat there with closed eyes letting the wind ruffle up my hair. The occasional splashes from the sea water that hit my face were a lovely reminder that soon we would be in no man's land – or rather international waters – and it made me smile.

Wizard was sitting next to me looking out over the ocean we were about to conquer and for some reason he didn't seem so relaxed as me. I didn't really want to go into it but since we had a very long boat trip in front of us I decided to take the bull by the horns and ask. However, the answer was short as he just said that he would relax when we were in Amman. And that was the end of that conversation.

* * *

After a couple of hours we were in international waters. JAC was still the captain of the boat and Wizard ... well ... he was far from here ... sailing his own morphine ship. The rumbling sound of the engine made me sleepy and as the seat I was sitting on also reclined into a sun bed I lay back on it. It was quite comfortable and I must have dozed off because when I woke up I found that JAC had put his jacket over me. I looked to the front where I could see that Wizard had taken over the wheel and next to me JAC was lying in a chair like mine sleeping. I lay for a while gazing up at the dark sky. There were thousands of stars and they looked like shining diamonds on a black velvet robe. A feeling of being very small and insignificant in this endless universe washed over me but instead of making me uneasy it somehow comforted me. I could see what I suppose was a satellite moving across the sky and I for a moment I thought of what it would be like to fly around up there. I pictured myself in a spaceship zigzagging between stars and planets as I avoided asteroids and black holes. It was crazy but also so liberating. Being my own Captain. Being free. I put my seat back into the upright position and as the gusts from the sea hit me I shivered a bit. I looked to where JAC was lying and I could tell from the way he was hugging himself in his sleep that he was cold so I put his Jacket over him. Then I took the two steps towards the bow where Wizard was sitting steering.

"Hi," I said putting one hand on his shoulder and he turned his head towards me, saying,

"Hi".

"Where are we?" Wizard, who was sitting leaning casually back in the seat with only one hand on the wheel, sighed.

"Over 250 miles out," I stared at him in surprise.

"How long have I been sleeping?" Wizard looked at his watch.

"A little more than five hours. You should get some more. We will be here for a while." I didn't really feel tired so instead I took the seat next to him. He seemed kind of relaxed as he sat there just with one leg up on the dashboard and one arm resting comfortably on the armrest.

"Will you teach me how to steer the boat?" I asked hoping that he would say yes. I was always up for learning new things and since we had several hours to kill it seemed like a good idea. Wizard straightened up and slid over so I could sit next to him and for the next fifteen minutes I got a crash course in navy navigation. He was actually a very good teacher and when he was done, he got up and let me take the wheel. As he sat down on the seat next to me he lit a cigarette and went into his relaxed pose. I knew I shouldn't be asking but there was something that had been nagging me for some time and now that we had a peaceful moment I might as well try to get an answer.

"Wizard ..." I started a little warily, "there is something that's been bugging me and I don't know if you want to answer but I'm going to ask you anyway ..." Wizard didn't even look at me as his eyes were fixed on the bow waves the boat was making.

"Ask away," he just replied and I took a deep breath before I enquired.

"Why are you shooting up?" Wizard turned his head towards me and I could see a puzzled look on his face, "I mean ... you are one of the strongest people I know and ... probably the last one I would ever think to ... start that shit so ...." I stumbled through the sentence and the further I got the more I regretted asking the question but Wizard just kept staring at me.

"JAC hasn't told you has he?" he then said and now it was my turn to look surprised.

"Told me what?" A crooked smiled spread on Wizards lips.

"We didn't do this to ourselves. We didn't just start shooting up. This was done to us." I stared wide eyed at him as I mumbled,

"Why?"

"Why? We were captured in Afghanistan by some rebel group ... I don't even know the fuckers name ... and instead of giving us 'truth serum', which they probably didn't have, they pumped us full of this shit. They must have seen too many movies from the Vietnam War and thought that by turning us into addicts we would begin to talk when the withdrawals became too much but hey ... we are talking about us ... me and JAC. It is going to take a lot more than the shakes to make us spill the beans. You didn't know this?"

My chin dropped as I sat there starring at him in shock. They had been turned, and not by choice, into addicts. I was lost for words and I think Wizard could see it because as he continued his smirk faded.

"Anyway ... we managed to escape but by then we were hooked on the shit and the agency we worked for didn't care. They had already written us off when we got captured so there we were ... alone and hooked on this shit.

We then decided to go to east to Asia but that was a mistake. The shit was so cheap there that we did nothing but shoot up and ... well, you get the picture. It was over there JAC switched to heroin." Wizard snorted, "He had this idea that since heroin was cleaner than morphine it was easier to get out of. Well ... guess whoever told him that bullshit must have been a smack-dealer because it definitely didn't work. He almost junked himself to death over there, so I got us back to Europe and that's when we joined Liam's group." I was stunned and for once I didn't know what to say. "I'm surprised that JAC hasn't told you. I was sure he had."

"No. He hasn't." I felt like I had lost my voice and it was just coming back to me now because my answer came out in a low whisper.

"Well ... there isn't really much to say about it anyway. I'm glad he is out of it. He had it really bad." I almost choked but I managed to ask,

"What about you?" Wizard giggled as he looked down at the floor.

"Well babe ... that is a whole different story ... and there are not enough miles in the ocean to cover that one." He found my gaze and sent me a wink and a little smile. Then he got up and stretched before taking the wheel back.

The rest of the trip went smoothly. I didn't confront JAC about why he hadn't told me about his capture in Afghanistan and everything that followed. Somehow it didn't matter anymore. He was clean so I left the rest where it belonged: In the past.

* * *

In Dubai we 'dumped' the boat and continued in a 'borrowed' car to the airport.

The first flight to Amman departed an hour later, so we checked in after purchasing tickets. Since we did not have security clearance for our 'luggage', we had to let it all go in the hold, which meant that we did not have any weapons on us for the next few hours and as the situation was, this was by no means ideal, but we had no choice.

Luckily there were not very many people in the departure terminal but despite that we went straight to the gate and waited. Wizard, who during our boat trip had kept his addiction in hand by raiding the boat's first aid kit, had begun to show symptoms of withdrawal, sitting restlessly drumming with one hand on his thigh. On his forehead I could glimpse small beads of sweat, and even though there was some risk in going over and sitting next to him when he was like this, I did it anyway. He did not seem to mind, as long as I did not comment on his condition, and honestly ... the idea of doing that had not even occurred to me. Wizard knew the situation and how his body would react when he ran out of drugs, so to remind him of it was unnecessary.

"Here," I said, handing him my bottle of codeine tablets, "You better hold on to these until we reach Amman, do you hear?" His hands had begun to shake violently.

JAC, who had been gone for ten minutes, now turned the corner with three cups of coffee. There was no doubt that Wizard's withdrawal symptoms were getting worse by the minute. After I had taken my coffee cup, JAC sat down on the other side of Wizard.

Wizard's whole body now trembled and it was clear that he was not able to unscrew the top of the codeine bottle himself. I put my cup on the empty seat to my left and took the bottle out of Wizard's hand, opened it, and gave him five tablets. He immediately put them in his mouth and JAC gave him one of the cups of coffee. Wizard swallowed the pills and then leaned forward. He let his arms rest on his thighs as he bowed his head. It was as if electric shocks passed through his entire body.

"How many are left?" JAC asked, looking at the bottle. I unscrewed the top and poured the remaining pills into my hand.

"Four," I replied.

"Give them to him," he said and his voice reflected that he was really annoyed by this situation.

"He just got ..."

"Do it," he whispered, "He's used to something ten times stronger, so I'm sure he can handle it." I gave Wizard the last pills and he swallowed them.

"You have forty-five minutes to get yourself together," JAC told him coolly, "Otherwise we'll leave you here."

I had expected Wizard to protest, but no ... he nodded and replied,

"Okay."

Sweat sprang from his forehead and it was clear that he was fighting a desperate battle to remain calm both physically and mentally.

So far we had been alone at the gate but after a quarter of an hour more passengers started to arrive. They were people who were going to work in Amman and luckily most of them were already preoccupied with their iPads and laptops, so they hardly noticed Wizard's somewhat desperate condition.

When the flight was called, we waited until everyone had boarded before getting up. Wizard's tremors had subsided, but he was pale and sweating as if he had run a marathon. The gate stewardess looked at him and she was going to say something when JAC reassured her and Wizard and I handed over our boarding passes and went out to the plane.

We had bought first class tickets and I sat next to Wizard who seemed to have calmed down a bit more. JAC boarded and sat down in the row in front of us. He turned around and looked at Wizard, who had his eyes closed, leaning against the window. One of the stewardesses came over and asked if Wizard was okay and I apologized for him explaining that he had a fear of flying and a moment later she came back with a glass of whiskey for him. I thanked her for her gesture, because of course it was thoughtful, but with the ticket prices we had paid, there had to be at least one bottle of JD to offset them. I asked for a pillow and a blanket for Wizard, and she just managed to come up with them as the plane taxied to the runway.

Four hours later we left Amman Airport. I had to support Wizard so JAC had to handle the luggage. I managed to hail a taxi and put Wizard in front next to the driver while JAC and the taxi driver loaded all our bags in the back. When they were done, JAC jumped into the backseat where I was already sitting and as soon as the driver was behind the wheel, Wizard gave him an address.

Due to heavy traffic it was an hour later when we arrived at a small private residential property that was located in a narrow one-way street in the middle of Amman. JAC paid the driver and after unloading all our stuff he took off. As soon as he was gone Wizard started walking down the street. Although it was obvious that he was in a lot of pain he managed to walk by himself leaving JAC and me to carry the bags. We followed Wizard and approximately a hundred metres down the street he turned left and walked another fifty metres before crossing the road and turning right into a very narrow alley. Both JAC and I were on high alert as we moved down it, for it would have been a perfect place for an ambush, but Wizard did not hesitate or he was too sick to care. He continued relentlessly down to the end of the alley, where he went up a staircase to the first floor. Here he rang the doorbell on the left and shortly after it was opened by a young and very beautiful Arab woman.

"Alec," she exclaimed, smiling, but the smile quickly disappeared as it dawned on her what state Wizard was in. Wizard almost fell into her arms and it was clear that his weight was too much for her. I dropped the bags I was carrying and grabbed hold of one side of him and between us we got him through the hallway and into a small bedroom. We put him onto the bed where he immediately lay down and curled up in the foetal position gasping for air. The woman sat down next to him and he asked her something in Arabic. I did not hear her answer but after giving it to him he screamed out in pain. Then she asked him something else and to that he screamed "Yes", after which he clung to her thighs as the cramps incapacitated him. The woman remained seated quite calmly and stroked his hair until he relaxed his grip after which she gently freed herself and walked to the door.

JAC, who was standing in the doorway watching the whole scenario, got a little embarrassed when she smiled at him, and he moved slightly so she could pass him. Not unexpectedly JAC looked over at me with raised eyebrows asking if I knew who she was but I shrugged. I had no idea.

A moment later she came back with a needle and a bottle in which there was a clear liquid. JAC grabbed the bottle out of her hand and, after he read the label, handed it back to her. He indicated with his fingers how much she should give Wizard and the woman showed no sign of surprise at JAC's action. Her gentle expression remained as she put the needle in the bottle and extracted the exact amount JAC had advised. It was clear that she had done it before and the speed with which she found a vein in Wizard's arm was remarkable. A couple of taps on his arm and then she had it. She injected him and then bent his arm so that the small needle hole was closed. Within a minute Wizard had calmed down so the woman got up from the bed where she had been seated and left the room with the used needle and bottle. Silently JAC went to Wizard who despite being given morphine seemed remarkably coherent – tired but coherent.

"Okay, Wizard. Now we need answers. Where are we and who the fuck is she?" he said and without turning, he pointed in the direction the woman had gone.

"My name is Imeni and you are safe here," the woman, who had appeared in the doorway again, replied. The answer was by no means sufficient and I could see that JAC was just about to verbally attack her for her lack of explanation, so I felt obliged to cut in.

"Who are you?" I asked kindly doing nothing to hide my surprise over her presence here.

Normally I would have been a lot more sceptical, but there was something about her that just inspired trust, so I let it go. She smiled and that only enhanced her beauty.

"I'm Alec's wife," she said.

"Alec?" I enquired.

"Yes ... Alec." She pointed to Wizard.

At that JAC's and my jaws literally dropped. She chuckled a little but then she said, "Yes, we are married. I guess you don't know that we have children either?" JAC shook his head slowly.

"What? You have children?" Both JAC and I were completely in shock.

"Yes. Twin boys. Ten years old." She smiled and it was clear that just saying this filled her with love.

"Come," she said quietly, "We'll let him rest for a while."

Like two dogs, JAC and I followed her as she walked out of the room. It was completely surreal that Wizard had a family: A wife and two children. The most emotionally cold and insensitive of us was a father and a family man. I would never have guessed. He had never said anything. Never indicated it. I had always thought he was alone. No lover. No family. Nothing. Just him and that was one of the reasons he could live and do the things the way he did.

Imeni showed us into a small room next door and there was no doubt that it was the living room of the apartment. It was very Arabic-inspired with Persian rugs on the floor and walls, and big Moroccan seat cushions that surrounded a large low mahogany table inviting us to sit down.

She went out into the kitchen to get glasses and plates and shortly after the table was set. JAC and I sat and Imeni took a seat next to us. Her movements were calm, light and elegant and there was somehow something elf-like about her whole being.

It was very hard to imagine her and Wizard together because they seemed like two opposites. She was petite, feminine and elegant. He was big, masculine and rough.

"We apologize if we seem a little stunned," I said, "but we had no idea you existed."

"Probably none of Alec's colleagues know and it's best that way. But since you are the ones closest to him, I guess you had to find out one day. The mere fact that he chooses to bring you here shows how much you mean to him and how much he trusts you."

JAC was eerily quiet while Imeni talked and it made me a little worried. His facial expression showed a strange kind of mistrust and scepticism and it seemed to hurt him to find out about Wizard.

"How long have you been married?" I asked calmly and smiled.

"Uhh ... twelve years."

"Twelve years?" JAC said surprised, "It can't be. I've been working with Wiz ... Alec for nine years and had no idea he had you and ... kids? When do you see each other? That can't be often? I'm pretty much with Wiz ... Alec twenty-four-seven."

Imeni smiled indulgently at JAC.

"We see each other when it fits in with Alec's work. Sometimes he stops by and we are together for a few days, other times for an extended weekend. But we knew it would be like this and we have arranged our lives accordingly, so we are used to it. Sometimes it's a little hard on the boys, but Alec is always home for Christmas and on their birthday. We are very strict about that." She became serious for a moment but then she smiled again.

"We have never been together for a single Christmas." JAC suddenly alluded thoughtfully, "I thought he went on a drinking spree Christmas and New Year when the rest of us went home ... or wherever we went."

"No ..." Imeni said, "He came home and celebrated Christmas."

"So you are Christians?"

My question actually seemed a bit out of place but, after all that we had just been told, it was in a way pretty legitimate.

Imeni smiled and nodded.

I sat looking around and noticed that there were neither family photos nor religious effects to be seen anywhere in the living room. Imeni must have read my mind because she said quietly.

"We do not live here normally. This is ... just an address."

"Where do you normally live?" I looked at her curiously.

"That's not relevant," she said kindly before getting up and leaving the room.

JAC and I looked at each other and neither of us had any words for all this. The silence between us was much needed and it was only interrupted when Imeni came in again this time accompanied by Wizard. He had got the colour back in his face and seemed to be okay. Very calmly he sat down opposite JAC.

"Well, now you know. I am married and have a family."

Wizard looked at JAC, who was sitting and scowling at him. There was a long pause and the longer it got, the more the tension between JAC and Wizard grew. It was extremely uncomfortable, because when such a negative vibe between two contractors of their calibre grows stronger by the minute anything can happen. For the second time in all this, I was in doubt as to what they would do, for it was so obvious that JAC felt betrayed and let down by his best friend.

"Why haven't you said anything? How have you been able to keep your whole life a secret? What the hell is wrong with you? It's sickening, Wiz ... Alec. And Alec?" JAC got up and Wizard followed.

Imeni and I stayed seated but all my senses were on high alert.

"Goddamn. I had no idea you were named Alec."

JAC was furious and, by the look Wizard and I exchanged, it was clear that now was not the time to explain that Wizard's name was actually Oleg and not Alec.

"You knew perfectly well that Wizard is my call name and not my real one."

Wizard was obviously trying to stay calm but JAC's frustration affected him which I could understand, as it also affected me.

"A family ... Alec? Wife and children?" JAC began to walk around with his hands on his hips, "I thought I was your friend – at least you were mine. Why have you not said anything? Why keep it a secret?"

"To protect them," Wizard said calmly, "What you don't know, you can't tell – you know that. And yes, JAC. You ARE my friend ... my best friend and that's why I named one of my boys after you."

"What?" JAC momentarily stopped pacing. I could see that he could not cope anymore and I was pretty uneasy about what he would do.

Imeni got up and walked towards JAC but Wizard stopped her. It was far too risky to approach JAC now. There was a risk he could react irrationally and ...

Quietly, I got up and walked over to JAC. He had to be stopped as his attitude was unjustified and irrational.

"JAC, pull yourself together. This is not the end of the world. Wiz ... Alec did not do this to hurt you. He did it because he considered it to be the best thing for his family. You would have done the same." JAC looked up at the ceiling and took a deep breath.

"I need air," he said.

"Stop acting so sensitively," I replied, "If you need air, get out and breathe, but when you come back, we'll start afresh."

I was so tired of all this. Wizard had a family. A wife and two children, one of who was named after JAC. What the hell was the problem? If anything, JAC should feel honoured. Why he did not, I didn't understand.

JAC suddenly looked at me and I could see that all this was truly hurting him.

"Don't you get this shit?" he asked.

"Yes, I do, but you obviously don't. You feel let down and betrayed by your best friend and all he has done is to protect his family. Or rather his first family ... We are still his second family ... Yours and his relationship has not changed."

"She's right, JAC." Wizard said raising his eyebrows. For a minute no one said anything and this silence was almost worse than the foolish exchange of words. I watched JAC and slowly his facial expression changed from total frustration to something deeper and more hateful which invited a conflict. I made up my mind to break the silence but it was JAC who spoke.

"Okay," he said, "but since everything is so picture-perfect, why the hell do you take so much junk? Christ ... you have two kids ..."

"Don't go there, JAC." Wizard said loudly and I had no doubt that the shift in his tone of voice would seem like a red flag to JAC, who was just waiting for an excuse to explode.

"Fuck you." JAC snarled, "You may hurt us, but we can't say anything to you. Fuck you."

JAC's eyes flashed towards Wizard and I think everyone expected the worst until JAC suddenly turned and left the apartment. We all stood staring at each other and I could not help but draw a sigh of relief.

"Let him cool off," I said calmly, "He will be back. But honestly, this was a bit of a surprise, Wizard."

"Believe me, it was not my intention for you to know but now you do, remember that it does not change anything."

I sat down again to show that peace had been re-established and Imeni immediately followed my example.

"How did the two of you meet then?" I asked kindly and turned to Imeni.

"In Rafah. Alec was a good friend of my family." She smiled lovingly at Wizard, but then continued quietly, "One day my family was killed by a militia and I only survived because I was with Alec in his hotel room." They smiled at each other and it was clear that there was no reason for further explanation to what she was doing there.

"How old were you?" The question seemed somewhat irrelevant and it was only out of my own curiosity that I asked it because Imeni seemed to be much younger than Wizard.

"I had just turned eighteen."

She smiled at Wizard, who gestured that she should come over to him. So she got up, walked over and quietly bent down and they kissed gently and with a tenderness that I never would have imagined that Wizard could possess let alone show especially when there were other people present. It made me a little uncomfortable seeing them like that, so I smiled apologetically as I looked away.

A soft knock on the front door attracted our attention and Imeni, whose intention was to go and open it, was stopped by Wizard. I got up slowly and warily went to the front door. Carefully I opened it and there stood JAC. He had apparently cooled down and without saying anything he walked straight past me and into the apartment. Quietly, I closed the door and followed him into the living room. Imeni had sat down next to Wizard and was about to pour a cup of coffee for him when we entered. Wizard and JAC looked at each other and JAC was obviously about to say something when Wizard handed him the coffee cup that Imeni had just poured.

JAC took the cup.

"No hard feelings, okay?" Wizard asked.

"No hard feelings." JAC answered then he drank a mouthful.

Wizard looked thoughtfully at JAC, saying,

"On a rainy day, I will tell you the full story, but not now."

* * *

The stability between us was back and shortly after, JAC and I left the apartment. We strolled out into Amman's boiling heat without an actual goal but it did not matter. Normally neither of us would have ventured outside in the middle of the siesta but we had decided to leave the apartment so

Wizard and Imeni could have some alone-time together. It was several months since they had seen each other, so it was completely voluntary that we were now suffering in the heat.

JAC was completely chilled and as we walked down through the bazaar he casually put his arm around my shoulder. The smell of spices hit my nostrils and I took a deep breath. I had always loved bazaars like this one. As we passed one of the stalls where dried bay leaves, cumins and olive branches hung from the tent awnings and fresh figs, brown olives and cinnamon sticks combined with sacks of chili peppers and other strong scented herbs filled the air I simply had to stop. I don't think JAC cared much for it but he did dig into the bag of figs that I bought from the vendor so he wasn't completely uninterested. Despite the fact that on the outside we seemed like a couple of tourists who were just out enjoying ourselves we were constantly on guard and even though it was necessary I was honestly getting a little tired of it. I needed a place where I could just kick back and let my hair down and be myself like I had been in Kafka's house and on the boat coming here but I also knew that it had to wait. So, for now, I just strolled through the streets of Amman pretending everything was all right.

We had lunch at a small local restaurant and then we continued walking around in Amman well camouflaged behind sunglasses and hats. It was good to have this time together because then it gave us the opportunity to talk about everything that had happened during the last few hours.

"I feel a little bit like I'm dreaming and just waiting to wake up." JAC said as we made our way back to the apartment.

"I know what you mean," I replied placing one arm around his waist, "A father ... Wizard ... who would have thought it? And then married to an unbelievably beautiful woman. It's like we're in a Quentin Tarantino movie."

JAC chuckled as he chewed his gum. "Yes ... I wouldn't be surprised if John Travolta was dancing around the apartment when we return." We both laughed and honestly it would not have surprised me either.

By seven p.m. we were back at the apartment. Wizard greeted us at the door with a bare torso, military trousers and his Glock. Imeni was in the kitchen cooking so we went into the living room and sat down.

"Knox is arriving tomorrow night," Wizard said seriously, "We can't stay here so I suggest we pick him up and move on." JAC, who had thrown himself on top of some of the large pillows on the floor took off his sunglasses.

"Okay," he replied nonchalantly patting one of the pillows to signal to me to sit down, but I ignored him.

"JAC and I are taking a hotel room tonight," I said looking at Wizard.

"Why?" The wrinkles between Wizard's eyebrows reflected that it was not exactly what he had expected to hear and that he was actually quite perplexed by this seemingly friendly gesture.

"So you and Imeni can have some time together."

"Imeni will leave when we have had dinner," he said, "so you do not have to go anywhere." I tried to read Wizard but neither his voice, his face, nor his body language showed any signs of emotion about the fact that he would soon be separated from Imeni again. It was admirable – and at the same time also a bit thought provoking – but I threw all my preconceptions away.

"Why?" JAC asked.

"Because she needs to be with our boys." Wizard replied and we knew all too well the assertive tone of voice which indicated that the subject was not up for debate.

"Okay," JAC replied, "Do you have a picture of your kids?" The question came as a surprise to me but my curiosity was not so obviously guarded by it because I actually wanted to see a picture of them too.

"No." Wizard replied snarling. Deep down we all knew that we never had any effects on us that could be traced back to anyone. It was not because we did not want to but because it could simply be too dangerous for us and for those we cared about if they fell into the wrong hands.

"I hope they take after their mother." JAC joked as he smiled wryly to Wizard.

"Oh, shut up." Wizard replied smiling.

"One is called JAC – what's the other called?"

Despite the fact that Wizard clearly did not want to continue this conversation, understandably, JAC did not let it go. Like me, he wanted to know more about his best friend and his family – now that the topic had been broached.

"Nico." Wizard replied looking at me.

"Nico and JAC. Cool. Do they know what you are doing?" Wizard turned his eyes to JAC.

"They are children, JAC ... so no. Imeni knows. Not in detail but in broad outlines." As if she had heard her name spoken Imeni entered the room.

"Food has been prepared for you all." She smiled at us and walked over to Wizard. They talked in Syro-Arabic and during the conversation he looked at his watch. The moment after Imeni left the room, Wizard picked up his jacket.

"I'm just going to take Imeni to the airport," he said and at the same time Imeni came back with her luggage and said goodbye to us. Wizard took the luggage and a few minutes later the front door slammed shut after them. JAC and I were alone in the apartment that smelled heavily of curry and chilli and slowly my hunger emerged.

"Do you want something?" I yelled to JAC as I stood pouring curry, rice and chilli sauce onto a plate out by the stove.

"Yes please," he shouted back and a few minutes later we were both sitting in the sea of pillows eating.

A key was put in the front door indicating that Wizard was back and it wasn't long before the three of us were sitting enjoying Imeni's cooking skills.

"Not to pry ..." I said to Wizard and was expecting to ask him some more questions when, out of the blue, he answered me.

"Then don't."

And that was the end of asking questions about his private life.

Chapter 26

The evening and night passed calmly.

While I sat with the laptop reading through documents as well as working on the setup, JAC and Wizard explored options. After a few hours and several scenarios presented about our further journey, JAC and Wizard had still not come to an agreement and, it seemed, it was time for me to get involved.

"Maybe we should look at it a slightly differently way? No matter where we are, we will never be safe, so why not turn it to our advantage? Why not make it attractive to employ us? We have each managed to stay alive, despite the fact that we are wanted and have pretty much everyone breathing down our necks. We must be able to market ourselves on that basis. Let's go public with it. Let the clients come to us instead of us spending all our time hiding from them." My idea made the guys shut up and for a while there was complete silence in the living room. But in my opinion, it was actually the only thing to do ....

"You're crazy," Wizard finally said, "Nobody will want to contract us. No-one. We are a liability."

"No, we are not," I said a little annoyed that he had not grasped the point of what I had just said, "We have what they want. The ability to fight and fight back, and last but not least to survive. We need to move away from assassination assignments and just concentrate on teamwork." JAC and Wizard looked at each other. They did not say anything, but they did not contradict me either, "We offer ourselves as a team – and only as a team. We know we are more vulnerable than others because we are wanted and even have bounties on our heads, but we also know how to protect ourselves. We have proved that if they get too close, then we are able to disappear – and disappear for good – if it suits us."

"We have been unbelievably lucky so far." JAC said quietly looking at me as I closed the laptop.

"No, we have been incredibly talented. Used everything we have learned. Been creative and innovative and solved the problems we have been faced with. We have delivered on what we have promised despite the fact that we have been betrayed and stabbed in the back. We've avoided elimination by those we trusted the most and whom we thought were our colleagues ... yes even our friends. Despite all this, we are still here and therefore the best at what we do."

It was so quiet in the living room that you could have heard a pin drop.

"If we do this, we need a bigger team," JAC said quietly, "The four of us are not enough."

"Then we find four more. Who would you suggest?" I looked at them both as Wizard got up.

"If we really do this, then the other four must be as 'wanted' as we are." Wizard said.

"Or someone we trust a hundred percent," I said, noticing out of the corner of my eye that Wizard was challenging me.

"I do not trust anyone a hundred percent," he said calmly.

"You trust Knox," JAC replied, "Knox has proven his loyalty and worth and is a good and stable colleague who works like a horse in the field." He took a deep breath and was about to continue praising Knox, but I interrupted him.

"We all agree on that and we must all agree on whoever joins the team, but can we agree that this is how we are going do it? Offering ourselves as a team – mind you without our names showing on any contract?"

"It doesn't matter if our names are on the contracts. The rumours will soon be that we are back," said Wizard and went out into the kitchen for a bottle of JD and some glasses.

"Leave the setup to me," I told him when he returned, "But do we agree that this is what we are going to do?" I asked both of them.

"Okay." JAC said and I turned to Wizard, who was just staring at me. Then he nodded. I took a deep breath. It was decided. To move on we needed to find a name for our team. We searched far and wide in our quest, but suddenly JAC asked,

"What are the initials of our first names in civilian life?" JAC looked at Wizard, "Yes, yours is an A." Wizard and I exchanged a quick glance, but neither of us corrected him. JAC looked at me.

"Mine is a C," I said, not wanting to reveal my birth name. It had been so long since I had thought of myself as a civilian and even longer since anyone had called me by my 'real' name. It belonged to a completely different life that I – in so many ways – had put behind me. I was not that person anymore and therefore did not feel that the name was mine. In fact, I felt more like a phone book. Look on a random page and stop your finger at the tenth female name, then you knew what my name was this week. OPUS was the name most people knew me by, but for me it was not my name either. That was more like the synonym of my survival.

Luckily, neither JAC nor Wizard inquired into my civil name, so I left it at that.

"Okay, mine is an O for Olivier," JAC replied, "What do you think about ACO?" Both Wizard and I raised our eyebrows. It was not bad.

"ACO Enterprise?" The question came from Wizard and as the smiles slowly spread on our lips, we looked at each other.

"That sounds like something from Star Trek," I said, and then we all burst into laughter.

"We boldly go where no man has ever gone before." JAC said almost crying with laughter and then we literally rolled around on the pillows laughing. It was so unbelievably liberating just to lie there and laugh and I think we all felt that way.

The laughter died out slowly and, when various sniffles were over, JAC scowled over at Wizard.

"I always thought there was a little Klingon in you, Wizard," he said and we were back in almost hysterical fits of laughter.

"No. Seriously?" asked Wizard, wiping his eyes with the edge of his t-shirt.

"It's serious." JAC replied.

"At least that would explain a lot of things," I said, smiling at him.

"You fucking Romulan," he replied, throwing a pillow at me and then we were back where we started – in fits of laughter once more.

Before we turned off the lights that night we had agreed on our new name. We were called ACO Security Service or simply ACOSS.

* * *

I spent the next day in front of the laptop. I used some of Liam's customer contract setups as templates for our own, and I set ourselves up as a Limited Company with a mailbox as an address. Next, I contacted a bank in Grand Cayman and set up a temporary master account with ten associated sub-accounts. Within ten working days one of us had to show up in person and sign the papers. We drew lots about who was going to go and it was me. Wizard had a contact in Damascus who could arrange 'travel documents', so we decided to go there as soon as Knox landed.

As the day progressed, it became more and more clear that if this was to work, then we had to have one person who would take care of all the administrative work in the future. I could not look after the 'office' and be out in the 'field' at the same time.

"It must be someone who knows how to research and undertake

background checks on all the clients and affiliations. One who can access various relevant databases. What about Hendersson?" I asked Wizard, but he shook his head resolutely.

"He goes to the highest bidder and is by no means loyal. He is a contractor, just within the IT world, so it is too risky." Unfortunately, Wizard was right and, with the relatively stable situation we had now, there was no reason to take such a chance.

"What was his name, the young boy we met in Benghazi?" JAC suddenly said, looking at Wizard, "Akram? Akim?"

"Aslan," replied Wizard, "Yes, he would be okay if he's still alive." There was a moment of silence, as it was not one of the sentences we used, but sometimes ..., "But he was actually a terrible soldier. You have to agree with me, JAC?" Wizard stood in the doorway to the living room with a bottle of water in his hand. He unscrewed the top and sipped.

"He was ... no he was not ... he was miserable, but he had the will." JAC replied.

"No, he did not," Wizard said, "Maybe the will to get out of it alive, yes, but no more than that."

"And why would he be the right one?" I asked sceptically looking at them.

"He was a trained programmer and had worked for Microsoft, but his father had, on behalf of their family, called him home to fight. The family was from Libya, Al Khums I think, and as the eldest son, he should 'uphold the family honour'. Completely insane. The kid had no idea which way was up or down regarding an AK 47."

I shook my head and smiled to myself.

"He really did his best, but had it not been for us ..." JAC looked at Wizard, "he wouldn't have lasted an hour."

"If you think we can use him, find him," I said calmly and continued working on the laptop. As if it were a cue, JAC left the room while Wizard walked over and opened a window. As he fastened the window hook, prayer was called from the minarets, and the narrow alley the window overlooked made it echo.

In my search of the various folders on the USB, I had come across one that contained a lot of documents written in the Cyrillic alphabet, so I turned the laptop towards Wizard asking him to translate them.

"Do you know what they say?" I asked hopefully, as he sat down and began to read them. He flipped through the various documents and when he had read them, he looked at me and his facial expression clearly showed that the knowledge he had just gained, he could well have done without.

"The weapons in the barrack were intended for ISIS," he said quietly,

"They came from Zagreb." We were both silent.

"Then we have done something right by preventing the fucking Islamists extremists from getting them," I replied smiling.

"How the hell did Liam get involved with them? That would be like saying yes to fighting for the terrorist group Boko Haram," Wizard snorted, "Fucking idiot."

I took the screen back again and for a while sat considering Wizard's interpretation of the document. It was obvious that Liam had been mixed up in some shit, but why ISIS? Why not some of the Chechen rebel groups? They were at least reputable and judging by the information on the USB, they paid just as well.

No private companies in our industry would want anything to do with either Boko Haram or ISIS. Some paramilitaries fought on their side, but if you were a serious enterprise, you said no to fighting for them. Because even though they had enough money to buy an entire elite army, there were limits to what we – the professional soldiers – wanted on our CVs – and these two organizations were not ones we wanted to be associated with – regardless of the size of the cheque.

Despite this, I now knew individual contractors, like Liam, were hired by both organizations and took an active part in their fight, but this was not something we – ACOSS – wanted to be a part of.

* * *

I opened the document with the drawing of the isotope and then pushed the laptop back to Wizard. He looked closely at it and began translating the Russian words. Suddenly he stopped and the furrows between his eyes had become deep and very marked.

"This is something JAC must have a look at," he said as he scrolled down the page calling for JAC, who, within seconds, appeared in the doorway with the phone to his ear. Without looking at JAC – and seeing that he was talking on the phone – Wizard continued to scroll up and down the page, saying, "Just check this out."

JAC walked over to him, bent down and looked over Wizard's shoulder.

"I have to call you back." JAC said, ending his call. With an elegant movement that seemed completely out of place, he pushed Wizard, who moved, and then sat down, "Where did you get this from?" he said seriously.

"From Liam's USB," I replied, and Wizard began translating the document.

"It is not necessary. I know what it is. These are the drawings for AR – 'Acid Rain'," JAC said. My expression must have shown that I did not have the faintest idea of what he was talking about, for after a brief glance at me, he began to explain. "It was for use in chemical warfare, but it was banned – strictly forbidden. Rumour has it that the Americans 'withdrew' it when it turned out to be a viral mutation." I looked at him.

"Acid can't mutate?"

"It has nothing to do with acid. It is a virus that does the same thing as acid when it hits the skin, only with the small difference that instead of etching through the skin from the outside, it does it from the inside." He got up again, "But you can take it easy. If that was what was in the metal box that I handed over to Mossad, then it's in their hands now – or rather in Kafka's." JAC left the room again with two sets of eyes following him.

"Then I'm immediately completely calm!" Wizard announced sarcastically. I turned the laptop back towards me again. Strange as it may sound, I was not in the least bit worried, because if that was what was preoccupying Kafka then he probably did not pose a threat to us for the time being. So unless he blew Mossad to hell, the danger from him was minimal. And when it came to Kafka that was the only thing I was interested in.

My search between the documents continued and a few hours later, JAC entered the living room again.

"He's alive," he said in astonishment, smiling all over his face.

"Who?" asked Wizard frowning as he chewed on a Nutrilett bar.

"Aslan ..." JAC looked at him and wrinkled his nose, "What the hell are you eating?"

"Lunch. You don't think all this comes naturally, do you?" He replied pointing to himself.

"No, with that wife, you have something to live up to," I said, smiling.

"Shut up now," JAC said, "What I wanted to say was, that Aslan is alive and believe it or not, he's in Damascus."

"What is he doing there?" asked Wizard, crumpling the paper from his health bar.

"He's hospitalized with gunshot wounds." JAC replied.

"Beautiful," replied Wizard swallowing the last mouthful, "As long it is not his head or hands that he has shot off, it will work."

"I have booked a hotel for you in Damascus," I said dryly as I sat with my eyes glued to the screen, "Three rooms and then you have to promise to behave nicely ..." I closed the laptop and got up "because I'm flying to Geneva early tomorrow morning to talk to a lawyer about setting up secondary accounts because we should not keep all our assets in one place."

"Then we must hope the passports are ready." Wizard said slightly teasingly while winking at me.

"With your fabulous 'persuasive abilities', I know they will be," I replied winking back. He smiled wryly before I left the room.

* * *

Day passed into night and the time to pick up Knox was approaching.

Wizard had made sure the passports were delivered in Daraa, so at seven p.m. he drove off to pick them up. It gave JAC and me four hours alone and those we spent eating and having sex. My pain had largely disappeared, which meant that we did not have to be limited by it.

In fact, being limited was one of the things I hate the most. I have always believed that being able to choose was a human right, and being deprived of that right – although for just a short period of time – made me almost desperate. It was pretty two-faced of me, because if there was one thing I did not do in my job, it was to support this right in relation to my marks. My choice here was in accepting the task or not. There was, of course, the possibility that I chose not to perform the accepted task, but that would have seriously limited me in terms of getting future tasks, so it was not a real option – and that would have been a limitation for me. But, despite this, it was at the same time this limitation that set me free. To have freedom of choice was the ultimate goal. In many of the countries and cultures in which we operated, the individual did not have this opportunity, and once one has seen what this can do to people, then the relatively few rules we had to live with were acceptable. After all, we had the choice, which was more than many people had.

At ten forty-five p.m. Wizard was back. He had not only obtained new passports but also new license plates for the car, which made it safer for us. JAC and he left immediately to pick up Knox at the airport and I was left with the laptop and my new passport. There were six hours until I had to catch my flight and I spent them sleeping, showering and packing. It was nice to finally be alone in the apartment, and where I would normally have seen news on the laptop or heard music, I felt more like just enjoying the silence after all these hectic days.

* * *

The trip to Geneva went as planned and so did the meeting with the lawyer.

He had previously worked for Liam and therefore knew the entire setup. The agreement he had with Liam included a 'transaction fee' of one and a half percent of the amount of each transaction. For security reasons, I increased that to three percent and when that happened, I had the lawyer exactly where I wanted him. Before I left, I gave him an address and phone number I had found on Liam's USB and asked him to check them. When he was in possession of the information, he should contact me, and only me. If I did not answer him within twenty-four hours, he should destroy the information. We then said goodbye and I took the next plane back to Amman.

I was picked up at the airport by Wizard. We used the trip to Damascus to bring each other up to speed with what had happened in the last one and a half days so I was prepared for both Knox and Aslan to be at the hotel.

It had been no problem to persuade Aslan to come and work for us. He had actually been extremely eager to replace his weapons with a keyboard and, having discharged himself from hospital, he was already sitting and waiting for me with the laptop and the USB. Knox had suggested that one of his former teammates, with whom he had worked in Sudan, join the group. He was a former legionnaire, but had worked for the last nine years as an individual contractor for several organizations, and JAC had already checked him out and, luckily for us, he was not currently contracted. His name was Christo and he was a native Southern Sudanese.

"When do you think I should be introduced to them?" I asked, for it seemed rather pointless to me to wait.

"When we have a secure base. We can't keep moving around from hotel to hotel. There is too little security in them and yes ... our situation is too insecure." I nodded in response to Wizard and took the opportunity to come up with a proposal for a safe 'port'.

"What do you think about Frankfurt? It is in the middle of the EU and with one of the largest airports and military bases just around the corner. In terms of infrastructure, it would be perfect."

Wizard had become completely silent, which was usually a good sign.

"Frankfurt?" he finally said, "I was hoping for Bogotá or Caracas, but Frankfurt is actually not that crazy."

"And who the hell is going to look for us there?" I asked rhetorically, but Wizard took the question literally.

"All the usual. For them, borders do not exist. You know that damned well. Do you speak German?" The question came as a surprise to me and I could not help but smile.

"Wizard, I'm half Swiss. I speak Swiss German."

Wizard started laughing. "It's not the same thing. Swiss German is completely incomprehensible."

"Shut up," I said, but could not help but giggle, for he was partially right.

"Well, then you know what language course you have to listen to on your iPod during the next missions," he said sarcastically, but I had no doubt that he meant it positively.

* * *

The trip was uneventful and we arrived at the hotel according to plan.

Wizard sent a text to JAC that we were outside and after leaving me there he drove into the gloomy Damascus night.

While waiting for JAC I looked up at the façade of the hotel I had booked. It was a small and very typical cheap Middle Eastern hotel which made it perfect for us as it didn't attract any attention in its appearance. It did not take many minutes before JAC came down the stairs smiling and, before he reached me, he threw a room key to me. It was a big old iron key and I did not think that hotels still used such things.

"Welcome to Hotel Shangri-La," he proclaimed grinning and gave me a hug, "An ingenious name for this dump." And I tended to agree with him, but as a temporary base for us, it was perfect. No one cared who came and went, so we would hardly be asked any questions.

We walked up to the floor where the rooms were and when we entered the room where we were supposed to stay it was clear that JAC had already moved in.

If you did not know better, you would think that we were in a military supply warehouse, because there were stacks of camouflage clothing in different colours and patterns, boots, bags, backpacks, caps, helmets, armbands and cartridge belts everywhere. In addition, there were bags with weapons, three of which were partially pushed under the bed and the rest were stacked along a wall next to it. I stood for a while taking in this organized chaos.

"Are you planning on having a yard sale?" I asked with a slight astonishment in my voice.

He laughed. "I wish. It's mostly stuff Knox brought with him. Not bad – especially this." He went to the closet and pulled out a Dragunov sniper rifle. I put my bag down and took it out of his hands. It was the latest model.

"Lovely," I said, "Has Knox become a sniper?"

My question was particularly relevant because why else would he have a rifle like this? It was a special weapon and it was expensive.

"Have you swept all this?"

JAC smiled at me and, unaffected that I was standing with a sniper rifle in my hands, he gave me a quick hug.

"Of course and it's all clear."

"Including the rifle?"

"Yes, the rifle too. And no. Knox has not become a sniper. There was one 'going spare' so he grabbed it." JAC sent me a smile and winked.

"He must have had quite a bit of overweight," I concluded as I let my fingers wander up and down the rifle. Touching it awoke something in me and I suddenly realized how much I had missed this. Missed the missions. I was not born to be sitting behind a computer. No. I belonged out there in the rough terrain hunting down marks. I needed it to feel alive. Needed it to breathe. And this ... this was my oxygen. My fingers took a firm grip on the rifle's barrel and a warm shiver spread throughout my body.

"It was sent as special cargo. We were two hours getting it through customs. Fortunately, the rifle was in his suitcase, otherwise ..."

I turned to JAC.

"JAC, we need to get started. I cannot stand this. It feels like we are constantly going in circles. We have to get out there. I have to get out there." I nodded towards the window and alluded to what seemed to be our 'old' world.

"I know. I feel the same way. It's the damned restlessness."

"It's the urge to get my heart rate up. The urge to feel like I'm alive. I'm going insane just waiting. Get me out there, JAC," I said, looking at him almost pleadingly. My desperation must have been evident because he grabbed my shoulders tightly with his hands and squeezed them.

"You will get out there. I promise you. I am going crazy too from being 'the zebra not the lion'," he replied.

"It's almost two months since I've last worked, JAC. Two months. It is ..."

"A fucking a long time ... I know, but we'll be out there soon."

He pulled me into him and kissed my hair.

Holding the rifle in one hand I wrapped my arms around his waist and put my head against his chest. His dog tags felt cool against my skin and the thought crossed my mind that if I pressed my head extra hard against him, his name from the dog tag would be copied to my temple. It was actually a silly thought, but I needed to have him with me, and what better way than to have him imprinted into my skin. The two dog tags that I had taken from Aussie and Liam, I had put on the chain with my own, and even though it was a bit sick, it gave me a strange reassurance to know that in a way they were always with me. When it came to JAC I did not want him to be part of this chain, so a print on my temple of his, was the closest I wanted his dog tag to me. I was abruptly torn out of my thoughts by a knock on the door and we let go of each other.

I threw the Dragunov on the bed and, at JAC's signal, I went into the bathroom and closed the door. I was tired of this. Tired of hiding. I closed the white toilet lid and sat on it. It was so fucking grotesque. I should be out there making a difference. There were lots who needed me but instead I sat here – one of the world's best snipers – on a white toilet lid in a cheap hotel in Damascus – a hundred metres away from an actual combat zone hiding and also from some of my own teammates.

It was foolish. STUPID. I had just reached this conclusion when JAC opened the door to the bathroom.

"Is Wizard back?" I asked, sincerely hoping that was the case, but JAC shook his head.

"No." He crouched down in front of me, "Promise me you will not do anything hasty. Wait until he comes back and we'll figure it out, okay?" There was an honest and real concern in his voice because he knew I was right, and with my knowledge of him, he would agree with me. We had to be out there. That was what we were trained for. That was where we were most comfortable.

Being in action.

There was a knock on the door again and this time it was Wizard. I could hear JAC speaking quietly to him, and his words were so true,

"We need to stop hiding her. She's very near the edge."

"No time like the present." Wizard replied and then he called me.

I got up and left my 'toilet exile'. For some reason I suddenly felt like a little girl being let out of detention. I entered the room and as I stopped I looked directly at Wizard.

"Wizard, I ..." I began, but he immediately raised one hand indicating that I should keep quiet.

"Here's what's going to happen." He looked at me and I immediately recognized the emotionally cold eyes that lay just below the surface and that occasionally appeared and flashed towards me.

"You and Aslan get the setup running and, if you assess that it is something he can handle, then you hand it over to him. In the meantime, JAC and I are getting ready to leave." JAC looked at him in surprise, but chose not to comment and asked,

"Where the hell are we going now?"

I had expected him to say Frankfurt, but ...

"Luc is north of Aleppo and they need a little help up there," he said, not really expecting any objections from us. This was the best news I had received in a long time because finally, I could look forward to a little normality coming into my life again.

"Who pays?" JAC asked.

"It's Luc, JAC. If he needs our help then ..." I said almost desperately because I did not want him to take away the chance of me getting back in the field again. I did not care that Luc needed us – so many did – but I needed this ... Or rather – we all did.

"No payment ... No help." JAC said coldly and I was about to lose patience that he in his own super-capitalist way stood in my way.

"Hell, JAC," I said annoyed and frustrated, but I knew even before the words left my mouth that it would be of no use.

"That's the way it is," he said, and I was well aware that it would be futile to argue with him. It hurt me to have to admit that he was actually right. We had not come here to fight the wars of others without getting paid for it. The motto 'Pay or Perish' remained valid.

"Okay," said Wizard, looking at me, "but then you'd better get started and find a job for us and take Aslan with you ... because there are bills that need to be paid ... NOW." He got up and opened the door to the corridor. "Are you coming?"

I looked wide-eyed at both him and JAC, because it seemed to me as if his gesture had come out of thin air and besides, we had not even discussed introducing me to the others, so ... JAC smiled,

"What are you waiting for? Would you not like to meet the group?"

I nodded like a schoolgirl who had just been told she was going up to the blackboard, and without further delay, I followed them.

When we entered the hotel room two doors further down the hallway, we almost gave Knox a cardiac arrest. He was sitting on a bed talking on the phone when we came in, but stopped in the middle of a sentence when he saw me and slowly lowered his phone from his ear while staring at me.

"Knox?" it came from Wizard, referring to his unfinished conversation, and Knox immediately picked up the phone again.

"Call you back," he said, ending his call.

Aslan was sitting on the other bed zapping TV, but when we stepped in, he promptly turned it off. Christo, who had apparently just been in the shower, came out of the bathroom wearing one towel around his waist while rubbing his hair with another and he also stopped when he saw me.

"What the hell ... We have a woman on the team?" he asked, smiling broadly. His black skin made his teeth look like a string of gleaming pearls and it made his whole face light up.

"Knox," I said kindly, smiling at him, "Breathe." And it was as if my voice awoke him.

"OPUS," he exclaimed, "How? Are you ...?"

"Alive? Yes." I walked over to him and gave him a hug. It was the first time we touched each other, but it felt like the right thing to do, and he reciprocated. I was surprised that Knox felt more of a wiry build than muscular because he did not really look like that. He was a little bit shorter than Wizard, approximately a hundred and eighty-two centimetres, with short dark, almost cropped hair and his very classic features gave him a gentleness that in no way matched his deeds. I would guess that he was in his early thirties, which also applied to Aslan and Christo, but unlike Knox, they were both more muscular and where Aslan was the same height as Knox, Christo was slightly taller.

"OPUS?" The words came from Christo, "The OPUS?"

"Yes," replied Wizard, "the same."

"Holy shit," it came spontaneously from Aslan, who almost jumped off the bed, "everyone thinks you're dead."

I released my grip on Knox and turned to face him.

"That's the point," I said, smiling, shaking his hand, "but, as the person I am, I have chosen to be resurrected."

"Like a true saviour." Christo said almost poetically.

I walked over to him and calmly shook his hand.

"I do not bring much salvation with me – only eternal peace," I replied and smiled at him while JAC and Wizard stood watching in the background.

"To think I should meet you – a legend." Aslan was visibly very honoured, which annoyed me immensely.

"Listen," I said kindly. "If we're going to work together no more legend-talk, okay?" I let my gaze wander between Aslan and Christo.

"Okay," Christo replied, "but just give us a chance to get over the shock that you are alive and that we even have the opportunity to work with you. It's actually pretty incredible."

"How many people know this?" Knox asked alluding to my 'resurrection'.

"None, outside of this room." Wizard replied.

"And for now it must remain so." JAC continued and his answer was not one to be questioned.

"Yes, of course." Knox replied, while Aslan and Christo nodded in agreement.

"Oh, by the way, Christo. This is Wizard." JAC pointed at him to introduce them.

"Wizard? OPUS and Wizard on the same team? Holy shit."

"Relax," Wizard said, holding out his hand, "Where the hell did you find this cheerleader, Knox?"

"On the savannah. He ran around with a bunch of Hutus." Knox sent Christo a wry smile and winked.

"Just be glad I haven't made soup from you yet," he replied sarcastically, tossing the towel he had wrapped round his hair, at Knox. We all stood and looked at Christo's hair because, it was really only now that we saw what it looked like. It was huge, curly and like a halo on the top of his head. At the same time, we all burst out laughing.

"That's some afro." JAC shouted and had to squat on the floor laughing.

"Can I just ..." Aslan reached out to touch Christo's hair while laughing.

"Hell no," it came from Christo as he slapped Aslan's hand away.

Wizard laughed so violently that he had to lean against one of the walls while tears ran down his cheeks. Knox lay on his back, chuckling as he held both his hands up in front of his face.

"You'll have to do something about it," I snorted as I wiped my eyes, "What will you do if one day it starts to rain and we are on a mission? We cannot risk your helmet suddenly popping off." Fortunately, Christo could see the humour in this situation and started laughing.

"Maybe I should let you cut my hair," he said slightly hopefully, looking at me.

This, however, only elevated the laughter even more.

"Try Aslan. He's obviously crazy to touch it," I cried from laughter.

"Hell no, it needs a woman's touch." Christo replied.

"That's why I suggested Aslan," I replied, and now both JAC and Knox were crying with laughter.

"I think I'll get a bottle of JD." JAC said in tears before disappearing out the door only to return two minutes later with a little 'fire water'. The laughter was dying down, but there was no doubt that it had helped to create an absolutely fantastic atmosphere between us. All barriers were gone, humour can do that to people, so now the real work could begin.

Chapter 27

We had arranged ourselves in the rooms so that JAC and I slept in the first one, Wizard and Aslan in the next and Knox and Christo in the last one. Since mine and JAC's resembled an army storage depot, breakfast was consumed in Wizard's and Aslan's quarters.

Aslan, who was a Muslim, had been up since five o'clock to pray, and for some reason it became custom that he made breakfast for all of us. I have often worked with mercs who were devoted Muslims, and it has never been a problem.

When I was hospitalized in the US, I had had plenty of time to expand my horizons and one of the books I got to read was the Koran. I simply had to know what it was that made people go to war for it. To my surprise, I had to conclude that Islam was not a religion that preached war and violence – quite the contrary. Now, I have also read both the Old and New Testaments, and in fact there was more violence, death and destruction in the Old Testament than there was in the Koran, so to me it seemed completely insane that someone could legitimise their terrorist acts with reference to the Koran. From my sickbed in the US, I could not help but think that the crusaders of ancient times were the jihadists of today, and considering that there had already been mercenaries in the time of the Crusades, then our profession was already a reality at that point in time

* * *

After breakfast, Aslan and I stayed in the room. We spent the whole day in front of the laptop, and if I had ever had the slightest doubt whether Aslan was the right one for the job, it was put to shame now. He was perfect for it. The combination of IT nerd and soldier was ideal for the job and what was more, I could see that he really enjoyed all the tasks. His work was structured and purposeful, and he was thorough, especially when it came to the research of the individual customers, weapons, hotels etc.

Since Aslan did not have to join us in the field, and therefore could not make money as a merc, his salary was a set percentage of our income, and despite the fact that he, for security reasons, did not have access to the individual accounts, he was the one who distributed the salaries of the individual team members to their respective accounts. He could also create accounts and check if transfers had gone through, but other than that, only us mercs had access to our own accounts. Each time a transfer went through, a percentage of it was automatically deducted to cover expenses related to the individual missions as well as administration costs which covered Aslan, the lawyer and the bankers. In time, we also had to find an accountant, but for now the most important thing was to get some assignments.

In the evening, Aslan was able to present the team to ACOSS's website and when the clock struck midnight, he pressed the button so that it was officially on-line.

The next day, JAC, Wizard and Knox spent most of their time attached to their Blue Tooths and around four p.m. the first assignments started arriving. Aslan immediately researched the customers who were behind the requests and if there was just the slightest chance that a customer had any connection to the FSB he or she was excluded.

At around eight p.m., a task came in from a private overseas company that wanted to hire us to protect a convoy from Damascus to northern Syria. It sounded really interesting and seemed to be a good mission to start with. To determine the cost of it, everyone in the team had verbally stated their daily wage and based on this, we set the price for the customer. Our total weekly price for the team was a hundred thousand Euros or fourteen thousand two hundred Euros per day, which included transportation, weapons, ammunition, wages, and administration fees.

As expected, the customer tried to negotiate the price, but our rates were not negotiable, and they ended up accepting the deal.

The task was estimated to last exactly one week and was to begin two days later. The money was to be paid when the agreement was signed after which we began the detailed planning. It took an evening and it was primarily Wizard and JAC who were in charge.

Meanwhile, Knox, Christo and I went through our equipment, such as phones, headsets, weapons and ammunition as well as clothing and field equipment so that everything was packed and ready for the next day's departure.

The night before we were to leave, we were in Knox and Christo's room and at one point I got up and signalled to JAC that we should go.

Wizard and Knox paid no attention to this but both Aslan and Christo looked curiously at us. The next morning as I was going over the last things with Aslan, he asked me if it was true that JAC and I were a couple.

I looked at him.

"As much as you can pair up in this industry," I said quietly and smiled.

"Do you want to die for him?" he asked and the question totally took me off guard. I sat for a while thinking.

"I would die without him," I said thinking of being alone on the island in Thailand. Aslan smiled and then he became serious again.

"What if something happens to you on a mission? Have you written a will?"

"I don't know about the others, but I have. I assume they have."

It was one of the practical measures that one automatically took before signing one's first contract, and in fact, there were many organizations that had lawyers attached, who took care of this very area. Aslan looked at me.

"IDs and kill pills are over there," he said then, nodding toward his nightstand.

I patted him on the shoulder as I got up and went over to take them. On missions like this, where there was the possibility of bumping into enemy troops like ISIS and Al Qaeda, we always had cyanide pills on us, because if you were captured, then you at least had the choice if you wanted to take your chance or ...

"See you in a week," I said smiling at him.

"You bet," he replied, as I went out and closed the door behind me.

* * *

Despite the fact that none of us had experience of guarding convoys, the mission went well. Knox had previously guarded oil pipelines in northern Iraq and, although it was not quite the same, there were certain similarities.

The mission brought us very close to the front line between ISIS, the YPG (Kurdish freedom fighters) and the government troops, but, in spite of that, we did not take part in any actual combat operations on the way to the destination.

The contents of the convoy were medical equipment for a hospital in Aleppo and, even though fighting was taking place in certain parts of the city, we did not fire a single shot.

The equipment was thus delivered safely, and although the hospital building shook a few times while we were there, due to grenade blasts, there was no real danger, judging by the reaction of the hospital staff. They just continued their work as if nothing had happened – for them it was just routine.

Once we had delivered the equipment, we agreed to take a few hours break before driving back, so Knox and I went in search of coffee in what constituted the hospital kitchen. The kitchen was in the basement and when we got there, two nurses were sitting chatting and eating something that looked like grey porridge. They abruptly stopped when we entered, but I reassured them that we did not mean them any harm and they resumed their lunch.

Knox found a couple of cups in a cupboard, but there was apparently no coffee. One of the nurses went to him with a jug of tea and out of courtesy he accepted and she poured it into the cups. We drank a few mouthfuls each and then put the cups down. Once you have set your heart on coffee, tea is not exactly what your taste buds need.

After the taste, Knox jumped up and sat on the kitchen table and lit a cigarette. For a while we did not say anything but the nurses had resumed their conversation.

I had mentally surveyed the room and had immediately concluded that there was no reason to be alert about anything in here. Therefore, it came as a surprise when the door to one of the big cold stores suddenly opened and a doctor and a nurse came out. Knox and I had noticed the door, but we had not anticipated that people would suddenly come out of it, so therefore we looked with surprise at them and at each other. It was not every day that we saw that scenario. The doctor disappeared immediately, but the nurse stayed. She obviously knew the two girls, because they smiled and talked cheerfully together. Knox jumped silently off the kitchen table while I pulled my Glock, and together we walked calmly towards the cold room. The nurse, who had come out of it, shouted something at us and then pushed the other two girls aside to get to us but Knox stopped her with one hand while I continued to the door.

Knox signalled to the nurse to be silent and, after a few protests, she was. Carefully I slowly opened the door. The room was lit by a fluorescent lamp in the ceiling, so it was not a problem to see what or rather who was in the room. On a thin mattress in the farthest corner lay a soldier. He was not conscious and judging by the attached IV equipment he probably would not wake up for the time being. I signalled to Knox that he should stay outside and then I disappeared into the room. It did not take me many seconds to realize that it was one of Luc's legionnaires, because I recognized him as the little Arab guy who had stood in the doorway of Luc's tent in Afghanistan. He was badly hurt, but he was alive, so I secured my Glock and went out to Knox without worries for my safety. As I came out, the nurse looked at me desperately and I signalled that everything was okay and gave her access to the room, which she took advantage of immediately. After she disappeared into it, I closed the door, and via my headset, I asked Wizard to come down to the kitchen.

Wizard arrived two minutes later and while Knox stayed by the cold room door, I walked over to him.

"One of Luc's boys is in there and he does not look too good," I said quietly with a stoney face. Wizard walked to the door and disappeared into the room. Shortly after, he returned with the nurse having evidently said something to her because she hurried out of the kitchen. The other two nurses had already left, so we were the only ones here.

Wizard called JAC over the headset and then we all stood silently. No need to say anything. In a few minutes, the situation would be resolved, whatever the solution might be.

"One of Luc's legionnaires is in there," Wizard said seriously as JAC entered the kitchen, "We have to get him out of here."

Without commenting on Wizard's words, JAC went and looked in the cold room, then turned to face us.

"Why? He seems to be doing okay." JAC obviously had no intention of getting mixed up in this mess and I could see his point but my initial reaction was that we could not leave him here. It could turn out to be extremely problematic, which we certainly did not need right now that we were getting out and back to Damascus.

"We cannot leave him here. If ISIS comes, he will be a head shorter."

Silence. I was just about to break it when JAC got ahead of me.

"What does the doctor say?" he asked slightly dismissively and without any great empathy.

"He's on his way." Wizard replied in his usual monotonous voice, scratching his hair.

"Good ... If he can be moved, we'll take him with us otherwise ..." JAC's eyes were directed at Wizard and they were firm and rock hard. I could not help but think that if these two men had really become enemies in the apartment in Amman, then it would have cost more than just blood, sweat and tears. JAC grabbed his AK 47, and without looking at us, he announced that we were leaving in ten minutes as he left the kitchen.

Judging from Wizard's blank stare, he did not seem thrilled with this message and, knowing him, he was weighing up every possible option and outcome to the present situation; calculating risk factors and potential injuries depending on the solution. He only put his strategic thinking on standby when the doctor and the nurse entered the kitchen. Together with the doctor he disappeared into the cold room only to come back two minutes later pursued by the doctor, who was protesting loudly because of Wizard's decision to take the legionnaire with us. Standing back, I watched Wizard let all the doctor's admonitions bounce off him, while words like 'irresponsible' and 'risky' were repeated constantly.

Suddenly Wizard turned to the doctor and, it was clear that he had had enough of listening to all his objections, he grabbed the collar of the doctor's coat, and pretty much lifted him off the floor. A few Farsi words were spoken by both of them and Wizard then slowly released his grip. After the doctor had solid ground under his feet again, he straightened his collar and told the nurse to get some extra drip bags of antibiotics and painkillers and, clearly shaken from witnessing the little incident between Wizard and the doctor, she disappeared out of the kitchen. The doctor and Wizard looked at each other, but it was an unequal battle; Wizard weighed the survival odds for the legionnaire, if the hospital fell victim to an ISIS attack, while the doctor assessed it from a medical point of view and only that. The doctor eventually withdrew, and at Wizard's signal, I went with him to the soldier. I removed the IV bag from the rack and held it up in the air while Wizard lifted the soldier up and together we left the cold room. On our way through the kitchen, we passed the nurse who was giving Knox the extra bags and some ampoules of morphine and three minutes later, we were out by the Land Cruiser. Christo, who had been guarding it, stared when we came out with the soldier, but without comment he opened the back door and made room for us to put the soldier in there.

Wizard put him in and I handed the drip bags in to Knox, who had placed himself in the back seat and was rigging the bags so they could be hung up.

A mortar shell exploded two hundred metres further down the street, and in its wake, a group of Dashers (soldiers from ISIS) came running. They were moving across the street and had obviously not seen us as they just continued their journey.

Immediately, Christo, Wizard and I went on high alert and Wizard called JAC over his headset. We were all aware that we had to leave now if we wanted to avoid a direct confrontation with the Dashers, and JAC came running out of the hospital's main entrance and jumped into the car's passenger seat. Christo started the engine while Wizard and I sat in the back seat each by the windows with Knox, who was still attaching the drip bags to the roof, between us. In fact, his venture with the bags looked miraculously successful because of the help of a few zip ties and a roll of duct tape.

Christo accelerated, JAC shouted, "Lock the doors." In a few seconds we were at the end of the street, where he turned sharply to the right and whether that was a good idea, we actually did not have time to wonder, because a bunch of Dashers came running straight towards us with raised guns.

"Fuck," Knox, who was sitting facing the rear window, called out and his outburst caused Wizard and me to turn our heads simultaneously to see what it was all about. Apparently, we had ended up in the midst of a fight between government troops and Dashers. The Dashers coming from the front of the car started shooting at the windscreen with little effect and soon we were surrounded. The whole car rocked, as soldiers, from both sides, slammed their rifle butts into the body of it and in my mind, I thanked Wizard for our armoured vehicle.

"Drive." JAC shouted and Christo floored the accelerator. The car hit some Dashers in front of us but honestly, we didn't care. There were gunshots everywhere and fifty metres to the left a couple of hand grenades exploded. Christo hit several Dashers with the car as he raced to get clear of the combat zone and what to begin with seemed to be a confrontation between two warring parties, now seemed to be more of a fight between two rival gangs. At the end of the road we almost collided with a tank as it came round the corner and fortunately Christo managed to dodge it. Behind it we could see another fifty Dashers with raised rifles.

Christo speeded up and a few Dashers bounced off the vehicle but there was nothing to do about it. Better them than us.

We drove at breakneck speed through the narrow streets of Aleppo, and it felt like we were in a maze surrounded by white walls. We had no idea where we were, but we had to keep going. Sometimes streets were blind alleys giving us no alternative but to reverse.

It was hell and not the least because the fighting was literally all around us. It felt like we were just driving blindly round and round without getting anywhere in these little alleys. JAC cursed loudly that the navigation equipment did not work here, but there was simply no signal – or the signal had been scrambled – who knew?

Leaning forward, I could see a five-story building in the distance and, if I was right, it could be our salvation.

"Get me to that building," I said to Christo pointing in the direction of it, "I'll go high-ground and direct you out."

"No." JAC shouted, while he was still messing with his GPS.

"Yes," I replied placing my hand on his shoulder, "The odds of ISIS getting us when we are driving blindly are far too high. Let me go."

Christo braked hard as I took OPUS and the box of bullets that lay at my feet and opened the door. JAC tried to grab me, but I was already out of the car and slamming the door.

To the sound of the tyres squealing as Christo hit the accelerator and with mortar shells exploding nearby, I disappeared like lightning into the building.

It was old and judging by the amount of papers and folders scattered across the landings it had been some sort of official building. I ran up the stairs and on the way I turned on my headset. I met no one and one minute later, I cautiously eased the door to the flat white roof open. I could see most of the surrounding area from up here and, what was better, there was GPS signal on my phone. I ran over to the edge of the roof, and positioned OPUS so it was supported. Then I started scoping the terrain.

"Talk to me, JAC," I said and JAC described their location. Ten seconds later, I had them in my telescopic sight, and calmly and safely I guided them out of the maze via GPS and OPUS. When JAC announced that they were out I rolled over so I was lying flat on my back with OPUS pressed against my chest. I closed my eyes and let the sounds around me form an inner picture of my situation. As I lay there, it really dawned on me how much I had missed being out in the field again. It was wonderful and filled me with an inner calm and contentment.

"OPUS," JAC's voice in my headset tore me back. It was clear that maximum range on it was about to be reached, "Fo ... fin ...."

The signal disappeared. I lay for a while waiting, but then I turned off the headset. Like so many times before, I was now alone, but it did not bother me. On the contrary. It was a nice familiar feeling that seemed almost intoxicating and made me smile.

I was engrossed in the moment but then reality reappeared. I had to get out of the city, and via the GPS I could see that it was approximately one hundred kilometres to the Turkish border. As prescribed by procedure, I entered the co-ordinates of my current position, followed by those of the border crossing west of Idlib, and then I sent the information to both Aslan and JAC. With the GPS in hand, I then ran back to the door, and I disappeared down the stairs.

For safety reasons, it was best if I waited until it got dark to move through the city, so I stayed on one of the lower floors of the building until evening. Throughout the day I could hear the shootings wavering back and forth in the surrounding streets, and despite the fact that the building was occasionally passed by running soldiers, none of them sought refuge in it.

As darkness descended over the city, I prepared for my exit.

Aslan had replied to my message, but I had heard nothing from JAC, which I did not find alarming. Mobile coverage was not always stable in war zones and sometimes it could take hours or even days before you got through. I finally turned off the phone even though I still had not heard from him and ventured out into the evening. The streets of Aleppo now only resounded with sporadic bursts of gunfire coming from the south-east and therefore posed no direct risk to me.

Silently, I sneaked along the walls of the houses and, as it got darker, bonfires were lit in various places in the empty and sometimes shattered buildings. Whether it was soldiers or civilians, I had no idea and I had no intention of finding out. I was just going out of town and to safety so I could meet the team again.

The sound of my pounding heart was the only thing that accompanied me as I moved quickly and almost cat-like through the streets. For others, it would have been natural for their heart rate to gallop away, but I took it that I was out of training and it annoyed me quite a bit. Along the way, I had to seek cover several times in or between buildings when soldiers and tanks crossed my path, but at no point was I spotted.

It took me three hours before I was so far outside Aleppo's city centre that I thought I could afford to take a rest. The landscape outside Aleppo was flat, barren and slightly sandy and it suited me really well after having to climb Aleppo's streets, which were often nothing more than rubble, shattered stones and pieces of concrete walls whose edges could be razor sharp.

The sky was illuminated by a sparkling sea of stars and only the sight and sound of a pair of random passing F16 planes broke this otherwise spectacular night. It made me think of the boat trip to Dubai and for a minute I closed my eyes as I recalled its slightly rocking movements of the speedboat. My memory was so vivid that I could almost smell the saltwater and feel the breeze on my face. Not often you can do that in the middle of a desert but it was kind of lovely.

By two o'clock I had reached a rock formation and made a short stop again. I needed to rest, so I sat down on the hard sandy ground with my back up against a rock. It was completely quiet and as I felt relatively safe I took the time to check my GPS. The moment I turned it on, a message from JAC appeared. I smiled to myself. They had reached Homs, but the message was several hours old, so they were probably closer to Damascus now. I read my co-ordinates and sent them to him and Aslan and – as I used to – I left the phone open for approximately three minutes afterwards. A message came back from Aslan containing a set of co-ordinates followed by the name – Luc. I smiled and responded by sending the co-ordinates back. Then I got up and started my journey towards Idlib – and Luc.

Chapter 28

Four hours later I arrived in Idlib. The sun had risen and the first prayer of the day in the mosques was coming to an end. I moved quietly along the houses of the shattered city and slowly I approached my destination.

The co-ordinates led me to a district and here, there was no doubt that the morning prayers were over, as the first mortars of the day were already flying round the streets. I sought refuge in one of the buildings, which at first glance seemed empty. On closer inspection, however, it revealed that there were two snipers on the roof, so inconspicuously I slipped onto it. Which side they belonged to, I had no idea and didn't really care either. What I had to make sure was that they were NOT from Luc's team. After confirming that they were not, I eliminated them – quickly and painlessly – with a single shot to each.

The coolness of the dawn and the opportunities the darkness of the night had given me to get cover disappeared as the sun rose in the sky. Therefore, I snuck back down the stairs and managed to slip into a room off the stairwell when I heard footsteps come running. It was a couple of Syrian soldiers, so I waited until they had passed the room and then I continued down the stairs and out of the building. For the next hour, I went from building to building hoping to find Luc and his team, but without any success. Another hour went by and still no sighting of either Luc or for that matter other legion or merc units. I gradually began to consider forgetting about Luc and instead heading to Homs, from where I could possibly get a lift to the Jordanian border with one of the international aid organizations.

I had decided that this was what I was going to do when I felt the muzzle of a gun against my temple. I had no idea why I hadn't heard the soldier coming up behind me and now I was about to pay the price. As I slowly began to raise my arms I felt a hand grab OPUS and take it from me. I was told to turn around slowly and I immediately recognized the voice.

"Fuck you, Luc," I said, spinning around so we were face to face. Maybe I should rather say my face to his chest, because Luc was as tall as JAC.

"What the fuck! OPUS?" He was obviously very surprised, that not only was I alive, but I was there, right in front of him.

"Yep," I replied, smiling, "for a division that needs help, you are fucking hard to find." I grabbed OPUS out of his hand, "Give me that," I said and Luc chuckled a little.

"Now we're even," he commented with reference to our last encounter in Afghanistan where I surprised him by taking his Glock from his waistband. It was when I wounded Kafka in the legionnaires tent by throwing Luc's hunting knife so it punctured his lung.

A mortar blast a hundred metres from us broke the 'idyllic' welcoming and made us both duck. I felt Luc touch my arm, but the gesture was not out of care. It was solely that he wanted to indicate the direction we should take and we immediately disappeared through to the back of the building. Here it was not so noisy and Luc, who had let go of my arm, ran across the narrow street and into another building and down into its basement. Down here he opened the door to a room and we slipped in leaving the door open.

"How many are you?" he asked and there was a glimmer of hope in his voice.

"Only me." I could see the disappointment in his face and I did not blame him. It did seem completely insane that I should be alone in the middle of this battle zone.

"Where are the rest?" he asked.

I shook my head.

"Long story," I replied, "Haven't you been told that I was coming?" I was kind of surprised because I somehow had imagined that Wizard would have contacted him.

"No," he replied, "Who would have told me that? "

"It doesn't matter. Can I stay with you guys until I figure out how to get back to Damascus?" Deep inside I hoped he was going to say yes but I was not sure. It was not something the legionnaires did – take on board women – but I hoped Luc would look past my gender and see me as just a soldier. He stared at me for a second and then he smiled.

"Of course. I wouldn't dream of saying no to a lady holding a sniper rifle." He winked at me as he smiled broadly. I couldn't help smiling back because even though Luc was a bastard he was a likeable one. But now that I was officially in his team, I saw no reason delaying what we were there for.

"Perfect. Let's go and get some Dashers, shall we?" I raised OPUS as a signal to move on. We could small-talk later. He chuckled.

"You're fucking incredible, you know that?" he replied, smirking while shaking his head a little.

And that's how I became a part of the French Foreign Legion for a while.

Chapter 29

All day long we fought in the streets of Idlib and, in the heat of the house-to-house battle, it was not always easy to identify who was the enemy and who was a 'friend'.

Luc and I had agreed that I should primarily support his legionnaires, which in practice meant that I only shot at the enemy when the enemy fired at them. It suited me well, because the target was easily identifiable so my task was mainly to return enemy fire.

It was nice to be back in the field again and I could not have had a better baptism than with Luc and his team. They were ultra-professional and their teamwork exemplary.

In the evening we pulled out of the city centre and entrenched ourselves in a small house that appeared to have been abandoned by its previous occupants.

Judging from the interior and that there were several animal remains outside, I would think that it had belonged to a farmer and his family. However, they were long gone and had only taken the most necessary things with them, implying it had been a quick exit.

The surrounding landscape was flat and barren with only a few rock formations to the east, which made the house very easy to guard. Should anyone try to sneak up on us, we would be able to see them coming from a long distance.

Two of the legionnaires swept the area in and around the house before the rest of us made our entrance. It was a small farm cottage consisting of three rooms. Two of them were bedrooms, and judging by the beds, at least two adults and five small children had lived there. The living room was approximately fifteen square metres and except for some broken chairs and glasses there was nothing.

The temperature had started to drop, so together with one of the team I lit a fire in the middle of the living room floor. We got the firewood from the broken chairs as well as some dried twigs collected by the legionnaires when they had swept the surrounding area. Shortly after, we all sat around the fire. The legionnaires shared their field rations with me and the conversation was lively but low-key in volume.

Luc had divided them into teams of four, so that each team stood guard but changed at two-hour intervals throughout the night. Since I had not slept in the last thirty-six hours, I was exempted from this shift, and I quickly withdrew to one of the bedrooms to sleep.

I took the empty bedroom furthest from the living room as five legionnaires had already bunked down in the room next to me. The room had obviously been the kids because the beds were so small that not even I could fit into them. I therefore flipped two of the mattresses onto the sandy floor before collapsing on them.

After a few hours, I woke up with Luc lying next to me, spooning me. He had unfolded his sleeping bag and laid it over us. His right arm was around me but he was not holding on to me. It just lay there as a visible shield telling the world that I was claimed. I could feel the heat from Luc's body and his steady rhythmic breathing above my ear. Although we were both fully dressed there was something intimate about it and, even though I liked it, it also made me a bit wary. I didn't know Luc, at least not so well that we should be spooning, and therefore began to dislike his closeness so I pulled away. My movement woke him up and instead of letting me go he pulled me closer to him. His grip was firm and made me feel like he was trapping me and I could have made a scene about it but I chose to turn to face him.

"Luc," I said, just about to object to his tight hold on me, but he stopped me.

"It's best this way," he said, almost whispering, "The others do not touch you as long as they think you are my bitch." His voice was not exactly cold but there was no emotion in it either, and for a brief moment it reminded me of one of the officers in Belize. Momentarily I was stunned and while trying to regain some sort of control, a fierce doubt washed over me. Where was I in relation to Luc and what were my options in this situation? There was no doubt that he could sense it, but he did not either elaborate or assure me that nothing would happen to me.

The insecurity of the situation made me decide to get up, but when I tried, he held me so tight that I almost panicked. Nobody should do that to me without my permission and in pure reflex I grabbed for the hunting knife in my boot. In a split-second Luc had pinned me down on my back and rolled on top of me. However, in the heat of the moment I had managed to place my hand with the dagger in his crotch and he definitely could feel it. He looked at me with a crooked smile and then I heard the click of the safety catch being released from his Glock. We lay there completely still and just stared at each other. Me with my hunting knife inches from his manhood and him with his Glock pressed against my temple. His gaze was calm and in no way threatening, rather the opposite. In his eyes lurked a deep respect and for a moment I thought I saw a glimpse of a sincerity that I had not expected to see. While we were lying like this, one of the legionnaires suddenly entered the room, but only for a brief remark.

"*Disparaissez.*" Luc commanded harshly and sharply, without looking at the legionnaire, and at the sound of Luc's voice he immediately left the room. We lay like that for ten to fifteen seconds locked in each other's gaze and I could feel Luc getting aroused. To be honest he wasn't the only one. But then suddenly Luc secured his Glock and rolled over on his back next to me. The minutes went by and neither of us said nor did anything. I could barely breathe. Not because I was scared or felt offended. Just the opposite. I was wildly turned on and I knew Luc was too. The mere thought of what had just happened between us – the power struggle – made me gasp for air. This is what I wanted. This is what I had been looking for – equal control. And if anyone could give me that it was Luc. I had to see if it was true. That he wanted this as much as me. In a flash, I rolled over so I was lying on top of him and I placed my hunting knife between his legs again. He looked at me in surprise and I could feel him getting even harder than before.

"Take your Glock ...," I whispered in his ear, "and put it against my temple." Luc's eyes didn't even flinch when he lifted the gun and a second later I felt the cold metal of it in the small recess on the side of my head.

"Take the safety off," I whispered as I smiled, not that he could see it but it didn't matter. It was a smile for me and for the fact that I was right. He was just as much into it as I was. I heard the click from the gun and a warmth rushed through me as if Luc had just thrown gasoline on my already burning fire.

"Don't you fucking move it," I said hard and commanding. Then I moved my lips from his ear to his neck and started to kiss him. As my lips found his I clenched my thighs hard against his waist. With my free hand I started to loosen his belt and unbutton his waistband while our kisses became wilder and more aggressive. As I unzipped his pants I bit his lower lip so hard that it drew blood but he didn't care. He just rolled his tongue over it and tasted the blood. The look in his eyes and the smirky smile he sent me as he did it made me even more wet for him. I took a firm grip on his hard cock and then and only then did I remove the knife. But by doing so I gave him all the power and he knew it. Eyes locked he rolled me around, still with the Glock at my temple. I let go of his cock as I kicked off my boots and got out of my pants. As I wrapped my legs around his waist I could feel him direct his cock into me. Our eyes never left each other. Not even once. This was no longer just about lust and fucking. No. This was a game of power. Real power. The kind of power you can take but only if you trust and respect each other. And in that instant I knew we both did. There was no overpowering. No teacher/student relationship. Just pure enjoyment of the power game. I could see in Luc's eyes that his sexual preferences were the same as mine so now it was up to me to show him that I was there with him.

"Fuck me, Luc. Fuck me hard," I commanded, "but don't let go of the gun." He pressed the Glock even harder to my temple and then he thrust into me. Again and again and again. And not even for a second did we lose eye contact. It was so extremely life-affirming in its own perverted way that I could barely breathe, and judging by Luc, he was in exactly the same place. He knew he could pull the trigger any time and kill me and there wouldn't be a damn thing I could do about it. I had put my life in his hands. Put all my trust in him that he wouldn't do it. He knew I was completely at his mercy. That he held my life in his hands. As I stared into his eyes I realized it was not the power that was the most important thing to him. It was the trust I placed in him. The trust in him to decide whether I should live or die. The ultimate trust.

To outsiders it might have seemed like a rape, but to us it was anything but. Luc and I exploded at the same time and we had to bite each other's shoulders so hard not to scream from ecstasy. When we were done, we both lay gasping for air.

"Jesus," he said after a minute, shaking his head still gasping, "I've never felt anything like this. I had your life in my hand." His body trembled from his physical and mental rush, "I'm never going to let you go," he said softly, staring at the ceiling while still catching his breath. The sincerity in his voice made me smile.

"Does that mean you want to be my bitch?" I said teasingly, but there was an underlying note of truth to it.

"Any time," he replied smiling, "Any time."

Then he turned so that he was lying on his side and with one hand he caressed my cheek. His gentle touch was in such stark contrast to the rape-like sex we had just enjoyed that it somehow made me a little insecure.

"Don't get all soft on me," I said quietly, "I'll be gone in a few days."

He seemed not to have heard my statement, but continued to caress me. Then he suddenly stopped as if it was only now that he had realized what I had said. He grabbed my jaw hard and turned my face towards him.

"Well, we better make the most of it then." Our eyes met and behind his cold gaze, I glimpsed the inner passion that only a few of us, who literally live from day to day, know. It is a passion that transcends everything and that makes everything else fade in its presence. It is the very nectar of what we do, whether it be killing or making love. With its intensity, it makes our presence in the present even greater, and with its harsh caresses, it makes us love more passionately and wilder than we had ever imagined possible.

* * *

It was 5.30 a.m. when I woke up with my head lying on Luc's chest and his arms wrapped around me. If some of the legionnaires had seen us lying and sleeping like this, they would not have been in doubt that what had taken place that night had nothing to do with rape.

I had been awake a few times during the night, and every single time Luc had been lying holding me. Normally I wouldn't have liked this but much to my surprise I didn't mind at all. His warm muscular chest against my back felt like a wall shielding me from the rest of the world and for the first time I felt truly protected. It was as if being in Luc's arms no harm could come to me and, although it was such a new and strange emotion, it wasn't unpleasant. Had it been anyone else I would have perceived it as clingy and moved away but with Luc it was different. It was the most natural thing in the world to have his arms around me and I therefore had no problem sinking deeper into his embrace. His steady breathing had been so soothing and meditative that it had rocked me to sleep every time I had woken and I could easily had gone back to sleep now if it wasn't for the fact that my throat was burning from thirst. Quietly, I freed myself from his arms, got up and dressed.

A couple of the legionnaires sat inside by the crackling fire talking, but when I approached them, they stopped. Quietly I sat down and, as if it were a signal, one of them handed me a bottle of water. I took a few sips and then gave it back to him.

"Are you okay?" he said and there was a hint of concern to be spotted in his voice.

"Of course she's okay." The voice belonged to Luc and it came from the doorway where he was standing only wearing his boots and sandy coloured camouflage pants.

I looked at him as he stretched and yawned, and I couldn't help smiling. But then I turned my head towards the legionnaire.

"I am just fine. Actually, I'm better than that," I replied still with a crooked smile on my face.

The legionnaire had no idea how to respond to that comment and therefore chose very sensibly to look into the flames. Luc walked around the fire and as he passed me, he discreetly let a few fingers touch my neck. It was as if his touch sent a chill through my body but it was a nice chill. He sat down next to me and ran one hand down my back. I shuddered, which immediately made him put his arm round my shoulders. There was an odd silence around the fire so it was almost a relief when my phone beeped.

Everyone looked at me, while I was checking the message from Aslan. It was co-ordinates as well as a date and judging by the GPS, the co-ordinates were for the city of Erbil in northern Iraq. I answered by sending the co-ordinates back and then I turned off the phone.

"It seems like I'm going to Erbil," I said in the most neutral voice I could possibly come up with, "Any suggestions on how to get there?" I looked around at the legionnaires, but they were all stoney faced. Luc quietly removed his arm from my shoulder and stood up. He indicated that I should follow him and we walked out of the house ending up behind it before he suddenly stopped and turned towards me.

"If you can wait a few days, you can have a lift with us. We're going to Mosul. It's not that far from Erbil."

I nodded. It was far safer to travel with them than it was to go off on my own, so yes ... I could easily wait a few days. I took a few steps towards Luc so we were pretty much face to face and, despite the fact that my inner voice told me to keep my distance, everything else in my body screamed for him.

"I don't know how you work your team, but ..."

He smiled.

"Don't worry. You're safe. No one touches you until I give the green light."

"Green light?" I raised my eyebrows.

He raised his hand and caressed my chin.

"I always 'test drive' all women in our company before the 'boys' get access to them." He leaned in over me and kissed me gently and superficially on my lips. "But don't worry," he whispered, "It's me who's your bitch and not the other way around, so ..."

He spoke softly, almost mesmerizingly, and it turned me wildly on. I took a step towards him and pressed him up against the wall of the house.

"Don't let me fucking regret this, Luc," I said, sliding one hand down to his crotch. There was a short glint of surprise in his eyes but it quickly turned into a wanting desire. While opening his pants with one hand my other hand retrieved my Glock from my waistband. I shoved the gun into his hand and just before I let go of it I unsecured it. We stood like that for a moment and, as I started to rub his already very hard cock, he put the gun to my head.

And with the pistol against my skull, I went on my knees and breathed through my nose until he came in my mouth.

* * *

An hour later we were in the centre of Idlib.

If there was a war zone in Hell, it would have been moved to Idlib for a short time, or more specifically, to where we were. Luc had led us into a sector of the city where some of the fiercest battles were being fought, and that day was no exception.

As we moved from building-to-building mortar shells rained down on us spiced up with salvos from machine guns and rifle shots, and pieces of concrete, dust, rubble and rebar flew around us; we were pretty busy.

The group got separated along the way and I ended up on the first floor of an empty building with one of the legionnaires. The outer wall facing the street was blown to pieces, and there was therefore a clear view of the building opposite, from where we were shot at with an intensity that can only be described as fierce. We sheltered behind a pile of bricks and we managed to get an M16 rifle on a tripod before the legionnaire started returning fire. I had OPUS, but a sniper rifle in this inferno was not exactly ideal as the buildings opposite were far too close, so the noise from the shots and grenade blasts formed a violent resonance that was deafening. We therefore both lay with slightly open mouths to counteract the explosive pressure that would otherwise be in our heads. Our headsets were off as the reverberation around us prevented us from hearing anything in them anyway so we were out of contact with the rest of the team.

* * *

At noon the offensive calmed down a bit and therefore gave us the opportunity to move position to another building as well as to get an overview of our situation – both strategically and in terms of ammunition. We had turned our headsets on again and through them we could hear that the rest of the group had ended up in one of the streets close by. They were on their way to us, but the fighting near them had not yet subsided, so we were asked to stay where we were and wait. We were now on the third floor of the building next to the one we had left, and even though large holes had been blown in the wall towards the street, there was significantly more cover here. I had taken up position behind a part of the outer wall, which had only been shot halfway to pieces, and from here I had a good view of the neighbouring buildings on the opposite side of the street. The shots had almost completely stopped and, judging by the clock, it was time for the noon prayer. The legionnaire came over to me and sat down next to me and signalled with his hand that I should turn off my headset. I had no idea why he wanted me to do this particularly as I was in the middle of a reconnaissance of the neighbouring buildings, but I quickly found the button and switched it off.

"We talked a little bit in the group," he said with a thick French accent as he looked seriously at me. Without moving my eye from OPUS' telescopic sight, I replied,

"Yes, and?"

"If Luc does something to you that you don't want him to do, you tell us. Okay?"

I turned my head and looked at him. It was not exactly the words I had expected to come out of his mouth. In fact, it seemed strange that a group of foreign legionnaires had discussed my well-being.

"What's your name?" I asked quietly because somehow it would only feel right to talk about such things if I knew his name.

"Icos, ma'am ..."

"Honestly," I replied to him, "What would you do if he did? I mean if he did hurt me?"

"Stop him," he replied shortly, looking over at the building opposite us, "We know we do not have the best reputation for how we behave when we 'have time off', but ..." He hesitated for a moment, "we do not want to passively watch him while he ... hurts you. Not you ... of all people."

It was obviously hard for him to talk about, and I did not particularly like this conversation either, so I interrupted him.

"Icos, you ... I can assure you that there is nothing going on that I do not approve of, but if at some point there is, I promise you that you will be the first to know." I gave him a pat on the shoulder and smiled, "But thank you for your concern. I appreciate it ... A LOT."

He looked at me and nodded and I could see that this statement meant something to him. There was no need to talk about it further and it was never brought up again. We returned to our war mode and continued the 'party' now that the noon prayer was over.

* * *

Two hours later, the group was reunited. One of the legionnaires had been wounded and was therefore partially out of the game. The battle had escalated, so we fought like crazy, but it was difficult to say who it really was that we were fighting, because it could just as easily be Syrian government troops or a local militia or ISIS, so in fact we fought just to survive. Normally I preferred to have a clearly defined target, because then I knew what I had to deal with, but right now it was just a matter of keeping myself and the team – Luc's team – alive, so the target was irrelevant.

We had fortified ourselves in a low residential building and were under constant fire from the corner building opposite us. For good reasons, we had spread out on each floor of the house and I had of course 'crawled' up to the roof of the building. Then suddenly all local hostile activity stopped and even the individual shots that could be heard in the distance gradually died out until they too had finally completely disappeared. There was a strange silence that was almost noisier than the inferno of mortar shells that had echoed around us less than two minutes ago. Quietly I began to climb down from the roof.

"*Sortez, sortez*." I could hear Luc shouting to us through the headsets and like a machine gun salvo we all ran through the building and out of the back. We continued through another building and ended up in a narrow alley that was, in fact, a really bad place for us because it was perfect for an ambush. Luckily for us, no enemy troops had got that idea.

We moved slowly alongside the wall to the end of the alley. Then Luc – who was leading the way with six of his men – suddenly gave us a silent command to stand completely still. The whole row of soldiers froze and not so much as a crackle from a backpack or a change of grip on a rifle was to be heard.

There was a faint rumble that slowly got louder and louder and deeper and deeper, and with the sound came tremors that resembled an incipient earthquake that shook the earth and the surrounding buildings. We stood up against the wall, while dust, plaster and rubble fell down in front of us and, while all the crap came tumbling down, the sound got louder and louder. At the end of the alley, a Leopard tank suddenly appeared and it was followed by a train of nine more and five trucks with soldiers. Judging from the flag waving on the first tank, they were Syrian pro-government troops, but whether it was one or the other 'faction' in the conflict was at this point in time really not relevant to us, as we just had to leave. We waited until the train had passed and, when we were sure that it was far enough away from us, we left the alley. We ran in the opposite direction from the tanks, as if we had a pair of aggressive Rottweilers right on our heels. After two hundred metres we turned into a narrow street. As we ran, I could hear Luc talking over the headset to a pilot and judging from the conversation, we would be picked up in twenty minutes. The pilot might as well have said twenty hours, because in our situation, it would feel that way.

We came to an open square that had once been a lively bazaar but like so much of the city it now lay in ruins. At Luc's order we entered a small building. To the right of the entrance was a small room and here we had the opportunity to catch our breath. As we stood gasping for air, we could hear the tanks firing repeatedly and even though we were approximately four hundred metres away and there were several apartment blocks and office buildings in between, the sounds were unbelievably loud. It was clear that they were levelling one building after another to the ground, for the repercussions of the shells being fired and the subsequent tremors from collapsing structures shook the small building we were in so dust and pieces of plaster sprinkled down on us.

I was standing next to the wounded legionnaire, who was leaning against one of the walls, when without warning he fainted. I managed to catch him before he hit the concrete floor, and immediately Luc and one of the other legionnaires were next to us. We put him on the floor and while the other legionnaire took his pulse, Luc removed his jacket, vest and various equipment and weapons. He was hit in the shoulder, but it was not the only place. He also had a really 'ugly' gunshot wound in his side and, from my position, I could easily see the bullet hole. There was no doubt that by the entry location the shot was from a sniper, and Luc and I exchanged brief glances.

Gunshot wounds like this were serious and often caused internal bleeding; in this case to his lungs. He had obviously suffered tremendous blood loss, which explained why he fainted and as his heart rate slowed down his face turned completely ashen. I slapped him on the cheeks a few times and after a while he woke up a bit. I looked at Luc seriously.

"We have to give him blood," I said quietly, "Or else ..."

Luc ripped off the soldier's bloody t-shirt, and from the bullet hole in his side and the shoulder, blood ran out – not fast, but it was presumably because his heart rate and therefore pulse was so low.

"Check his left shoulder," he replied, and what I found were the letters AB+, "All the soldiers on my team have their blood type tattooed on their shoulder."

Luc looked intensely at his watch as he said it, almost as if he expected it to answer him.

"AB+," I replied to him, which immediately made him turn to the other legionnaires and ask if there were any who were AB positive. One of them came over to us and without speaking started to roll up his jacket sleeve. As we had no IV equipment, we had to practice 'the bad doctor's emergency solution', which meant that we drained blood from the legionnaire via two disposable syringes and injected it directly into the wounded person. It was Luc and I who did it, and while I was draining the blood, Luc injected it. We managed to transfer about half a litre, I would guess, before we heard the helicopters in the distance and a few minutes later, we were airborne.

Luc sat behind the pilot and started to direct him to the hospital in Aleppo, but understandably I interrupted him before he finished his order.

"Luc," I shouted and he turned his head towards me, "Not Aleppo. The hospital is not safe." He looked at me sceptically, "I was there. The hospital is, in all likelihood, now in a hostile zone."

Luc shouted back at me,

"I have one of my men there."

I leaned forward and said calmly into his ear,

"No, we took him with us when we escaped. He is with JAC and Wizard in Damascus now." Luc stared at me and, as I leaned back again, a smile spread on his lips. He turned to the pilot and had both helicopters redirected to Damascus. Now it was his turn to lean forward towards me and with a firm grip on my neck, he put his mouth to my ear.

"Thank you," he said before releasing his grip.

I nodded briefly and smiled at him. Then I picked up my phone and messaged Aslan that we were on our way to Damascus with a wounded legionnaire and that we would touch-down in one and a half hours. Shortly after, a set of co-ordinates returned, which I gave to Luc, who then instructed the pilot that this was where he should land and the rest of the trip I sat and looked down at the cities we flew over.

The city of Homs was destroyed. There was pretty much nothing left except for crushed exposed concrete and rubble of the once beautiful city, and then it suddenly hit me. Was it not really such cities that testified most to our presence?

As they lay there – bombed and defeated – they told stories of the unimaginable battles we had fought for them and in them. We wrote their wills in the rain of bullets that hit the house walls, and by their fall, we sealed their concrete graves. But their ruin justified our existence, so what was best – theirs or our survival? Holistically and humanely the answer should be theirs ... but rationally and selfishly it would always be ours. I leaned my head back and closed my eyes. The rotors of the helicopter had a calming, yes, almost sleepy effect on me and in my mind I quietly concluded that as the world looked right now, many concrete graves were waiting out there as were more zeros on the cheques. A wise man once said 'War is Business and Business is good.' I could not agree with him more.

* * *

We landed in a meadow on the outskirts of western Damascus, and Wizard and Christo were already waiting in the Land Cruiser and what appeared to be a beaten-up old truck. Where they got the truck from I don't know and I didn't ask.

The wounded legionnaire was put into the Land Cruiser, and within two minutes, the helicopters were gone and we were heading south. I was sitting in the front of the truck next to Icos and Christo who was driving. Luc was riding with Wizard in the Land Cruiser with a couple of legionnaires.

"Where are we going?" I asked when I could see that we were not heading towards Damascus.

"Amman," Christo replied, "and welcome back." He smiled.

"Thank you, but have you cleared this with Luc?"

"Who gives a shit," he replied, "It's Amman or I'll drop them off right here."

I was in no mood to discuss it with Christo, who apparently did not have much time for Luc and his team. Why that was did not interest me. The most important thing was that JAC and Wizard trusted them.

Two and a half hours later Christo stopped the truck at an intersection and having left the wheel to Icos, we proceeded on foot to the apartment. Where the legionnaires were going was none of my concern but I guess they had their own connections in Amman when it came to sleeping arrangements.

As we walked I asked Christo,

"Why are we back in Amman?"

"Wizard didn't like the lack of security at the hotel in Damascus so between us we moved Aslan's office and all the kit to here. It's a bit crowded but Aslan is sorting out some storage for the kit."

Wizard, Luc and the others had driven to another address with the wounded legionnaire – an address that, according to Christo, was a private clinic where the wounded soldier, whom they had brought from Aleppo, already was.

As we entered Wizard's apartment we were greeted by JAC who was drying his hair with a towel, having just stepped out of the shower. Knox suddenly appeared at the entrance to the living room and waved us down there with a big smile. Both Christo and I started to walk towards him but as we passed the first bedroom, JAC grabbed me and pushed me in slamming the door behind us.

"I need my fucking fix," he said coldly and threw me on the bed like I was some piece of equipment just there to please him. In pure reflex, I made a backward roll, so I ended up standing on the opposite side of the bed, with my Glock pulled. JAC looked at me rather surprised but then started smiling as if this was a joke.

"Don't even think about it," I said with the same coolness in my voice as the one he had just used with me and for a moment his gaze hardened. Then, slowly and with his hands slightly raised, he began to walk towards me.

"Hey, relax. It's me," he said, but in his voice lurked a strange false sweetness that was emphasized by the slight tremor in it.

I clicked the safety catch off on my Glock and he stopped abruptly. His eyes became icy cold and almost psychotic and once again the thought occurred to me, that he might want to hurt me. I strode round the bed and walked towards the door while our eyes were locked on each other's and it wasn't until I opened the door that I secured the Glock. JAC's gaze was now incomprehensible and it intensified when I put the Glock in my waistband.

"Whatever happened to 'Thank you for staying in Aleppo and saving our asses and by the way welcome back'." JAC stared at me like I had spoken in a foreign language he didn't understand and his whole attitude got me so fucking furious. Who was he to think of me as a sex toy that was only here to satisfy his needs.

"I'm sorry .... Welcome back; is that what you wanted to hear? Now I have said it so get your ass in here ... please, Your Highness." He made a courtesy gesture with his hand but if he thought it was funny he was wrong. It came across as mockery and it made me frown.

"Grow up, JAC," I said and turned around to leave but he grabbed my arm and yanked me back in the room.

"What the fuck is wrong with you?" I yelled angrily, "Don't you fucking get it? I don't want to have sex with you. I have had enough."

"Enough?" he repeated frowning so his entire face looked distorted.

"Yes. Enough. You are so fucking selfish."

I moved towards him aiming for the door behind him as I wasn't in the mood for this now. I was hungry and tired and just needed to rest. I had thought he would push me back into the room but he just stood there non-plussed. As I walked towards the living room, I couldn't stop thinking what a selfish bastard JAC was: No kindness, no empathy just a mere desire to obtain sexual gratification through me. I was not his fucking little sex-toy and I was definitely not going to obey him for whenever he wanted 'a fix'.

As I approached the living room I could hear JAC's footsteps behind me. He walked fast and I knew he was trying to catch up to me before I reached my destination. But that didn't happen.

The sight that greeted me in the living room was of Christo and Knox sitting in the midst of all the pillows drinking Red Bull and eagerly devouring a couple of pizzas. I couldn't help but smile. All they needed was a PlayStation and the image of two teenage gamers would have been completed.

I could feel JAC's hand on my shoulder but it didn't make me turn round. I had had enough of him.

"What the fuck was that all about?" he whispered in my ear but I pretended I hadn't heard. Fully aware of his eyes piercing me from behind I walked across the living room and took a Coca Cola from the table in front of Christo and Knox.

"I can't do this anymore, JAC," I said as I opened the can. Although in the middle of a bite Knox and Christo had stopped eating and were now watching us.

"What the fuck do you mean by that you can't do this anymore?" he said loudly, shaking his head slightly.

"I can't, JAC. I'm done with this. Done with us. Do you understand? We are finished. Over. I have had enough."

"What do you mean by had enough?" It was as if he didn't want to understand that I was ending our affair. And it hadn't really been my intention to elaborate on it but if that was what it took to get it through his thick skull well ....

"I need more, JAC. More."

"Okay. I'll give you more. I'll ..."

"No, JAC. You can't. You can't give me what I want so stop it. We are done."

"I don't know what you want. Tell me!"

There was a real vulnerability in the way he expressed the words, but even though it touched me it was not enough to change my mind. As much as I loved, cared and trusted him something had changed in me. And that something was Luc. With JAC I had somehow always been the master in our sexual exploration: Not that he didn't take control because he did but I had been the teacher and that had been fine for that moment. But meeting Luc I suddenly found myself being sexually equal with someone and that made me see how much I had longed for it. Luc took charge but he did it in a respectful manner and with little to no opening for me to reverse his attentions. I liked that. With him sex was more of a mind game and not so much about the physical act itself although it would naturally end with it. But there was also something else about Luc, something that attracted me to him. I couldn't quite place it but it was something I had to have more of.

I took a sip of my Coca Cola then I looked at him. I was about to say that we would talk about this later but then I heard Wizard's and Luc's voices chatting cheerfully as they walked through the hallway.

"That was fast." Christo stated with his mouth full of pizza and I could hear the relief in his voice, that JAC and I had been interrupted. We had only been in the apartment for twenty minutes and Christo and I had both thought that we wouldn't see Wizard for at least a few hours. As for Luc none of us expected to see him here with us in the apartment at all.

"No need for us to stay. The doctor has taken over so we might as well wait for news here rather than hanging around there. I'm also a bit tired ..." Luc ended his answer smiling at me and I couldn't help but smile back.

JAC who had gone into the kitchen to fetch some beers, now appeared in the doorway. He gave a can of Heineken to Wizard and offered one to Luc. Luc declined and instead he walked over to me. Discretely he touched my back as he leaned in and whispered in my ear,

"I came back to see you." I couldn't help myself as I smiled but I should have guessed that JAC would pick up on it immediately. I didn't have to look to know that JAC was staring at me and when Luc and I sat down he monitored every move we made. While sitting between a couple of large orange-coloured pillows Luc started to slowly caress my back and JAC's stare turned from mischievous to angry but he didn't get a chance to say anything or act upon it as Wizard, who was totally unaware of the situation suddenly interrupted the little scenario.

"Luc has offered us a lift to Mosul tomorrow. So Aslan will .... Where the fuck is Aslan?" Wizard looked around questioningly but it was Knox who answered.

"He was tired so he went to bed after getting the pizzas."

"Okay. I'll talk to him in the morning about transportation from Mosul to Erbil." Wizard sat down and took a slice of pizza but JAC remained standing and staring at me and Luc. Then suddenly he turned and a few minutes later we could hear the front door being slammed. I don't think there was a single person in the room who hadn't noticed the way he left but nobody said anything and five minutes later we were all talking and laughing and it was as if it had never happened.

The rest of the evening passed quietly. We ate, drank beer and had fun. Aslan had been woken up when JAC had slammed the door and he had now joined the party. At one point Aslan and I went into the office as he had a couple of questions regarding requests from customers that had come in. We ended up sitting for a few hours in front of the laptop working and it was really nice.

That night I went to bed alone in mine and JAC's room but I was awakened at half past two in the morning by JAC entering.

He immediately took off his clothes and went straight to the shower and then to bed. I was well aware that he had been with someone else, and oddly enough it did not bother me at all. If it had done, I would actually have been a hypocrite, but I was perfectly okay with it.

"How hard were you on her?" I asked with my back to him.

"Too hard," he replied without any remorse or empathy in his voice.

I turned over and looked at him.

"Is she alive?" My question might seem absurd, but it was extremely relevant because JAC was able to kill to obtain his satisfaction.

He lay with his arms behind his head and looked up at the ceiling. He did not answer my question but I knew she was. JAC would never have killed her. Not over this.

"Why Luc?" he asked without looking at me.

"Because you were not there," I replied, and that was partly true. There was no reason to tell him that Luc turned me on in a way that no man – not even JAC – had ever done and that the kind of 'death sex' we had had was so intense and life-affirming, that it had been all-consuming. In our job we risked dying, we knew that, and we were also aware that we had little or no control over the circumstances if it were to happen.

To suddenly have the opportunity to control whether we should die – that was the ultimate rush. We were daily masters of the death of others, but now we were suddenly masters of our own destiny, and at the same time we put that decision in each other's hands. Greater trust and confidence could not be given to another human being than letting that person choose when one's life should end.

JAC looked at me.

"I can't do this," he said quietly, "I'm not like you. I still have feelings – at least at the moment." His words stung me, for if there was something I did, it was to feel. I felt the whole world and even more so when I was with Luc. But maybe the world was just not enough anymore.

"JAC. I love you."

"I know, but you just don't love me enough – and that's okay, but I don't want to share you anymore, so you have to decide – and decide now."

We looked at each other and inside I was screaming for him: My friend, my lover, my confidant, my saviour, my rock. I would never have survived what I had been through if it had not been for him, but right now I would not survive if I stayed with him. It hurt so terribly, but I had to admit that it would emotionally be the death of us if we stayed together.

I got up and put on my t-shirt.

"One day you will thank me for this, JAC," I said and my voice was about to crack. As JAC put one arm over his eyes, I continued, "You know you can trust me on missions – I would die for you out there, but I can't give you more than that – not now."

I would have loved to have walked over to him and hugged him and held him, but it would have seemed pathetic and artificial, so I just left the room.

When I had closed the door behind me, I stood quietly in front of it for a brief moment.

Should I go back in and kiss him and say that everything was forgotten and that we were together again – him and I – or should I just go? Maybe deep down I was hoping he would open the door and pull me in there, where I was so unspeakably safe. But nothing happened. He did not come storming out and I did not go back in.

I walked quietly down the hall and into the office, where Luc was lying asleep on the floor in his sleeping bag. Next to him lay his Glock with the safety catch off and quietly I bent down and put it on. As soon as he heard the click, he opened his eyes and we looked at each other. There was no doubt that everything that had happened was painted on my face, so just as quietly he unzipped his sleeping bag and I crawled in. Somehow, words were not important and when he put his arms around me and kissed me very gently, I could not hold back my emotions any more. I started sobbing heartily and he comforted me with kisses and caresses. It was only in the early morning hours, that I fell asleep in his arms, and at no point did I feel the situation was awkward or wrong. On the contrary. Everything was as it should be. I had made the right decision.

* * *

By nine o'clock in the morning I was in the kitchen with Knox. We stood chatting, drinking coffee and the atmosphere was nice and cordial – just an ordinary morning coffee. Wizard and Luc had gone to the clinic to check up on the two legionnaires and JAC was sitting in the office with Christo and was in the process of viewing a virtual reconnaissance of the area around Erbil.

Aslan, who had been walking around the living room for the last half hour with his phone glued to his ear, came out into the kitchen and he seemed more than a little annoyed.

"Does anyone know when Luc and Wizard are going to be back?" he asked looking at us, but neither Knox nor I had any idea. Knox subsequently went in to JAC and Christo, and despite the fact that I did not feel like joining them I felt obligated to do so. I put my half empty coffee cup on the kitchen table and went after him.

JAC and Christo were completely engrossed in their visualisation programme and did not immediately notice when I came in and stood behind them. It was quite fascinating to see how they had got the whole area around Erbil included and how they could manoeuvre around the terrain with co-ordinate indications. Aslan had sat down on the other side of the desk and was in the process of entering a lot of names, times and co-ordinates on his phone.

My eyes wandered from the screen to JAC, and I had to admit that I had an incredible urge to touch him. My whole body longed for him to hold me and the more I looked at him, the greater the tension in my stomach got. A violent nausea struck me and I wanted to scream at him that if he just wanted to see this from my point of view then he might understand, but I remained silent.

It hurt me so much to look at him that I had to go, so I went into the room that JAC and I had previously shared and closed the door. As I stood there by the bed with its crumpled bedding, there were tears in my eyes. It was completely silly, but I actually missed him so unspeakably much. Not sexually but as a friend.

The last time I had felt this way was back in Karachi, where I thought I would never see him again and now ... now he was sitting in the office a few metres from me and I still missed him, and if possible, even more.

In the past, I would have pushed such feelings away, but it was not possible for me anymore. Maybe I really was getting emotions – not just some that were prefabricated, but real honest emotions. Suddenly I understood what Liam had meant, when he said that he hated me for making him feel because it was really horrible to be able to feel the unrequited longing and sadness that, through all these years, had been hidden away, and which now suddenly reappeared with an unparalleled strength and intensity.

I went and sat on the edge of the bed and looked blankly into the air until the door opened and JAC came in. It was as if he had expected to find me there, for he did not seem surprised to see me. Silently he closed the door then squatted down in front of me. He took my hands in his and kissed them gently while we looked at each other.

"I can't do this, JAC. I miss you like I have never missed anyone before. I can't breathe. I cannot lose you, because then I will lose myself." I wrapped my arms around him and he reciprocated my hug – thankfully, "I'm sorry for what I did and said yesterday. I'm so sorry." We held on to each other like it was the last time we would ever do so.

"We both did really stupid things yesterday," he whispered and slowly we let go of each other. He smiled at me and moved some of my hair to one side, "I think you should sit this mission out and stay here in Amman with Aslan."

I looked at him quizzically.

"Why? We are a team, we ..."

JAC put his fingers on my lips and I was silent.

"Because we need some time away from each other, or rather, I need some time away from you. Will you give me that?"

"If that's what you want – then yes, but I do not understand ..."

"You don't have to understand ..." he said, "Just do this favour for me."

He smiled at me and we bumped our foreheads gently together.

"Okay," I said quietly, "Okay."

He kissed me on the forehead and got up.

"The contract in Erbil is for one month, so we have time to get a little distance between us and then we have to see." He went over and took two large empty bags and threw them over to me.

"Want to help me pack?" He smiled at me again just as I laid the bags on the bed, after which I walked over to him.

"Thank you, JAC," I said quietly. He put one hand under my chin slowly lifting it up.

"*De nada*," he replied smiling.

* * *

By twelve o'clock Wizard and Luc were back, but it was only to pick up their gear. JAC explained to Wizard why I was sitting this mission out and despite some doubts from Wizard and the rest of the team they accepted it.

Since the two helicopters were to pick them up at a small airport outside Amman, Aslan and I drove the boys out there. The truck with the rest of the legionnaires was already there and it soon became clear that thirty-two men with full gear was the limit of what the helicopters could take, but no one raised an eyebrow. Luc did not ask why I wasn't going, as our communication was very sparse, which in many ways helped in the somewhat strange situation that existed between JAC, him and me. JAC did his best so that no one would notice that there was anything different between us, and to some extent he succeeded.

As the last of the legionnaires was getting onto the helicopters Luc pulled me aside behind the truck and as soon as we were alone, he kissed me. His kiss was deep and filled me with such a need for him that I didn't think it was possible. I wanted him so badly and as I stood pressed up against him I could feel his hardness against me. But there was so much more in that kiss than just the physical part. I wanted to devour him. To possess him. Wanted to give myself completely to him. I wanted him to invade my body and mind to .... Luc broke the kiss and I could see we were both a little breathless. Then he leaned in and whispered in my ear,

"I'll be back. I promise." I smiled at him and – oh my God – did I hope so because I was not ready to lose him.

We walked together to the other side of the car just to see that everybody was waiting for Luc. I watched him as he ran over and jumped into the helicopter and as it took off he smiled at me. The smile made my entire body long for him and when I looked at JAC in the other helicopter I have to admit that that feeling was just not there.

As the spinning rotors disappeared over the horizon, Aslan and I got back into the vehicles and drove through Amman's bustling street crowds and back to the apartment.

The place felt very empty after a day full of people, but it was also nice that it was now just Aslan and me. There had been so many people around me all the time, which had felt pretty noisy and cramped in the small apartment, so a little peace and quiet was welcome. The rest of the day and evening we spent cleaning up and getting more RAM for the laptop.

The days slipped away and despite the fact that I ran twenty kilometres daily, lifted weights in the local gym, shopped and cooked for us, I was going crazy. The thought that the team was in one of the worst combat zones in Iraq and that I was not there to help them, was getting to me.

We regularly received reports from Wizard which showed clearly that they were all pushed to the limit. Our client was a local militia who desperately needed help from professional soldiers to protect a refinery they owned, but the fighting often took place so close that one could hear the bullets whistling through the air when Wizard Skyped us. According to him, only the militia, which consisted of sixty to seventy men, took part in the fighting, but he wondered whether they would have benefitted more from hiring the team as a combat unit and not, as was the case – a security unit. His reasoning was that the militia had shown that they had little or no military experience. Although he admitted that they had a will of iron, which he compared to the Palestinian militias, that the majority of us, who had been on missions in the West Bank, had encountered.

The militias in Erbil were fighting fierce battles against ISIS, and while ISIS fought for their religion and Caliphate, the militia fought for their families, which made them incredibly loyal. From our conversations with Wizard, he said that to him that was reason enough to teach them basic strategic combat techniques.

One night, while Aslan and I were surfing the web for some new weapons, a Skype call came from Wizard's phone. However, it was not Wizard but JAC and, even though he looked very tired and worn out, it was nice to see him. After a few minutes of status reporting, he asked to speak to me in private, so Aslan immediately left the office and closed the door. When we were alone, JAC said calmly,

"OPUS, I will not return when this mission is over. I have decided to stay and help the militia fight ISIS without a contract." It was quite strange to hear these words coming from him, for he was the one who was most focused on money and, therefore, generally did not lift a gun without payment.

"Okay," I replied very puzzled, "And why this sudden idealism?"

"These people are fighting with everything they've got and to see an enemy who is so barbaric that ..." He looked away from the phone, "They are horrible, OPUS. It beats everything I've seen." It was clear that he was moved by it, and that was far from good.

"JAC," I said calmly, "When the contract expires, you come back here with the team and then we make a plan for how we can help these people in the best possible way. And if you still want to go back, I promise I will support you – no matter what."

"You are welcome to sit down and make plans, but I will stay here." His eyes revealed that he had made his decision and that any attempt to talk him out of it would fail, so I had to play the 'Wizard Card'. Wizard was the only one of us capable of talking JAC out of his most insane ideas, and in my view, this was definitely one of them.

"What does Wizard say about this?" I asked.

JAC looked over the phone.

"Judging by his facial expressions, I think he will kill me when I hang up." He laughed.

"Fuck you, JAC." Wizard said in the background, "You are coming with us to Amman. Even if I have to put you in a body bag."

Wizard appeared on the screen behind JAC.

"OPUS, I promise you I'll bring him home. Whatever it takes." Wizard gave JAC a nod while calling him an idiot and JAC chuckled.

"JAC, do you want me to come over there?"

I could see that he was glad I offered it, but he refused on the grounds that there were only five days left of the contract, so that would be foolish.

"Before you got here, you'd have to go home." And that sentence alone showed me that he had made his decision. He had said, 'You are going home' and not 'we are going home'.

"Take care," he said sending me a screen kiss, "And by the way ..." He leaned forward towards the screen, as if he wanted to whisper something, "If I had come back, we would have continued and let bygones be bygones."

He smiled and moved back from the screen.

"Okay, JAC. Get it out of your system and then come back."

His eyes shone with joy that I had accepted his decision, and his voice sounded happy when he said,

"Got to go. Take care, babe."

He sent me a finger kiss and then the conversation ended.

I sat for a moment in front of the blank screen, but then I suddenly got a weird feeling in my stomach and several massive chills wavered through my body. The door opened and Aslan entered the office with a mug full of coffee.

"JAC is not coming back," I said shortly and Aslan looked at me wide-eyed, "He has become a partisan."

"You are fucking kidding me. Mr. Capitalist himself. I don't believe that." He went to the laptop. "Move," he said loudly and his tone made me obey.

I had never heard him command anyone, so in 'shock', I got up and made room for him. To my surprise, it was his intention to go into ACOSS's bank transfers.

"I do not have access to his accounts, but I can still withhold his money for this mission," he said authoritatively as his fingers danced across the keyboard.

"Don't, Aslan. It's JAC's money."

"Yes, it is," replied Aslan, "and he will thank me, when he has spent all his fortune helping the militia and its blood-sucking families, for believe me

OPUS, they will throw themselves at him and exploit him when they find out that he has money."

"Aslan, for fuck's sake. You can't do this. It's ..."

"It's already done," he said briefly, pressing Enter, "Sue me if you want. I do not give a fuck."

His face was hard and he deliberately avoided all eye contact with me. I had never seen him like this before, and the impulsiveness and determination he displayed suited him, I thought.

"Aslan, when he finds out – and he will find out – he will come after you. You don't want that, do you?"

"Just let him come," he said, closing the laptop, "I'd love to have that fight with him." His courage was admirable, but it was unrealistic that he would win over JAC if it came to a physical confrontation. If, on the other hand, it was a more argumentative one, then the outcome was more uncertain.

"You are crazy," I said calmly and only now did he look directly at me, "I only know one person who has a small chance of stopping JAC if it should come to it and that's Wizard." I turned around about to leave for the kitchen.

"Or you," he said quietly and in complete surprise at his comment, I turned back and looked at him.

"No, Aslan. Not even I can stop him. It has just been proven." Aslan looked at his hands,

"You don't know how much he loves you, do you? He would go to hell and back for you." He looked at me and his expression was highly unpleasant, "Your behaviour would never have worked with me. NEVER. You don't deserve him." His words were accurate and they hit home, but not enough to hurt me.

Aslan knew nothing about JAC's and my story, so how could he know better? But he was right about one thing. JAC would die for me and I would die for him – no matter what relationship we would have with each other in the future. But whether I deserved him? That was a different matter. Basically, we probably deserved each other. We were both so screwed up – in our own diabolical way. I went to Aslan and patted him on the shoulder.

"You're probably right," I said, smiling, "but before you draw your conclusions, know that I would die for him. Die, Aslan. Can you say you would do that for anyone?"

Aslan got up without saying anything and went into the living room. Shortly after, I could hear the television. The conversation was over.

Chapter 30

Five days later, Aslan drove to the airport to pick up Wizard, Knox and Christo. The mission was over and, although they had not been directly involved in any fighting, they had been close to the areas where it took place.

During the time they had been away, I had realized, that even though it was nice – for both for my body and soul – to have a break from combat, I felt best when I was with the team. No doubt my urge to protect and have control of the situation played a massive role in this, because how was I going to help them if I did not know what was going on. The thought of them being in a fight without me being there to give them cover, had often led to an inner restlessness that had affected both my sleep and my daily routines.

The weekly reports from Wizard, that the task of looking after the refinery had been uneventful, were reassuring, but I knew only too well, that it was only a matter of time before they would encounter the first rain of bullets, and the longer they were there, the greater the risk. It was like the silence before the storm. This strange wait for something, which in this case never came, had been horrible for me, and if anything, it had only confirmed that I belonged in the front line and not behind the scenes. The clarification I had regarding this, was in fact a great relief to me, and the doubt whether an ordinary civilian life would be better for me, was gone. I simply could not work properly if I was not in the field.

That JAC had remained in Iraq was in many ways very out of character, but I had chosen not to speculate about it, because basically it was his choice. If he really thought that it was what he needed, so be it. As long as he did it of his own free will, he had my full approval, but it was strange.

At 1.30 p.m. Aslan entered the apartment. He was followed by Wizard and a talking and grinning Knox and Christo. I was standing in the living room where I had put a bottle of JD and five glasses on the table. Knox was the first to enter the room and he walked straight to me. As we were hugging each other, Christo entered and at the sight of the bottle on the table, he rubbed his hands together and smiled,

"Damn. You know exactly what a man needs, don't you!" he said grinning as he took the bottle and removed the top. Knox and I let go of each other.

"You bet I do," I replied winking at him. A huge smile spread across his lips and without letting go of the bottle, he opened his arms.

"Come here, you gorgeous woman," he shouted happily and the hug he gave me almost squeezed the air out of me.

"So? How has it been to get paid for walking around in a refinery?" I asked a little teasingly looking at Knox and Christo.

"Fucking boring." Wizard replied from the doorway. He was standing leaning against the door frame, with both arms stretched as if he were about to do an abdominal exercise. I turned around and saw the familiar smile on his face.

"Hey, babe," he said stepping into the room. We hugged and it was great to have him and the rest of them back.

Christo had put the bottle of JD to his mouth and was gulping the whiskey. As Wizard passed him he gave him a hard thump on the back of his neck so he spilled some drops of the golden liquid.

"Use a glass, damn it," he said and the words made Christo remove the bottle from his mouth as he swallowed, followed by him wiping his mouth with his sleeve. Then he bent down and poured some in all the glasses on the table. When Aslan entered the living room the group was complete and we all took a glass and toasted ourselves. After the toast Knox threw himself onto the pillows.

"Fuck, it's good to be back," he said closing his eyes.

"Yes, and enjoy it while you can." The words came from Aslan, "The requests are coming in like crazy." Wizard put his hand on Aslan's shoulder.

"Relax," he said, smiling, "We'll have next week off so no more talk about work till after that." I looked at him, because it was not like Wizard to 'take time off', but he probably wanted to go home.

"Fine by me." Knox replied while closing his eyes and putting his hands behind his neck.

"I need a couple of women or three." Christo stated as he walked around filling our glasses. Knox opened his eyes and sat up abruptly.

"Too right. I'm up for that," he replied emptying his glass, "A bath and then we are on the move." The seemingly newfound energy in Knox made us all laugh and we toasted it.

"Relax, Knox." Aslan chuckled.

"It's easy for you to say. I have not had anything since Karachi. Fuck I need it. Are you coming with us, Wizard?" Knox looked questioningly at Wizard and mentally I could not help but smile. Knox did not know anything about Wizard's marital status.

"No," he replied, emptying his glass, "I need to fix some things so ... you have fun." And then he put his glass on the table.

"Will fucking do." Knox replied without asking what it was Wizard needed to fix. To be honest I think he knew he would not have got an answer anyway.

"Aslan?" Knox looked at him.

"Yup. I'm always ready for a drink and some LADIES." Christo looked at him and laughed.

"I never thought I would hear those words from a Muslim." He raised his glass.

"Islam has many faces." Aslan replied and the answer made Christo gag on his whiskey.

"I love the way you practice Islam. Drinking, fucking and killing. A role model for all Muslims." He laughed as he put his empty glass on the table, "And with these words, gentlemen ..." He turned to me and nodded, "and lady, this magnificent specimen of a man will slip into the shower."

We laughed out loud and a few minutes later Wizard and I were alone in the living room.

"Do you want a cup of coffee?" I asked as I gathered the glasses from the JD party. Wizard took off his jacket and threw it on a chair that stood in the corner.

"It would be great. I've been drinking sweet tea for a month – and I hate tea." We smiled at each other before I went into the kitchen and put on the coffee. Wizard came into the kitchen a couple of minutes later and while facing the kitchen table he lit a cigarette. Then he turned to me.

"When are you leaving?" I asked as I took two mugs from one of the kitchen cabinets.

"Tomorrow morning." He exhaled the smoke from the cigarette through his nose, "Damn it, OPUS. I'm genuinely sorry we lost JAC. I don't know what happened. He ..." Wizard shook his head, "He started talking to some of the Kurds who work at the refinery and ... yes ..." He took a puff from the cigarette.

"Do you think he will stay there?" I asked knowing JAC well enough to know that he would.

"Yes ... at least for now. He has found a cause to fight for. He has never really had that." Wizard knew all too well what he was talking about because fighting for an ideology, whether it was political or religious – often it was both – was originally, how he had started his military career. He therefore knew the mechanisms that put you into such a situation all too well.

"What will it take to get him back?" I asked.

"I have no idea ... When the cause he is fighting for wins or loses? That the war against ISIS stops?" Wizard sighed, "I don't understand him. It's not his war. It's nothing to do with him."

"He probably sees the war against ISIS as a mutual war and now he wants to make his contribution." As I said it, I could hear how hollow it sounded, for the JAC I knew would never contribute anything without getting something in return, whether it was cash or personal satisfaction. JAC was not the type who would fight for a cause – perhaps for a person, for his team or to get revenge – but not for a cause. If it had been a long time since he had been on a mission, I could have understood that he needed to get out there and accomplish something, but we had just been to Aleppo. On the other hand – it had been months since he had a real kill, so maybe ...

"Come on," Wizard snorted, looking at me, "You don't believe that. It's JAC we are talking about. The man is a rock, both physically and mentally. If he sets himself a goal, you know he will go all the way to achieve it."

"Exactly, and now he has this idea. Wizard, we have to let him fight for his 'ideology'. When he is done, he'll come back. Let him run his 'partisan wild oats' off."

Wizard smiled, "Maybe you are right." He stubbed his cigarette out in the ashtray next to him while blowing smoke from his nose, "And if he doesn't come back, then fuck him."

He disappeared out of the kitchen with his cup of freshly brewed coffee and left me standing blowing on my steaming cup of mocha.

Wizard was right. Fuck JAC.

* * *

The next morning Wizard left and I was alone in the apartment. The boys had not returned from their party trip yet, so I had the whole place to myself and it was not so bad. A long bath, Mike Oldfield on the iPod, and a cold glass of wine was how I spent my morning. At 2 p.m. Knox showed up. He had had a terrific night and had ended up with a blonde model in the Hilton Hotel. Somewhere along the way he had lost Aslan and Christo, but judging by where he saw them last, they were 'in good hands'. I smiled and laughed at his amazing visual account of the events of the night and it was great to see him so happy and relaxed. Four hours later, Christo and Aslan entered the apartment laughing and boisterous. They had been partying for almost a day now and they were clearly not done yet.

"Hey, babe." Christo shouted from the hallway and I smiled to myself as I put down Stephen King's *The Stand* and got up from the soft sea of pillows in the living room. Knox had gone to bed a few hours ago, so there was only me and my book to receive the boys. I went into the hallway and saw Aslan sitting on the floor up against the wall laughing while Christo stood leaning against the front door doing the same.

"Hey, babe," Christo said again when he saw me, "We thought it was a shame you sitting here all alone now that JAC is out fighting in the name of ..., so we have something for you."

He walked swaying slightly towards me and placed a little white envelope containing what I presumed was cocaine in my hand. Next to the white powder were also some multicoloured pills.

"We didn't know what you liked, so here is a bit of everything. A small buffet. Have a blast – we certainly have." He patted me on the shoulder and laughed.

"Where's Knox? Is he here?" I looked at my gift, shook my head and smiled.

"He's sleeping," I replied.

"Bull shit," Christo replied, "He's not going to fucking sleep," and with the best of intentions, he went and grabbed the door knob to the room where Knox was sleeping.

"Wakey, Wakey," he shouted loudly before slamming the door behind him.

I shook my head again and chuckled. And then my gaze fell upon Aslan, who was still sitting up against the wall. He was looking up at the ceiling while chuckling.

"Are you okay?" I asked loudly and without looking at me he gave me a thumbs up.

I left Aslan to his own devices and walked back into the living room still looking at the colourful pills in my hand. It certainly was a selection if you wanted to get high but I had no interest in it. Suddenly Christo appeared in the door.

"Fuck ... he almost shot me," he said before throwing himself onto the pillows. He was clearly wasted.

"What were you expecting? You stormed into his room." Christo, leaning towards the table, took a small bag of cocaine out of his pocket, opened it, cut it, and sniffed it.

"Do you want some?" he asked when there was one line left. He looked up at me with raised eyebrows. I shook my head and waved dismissively with one hand.

"No thank you. It's all yours." And then he sniffed the remaining line before licking the paper clean of the little that was left on it.

"Do you want to go out?" he asked smiling.

"I think I'll take a rain check," I replied sending him a wry smile, "but please ... party on."

"Will do, babe. Will do." Christo leaned back, "Knox, what the hell is taking you so long?" he shouted as he looked up at the ceiling. Knox appeared at the doorway.

"Relax. I just needed to look human," he replied as he tucked his t-shirt into his light camouflage trousers. Christo got up and went over to him grinning,

"We don't have that much time." As Christo passed Knox he shouted to Aslan that they were leaving. When Knox had finished fixing his t-shirt, he looked at me.

"Do you want to join us?" he said quietly and I actually think that he would have liked me to.

"No, Knox ... but thank you for asking." He caught sight of the empty cocaine paper and looked at me, raising his eyebrows as if asking if it was mine. I smiled.

"It's Christo's." He nodded and smiled back.

"I thought so. See you later," he said and went to join Christo and Aslan, who were standing by the front door discussing which party they should crash now.

After they had gone, the lovely peace and quiet I had had all morning, returned so I just sat and enjoyed it but then there was a knock on the door. My first thought was that it was one of the boys, but my intuition told me something else, so with my Glock in one hand, I slowly opened it. There stood Luc.

"Hey," I said smiling, "Come in." He stepped in with his bag and put it down on the floor.

"Are you alone?" he asked, closing the door with one foot.

"Yes," I replied, "The boys have just gone out to party. Wizard left this morning and JAC ... JAC did not return from Iraq." Luc's smile hardened as he looked at me seriously. He was just about to ask ... but I beat him to it, "No, he is not dead. He decided to stay and fight with the Kurds against ISIS." Luc shook his head.

"That idiot," he replied, but I immediately sensed the relief in his voice. Luc's arms curled around my waist as he pulled me into him and our kisses quickly escalated from soft and gentle to hard and aggressive. He pushed me back against the wall and we began to rip our clothes off. Wrapped in each other, we stumbled into my room – the room that had been JAC's and mine – and rolled onto the bed. He lay on top of me and with a firm grip on both my arms he pinned them above my head so I could not move, despite the fact that I tried fiercely. It quickly dawned on me, the more I moved, the harder he held me and the harder he became. It was fantastic. With his legs he spread mine and then ... he was inside me. I realized, that he must have done this countless times before, because otherwise he would not have been so good at it. I resisted, not because I wanted him to stop, but because it was part of the 'game', and I could feel that it excited him even more and honestly ... it also turned me on. That I could control his degree of arousal this way was exciting. Our sex was rough and carefree but also tentative and with full respect for each other. The way he dominated me but always left the mental door a little bit open so if I didn't like what he did or wanted to do something else I was welcome to kick the door in. And then the roles would be reversed. We switched back and forth several times and it was awesome. He knew how to be both dominant and submissive and so did I. It was as if we had known each other for years and it was amazing how our bodies moved together. At no point was there any awkwardness or fumbling. We were like two bodies moving as one never denying each other any kind of pleasure. What he wanted I gave him and what I wanted he gave me. No turning away. No questions asked. And so we switched back and forth. His desire versus my desire. It was so liberating that I couldn't get enough of him. He was what I had been waiting for. He was everything I needed and I couldn't wait to explore our deepest sexual fantasies together.

* * *

Afterwards, I went into the kitchen and fetched two bottles of water and when I got back to the room, Luc was sitting up in bed, with the sheet half covering him. He had lit a cigarette. I went over and handed him a bottle which he drained as I threw myself on my stomach next to him. I unscrewed the top of my bottle and drank a mouthful, after which I took the cigarette from him and had a puff before giving it back.

"What have you done with your team?" I asked.

"We needed a little R&R after a month in Mosul. The boys were getting restless and so it is better to give them a few days off to get it out of their systems." He looked at me and smiled knowingly.

"And you came here to get it out of your system?" I said, smiling back at him. He lay down on his side and looked me in the eyes while gently letting a few fingers wander from my shoulder and down my arm. His touch was so gentle and caressing that it was hard to imagine that the very same hands had killed countless times. When he touched me, it was as if he was waking me up – he was giving me life – and that did not make my thoughts any less absurd.

"Yes. I told you I wouldn't let you go," he said leaning forward and we kissed with the same gentleness as was in his caress.

When we finally let go of each other's lips, he shoved the cigarette into my water bottle, after which I screwed the top on and threw it down on the floor. Luc caressed my neck and back and I could feel how he let his hand run all the way down my spine to my butt and back up my spine again. When his hand reached my neck, I gently placed my hand on it, thereby stopping his movement. I looked at him and said quietly,

"Luc, I want you so fucking bad," and he was about to say something as I pushed him over so he was lying on his back and the second after I sat across him. Slowly I bent down and kissed him, all the while I could feel him penetrating me. We kissed and as his hands caressed my neck, our kisses became more and more harsh and raw. The gentleness and roughness that was in this incipient lovemaking was absolutely amazing, and it only intensified when I slowly started riding him. I could feel his hand move from the back of my neck to the front of my throat and to my chest only to wander back up to my neck.

Suddenly he took an iron grip around my throat and began to squeeze, all the while slowly stretching his arm so I ended up sitting vertically on top of him, and in sheer excitement I set the pace. His hand squeezed my throat and it quickly dawned on me that the harder I rode, the more he squeezed. In fact, it was only when I was about to lose consciousness and slowed down that he loosened his grip. The feeling that I, depending on how hard I rode him, could decide how hard he strangled me was so fantastic.

It was as if I decided whether I wanted to live or die. Even though I knew perfectly well that Luc would never kill me, he actually gave me the opportunity to let him do it, and that turned me on even more. And there – in the midst of excitement and semi-consciousness – I rode us both hard to the point where our bodies trembled and we both screamed in pleasure before exploding at the same time.

Shaking, sweaty, and gasping for air, I fell down over Luc, and as my cheek hit his naked sweaty chest, I could feel his heart pounding almost at the same pace as his fast and furious breathing.

Slowly I slid down off him so I was lying on my back next to him. Still gasping for air, I tried to regain control of my trembling body, but it was impossible.

"Luc ..." I gasped as I lay staring at the ceiling, "You'll probably have to extend your R&R." He was still gasping for breath, but couldn't help but laugh.

"I think you're right," he said and we turned our heads and looked at each other in agreement that this was ... unbelievable ... and would certainly not be the last time, that we practiced this kind of sex.

When I woke up, it was dark in the room. Luc lay on his stomach next to me with one arm across me and slept. My mouth and throat burned so violently that I simply had to find something to drink and since both of our water bottles were empty or contained cigarette butts, it forced me to get up. Slowly I unwrapped myself from Luc and found a pair of pants and a t-shirt. The door to the room was closed and I did not remember us having done that, so I went quietly into the hallway.

There was light coming from the living room and the kitchen and I could hear the voices of Knox and Christo talking and laughing, and at the same moment my gaze fell upon mine and Luc's clothes, which were still scattered in the hallway. Quietly I gathered them and threw them on the floor in our room. Closing the door behind me, I walked calmly down towards the light.

Glancing into the living room, I caught a glimpse of the boys lying sprawled out amongst the pillows while drinking JD and smoking. Before joining them, I grabbed a few bottles of water from the kitchen and as I entered the living room their conversation fell silent and they both stared, smiling at me without saying anything. I unscrewed the top of one of the bottles and drank almost the whole thing in one go, after which I threw myself on the pillows.

"What's up? No more partying?" I asked. Knox raised his eyebrows.

"Judging from the clothes in the hallway, it seems like the party was here," he stated, smiling. I smiled back at him and took another sip from the water bottle.

"It was a party for two," I said as I drank the water, "Where is Aslan?"

"We have put him to bed. He went cold at the party we were at, so ... yes ... here we are," Knox replied, "By the way, greetings from The Kid." I stared at him eyes wide open because I had not thought about The Kid for a long time,

"The Kid? Is he here in Amman?"

"Yep. He has gone solo with one of the big security companies." Knox winked at me, "Don't worry. He doesn't know you're here. He just asked me to greet everybody around me that he knew."

"Fuck ... The Kid." I unscrewed the top of water bottle number two and took a sip, "He's probably pissed at me."

Knox and Christo looked at me in surprise, and I was about to tell them why, when Luc suddenly appeared in the doorway. I could not help but smile as he yawned. He was wearing pants, dog tag and his Glock as he stretched. Knox and Christo nodded to him and smiled, and he reciprocated with a 'Hey boys' as he ran his hand through his short dark-blonde army cut hair.

I got up, walked to him and handed him a water bottle. The way he looked at me totally turned me on. No doubt he could see it and I could see he enjoyed it. Still with our eyes locked on each other, I ran my hand down over his chest and his six-pack and even though I was aware that it turned him on, he did not let himself be bothered by it. He simply unscrewed the top of the bottle and drank a sip – still with his eyes locked on mine.

"Do you want to get pizza? I'm fucking hungry," I said half-whispering to him and the water bottle at his lips was replaced by a warm smile that made me want to rip his clothes off again.

"Of course," he replied, "Is there anything else you want at the same time?" He sent me an extremely suggestive smile that said, 'Bring it on.'

"Oh yes, but you will find out when we have eaten." The words had barely left my lips as he tore my head back with a firm grip on the hair on the back of my head. I indulged him and I could see he enjoyed it.

In response to Luc's rather demonstrative action towards me, Christo secured his Glock, but I signalled that he should leave it and Luc did not appear to be bothered by it. Instead, he kissed me aggressively and I reciprocated. Then he let me go.

"Are you hungry?" Luc asked turning to Knox and Christo.

"Not if I have to kiss you like that to make you get me a pizza too." Knox said, dryly wrinkling his nose. There was a moment of silence, but then we all broke out in laughter.

Five minutes later Luc went for pizzas while I took a shower.

The next three days I spent with Luc and they were amazing. We had sex, ate, drank, had more sex, slept and the first thing we did, upon waking, was to have more sex. Our passion for the raw and violent was so intense, that at times it was difficult for us to distinguish between what was physically possible and impossible. With Luc, I found myself in a sexually boundless world where desire and passion fused together and where everything was allowed and nothing was too extreme or perverse. It was a pure and raw worship of ourselves as individuals as well as an expression of mutual care and true compassion. We used and were used by each other to obtain satisfaction but we only released it when the other was ready to culminate at the same time.

In the end, it was only our physiques that set the limits for what we could do because we had broken the mental barriers down piece by piece in our desire. It was as if we channelled our mental energy into physical endurance, which made us almost limitless in everything we explored.

There was no doubt that Luc and I had found the ideal sexual partner in each other, because we did not just go to the edge – we started at it and then we went beyond. Our appetite for what the next move would be had such intensity that we often forgot everything around us in our quest.

The limit had to be somewhere. We just had not encountered it yet. As the days went by, we realized that it was up to us to set the limit, because otherwise we would simply end up killing each other in sheer narcissistic passion.

On the fourth day Wizard returned to the apartment. We were all sitting in the living room eating lunch when he put the key in the door and I could hear him going straight to his bedroom and tossing his luggage on the floor.

"Hello," he said cheerfully as he entered the living room a moment later, "What the hell?" He looked at Luc sitting with us and a confused expression combined with positive surprise was painted all over his face, "Of all the people in the world you were the one I least expected to see here." Luc had got up with his mouth full of hummus and while he swallowed his food, they gave each other a hug.

"Unfortunately, the pleasure will be short, because I am leaving tonight." The others looked at him and then at me, but I already knew. Luc had told me or rather I could hardly have avoided finding out, because in the middle of our morning sex, his phone had beeped and he had been 'called to work'. Not that it had put a damper on the sex – on the contrary. It had made it even more intense, as we now had a time limit for our exploration of each other.

"Do I dare to ask how you have spent your time or should we just leave it at that?" Wizard looked at us all.

"Party, drugs and fucking." Christo replied, "You know, a typical Saturday night."

Wizard shook his head and chuckled a little before directing his attention to me and Luc. For some reason he assumed correctly that we had not partied with the boys. In fact, I had no idea what the others had been doing for the last three days, because I had only seen them sporadically and primarily in the kitchen when I went to fetch water supplies for Luc and me. Wizard kept staring at me, and even though I was trying to avoid his eyes, I knew he had seen right through me.

"OPUS," he said loudly, "You and me in the office – Now."

At the sound of his commanding voice, I was well aware that any kind of protest was pointless and I might as well obey, so I chewed my mouthful, got up, and went to him.

"I missed you too, Wizard," I said as I passed him in the doorway. I heard him ask the others,

"What the hell was that supposed to mean?" but no one answered him. Wizard followed me into the office and slammed the door behind him.

"What are you doing?" he said and there was an honest concern in his voice, "Are you fucking Luc?"

"You bet but it is none of your fucking business." Wizard had no right to interfere in that part of my private life and I think he knew he had gone too far. He put his hands on his hips and looked down at the floor, shaking his head slightly. Then he raised his head and looked at me.

"What would you think about me asking Luc to join ACOSS?"

The question surprised me because honestly, I had not seen it coming but it was actually a good idea.

"All right by me, but do you think the others will be okay with it?"

Deep down, I had my doubts, because Luc was not your average kind of soldier. On a mission he was indispensable, but outside he was undoubtedly a devil and I thought that it would only be Wizard who would be able to keep him in line. A bit like it was with JAC.

"You have to be okay with it otherwise it doesn't matter and don't worry about the others. They will follow," he said as if he had read my thoughts.

"Ask him – but I think he'll say no."

Wizard stared at me.

"Why do you think that?"

"He is a legionnaire at heart. He will never leave the legion."

"Are you sure? Not even if you asked him?" Again Wizard stepped over the line.

"I'm not going to ask him," I said quietly but firmly, before going back to Luc's and my room and closing the door.

Wizard had really stepped over my boundaries by putting me in a situation where my loyalty to him had to be measured by my feelings towards Luc. I did not want to be pressured by Wizard to pressure Luc, and that was exactly what he had done by asking me. I sat for a while and fumed that he had attempted to use me that way, but as time passed, I came to the conclusion that he probably had not meant anything bad by it. He just wanted to improve the team and Luc would be a strong colleague and team member. But it had to be Luc's choice and not because he felt pressured into joining.

I was sitting with my back to the door when Luc entered the room ten minutes later. He had lit a cigarette and I could hear his footsteps on the rug as he came over and sat down next to me.

"I declined Wizard's offer," he said quietly as he handed me the cigarette. I took a puff.

"I knew you would." Out of the corner of my eye I could see that he was turning his head to look at me, "You are a legionnaire in your soul ... and that's all right." Without looking at him, I got up and went over and opened the window and threw the cigarette butt out.

"These days ...," he said, "they have been completely ..." I looked at him.

"Yes, they have, but now it's time to go back to the real world." Luc snorted.

"Back to work."

"Exactly ... and who knows ..."

"If we will see each other again." He looked up at me, and my smile and raised eyebrows indicated, that those were my exact thoughts, "We have four hours before I have to leave," he said, and quietly I went and stood in the middle of the floor.

"Then will you do something for me?" I said gently.

"Of course," he replied looking seriously at me.

"Will you fuck me hard with absolutely no limitation but your own?" Luc's eye colour slowly changed to onyx black and his breathing became short.

"Are you sure you want me to do that?" he asked in a soft growling voice as he gently moved his hand to the back of my neck caressing it. I leaned my neck into his touch and breathlessly nodded yes. His bowed his head down so close to mine that our lips almost touched.

"I need to hear you say it," he then whispered almost purring. His gentle stokes on my neck had stopped and I could feel his hand grabbing the back of my hair. I closed my eyes.

"Please Luc. Please fuck me every way you like."

Two seconds later I was face down on the bed. He ripped off my clothes and while he pressed my head down into the pillows, he took me hard in the ass. The pain combined with the fact that I was about to suffocate was insanely arousing and then we reached the limit. I lost consciousness.

The next thing I remember is waking up in Wizard's bed with a blanket over me and Knox sitting next to me in the process of taking my pulse.

"Knox," I said and he immediately let go of my wrist.

"Jesus Christ, OPUS. What the hell is going on?"

"Where's Luc?" I asked.

"Fuck Luc."

"No, where is he?"

"Where do you think he is? Wizard is 'questioning' him." The words made me jump out of the bed just to discover that I was naked.

"Jesus, Knox," I said while wrapping a blanket round me.

"Wait." Knox said but I was already on my way to mine and Luc's room. Here I found Luc sitting on the bed wearing military trousers and dog tag and with his face hidden in his hands while Wizard paced in front of him. Aslan and Christo were also in the room and there was no doubt that they were monitoring the situation very closely.

"Stop!" I screamed and all four of them looked at me.

"Go back to Knox." Wizard snarled, but it was by no means an option for me.

"No. And don't you dare touch him, Wizard. Do you hear? He has done nothing wrong."

"Are you insane? Not only did he rape you, but he almost killed you." Wizard turned to Luc.

"Don't do it, Wizard," I hissed, assuming that he was going to beat him. If it came to that I had no doubt that Luc would succumb to Wizard's uncompromising methods after his many years of experience in interrogation. Resolutely I went over and put on pants and a t-shirt.

"It was a sex game that went wrong," I said as I got dressed and as I fastened my belt, my gaze found Wizard's.

"A sex game? Are you ...? Are you fucking crazy?" He looked at Luc and Luc nodded.

"Shut the fuck up." A resigned and somewhat annoyed Christo replied, "Can you no longer wait for the enemy to kill you? Now you have to do it yourselves. Fucking idiots." He shook his head, "But be my fucking guest ... I will not stand in your way." The words were still hanging in the air as he left the room. Wizard stepped towards Luc.

"If you ever do anything to her – whether it's intentional or not – I will guarantee you, that bloody anal torture is only the beginning of the things, I will do to you, before I kill you."

There was no doubt that Wizard meant it and he did not expect an actual answer to his statement either. Still angered, he left the room and, thank God, with the matter unresolved. The only one left now was Aslan, who was standing and just watching us. A moment later Wizard called him and it seemed as if it was almost against his will that he left. Luc sat staring a little apathetically into the air and it was clear that he was affected by the whole situation.

"Luc, it was an accident. It could have happened at any time. It was only a matter of time." I sat down next to him and gently began to caress his back.

"How are you feeling? Are you okay?" he asked as he put his hand on my thigh and caressed it softly. There was a sincere concern in his voice, so I leaned toward him and kissed him gently on the ear.

"I am just fine. And you?" I whispered, smiling at him as I continued to run my hand up and down his back.

"Fuck," he said, raising his hands to his face again, "I was fucking scared ... I thought I had lost you ... that I had killed you in the middle of my rush."

"But you didn't. I'm still here – and now we know where the limit is." He lowered his hands and blinked a few times.

"Yes," he said nodding quietly, "We do."

We sat for a while without saying anything.

"Come!" I said crawling into bed. He looked at me somewhat surprised.

"Have you not had enough?" he quietly asked.

"Come here." I patted the sheet and he crawled up next to me so I could lie down next to him. Lovingly, he put his arms around me and we hugged each other tight.

"It really was not my intention to hurt you," he whispered kissing me on the head.

"I know ... and you didn't hurt me. I enjoyed it – until you killed me." The sentence sounded completely absurd and made me laugh, and even Luc smiled.

"You are mentally damaged," he said kissing me on the head again.

"Yes, but at least I'm alive." We both started laughing.

"You know very well that they think we are raving mad." Luc said, alluding to Wizard and the boys.

"I don't give a fuck what they think," I said, "This sex is ..."

"Absolutely amazing." Luc concluded slightly dreamily.

I looked up at him and we kissed each other gently, intensely and for a long time. I loved the feeling of his mouth on mine. His soft lips that parted and the way his tongue danced with mine. It was all so right. So perfect. And for once I didn't miss his roughness. Slowly Luc let go of my lips. It was almost as if he didn't want to because it was done with such reluctance that it almost seemed painful for him.

"We have to figure out how we are going to see each other." Luc said suddenly and it surprised me. I had not given it a thought and it was probably because I lived in the present and not in the future. A possible future rendezvous was not something I dared think about for who knew what tomorrow would bring?

"I'll see you – like now – when we have time off – or when we 'share an office'." And here I was referring to when we were on missions in the same areas.

Neither of us touched on the subject again and for the next hour, we just lay and cuddled and chatted. Then Luc started packing and just as suddenly as he had appeared, he disappeared. His goodbye kiss was long and deep and this time neither of us wanted to let go. When he finally walked down the stairs I found myself following his every move. It was as if I had to have a mental imprint of them and even before the door to the street closed after him I was filled with a strange longing for him. It filled all my heart and for the first time I felt a true ache for someone. I closed the front door and went into the shower. Afterwards I went straight to bed. I did not really want to talk to the others, and it therefore suited me fine that they did not seek my company either. As I lay there in the incipient twilight, I could smell Luc. His body scent hung in all the pillows and sheets, and as I lay my face down on one of the pillows and took a deep breath, my whole body began to throb with excitement and deep longing for him.

And there – right there in the middle of missing him and the powerlessness in relation to the fact that I did not know when I would see him again, I promised myself that I would never let him go. Never.

Chapter 31

The hectic start of the next day indicated that party time was over and that everyday life was back. Wizard had contacted The Kid and persuasion had not been necessary to have him join us. Evidently he would love to be a part of the team but for security reasons, we chose not to say anything about me being present.

Aslan had selected five missions that could be of interest to us, and new passports had been ordered for all of us – including The Kid. They were due to be picked up later that day. As our arsenal of weapons had gradually become bigger, Aslan had rented an external storage room in the city for them, and while Wizard and the boys had been in Erbil, Aslan and I had secured the room according to all regulations before moving the weapons into it.

The fact that we had to do this, had made finding a new and more permanent base even more relevant to us. We had now stayed in Amman for little over a month and the apartment was no longer ideal in terms of size or security. The first time Wizard and I talked about getting a new permanent base was when we were driving from Amman to Damascus, and here the choice had fallen upon Frankfurt, but now suddenly another city had come into play. Aslan had suggested Barcelona and honestly, there were a lot of good reasons why we should choose that over Frankfurt. It was in Spain or rather Catalonia. The Catalans were known for their nationalism, they basically wanted the region to secede from Spain, but that did not seem to be realistic in the near future. But the nationalist feeling made them cherish everything that was 'within the walls', which was positive for us. Barcelona's location was perfect in many ways. Not only was it directly on the Mediterranean coast with a large port, but it also had a large international airport and was only a few hours' drive to the French border.

Before the noon prayer had sounded from the mosque, we had agreed upon Barcelona, and Aslan was given the task of finding a suitable property in the area. It should meet all our requirements for size, isolation and training facilities and be maximum thirty minutes' drive from the city, airport and port.

After dinner, we gathered in the living room, to be introduced to the new missions. The five missions that Aslan had selected were, respectively: in Gaza, Lithuania, Italy, the Persian Gulf and Ukraine. After some discussion, we chose Gaza.

The mission was for a private company that had won a construction contract in the area and they wanted protection of their material convoys to and from the construction site as well as protection of their employees while on the building site.

The security on and around the construction site itself would have nothing to do with us, as it was Israeli soldiers who were in charge of that, so basically it should be a mission that we could handle easily. The assignment was to begin in two weeks and last for three months with the possibility of extension, as the company was awaiting an answer as to whether they had won more contracts in the area. If that happened, we could choose to commit to another period or move on to another assignment.

After Wizard and Aslan had assessed the mission in more detail, it became apparent to them that we needed two more men. The reason for their assessment was that the area we were going to was highly unstable, and even though we had a huge advantage, as Wizard for long periods of time had worked there before and therefore had contacts all over the place as well as spoke the language fluently, we needed more firepower on site. So while Aslan arranged all the practicalities related to our departure – permits, clearances, transportation, tickets, etc. – and Knox and Christo drove to the warehouse and did an inventory check, Wizard and I went for a walk. We needed to brainstorm who could be the new members of the group, and what better place to do it than in a small local café? – so we did just that.

* * *

As always, we sat in the back of the room so we had a full view of everything that was happening around us. We ordered Coca Cola and some snacks and then we got on our phones. After an hour, we had selected Ben – a former French Foreign legionnaire – and Castro, an ex-US Marine. I had only heard of them, but Wizard knew them both and could vouch for them – as much as you can vouch for anybody in our industry.

Ben was British and his military background was as long as it was varied. He had been to Corsica when he was in the Foreign Legion, but despite the fact that he had been at the top of his class, he had never really fitted in because he functioned best when he had influence, and this was not possible as a legionnaire. Therefore, for the last eight years he had worked for a large private security company, but he was now bored and looking for something else. Castro was almost his total opposite: An ex-Marine explosives specialist who had only recently gone solo after fourteen years in the US military. Rumour had it that he had turned down some of the big security companies' job offers because he no longer cared for the heavy and bureaucratic organizations. As a person, he was quiet, introvert, but stable and very loyal.

After sorting our personnel requirements, Wizard and I knew, we had to talk about the situation with Luc. Neither of us wanted to, but it was necessary, because there were only two weeks left of the period that Wizard had bought from him and if unresolved by then it ultimately could become a security risk for all if Luc were to visit. We agreed that the location of our new base in Barcelona, should be kept secret for as long as possible.

Our conversation then took a more personal turn, as it was very important that Wizard understood that ACOSS was paramount to me above all, including Luc. At the same time, I would be sorry to lose him, but if that was what was needed, so be it ... Wizard must never be in doubt about where my loyalty lay and I could see that he was relieved at my declaration. The conclusion was that we would review it when we came back from Gaza. A lot could happen in three months and the possibility of Luc going to Gaza to find Wizard, we calculated as minimal.

After consolidating our agreement over lunch, we went back to the apartment. As we entered, we could hear The Kid's voice and Wizard and I quickly exchanged a few glances before walking into the living room. Here we found Christo, Knox and The Kid sitting and drinking JD. Aslan was out fixing some things in the city. The Kid's facial expression when he saw me was worth a million in gold. He stopped in the middle of a sentence and his jaw dropped.

"Hey," I said casually to him, "I owe you an apology for last time I just disappeared."

"Fuck ... you ARE alive," he said, smiling all over his face, "Come here."

He got up and we met halfway with a long hug.

"I really did not believe that you were dead. You're like a cat. Isn't it the third time that you've supposedly died?"

"Yes, I guess," I replied, laughing, "I really mean it when I say I am sorry."

The Kid looked at me still smiling.

"Don't worry. You had your reasons and I am sure they were good."

"The reason is him," I said, nodding toward Wizard, while The Kid, of course, was uncomprehendingly watching us.

"We came face to face with each other and ... yes ... now we stand here ... not facing each other but next to each other." Wizard replied and looked as if he expected The Kid to fully understand what he had just said. The Kid had obviously not grasped any of it and, in his defence, it was not the best explanation Wizard had given in his life.

"We fought on opposite sides out on the Farm and we made the decision to go AWOL instead of killing each other. If I had found you then, we would have taken you with us," I said as an explanation of Wizard's somewhat garbled statement, and it seemed that The Kid understood what I meant.

He stood for a while and then he said,

"If you had found me, I would have come with you. But now we are together again and how cool is that?"

He went over and took his glass of JD.

"To the ACOSS team," he said raising his glass.

"To the ACOSS team." Everybody in the room lifted their glasses and drank.

Wizard and I smiled at each other because this was exactly how it was supposed to be. Unity.

"Well," Wizard said seriously as the boys put the empty glasses down, "The Kid is our newest member, but he is not the only one. What do you say to Ben and Castro joining the team?" There was silence for about half a minute.

"Why not?" Christo finally replied, "I do not know Castro, but I know Ben from the Legion and he is okay. He's crazy. Super in battle and a party animal in his spare time so ... Perfect."

"He's fucking erratic and a mental case." Knox said, "You will probably have to sleep with your Glock unsecured if he joins us." Knox nodded towards me as he said it and there was no smile on his lips.

"It's okay with me," I replied.

"Yes, it is," Christo said, "With a little luck, you can get Luc to kill him. Ha, think about it ... two foreign legionnaires and a contractor ... a 'three's a crowd' drama ... Fuck, we can step out of the industry and sell the movie rights."

"You can be absolutely sure that you would never get to the première if you don't shut up," I hissed and I could feel my inner rage rising.

"Fuck you!" Christo said as he got up, "You don't scare me, you just need to have some ..."

"You do NOT finish that sentence." Wizard wisely stepped in and his voice was harsh and determined as he silenced Christo.

"Whatever ..." Christo said, "For my part, Ben is welcome and I don't know Castro, as I said, so ..."

He shrugged and left the room.

"Someone explain to me what's going on?" The Kid asked rather hopefully.

"One day when it's raining and we have got nothing better to do, I probably will." Knox said sighing.

"Okay," The Kid replied, smiling, "Then I have something to look forward to."

That attitude was one of the things I had always liked about The Kid. That he did not indulge in unnecessary trifles was the very essence of who he was, and I admired it.

As Wizard took out his phone and disappeared into the office, I took the opportunity to sit down opposite The Kid and drink some JD. He looked older, even though it was no more than five months since I last saw him. It suited him. Gave him more character.

"Is JAC here?" he asked as he lit a cigarette.

"No," I replied, "He is fighting ISIS in northern Iraq."

"Who the hell hired him to do that? It can't be a local militia. They don't have any money." He asked as he inhaled.

"No, he is there as a volunteer – unpaid volunteer."

The Kid's eyes told me that he clearly did not believe me.

"Volunteer? You are bullshitting me. JAC has never done anything voluntary in his entire life. It's always been something for something." The Kid handed his glass to Knox, who was about to pour more JD in his own. Once he had filled The Kid's glass, we raised our glasses to each other and Knox drank half of his while The Kid emptied his.

"Well ..." He took another puff from the cigarette, "We will do fine without him, so ..." The front door opened and a minute later Aslan passed by in the hall. He went straight in to Wizard, but was immediately asked to leave, because a few seconds later, he was standing in the living room.

"You must be The Kid," he said, shaking his hand. After a short greeting, Aslan picked up a glass and then sat down next to me.

"Aslan and Wizard know each other from North Africa," I told The Kid, just to get him up to speed, which he acknowledged. With a slight nonchalant motion, Knox pushed the bottle of JD over to Aslan and as he poured whiskey into his glass, my phone beeped. It was the response of the lawyer in Geneva, so I withdrew to my bedroom and left the boys to bond.

My bedroom window had been open all day and it had made the room a little cooler than I had expected, so I put on a long-sleeved polo shirt and sat down on the bed.

From the lawyer's email it had apparently been very difficult to find the address I had asked for, but he had succeeded and it was an empty plot up in the mountains belonging to a limited company registered in Jersey, but it had not been possible to find out who was behind the company. I smiled. It could only be Liam or someone close to him who owned it. Who else? According to the lawyer, a building permit had been issued for a six hundred square metre house and the signature on these papers belonged to an 'Imeni M'.

My smile disappeared and my whole body stiffened. This land had evidently nothing to do with Liam. On the contrary. This was information about Wizard. Liam had tried to gather information about him, and then he had come across this. Whether Liam knew about the building permit, I had no idea, but the notary office in Geneva would have, because they registered all inquiries. I therefore immediately called the lawyer and after thanking him for the information, I asked him to contact the notary office immediately to inquire further.

When I hung up, I finished reading the rest of the email. Apparently, the phone number I had asked him to check did not exist anymore, and since it was a pay-as-you-go SIM, it was untraceable. I sat thinking for a while when suddenly the lawyer called back. He had spoken to the notary's office and informed me that there had been a request from a law firm in Lucerne. He even had the date of the inquiry. After hanging up, I checked my phone and it had been four days before we blew up the barracks in Afghanistan. I had to inform Wizard about all this so I went straight to the office to find him still engaged in a phone call. His conversation was coming to an end so he did not mind my presence. I sat down on the chair in front of the desk. Wizard hung up and looked at me.

"What's up? You look worried."

"Yes ..." I replied, "Could you close the door?"

He looked at me briefly before doing so. Then I started to tell him what I had found. As I spoke, Wizard had sat down in the office chair, without saying a word. When I was finished he just stared at me. Then he smiled,

"And now you think that ...?"

"I have no idea what to believe. I just wanted to tell you that Liam was investigating you." Wizard leaned forward on the chair and put his elbows on the desk.

"I have no doubt that he was investigating me, but he was never close. At least not close enough for me to do anything about it."

"But if he knew about Imeni ..." To me it seemed like Wizard took this too lightly.

"Imeni and the boys are safe. He would never have found them. NEVER. And I can assure you, that they have never been to Geneva and it has never been my intent for them to go there." He got up and walked round the desk to me, "Forget it. Liam is dead and so is this topic."

I should not have been surprised by his reaction, but I was. Strange as it may sound, I somehow felt that Imeni and his children were also my responsibility. Wizard had shown me immense confidence by introducing me to Imeni, and by doing so he had invited me into his private world. It was not normal for someone with his portfolio to do that, but he had chosen to do so and therefore he had mixed the 'two families'. In my mind, Imeni was now a part of us and I would at any time help her and the boys if needed. I got up and walked to the door.

"Okay," I replied without looking at him, "But hopefully you know that if you need me, I ..."

"I know," he replied, "And Imeni knows it too. She has your contact information if ... if it should be relevant."

We looked at each other briefly and our eyes indicated that there was nothing more to say – at least not for now.

* * *

The remaining time in Amman was spent preparing for the mission. We did cardio fitness training in the mornings, studied the area and set up strategies and battle scenarios on the laptop in the afternoons and refreshed our Arabic in the evenings by reading, listening to audio tapes and watching TV or movies.

Aslan had prepared training and diet plans for each of us, and even though we were already very structured, it was actually a huge help.

Five days into our routines, Castro arrived. He quickly joined the group, especially thanks to The Kid, who, with his relaxed and straightforward manners, made him feel right at home. Christo and I had buried the hatchet and had become such good friends that we were each other's sparring partners during training and it was great.

Since the space in the apartment was limited, we had to share rooms. Wizard and Aslan shared one room, Knox and Castro were given the pleasure of the living room and The Kid had moved in with me. Christo was assigned the office which he was going to share with Ben when he eventually arrived. The first evening The Kid and I shared the bed, we did not get much sleep because we lay talking all night. He told me about his missions and I told him about Belize and the time in Islamabad with Kafka. Of course, we avoided all the gruesome details, because there was no need for that. In truth, neither of us needed to relive the horrors we had endured.

The night before Ben's arrival, I was given a refresher course in self-defence techniques by The Kid. Knox had asked him to do it, so we practiced all evening in the living room and it was great fun for everyone. The Kid would show me how to perform a different technique and then I would choose one of the boys to try it on. There was laughter and crying as I tossed them around and the biggest applause sounded when I made Wizard fly through the air and land out in the hallway. After four hours of intensive training, and with several bruises on both me and my 'victims' bodies, we stopped. It had been an incredibly cozy evening and we had all needed the practice.

The next morning Ben arrived while Christo and I were out running. We ran twelve kilometres every day at a moderate pace and finished with three sprints of a hundred and fifty metres each. The air temperature was twenty-seven degrees so we were short of breath and sweaty when we got back to the apartment. As usual, Christo and I went straight to the kitchen and drank one and a half litres of water each and, as we were standing there cooling off, Wizard suddenly called us into the living room. Sweaty and still catching our breath, we went without knowing what was waiting for us. But we were soon to find out.

"Say hello to Ben," he said and I saw his crooked smile. Since I was standing behind Christo, I could not see Ben, but I heard Christo say 'Nice to see you again, man' and, after they shook hands, I stepped in front of him and there ... there was a live blond Barbie Ken facing me. He was just as tall and wide as JAC, and he had a smile that could make any woman weak at the knees. It was safe to say I did not know what I imagined Ben would look like, but it was definitely nothing like this.

As we shook hands he calmly asked in a velvety voice, "What's your name?"

In the midst of all this, I had completely forgotten to introduce myself.

"Uh ... OPUS," I replied, trying to seem unaffected by the fact that a Greek Adonis was standing in front of me. However, my attempt totally failed and my awkward behaviour triggered laughter from The Kid, Knox and Aslan.

"Guess you didn't expect that ...," laughed The Kid.

"Noooo," I said, "But it's not really me who should feel surprised. It's Knox and all his fair-haired models. You've got some competition now, Knox."

I winked at Knox, who loudly proclaimed that he had a few girls in reserve, if Ben wanted to borrow one. Ben smiled.

"Thanks, but no thanks. I prefer brunettes. Are you available?" he looked questioningly at me as the laughter in the room slowly died out.

"Now, available is a broad concept, but no, I'm seeing someone."

"Hmm ..." Ben replied, "Too bad. It's always easier when the bitch is in the team. Then you always have access to ..."

There was a moment of silence and everyone waited for my reaction, which came promptly. I took a step towards him and wanted to slap him right in the face, but he grabbed my hand and ... thanks to my training the night before, he flew through the air and landed at Wizard's feet.

"I'll teach you who the fucking bitch is here," I snarled and was about to do so but then I stopped. I had never seen such a look in anyone's eyes. There was a fierce hatred in them that for a split second made ice run cold down my spine.

"Stop," Wizard shouted, "Stop, OPUS." But there was no need for him to say it. I had already stopped. The room was silent for a minute. Then I took a step back and Ben got up. He straightened his jacket and then smiled at me. I tried in vain to return one.

"Well, since everyone has said hello," Wizard concluded, "Shall we move on?"

Everybody went back to normal. Except for me. I went to my room to distance myself. I was very uncomfortable with what had just occurred between Ben and me so I thought a cold shower might wash my memories away. Before I turned on the shower I locked the door to the bathroom. It was the first time since we had arrived at the apartment, I had done that. Then I let the water hit my naked skin.

The glimmer of hatred that had been in Ben's gaze was frightening, and I had never seen it so true and pure before. Maybe Knox was right. Maybe Ben was completely mental? I actually used to be pretty good at reading people, but him ... his hatred ... I did not want to explore it any further.

When I came out of the bathroom, The Kid was sitting on the bed and, only wearing a towel, I sat down next to him.

"That was not a good start," I said, annoyed at what had just happened between me and Ben.

"It could have been worse," he said quietly, starting to unlace his boots.

"What do you mean?"

"You could have killed each other."

"Oh ... Shut up," I said and The Kid laughed.

While I was trying to find some clothes in a drawer, there was a knock on the door and The Kid shouted loudly, "Come In." A few seconds later, Ben stepped over the threshold.

"May I speak to OPUS in private?" he asked calmly, while The Kid kicked off his boots.

"No," he replied, and for the first time there was a firmness in his voice that I had never heard before. Ben took a deep breath.

"If I wanted to kill her, I would have already done so," he said unaffected by The Kid's protective way of acting.

"If you had killed her, you would be dead now." The Kid stated, getting off the bed.

"Give me five minutes," I said to Ben, "and then come back so we can talk." I sent him a smile and after returning it, he left the room.

"You leave the damn door open, you hear." The Kid said resolutely when Ben was out of sight.

"Yes, yes ... relax now," I replied slightly annoyed and went into the bathroom to put on my clothes. If I wanted someone to help me, it would probably not be The Kid ... no ... not when it came to Ben. It would be Wizard.

Five minutes later, Ben was back. The Kid had left with a few protests hanging in the air, but we were alone – and the door was open.

We both quickly agreed to delete our first encounter and start over. After the obligatory handshake and 'welcome-to-the-group' hug, we each lit a cigarette and sat down.

There were no chairs in the room, so we sat on the floor with our backs up against the end of the bed. As we sat there, it almost seemed as if we had just performed an old Native American greeting ceremony – 'How, a handshake and then a sit-down to smoke a peace pipe'. When I said that to Ben, he snorted loudly and afterwards he leaned back and blew smoke rings up into the air.

"Can you see what I'm writing?" he said, alluding to the fact that the tribes in the old days use to send smoke signals. I leaned back and looked up at the rings. Then I took a puff of my cigarette and blew smoke rings too.

"And here is my answer." He said nothing but smiled. We sat like that for a while without saying anything and strangely enough, the silence between us was perfectly okay.

"I know it sounds pathetic, but I always wanted to meet you," he said softly without looking at me.

"Do I live up to your expectations?" I asked a little sarcastically. Actually, I was totally indifferent to his answer and what he thought of me, but the glimmer of intense hatred I had seen in his eyes earlier, intrigued me.

"I had imagined you taller and more butch," he replied sardonically.

"Sorry to disappoint you."

Ben did not show any emotion and, oddly enough, I did not expect him to.

"Are you as hardcore as rumour has it? Rumour also says that you are dead, which you obviously are not." He looked at me, but I just stared at my feet.

"It depends on how you define hardcore. The number of kills? The way they are done?" Ben shook his head and looked away.

"No, I meant your mentality. You are cold, calculating and without empathy. Is that true?"

With a little sigh I got up. It was unbelievable that these labels were still attached to me, for I had never really done anything to earn them. In the past, I would not have cared, because I could not relate to them, but they allowed me to move around undisturbed in the camps. But as time had passed, such synonyms regarding my personality had begun to annoy me, for who would basically be with someone like that? Maybe someone similar? I smiled to myself and looked briefly at Ben.

"If so, we have something in common," I replied, taking a drag on my cigarette.

Ben was silent for a moment.

"Are you saying I'm your male counterpart?"

The conversation had started to bore me.

"No, I have already met him."

I smiled and with Liam in mind, I finished my cigarette.

"Did he survive that meeting?" Ben asked in a voice signalling that he already knew the answer. When I shook my head indicating 'no', he stared at me and, for the first time, I sensed a kind of respect from him. I smiled at him.

"Come," I said, "I think it's time for lunch."

He got up and without any physical contact – not even a glance – we joined the others in the living room.

Now that the team was complete, we quickly returned to our daily routines.

Aslan had increased our physical training schedules, which caused the majority of us to go to bed early in the evening exhausted. Castro had suspected Aslan of having a drill sergeant hidden in his stomach, and I was inclined to agree with him, for at times it seemed as if he enjoyed 'tightening our bows' to the breaking point a little too much, but the results in only two weeks were impressive.

Since Luc had left, I had concentrated on the team but now, the night before departure, I felt restless.

Normally JAC would be here to take the edge off it, but without him and with Luc far away, I was like a lion in a cage. Around nine p.m., The Kid came into my room. I had already retired for the day and lay on the bed with my headphones on. Everything was packed and ready, OPUS was cleaned and my Glock was loaded, so I could relax. I just needed the morning to come and the plane to take off. Suddenly I felt The Kid touching my shin and I opened my eyes and took the headphones off.

"I know it sounds silly, but we drew lots and I won," he said as he stood while looking uncertainly at me.

"Won?" I asked getting up on my elbows.

"Yes ... I won you," he replied and, for once, I was completely speechless. Never had anyone drawn lots for me, and just the concept disgusted me.

"JAC is not here and the guy, Luc, you know, is not within reach either, so ..." The Kid looked insanely cute as he stood there and had no idea what to do with himself and just as abruptly as my disgust had appeared, it disappeared again at the sight of his insecurity. I broke out in laughter. In fact, I was lying and rolling around on the bed while holding on to my stomach in pure amusement. The Kid was completely confused and looked reminiscent of a little school boy who had just been caught doing something wrong. When the attack of laughter had subsided, I patted the mattress a few times and he promptly sat down next to me.

"It's sweet of you, but ... come on."

I got up and, like a kindergarten teacher, I took his hand and together we went to the living room where the others were. There was complete silence when we stepped in and I let go of The Kid's hand but remained smiling.

"You are amazing," I said to them, "and I really appreciate you thinking of me, but you do not have to draw lots for me."

"We're not thinking of you," Wizard said coolly, "We were thinking of ourselves. You are a better soldier in the field when you have sex before a mission." I must have looked horrified and it harmonized very well with what I felt.

"Do you mean it?" I asked him.

"Yep," he said, throwing a peanut up in the air, which he then caught in his mouth.

"Really?" It actually scared me a lot if that was the truth. I looked over at Knox.

"Really," he replied, nodding affirmatively. It hit me hard and no one in the room was in any doubt that it was news to me. I put my hands on my hips and started walking around.

"Why the hell have you not said anything before? It's some real shit if you're in danger because I'm not having sex."

Wizard laughed and Knox and Aslan joined him.

"Calm down now," Wizard said frowning a little, "There is plenty of expertise in the group to compensate for your possible lack of spark in the field. We do not die because you don't have sex." It sounded completely insane, as he put it that way, and it was clear that it triggered laughter in everyone, including myself.

"But tell me ... just out of curiosity ... are you rejecting The Kid?" The question came from Christo and there was a wondering tone in his voice.

I looked at The Kid and smiled at him.

"Even though it's tempting, I'm not sure it would be good for either of us." I winked at him and he sent me a little smile back.

"But that raises the question of who would be?" Aslan asked.

"No matter how much it hurts me to have to say it ..., none of you. And it has nothing to do with you bitches, but what I need ..."

I had an unbelievably hard time saying these things, because I did not want to offend any of them, but at the same time I could not do what they wanted, namely to have sex with one of them.

"Because it's something only Luc can give you." Christo interrupted saving me from further embarrassment. I nodded and smiled at him with relief.

"Then why don't we just hire that Luc-guy? Can he not get a contract as a 'sex slave' with us?" There was a moment of silence and then we all broke into laughter at Ben's suggestion.

"It has been tried," Wizard finally replied, "but he refused." We laughed even louder.

"Who is this Luc guy?" The question came from a choked-up Castro.

"A six foot two tall, dark-blond, highly-skilled French Foreign legionnaire." Knox replied, wiping a tear of laughter from his eyes.

"Luc?" it came from Ben and the surprise was painted on his face, "Luc ... as in Miss Lai and Miss Lou, Luc?"

"Yes," I replied.

"Fuck," he said, chuckling, "And you are in doubt about how to define hardcore. That, OPUS ... that's hardcore. Luc is one of the most vicious and depraved in the Legion ... Fuck of a cocktail you two make." He shook his head and laughed softly, "I don't want to face you two in a war."

The conversation had started to bore me, so I thanked all of them and went back to my room. Whether I wanted to or not, Ben's words had made me think. Was there something I had completely overlooked in Luc? Yes, we had wild and violent sex, but he did not do anything I did not want him to do. Maybe it basically said more about me than about him. In the beginning I had thought that the only thing Luc and I had in common was rooted in each other's cravings for perversities, but I knew now that it went deeper. Much deeper. Slowly I began to see common features and the conclusion was clear. We were in so many ways almost completely identical. But words like cold, cynical and unempathetic, I could not associate with us. Was my sense of reality so distorted that this was just something I imagined or was it everyone else, who just listened to old rumours and anecdotes about us? The perception that had become synonymous with me over time, was basically what I had always tried to escape, and now its hideous face reappeared. I went to bed and pulled the blanket over my head. More than ever, I needed to disappear into the world Luc and I had created. For in it, no synonyms or glory existed. It was clean and genuine and straightforward with all its presence and brutality.

And in the middle of my train of thought, my phone beeped with a message from Luc that he was thinking of me. It was not a 'miss you' or 'love you' but a 'thinking of you'. I smiled and put the phone to my chest. Thank you, Luc. Thanks for not complicating things. It made the whole thing a lot more believable and straightforward. Thank you.

Chapter 32

The next day, Aslan drove us to the airport. Since we had to bring a lot of weapons he had, to facilitate the 'processing time' at the airport, booked us on two different flights to Jerusalem. Normally I would not have given it much thought, but he was right in that the airport authorities probably would not mind a few AK 47s in the hold, compared to us converting a commercially scheduled aircraft into a 'weapons transport'. The first team, Wizard, Ben, Knox and Christo, departed at nine fifteen – and at eleven forty-five The Kid, Castro and I followed.

We cleared security in Amman pretty quickly and, during the half hour flight, we just about managed to drink a cup of unusually horrible airline coffee. However, it was a real nightmare to get through security in Jerusalem and, even with the clearances that Aslan had arranged, it took almost three hours.

When we finally walked through the bulletproof glass sliding doors that separated the cool airport terminal from the scorching afternoon heat outside, it was almost four o'clock. We threw ourselves and our luggage into a taxi and drove to a small hotel where the rest of the team was waiting. Or so we thought. But as it turned out, Wizard was still stuck at the airport.

Aslan was on his case and at six p.m. Wizard walked through the doors of the hotel. By that time Castro and I had found the hotel bar and when Wizard caught sight of us, he stuck three fingers in the air as a signal to us. I hurriedly ordered a triple JD and one minute later, he was standing next to us, downing the drink in one. He was sweating and pale and I had a feeling it was because he had not had the opportunity to take his 'medicine' on time due to the airport delay.

"Had a good trip, honey?" I said encouragingly to him as he ordered another triple JD.

"Like a walk in the park," he replied dryly after emptying glass number two. I put our room key on the bar counter and he took it straight away, "An hour," he said, putting his empty glass down before looking at me. I knew he meant he wanted peace and I nodded as he took his luggage and went up to the room.

After his exit, Castro and I ordered two more double JDs and then the scene was set. It was really nice to be in his company. He was not the greatest conversationalist, but that suited me just fine. The rest of the team could be pretty outgoing and borderline shouting at times, so being with someone who didn't say that much was a welcome change. We had been sitting in the bar for an hour and a half and during that time he had told me about his wife and daughter in Arkansas.

His wife knew what he was doing and was perfectly okay with it, and it was a great relief to him that he did not have to struggle with that on the home front, as so many other military personnel did.

I knew of other contractors whose partners had a hard time accepting their long absences when they were on assignments, but it was inevitable once one had chosen this kind of lifestyle. Many of the partners had known the conditions before entering into a relationship, but the romantic notion of 'An Officer and a Gentleman' quickly evaporated when reality intervened and they were left alone when the partner was on missions for shorter or longer periods of time. Unfortunately, a lot of relationships broke down because of insecurity and loneliness which led to jealousy and infidelity.

Thankfully, this was not the case for Castro and I actually admired him for it. Both he and his wife knew the terms before they married and they seemed like a good couple. From what I gathered they lived in the same small town as they grew up in. He and his wife had met in high-school which was the same school as his now eight-year-old daughter attended. The way his eyes sparkled when he spoke of her just showed how much he loved her and how proud he was of her, and for a minute I admired him and the way he managed to have a life beside all this. No doubt he was very dedicated to his family but to the question if he would leave the military life to be with them, he just smiled and said that that was a hypothetical question with too many facets to it.

If anyone had heard the way Castro and I had talked, they would probably have been surprised, for it was more reminiscent of an interview than an actual conversation. I asked questions and he answered in short and precise sentences with no long or deep explanations. But it suited me just fine. I think he appreciated my respect and acceptance of his introverted personality.

* * *

The next morning Wizard and Knox went to see our client, to agree the final details as well as collecting the two jeeps, which according to our contract, would be available to us.

At ten o'clock they returned and we packed the jeeps and drove to East Jerusalem.

Many years ago, I had an assignment in Jerusalem and it was remarkable how much the city had changed since then. Whether it was for the better could be argued, but at least it had become safer to drive through.

We drove to an area where some of the new settlements were being built and passed an incredibly beautiful landscape on the way there. Mountains all around us and roads winding at the feet of them like little snakes. The site in question was on the side of a mountain, and, like all the other settlements, it was surrounded by a high barbed wire fence with searchlights attached at appropriate intervals. It was clear that the construction had been going on for a while, but for some reason they had stopped abruptly, because cranes and trucks had just been abandoned. It seemed a bit ghostly, if anything, as there were still half-filled water bottles, and in one of the trucks the driver had left his lunch bag.

While Wizard and Knox talked to the head of the site security, the rest of us walked around to get an impression of our future work place. Some of the houses were four stories high and to get an overall view, I made my way up a staircase to the flat roof terrace of one of these buildings. From here I had a great view over the whole area and I could not help but be a little fascinated by it. In front of me, on the opposite side of the valley, lay small green and unspoilt mountain slopes, whose only inhabitants seemed to be a large herd of goats grazing. Behind me, the newly built houses climbed up a similar slope, however, there was not a blade of grass on this one, but instead around four hundred houses, which in their location, formed an entire labyrinth up the mountain side.

"It is beautiful, isn't it?" The words came quietly from Ben, who had come up on the roof as well.

"Yes," I replied without looking at him, "Have you seen the bullet holes behind you?" I was referring to the white wall next to the staircase where five black bullet holes disrupted the otherwise so immaculately plastered surface.

"Yes."

"Somewhere out there a skilled sniper with a Dragunov SVD has been lurking around."

My voice was wary and, as we stood there like two radar-equipped periscopes scouting the terrain, we zoomed in on all the elevations and outcrops on the slope opposite us that could form a potential cover for a sniper. After a few minutes we quietly walked back and as we passed the bullet holes Ben stopped and studied them.

"You are right. It's from a Dragunov," he said, sticking one of his fingers into one of the holes, "What the hell. Is the bullet still in there?"

"Yes, of course it is. The sniper has used the wall to set his range and elevation." Ben looked at me before turning completely round looking out over the terrain again.

"And you know that because ...?"

"Because I would have done that before I started to shoot." I walked through the doorway and started descending the attic's staircase. I could hear Ben's footsteps right behind me.

"I'm going to inform Wizard about this and until you hear anything further, I suggest you keep your head down." Although Ben didn't comment I knew he had heard what I had said. I did not go into any details about my worries as I wanted to speak to Wizard first.

Ben stayed behind, whether it was because he wanted to have a further look around the complex I didn't know and honestly, I was too preoccupied with finding Wizard to care.

* * *

I went back to where I had last seen Wizard and Knox talking to the security chief, only to find that they had moved into a portacabin that apparently was the office of the site foreman. As I walked in on them, they were in the middle of an argument about our patrol options but to me that had immediately become a secondary problem when I had spotted the bullet holes on the rooftop.

"And when was it you were going to tell us about the sniper attack you have been subjected to recently? I guess forty-eight hours ago?"

My voice was loud and penetrating as I stepped in, interrupting the security chief in the middle of his speech. Wizard looked at him.

"Is this correct? Have you been the victim of a sniper attack?" he asked with a seriousness in his voice that eliminated any kindness in their conversation.

The security chief nodded briefly and was about to continue from where he had been interrupted when ...

"Jesus Christ," Wizard exclaimed loudly, turning to me, "Is he still out there?" he asked, looking me straight in the eyes.

"Yes, he is," I answered. For even though I could not provide any physical evidence of it, my gut told me he was.

Wizard completely ignored the security chief and taking out his mobile he sent a collective message to everyone in the team. Then he turned his attention to the security chief again, who in the meantime had stopped talking.

"If we are going to work together, I need to have such information straight away. Understand? Because right now my team is walking around in a death trap. They are sitting ducks. Do you get that?"

His eyes flashed and his hands, which had so far rested casually on the table, were now clenched. The security chief tried to explain, but Wizard had shut him off.

"Where are our living quarters?" Wizard interrupted him and the security chief pointed to a spot on the map on the table, "We'll continue this meeting later." Wizard said firmly and together with Knox we left the office.

Outside the container, there was no one from the team to be seen, so we raced down to the jeeps. Wizard signalled that Knox and I should take one each, so after jumping into one of them I crawled across the passenger seat to the driver's side. Wizard and Knox had sneaked up to the one in front. When I could see Knox sitting behind the wheel, I turned the ignition on and we drove at high speed through the construction site and to the two residential containers located at the edge of it. We parked the cars behind them so they were hidden and I immediately crawled to the back seat and started rummaging around between the bags. I quickly found the one that I was looking for. It was the one with the purple sticker on it. It was our sweeper equipment. At the same time, Wizard opened the door to the back seat.

"I got it," I said, giving him the bag.

While Knox was our 'eyes', we swept and cleared the first container. When that was done I started to unload all our equipment into it. As Wizard had drawn the curtains it was relatively dark in there but I would rather work in almost total darkness than get a bullet in the head through the window. When I was done, I closed and locked the door to it.

Then I sneaked over to the other container where Wizard and Knox were almost done sweeping. I waited the few minutes it took them to call the place 'clean' and then I drew the curtains here too. It was now ready for the luggage from their jeep to be carried in.

Wizard sent a collective message to the others and then he drove off in the already empty jeep. While he was gone Knox and I carried in the rest of our luggage and we sorted it according to the sleeping arrangements. There were four beds in each container, so we split them up according to the teams that Aslan had assigned. Wizard, Castro, Ben and The Kid in one and the rest of us in the other. With almost military precision the moment Knox and I swapped the last bags, Wizard came hurtling round the corner with the rest of the team in the jeep. When they had received Wizard's first message – SNIPER – they all immediately took cover. Here they stayed until the second message – a set of co-ordinates for the pickup point – had shown. Within minutes they had all gathered and waited for Wizard.

Now together, we entered the container, that was the base for 'Team Wizard' – the other container Knox had named 'Team OPUS' – and even though the curtains were drawn, we positioned ourselves so that a possible shot through the window would not result in any casualties. Wizard told everyone what had happened – supplemented by my explanation from the roof and on Christo's response about how I knew the sniper was still there, I replied that it was something I could feel.

"So, heaven and hell are set in motion on the basis, that you think there is a sniper out there? That's ridiculous. Then why did he not shoot you on the roof? I would have done if I were him." Christo got up.

"I know he's out there. Believe me or not, I could feel him," I replied.

"Feel him? Fuck off." Christo walked towards the door, but Wizard stopped him.

"It's a sniper thing," I said coolly, "and the reason he did not shoot Ben and me was probably that he wants to find out who we are, how many we are and why we let ourselves be exposed in that way. Right now, he is awaiting his orders on what to do – believe me."

"Is it something you guess too or ...?" Christo looked at me suspiciously.

"It is what I would do if it was me," I replied. There was silence in the container, but then Wizard broke it.

"Well ... based on this new information we need to secure the area and, in the process, we will find him."

"Judging by the location and angle of the bullet holes, he should be three quarters of the way up the slope. I saw four possible positions where he could hide, but he could also lie on the ground and just wait, and if he does ... well, then he can be anywhere."

"Okay," said Wizard, beginning to point to the various members of the team. "Knox and Ben – The Kid and Castro – Christo and me. We take a closer look at the possible positions and you ..."

He pointed at me.

"I go high-ground," I said glancing at him.

"We are leaving in ten minutes," he said tapping on his watch and, as if it were the starting shot, everyone set about finding their equipment. I got up to go into the other container to 'saddle up', but as I passed Wizard, he grabbed my arm hard.

"I hope you are right," he said in a whisper.

"I am. Just wait and see. He is out there." Then he let go of me and, as if nothing had happened, I continued my preparations.

Ten minutes later we were all in full gear, and before we turned on our headsets, Wizard gave the final orders, after which we dispersed.

I looked up at the building next to the one with the bullet holes. It was located a bit geographically higher, and I noticed that there appeared to be a metre high wall all around its flat rooftop. Such a wall could provide me the perfect cover so I therefore climbed to its top and sat with my back up against the wall and waited.

The midday sun baked down on me and while I was sitting there sweating, my thoughts wandered from the impending mission to Luc. I missed him, his face with the cheeky smile and the heart-breaking laugh. The gentleness of his dark eyes that in seconds could become hard and cold as stone. His touch that was as unforgiving as his gaze. His scent, his ...

My thoughts were interrupted by The Kid's voice in the headset. He gave a set of co-ordinates and announced that they had located the sniper. I could hear Wizard answering that they should take him alive if possible. Mechanically, I turned around so I could look out over the terrain, and, via the co-ordinates, I quickly found the location of our target. Through my scope I saw The Kid overpowering the sniper and within seconds he had disarmed him and had zip tied his hands behind his back.

"Coming home with Charlie." Castro said and I could not help but smile. It was typical US Marine language, but it was perfectly okay as long as we knew what it meant. I got up and turned around to come down from the roof, and the very moment I stood fully upright, I was hit by a bullet in my left shoulder.

I fell forward and screamed into the headset:

"I'm hit. I'm hit. There's a second sniper."

As I screamed into the headset to warn the others, I started to crawl across the white concrete roof towards the door. And then it happened. I was shot again.

This time it was in my left calf muscle. I screamed that I was hit again in my leg.

"The shooter is on the left side of where you found the first one," I shouted into the headset as I crawled to the door. With difficulty I got it open, the pain from my leg and shoulder was unbearable and I was bleeding a lot, especially from the leg. Using the wall, I got up and stumbled on one leg down the stairs. When I reached the last landing, the pain in my shoulder increased even more and I lost my footing and rolled down the last eight steps. In the headset I could hear that they had found the second shooter.

"Where are you, OPUS?" Wizard asked in a calm voice and I gave him my position.

"Sit tight," he replied and I crawled to the nearest wall and sat up against it. I knew my situation was far from good, and the amount of blood that pulsed out of my leg spoke for itself. I took my Medical Survival Kit from the pocket in the left arm of my jacket and tried to stem the bleeding from my leg with some gauze. Unfortunately, it didn't work as the blood continued to spurt.

"Are any of you guys 0-rhesus negative?" I asked over the headset, but no one answered.

Quietly I started laughing.

"Well, guys, I think I'm in serious trouble here. Losing a lot of blood." I started to get dizzy.

"Getting pretty dizzy, guys." And then I lost consciousness.

* * *

Nine hours later, I woke up in a hospital bed in Jerusalem. My shoulder was taped up and my leg was wrapped in gauze. I thought my injuries did not feel so severe, but I guess it was due to the morphine they had given me.

Luckily, I was alone in the two-bed ward, seemingly they were taking no chances with me. In addition to three different drips, I found myself connected to a heart monitor as well.

The nurse's bell hung over my head, and after a little fumbling, I finally got hold of it. I had to get rid of all these electrodes and drips and get back to the team as soon as possible.

A doctor and a nurse walked in and after a long discussion which ended with me shouting and screaming at them, I was injected with something to calm me down. After the doctor had left the room, the nurse stayed behind with the guard they had called. It was probably very smart to have me guarded because I was furious. The injection had a rapid effect on my motor skills, and I eventually fell into a doze with the guard sitting on a chair at the foot of my bed.

When I woke, the guard was gone and instead Knox was standing next to my bed talking to one of the nurses. Through the door I caught a glimpse of Wizard's back and with these two near me, I felt an inner calmness regarding the whole situation.

"Knox," I said quietly and he immediately turned all his attention to me. I signalled to him to come closer and then I whispered in his ear, "Now, you're not running off with that fair-haired nurse there, are you?"

He smiled at me.

"Two more minutes and I would have," he said winking at me.

It was clear that he was relieved at my comment, because it showed that, after all, I had not suffered brain damage from having lost all that blood.

"Hey, chief ... she's awake." Knox shouted and, as if by magic, Wizard and a doctor suddenly stood by my side.

Like Knox, Wizard was happy with my return to the normal world, but his way of showing it was limited to a smile and a nod. His reaction did not surprise me. Wizard was like that and it suited me just fine. There was no reason for long explanations and sentimental outbursts. I was alive, so we might as well get the show on the road.

Explanations, on the other hand, were plenty when it came to the doctor's motives for NOT discharging me, and it was only when I grabbed Knox's Glock and pointed it at him that he signed the papers. After the harsh way of treating the doctor, he left the room, and the fair-haired nurse, with whom Knox had been talking, remained to remove all the electrodes from me and to help me get dressed.

"By the way," I said kindly to her, "My colleague you spoke to before, he really wants your phone number." She looked at me and I could see that the episode with the Glock, had shaken her. I could understand why because who the hell would put a gun to the temple of the man who just saved her life? "He's actually really sweet and in no way like me," I continued, smiling at her, "You really would have a great date with him. He is nice and thoughtful and ..." I waved her closer to me and she leaned forward, "rumour has it that he is absolutely incredible in bed."

She looked at me and I glimpsed a small smile on her lips. Just then, Wizard entered the room so I could not talk Knox up any more.

"She's ready," the nurse said helping me off the bed. Wizard did not look at the nurse at all but instead called Knox in and with his support, I staggered out of the room and down the hall trying to avoid putting any weight on my injured leg. Wizard caught up with us at the elevators with a cardboard box under his arm and I could see it contained several drip bags of both antibiotics and sodium solutions. It was part of my exit plan between the Doctor and Wizard, but whether the contents of the box would be used was up to me.

None of us said anything while we were waiting for the elevator and just as the little ping indicated it had arrived, the nurse came running.

"You forgot this," she said handing me a syringe of morphine. Unexpectedly, she suddenly took my hand and, while she wished me a speedy recovery, she pressed a note with her name and phone number into my palm.

She smiled and winked at me and then ran back to the counter where a couple of other nurses were standing preparing medicine for some other patients in the ward.

Once we were all inside the elevator, a smile spread on my lips.

"Here is her name and phone number," I said handing Knox the piece of paper. He looked at it and then he started to laugh,

"You are incredible, OPUS. You're half-dead, and yet you manage to get me a date. Fuck ... you are something else." Wizard also started laughing and I could see the absurdity of it.

"Yep," I said smiling, "but you damn well better live up to what I promised her." Knox stopped laughing.

“What the hell did you say?” he asked and I was well aware that various scenarios were running through his head right now.

“That you’re a hunk in bed.” Wizard was in stitches with laughter and honestly, I had tears of laughter rolling down my cheeks.

“It’s not going to be a problem.” Knox said confidently and with a cocksure smile on his face, he winked at me.

“And, Wizard ...” I said, as Wizard’s laughter slowly subsided while he wiped his eyes on his jacket sleeve.

“Now don’t you fucking say you got me a date too?”

“No, don’t worry. Here!” I gave him the syringe of morphine, “Do with it what you will. I won’t be needing it.” As expected, he did not say anything, but out of the corner of my eye I caught his little smile. Then the elevator doors opened and we were back in the real world.

* * *

After the episode with the two snipers, there was relative quiet around the construction site, so the work resumed a few days later.

Since I was not yet fully mobile, Wizard had moved Ben to my team to replace me. The two teams took turns either patrolling the construction site or escorting the trucks with building materials to and from it. The daily patrols took place from seven in the morning to nine in the evening, and they ensured that work could be carried out in peace. The task of accompanying the trucks was somewhat more difficult, as some of the materials had to be picked up in areas where Hamas had a lot of activity.

The first month we were only exposed to minor attacks which resulted in a few delays in the deliveries, but as the war intensified, it became more and more difficult to carry out this part of our task, mostly because the roads to and from the construction site were repeatedly blown up.

After a few weeks of my shoulder being taped, I was finally allowed to take it off. My leg was also improving and over the next five weeks I therefore started taking a more active role in the tasks. The two snipers we had caught were young boys aged nineteen and twenty, and at Wizard’s order, the team had detained them until they knew if I had survived. When sure, Ben and Knox had given them a ‘loving little talk’, after which Wizard had handed them over to the security chief. What happened to them next didn’t concern us.

Wizard had introduced a policy that we got weekends off. For my own part, I had refused it, as I felt that I had better make sure I was a hundred percent fit before visiting various obscure bars and cafés in Jerusalem. Luc and I had kept in touch via text message, but for security reasons neither of us knew where the other one was. I was somewhat surprised, therefore, when I received a message from Aslan on a Friday afternoon that Luc was back in the apartment in Amman. My body started screaming for him and after two minutes with Wizard, I packed a few things and got a lift with one of the trucks to the airport in Jerusalem.

I was back in the apartment in Amman by nine that evening and the first sight that greeted me, when I entered Luc's and my bedroom, was him sleeping, fully dressed, on the bed. I couldn't help but smile a little and I decided to give him an hour before waking him up. I spent the hour in Aslan's company and I think he enjoyed being updated regarding our work and not least my hospital stay.

After an hour, I went back to Luc, who was still asleep. After closing the door quietly behind me I turned on the bedside lamp furthest away from him and took off my clothes. I crawled onto the bed next to him and gently started to kiss him. It took less than five seconds, then he was awake and grabbed my neck hard.

"Careful. My shoulder," I said quietly, "I was shot."

I actually do not know how I had expected him to react, but he stopped abruptly and his facial expression showed concern.

"Shot? Can I see?" he said with a voice full of worry while frowning.

I pushed my shoulder forward, as far as I could and he let his fingers wander over the scar from the wound.

"The leg was worse. They hit one of the large arteries and I almost bled to death."

Terror ran over his face and then he kissed me tenderly on my neck.

"But I'm still here," I said in a whisper and with a true affection for him in my voice, "I won't leave you." Immediately his kisses increased and he let his lips wander all over my face, neck and breasts.

"Let me know what you want and how much you can take," he said looking up at me and his eyes ... his eyes were just mesmerizing: So full of compassion and desire at the same time that my heart skipped a beat. I had never wanted him more than I did in that moment. Never wanted anybody more. The thought of him pleasing me at my command made me lean my head back and as I put both my hands on the sides of his head I pressed him down to my crotch.

"Lick me till I scream and when I come you swallow my juices."

I didn't need to hear his response because a second later I could feel his tongue on my clit and as if he had done nothing else his entire life he sucked, bit, licked and tongue fucked me till I came so hard in his mouth that I thought I would faint.

He crawled up and kissed me deep so I could taste myself and then he said in a low sexy voice,

"Anything else I can do for you?" The corners of his mouth went up in a smile as he slightly raised his eyebrows.

"Fuck me hard," I gasped in a whisper, "Fuck me in every hole. Every single one." The last thing I saw before I closed my eyes was his turning black as Onyx and then I let him get to work. And boy ... did he work.

I lost count of the number of times we both climaxed but it was just what I needed. No more consideration or diligence. Just straight on raw sex. And the most fantastic thing was that it was with him.

We spent the following day having more sex and it was amazing.

Aslan knocked on our door a few times, but we sent him away, and it was only in the evening that it dawned on us that we had not eaten anything all day. Luc therefore went to get a pizza and while he was gone I took a shower and then spent time with Aslan in the office.

When Luc came back, we went back to the bedroom where we camped on the floor and started eating the pizza. In my haste to gulp down the food, I dropped half a pizza slice on my t-shirt, and in the light of Luc's grinning comment, we ended up in a food fight. As we lay there grinning and rolling around in sliced pizza, we started kissing. And there, right there – on top of the smeared tomato sauce and pepperoni pieces – we began to make love gently and passionately.

Our love was so present and intense that it completely engulfed me, and mentally I completely disappeared into it. It was as if I was lifted to a higher place where only sensuality existed. Whether it was the passion for each other's bodies, that had moved up to a mental level, I do not know, but for the next four hours, we made love like we had never made love before. We didn't just climax. No. We had orgasms that made our entire bodies tremble uncontrollably. How many we had, I do not know, but the last one, we had together, and after it we collapsed. We were lying on the bed, unable to remember how we got up there, as waves of energy washed through us. Luc found my hand and suddenly it was not just fingers we entwined but also both our psyches.

We looked at each other and we were in exactly the same place and could feel exactly the same things. As we lay the energy flowed through us, and when it had completely filled us up, it was as if it thanked us and slowly disappeared, leaving us with an inner glow that had not been there before.

"I'll never let go of you," Luc said smiling, "Never."

I smiled back, but then it suddenly hit me and I sat up.

A few seconds ago, I had been filled with such feelings of happiness, but now they were replaced with an enormous fear.

"Luc ... I'm scared," I said quietly and I could feel his hand cuddling my back.

"Why?" he asked calmly.

"Scared not to experience this again. To lose what we have. To ... to lose you."

He sat up, wrapped his arms around me and kissed me on the neck.

"You will not lose me. I mean it when I say I will never let you go. NEVER ... EVER." He hugged me, "I love you," he whispered into my ear, and for the first time in my life I could answer back honestly.

I closed my eyes and leaned into him.

"I love you too."

When I had said the words, it dawned on me, that for the first time, I understood what they really meant. For me, it had always been big words and some you only had to say when you really mean them, no matter how you loved another human being. I had told both JAC and Wizard that I loved them, but it was in different ways and neither of them came close to the way I felt for Luc. If I had been able to take JAC and Wizard and meld them together, they would probably have been close. But I had Luc. He had the character traits of all of them and more. He was like a diamond in my hands. Every time I 'turned' him a little, I saw a new facet and it was overwhelming.

We sat for a while and just held each other and in my mind I wished we could stay this way forever. I knew it was not possible but I was thankful that we were here now.

* * *

We woke up on Sunday afternoon and made gentle and sensual love. It was as if we just had to see if it was as amazing as we remembered it. And it was. It was the perfect end to an absolutely fantastic weekend and we could hardly let go of each other. Our farewell in the hallway was long and heartfelt, but strangely enough, in no way painful or full of longing. It was more like a feeling of happiness that we would see each other again soon, and when I closed the door, I felt unbelievably lucky and happy. Aslan appeared further down the hall and he looked at me in a completely strange way.

"Are you okay?" he asked raising his eyebrows.

"You bet," I replied as I walked back into the bedroom to pack.

Two hours later I was on a plane on my way back to Jerusalem and I could not stop smiling.

* * *

Knox, Wizard and Ben were sitting inside our container when I walked in. All three of them looked at me, but it was Knox who commented on my entrance.

"What the hell happened to you?"

I looked at him and just smiled.

"What do you mean?" I replied, trying to sound puzzled.

"You look completely different." I could not help but laugh.

"I cannot explain it, so let's just say that you will never have a better soldier to protect you. I am top notch."

Wizard, Knox and Ben looked at each other.

"Fuck!" Ben slammed his fist into the table. "Can we please get Luc on a contract ASAP."

* * *

The remaining time in East Jerusalem passed unbelievably quickly. The team worked better and better together and, after my weekend in Amman, I started going out with the boys at the weekends. Knox had had several dates with the nurse from the hospital, and he seemed to be really into her. Wizard had been home with the family for two weekends, and even Castro had begun to get a little more talkative. All in all, this task had been rewarding in more than just a work-related way, which was pretty unfamiliar to me. Maybe it was because Luc had opened up something in me that allowed me to feel okay about showing feelings for my team mates. Maybe it was just the circumstances of this mission or maybe it was the natural development in the team, I do not know. But it felt right that we got closer and closer to each other.

Chapter 33

The construction work was progressing according to plan, so our mission was not extended.

A week before we finished, Wizard announced, that we would have one month off before we had to reunite for a new assignment and, as expected, this information was well received. Castro hurried to book a ticket home to Arkansas, while Ben, Christo and The Kid agreed to go to London and 'let off steam' and Knox ... well, he was hit by Cupid's arrow, so he stayed with his nurse in Jerusalem.

* * *

Wizard and I booked tickets to Barcelona where we were to meet Aslan, who apparently had found a property that matched our requirements. It therefore seemed the most natural thing to say goodbye to the rest of the team in Jerusalem airport. There was no sadness about it only joy over a month-long break.

Wizard and I took virtually the entire team's luggage with us to Barcelona, so we had a huge amount of overweight, but there was no other option. Aslan had arranged for the clearance of the bags to Spain, so we went in cargo and got them checked in.

The three- and three-quarter-hour flight passed quickly. Aslan had sent a huge number of pictures of the property that he had found and I had to agree with Wizard that it looked like it was perfect for us. Evidently the current owners had had the idea of turning the place into a country club but for some reason the project was stopped and it was potentially for sale. From the pictures it appeared that it was only the final details that needed to be completed for the place to be up and running so we were quite curious to see if that was the case.

* * *

It was past two p.m. when we stepped out of the airport in Barcelona with all our luggage. Punctual as he always was, Aslan stood outside waiting for us. He had rented an SUV and it was just big enough to fit all our equipment in.

After greeting each other and loading the car, we drove off to the north-east of Barcelona.

The contrast from the warm and sandy desert climate to this very green and lush area was huge, and quite nice because believe it or not ... You can actually get tired of sand.

We drove out of Barcelona and up into the mountains, and after an hour and a half and several hairpin bends on narrow gravel roads, we parked in a courtyard. It's rare that I stare at something, but the house we parked in front of was ...

"That is not a house. It's a fucking castle," I said, looking out of the window of the car. Wizard and I opened the car doors and, as if in slow motion, we got out of the car. Our eyes were glued to the two-storey ochre-coloured building in front of us and, as if it were not large enough, it had a wing attached to each gable end. The 'U'-shaped building had been renovated beautifully and it really looked like the entrance to an exclusive resort.

"Where the hell did you find this?" Wizard took off his sunglasses.

"You are not the only one with connections." Aslan replied as a smile of satisfaction appeared on his lips.

"And it is for sale?" Wizard asked.

"Yes, seventeen million Euros. There is ten thousand square metres of living space, thirty-two hectares of land that consists of forest and best of all ..." We both looked at Aslan, "permission to build a helicopter landing site." Wizard and I looked at each other while Aslan took the keys to the house out of his pocket. Kafka's house had been impressive, but this one beat everything.

After a two-hour tour of it, we were back in the courtyard. I was struggling to visualise just how big thirty-two hectares was and Aslan offered to take us around the perimeter trail. As we got out of the SUV, having seen the extent of the land, Wizard said,

"Give them a bid of twelve million Euros and with an immediate takeover."

"Sold." Aslan replied and had we not been surprised before we certainly were now. We both looked at him in amazement.

"It's my father's," he said confidently as he got the papers for the property out of his jacket, "He just wants to get rid of it."

"Then maybe I should have said ten million Euros," Wizard replied, slightly shocked.

Aslan spread the papers on the car bonnet.

"He is my father. He's not an idiot." And the cynical way Aslan put it made me laugh. "He has had it for years but when I was wounded and hospitalized in Amman, he finally admitted to himself that me, as a soldier, was not a good idea. So, he started renovating this place. His plan was that I should run it when I recovered but by that time, I was working for ACOSS and had no interest in all this." By the tone of his voice, I had no doubt that he meant what he said and I'm sure Wizard noticed this as well.

"So, he just put it on the market?" I asked because I had a hard time understanding why it was still for sale. It had the perfect location and it was almost finished.

"No ... it's not on the market. My father held on to it in the hope that I would change my mind but that is not going to happen. So, in a way when you asked me to find us a property in Barcelona ... well ... Let's just say a future family feud was avoided when I told my father that he would get his wish of me working here ... and I got mine by not running a country club." A smile spread on Aslan's face, "ACOSS – A country club for mercenaries." He started giggling and both Wizard and I couldn't help smiling and while Aslan was lost in his own joke I turned to Wizard.

"Does ACOSS actually have twelve million Euros?" I asked in a very low voice as he stood reading the house deed papers.

"We do tomorrow," he replied dryly and then the discussion was closed.

* * *

Days later, when the deed had been signed and the money transferred, Aslan and I were in the process of looking at the drawings of both the house and the plot before Wizard sent Aslan back to Amman to arrange things in relation to the apartment and the equipment we still had there.

The house needed a loving and caring hand and it arrived in the form of a cleaning company and, later, Imeni. Wizard had asked her to come and help with the decoration of the 'castle', so the following week he picked her up at the airport. With Aslan away, Imeni's existence remained, so far, a secret between Wizard and me.

As it turned out Imeni was a fantastic organizer and, with our help knowing what the team needed, she got everything on track. Painters were ordered and colours were chosen for the walls throughout the house, the final touches were made to all eight bathrooms and in the kitchen specially designed kitchen elements were ordered.

Two weeks after Imeni's arrival, the house was largely finished and furniture and other equipment began to arrive daily.

We had planned it so one wing contained facilities for the team: bedrooms, bathrooms, training facilities in the form of an eight hundred square metre fitness room with various weights and machines, an entire spa area with jacuzzi, and massage tables, an infrared sauna and a games room. The last one was solely for The Kid's and Christo's sake, as we had often heard them talk about the games Counter Strike and Mortal Combat.

The second wing contained offices, conference rooms, a server room as well as additional bedrooms and storage facilities for our weapons and equipment.

The centre section was where Imeni's abilities as an interior designer came to the fore. The large kitchen had room for twenty people at the dining table. The three hundred square metre living room with fireplace and beautiful décor and furnishings adjoined a hundred and fifty square metre room, which she had arranged as a library. From the hall there was a wide stone staircase up to the first floor and here she had furnished five bedrooms – one for Wizard, one for me and three extra rooms, one of which had two beds. Neither Wizard nor I commented on it, but I assumed she had the twins in mind when she ordered the two beds.

Based on Kafka's house in Islamabad, I had requested bulletproof doors and windows be installed throughout the house, and within three weeks a massive iron gate would be erected at the entrance to the courtyard, to prevent unauthorized access. Wizard had ordered cameras and sensor equipment and Castro had been asked to come to Barcelona one week earlier than the rest of the team, to rig the whole area and the house with explosives, mines and booby traps. Everything was going as planned until the night before Imeni was to leave.

Imeni had cooked for us that night and when we had finished eating, I did the dishes while she and Wizard went into the living room to light the fire.

Suddenly I could hear Imeni shouting something in Syrian-Arabic to Wizard and he shouted back.

They quarrelled for the next half hour so much so that I was afraid the bulletproof windows would not hold. I deliberately did not go into the living room, as what was going on in there did not concern me, and besides, I was also tired after Imeni had made me move furniture all day.

At eleven p.m., I decided to go to bed with a bottle of water and an audio book in French, but as I passed the door into the living room, Imeni came running out crying. Carefully I went into the room. From experience I knew that Wizard's Croatian temperament was not to be taken lightly.

"Is everything all right?" I asked and had expected him to tell me to 'fuck off', but he didn't. He just stood staring into the flames in the fire.

"You were involved in JAC's detoxing, were you not?" he asked as he continued to stare into the crackling fire.

"Yes," I replied, walking slowly towards one of the two armchairs in front of the fireplace. When I reached it, I sat down.

“Was it bad?”

“Yes, it was,” I replied. There was no reason why he should not know the truth but I did not go into any specific details. That would not benefit anyone. If he intended to get clean, he would find out for himself anyway.

“Imeni wants me to ...” he stopped.

“If you want it, I’ll help you,” I said quietly, “But we have to do it now before the rest of the team gets back.”

“Aslan and Castro arrive early tomorrow morning.” He turned around but he did not look at me. Instead, he went straight to the other armchair and sat down, “In all the years we have been together, she has not once complained or demanded anything from me. She has always just complied and accepted the terms that come with being married to someone like me. Not once, OPUS.” Wizard sighed, “I have to do it. For her.”

“You will only succeed if you do it for you.”

“Believe me, it’s definitely for me too. I don’t want to risk losing her. She’s my whole life. She and the boys.”

It was the first time I had ever heard Wizard talk about his feelings, and it seemed so strange. He never talked about how he felt or about his private life, and now all of a sudden, we were sitting here, a cool evening in Barcelona, and ... I leaned forward in my chair and looked at him. He was sitting with his head leaning against the back of the chair and had his eyes closed.

“Does the team know you’re on morphine?”

“No, just you and Knox.” He opened his eyes and sat up straight.

“Then call Knox back. Castro will be busy outside with everything that needs to be rigged and I’m sure he would love to have Aslan as an assistant, so ...”

Wizard rose from his chair.

“I will do it at a later date,” he said then, stretching, “Next time we take time off, I’ll do it.” He yawned and walked out of the room with not so much as a ‘good night’. I snorted.

“Good night, Wizard,” I shouted after him and he shouted ‘good night’ back.

I sat in the chair for an hour and watched the flames turn into embers and eventually slowly then to ashes. It was clear that Wizard was not ready to be detoxed and when he was, I would of course be there for him, but it was also clear to me that it would not happen within the near future.

The next morning, Wizard drove Imeni to the airport while I stayed behind to receive the electric fencing that had been promised to be delivered before ten a.m. With ‘only’ a one-and-a-half-hour delay, two trucks finally rolled into the courtyard, loaded with fencing, poles and whatever else was needed to establish the external perimeters.

One of the drivers, a small, balding, middle-aged, chubby Catalan, jumped out of the cab of the lead truck with a true salvo of Spanish oaths. My Spanish was not the best and his strong Catalan accent didn't make it any easier, but from the words I understood, it seemed that he was mad about the road to the house and blamed it for their delay.

The driver of the other truck came strolling towards us as he looked around the courtyard and the buildings. When he reached us, he interrupted,

"Do you live here?"

The question was probably asked out of curiosity, but I saw no reason to answer him, as I continued trying to get the other driver to understand that the fence should go all the way around the plot and that they therefore had to drive out on the road again and follow the trail around and unload at regular intervals.

After a quarter of an hour of tug of war, I found that the language barrier between us was simply too big and I was about to give up when Wizard drove into the courtyard. With him in the car he had Castro so I could breathe a sigh of relief. Castro was Hispanic so spoke Spanish, so after a few minutes, explaining the situation to him ... 'the second Spanish Civil War' broke out.

Castro and the middle-aged driver shouted, screamed and gestured with their arms and after twenty minutes both drivers jumped into the cabs again and drove half a lap inside the courtyard before leaving. Castro signalled that he needed the car keys and Wizard threw them to him.

"You go with him, you've seen the trail, he hasn't" he said, smiling, "You never know what the crazy farm-boy is up to." Wizard laughed as he turned and walked towards the house.

A couple of wheel spins from Castro made me react and I only just managed to stop him before he would have disappeared out of the courtyard. As I jumped into the car, I was greeted by Spanish oaths that were clearly aimed at the driver. I was surprised to see Castro like this.

"Calm down, Castro. Turn right here," I managed to say as he turned the car towards the road. The second after he had turned, he smashed into the back of one of the trucks that had been parked round the corner hidden by a stone barn. With lightning speed, Castro jumped out and ran to the parked truck and before I could react, he had ripped the young driver out of his cab. After a lot of shouting and screaming from both sides, the older driver came over and it now developed into a violent quarrel, where Castro finally pulled his Glock. Less than five seconds later, I was standing next to them, but despite Castro aiming his gun at them, the two drivers were still in discussion, although at a somewhat lower pitch. Slowly I calmed their moods and Castro finally put his gun away.

Where before it had been impossible for the older driver to understand what I was saying, he now suddenly understood everything and within an hour, all the fence was off-loaded at the right places around the plot and both drivers were gone.

"Fuck, that's some temper you've got, Castro," I said on the way back to the house.

"Not really," he replied quietly, "But bad excuses and laziness pisses me off."

"Pisses you off? Promise me you'll tell me if one day you think I'm too lazy or make too many excuses. I don't want my head blown off because of it." I could not help but laugh.

"He was not worth a bullet. You, however, would be."

Abruptly I stopped laughing and stared at him, but then I could see that he could no longer keep his face straight and he began to smirk.

"Fuck you, Castro," I said with a touch of relief in my voice as we turned into the courtyard.

* * *

When we entered the house, Castro paused and whistled as he looked around the hallway.

"That ... that's damn nice," he said, "An entire battalion could fit in here."

"Come on, I'll give you 'The Grand Tour'," I replied with a little smile on my face and then we started walking up to the first floor of the wing where the Team was to live. Since he was the first one here, he would also be the first one to choose a room. He was visibly impressed as the tour of the complex went on, and we ended the entire session in the kitchen, where we found Wizard in the process of eating melon while talking on the phone. Not a very good combination. In fact, he had managed to cover the table, the board, the plate, his hands and phone in the juice from the melon. When he spotted us, he signalled that he had a problem, but neither Castro nor I had any intentions of helping him out of his mess. Instead, we hurried to the living room where there was a bottle of JD waiting.

"This is fucking nice," Castro said referring to the house. I poured whiskey into a couple of glasses, "Who decorated it? You?"

I smiled at him and let him draw his own conclusion. There was no reason to tell him about Imeni.

Wizard, who apparently had 'defeated' the melon, entered the room and patted Castro on the shoulder as he passed him.

"Is the fence in place?" he asked rinsing the question down with a glass of JD.

"Almost." Castro replied, taking one of the freshly poured glasses.

"What the hell is that supposed to mean? Either it is in place or it is not."

Wizard was clearly not in the mood to guess what Castro meant and the rather annoyed look he sent him demanded an explanation.

"The trucks have left everything where it's needed. Now we must erect it: ... put poles in the ground, roll the fence out, stiffen it and remove a few trees, but otherwise it's ready," Castro replied and drank half of the JD that was in his glass.

"In other words, we do not have a fence up at the moment?" Wizard seemed irritated by the answer, and, when he was in this mood, it was best not to contradict him.

"We must have the whole house and the plot 'prepared', so let's get started," he said sourly and then he left the room without looking at either of us. Castro, who was scowling, was well aware of what Wizard had meant by 'we', so he emptied his glass and put it on the table before going after him.

"Good luck," I said slightly sarcastically, because with the mood Wizard was in, he needed it.

For the next few hours, Wizard and Castro drove around the estate discussing options and solutions related to security of the house and the land. Maps were read, there was a lot of pointing and writing down on Wizard's tablet and, by five p.m., they had finished surveying the project. The rest of the day and evening, they sat in the office designing and calculating. In the meantime, I had spent the rest of the day connecting a surround sound system in the fitness and massage room as well as in the living room.

At six p.m. I drove to the airport and picked up Aslan, and three hours later the four of us sat in the kitchen eating dinner. Aslan was impressed with how far we had come in the two weeks he had been gone and, just as with Castro, Imeni's influence was not mentioned.

At ten p.m. I retired to my room. I needed some time alone so with Enigma on the iPod I threw myself on the bed. My thoughts flew away, and as many times before, they ended up with Luc. Suddenly my phone beeped. It was him. It was two months since we had last been together, and I had at times been going out of my mind with longing for him. Unfortunately, it had not been possible for him to take any R&R since they were in the middle of an offensive, but now it seemed that he could have five days leave. I wrote to him suggesting we meet in Nice and it suited him perfectly. After thirty minutes he wrote back that he would arrive there in two days, so I immediately booked a small hotel and sent him the name of it.

The thrill and anticipation of us being together soon, gave me a tremendous boost of energy, so I slipped into the gym to burn off some of it.

At midnight, I stood in the kitchen drinking a smoothie, which was badly needed after my recent physical burn.

I was completely in my own little world, so I got a shock when Wizard came into the kitchen to fetch some water. As we were standing there, I took the opportunity to inform him that I was going to Nice for a week and of course he had no objections. With Aslan and Castro in the house, he had plenty of help so I could travel with a clear conscience, which I did two days later.

Chapter 34

Normally I would have booked a room in one of the big international hotels down by the water, but I did not feel like being in a crowded place, so I had found a small cozy hotel right by the Nice Cathedral. My plane landed early, so I had most of the morning to myself before Luc arrived. For the first time in many years, I decided to go shopping for feminine clothes. It was a completely unfamiliar feeling to me, but it was actually very nice. Going into clothing stores where everything oozed femininity and sensuality was like entering a whole new world, and for a few hours I was seduced by its promises of achieving divine perfection by buying perfumes, makeup, shoes, stockings, dresses and accessories. For some reason being with Luc had awoken a feminine side in me. Not that I didn't see myself as such but I had always been a bit of a tom-boy and being in the military working with some of the toughest male soldiers had not exactly enhanced my femininity. But with Luc it was different or rather: I was different. Luc knew the tough side of me and what I was able to do and he didn't care. With him I was not just the sniper OPUS. No ... I was his equal in everything. He knew I was strong and could take of myself but in his presence, I didn't have to. Because he was equally strong – both physically and mentally – so for the first time I felt I could relax and explore other sides of me knowing that if I needed it, he would be there to catch me and vice versa. I had no idea what he would think about the 'feminine OPUS' but I just couldn't help her surfacing. It was as if something deep inside of me craved to show him that this was me too. So, if he wanted the whole package called OPUS, she would be a part of it.

* * *

Back at the hotel, loaded with shopping bags and wearing a large white straw hat which a street vendor had successfully imposed on me, Luc opened the door to our room. He started laughing when he saw me and then he took me by the waist and lifted me up. I threw the straw hat into the room and we kissed passionately while he carried me in and kicked the door closed behind him. I let all the bags fall to the floor and together we ended up on the bed, where for several hours we made wild and passionate love.

As we made love, we disappeared from our world – the real world – and into the normal world where ordinary people existed. You could say that Luc and I, in our own way, had figured out how we could build a bridge between the real and the normal world without having to give up what we liked most about either of them. We got the roughness and uncompromising environment that we loved so much in the real world, and could not do without, through the raw and brutal sex that we practiced. At the same time, we managed to weave the sensuality and normality of the normal world, which we really wanted to be a part of, into our symbiosis so that it became durable.

In fact, this combination of our worlds was ideal because we could live and enjoy both worlds as we became accustomed to the way we combined them. Somehow, he made me see that there was a real chance of us becoming a part of the normal world because our love on so many levels showed us what it could give us. Maybe it could even replace it? My thoughts about this were many, but not during these few days. These days belonged to Luc and me – and nothing was more important than that. Nothing.

That evening we went for dinner at a small local restaurant. Luc had no civilian clothes to put on, so he was wearing camouflage pants and a t-shirt, whereas I was in a floral summer dress, high-heeled shoes and full makeup. Luc was visibly proud to walk next to me, and throughout the evening we behaved like two lovers, who have just met. We talked and laughed throughout dinner and the topics of our conversation quickly went from being 'stories from the front' to becoming more personal.

Luc started to tell me about his childhood in Belgium, and then, as if the flood gates opened, his personal history poured out of him, undoubtedly the first time he had told anybody: He was born in La Louvière where his father had worked in the coal mining industry and his mother had been a packing lady in a factory. Before his first school year due to the fact that both parents lost their jobs, the family moved to Liège briefly before they ended up in Antwerp, where his father got a job loading ships at the port.

Antwerp had a harsh criminal underworld, and already by the age of sixteen, Luc was a part of it. He and his eighteen-year-old brother, Lenard, had been part of a hard-core gang, and before Luc turned eighteen, he had several convictions for violence and extortion on his record. For him it all culminated in a showdown with a rival gang, where he killed someone.

Subsequently, he received a mild sentence of five years, solely due to the fact that he was under eighteen years of age when he committed the murder. He started his imprisonment in a young offender's institution, and was moved to an adult prison when he turned eighteen where his criminal career took off. Luc quickly became part of the hard gang in the prison and for almost four years he beat, raped and blackmailed other prisoners. No one dared to touch him – not even the prison guards – and the one who tried, reported himself sick and was later transferred to another prison, after 'one night in the shower'. After that, Luc and his clique had largely free rein, and he, of course, had taken advantage. I would think that there were several prisoners and prison staff who were happy the day he was released, but what he came out to was by no means a fresh start. His brother was in trouble with some heavy boys in the criminal world, and they had chosen Luc to pay the debt. So, after being on the run from them for six months, he signed up with the French Foreign Legion and yes ... now he was sitting here eating dinner with me. It may seem strange, but his past and the things he had experienced and done were not something that either shocked me or made me look at him differently. The rumours about him were true and getting them confirmed by him – and then spiced up with a few colourful anecdotes – was okay by me. It was all in his past and, as Liam had said, 'We all have one.'

It dawned on me that as Luc sat there at the restaurant and told me his story, there was a glimmer of remorse in his gaze. When I inquired into it, he replied that the only thing he regretted was not having taken his brother with him when he ran off to the Foreign Legion. Subsequently, he had found out that his brother had been killed, but the information arrived in the middle of his sixteen-week initial training, so there was nothing he could do about it and later, well ... his life took a different turn and he had not seen either his family or Belgium again. In fact, he had not even visited his brother's grave in Antwerp. There was an air of regret about him when he said it, but it vanished as we walked down the *Promenade des Anglais* with our arms around each other. We stopped by some street musicians and suddenly Luc grabbed me and we started dancing. It was wonderfully liberating just to be able to give in and with his arms around me, I felt free. Free of everything. As two teenagers in love, we laughed as we jiggled around like a stray carousel. It was so wonderful. Liberating and wonderful. It was as if the dance broke the last inhibitions we had and the rest of the evening we acted completely silly as only two lovers can.

At one point we ended up on one of the piers in Nice's harbour. We had bought two ice creams and had found a bench from which we had a perfect view of the entire marina. I had taken off my shoes as I was not used to high-heels so my feet had started to hurt. I had swung my legs up so they lay across Luc's thighs and he was gently massaging my sore feet. The boats in the marina rocked gently from side to side when the little waves hit them and the lines from the sails, that were curled around the masts, made little 'pling' sounds as the slight breeze got hold of them. The sounds from the different masts almost made a tune and as I sat there in the beautiful night listening to their song, feeling Luc's loving hands on me while finishing my ice-cream I felt so happy.

When we got back to the hotel, he literally ripped off my clothes and we had wild and hard sex. There was only one word that covered all this and it was 'magical'.

The five days with Luc in Nice, was the closest I had been to having a life in the 'normal' world, and it was nice. But it was because it was with him and therefore, I did not have to pretend anything. I could be myself – on his and my terms – and it was fantastic. Slowly I actually started to believe that he and I could live like this and for the first time the thought crossed my mind that if this was what it was like to retire from the industry, then it was not really that scary. Not if it was with him.

The five days had felt like five hours when I reopened my suitcase to pack it. Luc was talking on the phone and when he hung up, he came in behind me and wrapped his arms around me while kissing me on the neck. I was standing leaning on my suitcase only wearing a white strappy t-shirt and with lace panties as I wanted to finish packing before getting dressed but Luc didn't seem to mind. Quite the opposite.

"Come with me," he said continuing to kiss me as his hands started to move over my stomach and down to the edge of my lace panties. I smiled but continued to put my clothes in the suitcase.

"The last time I checked, there was no access for women in the Legion," I replied leaning my head back against his chest.

"I'm going to Aubagne for a few days. Come with me. I'm not ready to let go of you yet," he whispered as his hand slid into my panties and down between my legs. No doubt he could feel how ready I was for him and it made his kisses more eager. I turned round and we kissed each other deeply and ended up in bed.

"Okay," I said stopping him kissing me, "but then you have to do something for me too?"

"What?" he asked looking a little surprised still with his hand between my legs.

"You have to delete Wizard from your list."

He stopped his hand from moving but he didn't remove it. There was a moment of silence and I had expected him to be offended, but instead a broad smile formed on his lips.

"How do you know I have a list?"

"Because we all do," I replied running my fingers over his lips. He kissed them.

"Okay," he replied, "but then you must do something for me too when we get to Aubagne."

"What?" I replied and he smiled.

"You will find out." He started kissing me on the neck again as his hand between my legs started pleasing me.

"What, Luc? I hate surprises," I mumbled as I started gasping for air.

It was necessary for me to find out what he wanted because I would not give him my word without knowing what I was agreeing to. Even though I trusted him, it was far too risky, especially considering what I had just asked him to do.

When he didn't respond I – much to my own surprise – grabbed his shoulders and wanted to push him away, but he was too strong and too determined in what he wanted.

"Relax," he said still kissing me, "I don't want you to kill anybody. You just have to tell me something."

"Can't I just tell you now?"

"No," he said as he slid two fingers inside me. I automatically spread my legs and it made his kisses more aggressive.

"Luc ..." I groaned as my back arched in pleasure but he shushed me and I knew I might as well stop. Besides, I was way too sexually aroused by his kisses and touches to be able to continue this discussion and we ended up having hard and rough sex.

* * *

At six p.m. we finally arrived in Marseille. Luc had rented a car in Nice and we had chosen to drive along the coast, despite the fact that there was a lot more traffic. I had sent word to Wizard that I was extending my stay by a few days and it seemed to suit him just fine.

If it had been up to Luc, we would have driven straight to the French Foreign Legion's headquarters in Aubagne, but I insisted that we went to Marseille first and he accepted it. I did not want to go to Aubagne because there was no reason to advertise that I was still alive. Rumours had spread that I was still breathing, but only a few could so far confirm it and I preferred it to stay that way.

Luc knew of my situation but was sure nothing would happen to me because I was with him. His arguments though could not allay my doubts so we went to Marseille.

We booked ourselves into a small hotel and our room had a balcony with a view of the marina. We went out for dinner at a local restaurant and then back where we made love all night with the balcony doors wide open.

When I woke up the next day, Luc had left for Aubagne, so I had breakfast alone and later lunch by myself at a small café in the area. After a few hours of shopping, where I bought some civilian clothes for Luc, I again put the keycard in the hotel room door. Luc was still not back so I went to the balcony with a glass of white wine and a local magazine I had picked up at a magazine stand. I could get used to this kind of life, I thought as I took a sip of my wine. Me and Luc living the good life in tranquillity far away from 'the real world'. I closed my eyes and let the last rays of the sun hit my face.

I must have dozed off because I woke as Luc put his keycard in the door. It was seven p.m. and the sun was long gone as he came out on the balcony. He had a huge smile on his face as he bent down and kissed me. Apparently, he had just been promoted to Captain, which immediately gave him a pay rise and some extra annual leave and I was happy especially because of the prospect of the extra days off.

Wearing new clothes, we went out to dinner, and afterwards we strolled down the beach. If you did not know any better, you would think that we were an ordinary couple, hand in hand and kissing, and at this time we were quite ordinary. We were too engrossed in each other to sense what was going on around us. If anyone had wanted to eliminate us, this would have been the perfect time; we were totally exposed and had forgotten all the potential dangers. We were just enjoying being 'ordinary' people – unaware, as they are, of our own destinies.

When we got back to the hotel, we took a shower and made love under the cascades of steaming hot water and it was wonderful. Afterwards we lay down wet and naked on the bed with only a sheet over us. Luc had turned towards me and his facial expression reflected that he had something serious he wanted to say and I immediately went into a defensive mode.

"So what is it you want to ask me?" I lay looking up at the ceiling while I asked him the question. I had deliberately avoided mentioning yesterday's conversation, because there was no reason to spoil yet another amazing day.

"Will you marry me?" he asked quietly. I turned my head and stared at him. It's hard to describe all the thoughts that went through my mind in the following seconds, and just as suddenly as they had appeared they were gone again. The only thing that remained was the true answer.

I smiled widely at him.

"Yes, yes, of course I will," I replied and a huge smile spread across his face. Carefully he opened his hand and there ... there lay the most beautiful gold ring.

"This sounds completely crazy," he said, "but when I bought it, I wanted it engraved, but I have no idea what your real name is, so ..."

We looked at each other and then we started to laugh. Fuck ... what a twisted world we lived in. We went to war, we killed and we made love with the same passion ... and we did it namelessly. I rolled on top of him.

"My name is Camille and yes ... I want to marry you." I kissed him fleetingly on the mouth after which we both smiled.

"Nice to meet you, Camille. My name is Lucas and I am over the moon that you want to marry me." We laughed, kissed and ended up making gentle and passionate love for several hours.

* * *

The rays of the sun fell through the balcony doors and they woke me up when they reached my face. Luc was already up and as he stood, leaning against the frame of the open balcony door wearing only jeans and smoking a cigarette, he looked like an American cowboy. I think he could feel that I was awake because he turned his head towards me and smiled.

"Camille," he said gently, "That's probably one of the only names I did not have in mind for you. But it suits you perfectly. It is sweet, gentle and warm. There is something almost magical about that."

"Sweet, gentle and warm? Are you sure it's me you are thinking of?" I inquired sarcastically and sat up on my elbows.

"Yes, when we are in the 'normal' world, it is. In the real world, you are anything but and you know what?" He threw his cigarette out over the balcony before he walked over and sat down next to me on the edge of the bed.

"I love them both ... and equally much." I somehow already knew this but to hear it from his own mouth was just so liberating for me. We kissed each other and I could not let go of his lips. He was about to be mine and I his.

"Let's do it today?" he whispered into my ear. "Let's go up to the mayor's office and do it ... now ... right now." We kissed again.

"Okay, but on our way to the mayor's office I want to buy a ring for you," I replied and Luc smiled,

"Absolutely," he said "And afterwards there is a place I want to show you." His smile became all boyish and mischievous and for once I didn't mind the secretiveness. We kissed again but didn't let it go any further as we both suddenly had a lot of things to do.

* * *

Much to my surprise it turned out not to be a problem to get married at the City Hall with short notice. Whether it was because the City Hall in Marseille was used to soldiers from The Legion having emergency weddings or it was because Luc's superior, who attended as a witness, had connections in that department I don't know. But four hours later we were married. Luc was in a sandy coloured suit with a white shirt, toning tie and white leather shoes. I wore an ivory-coloured long lace summer dress with matching high-heeled shoes. My hair and make-up had been done by a local hairdresser and it complemented the feminine outfit perfectly. My wedding bouquet was small and consisted of white lilies and jasmine both flowers I loved.

After the short ceremony Luc, me and the four witnesses – all Luc's friends and officers from The Legion – went to a local restaurant where we had a lovely lunch and then it was time for Luc's surprise. We said goodbye to the officers and then Luc drove us up into the mountains above Aubagne. It was a very winding road but the scenery around it was beautiful. Green slopes with small wooden or stone cottages spread out on them with the occasional vineyards that in some cases stretched for miles reminded me of why I had always loved France. The radio in the car was tuned to a local station that played songs by a typical French male singer who with his rustic voice sang local folk music. It sounded awful but instead of changing the station we ended up laughing at it and soon we started singing to help the poor guy get through the songs. It was such a blast that we only turned the music down when Luc turned into a very narrow dirt road. The road was more like a trail and if you didn't know it was there you could easily have missed it.

We drove through a pine wood with trees as high as three storey buildings. It was such a contrast to the landscape that we had left behind but I liked it. The wood ended in a small clearing that stood on a plateau with a drop of five hundred metres to the valley below and there ... right in front of us was a small stone cottage.

"What is this place?" I asked Luc, absolutely stunned over its beauty.

"It's mine," Luc answered as he turned off the engine, "I bought it seven years ago." He opened the car door and the fresh smell of pine and damp grass hit my nose. As I opened my door the first sound that hit me was birdsong and as I got out of the car I started to smile. It was so peaceful here.

Luc had opened the rear door and, much to my surprise, he produced a brown wicker basket that by the looks of it contained a bottle of champagne and a baguette.

"Come," he said with a grin on his face. His beautiful face that now was mine, "You don't have to worry here. Nobody but me knows about this place."

But as everybody knows old habits die hard so I scouted the surroundings but found nothing but trees, pine cones and bird song. As my gaze fell back upon the cottage, I could see that Luc had opened the front door and put down the basket next to it. I strolled over to him but was not prepared for him scooping me up in his strong arms and carrying me over the threshold. I laughed as he did it and so did he. It was so gentleman-like. And it was so him ...

After putting me down he started to show me the house. It was small – two bedrooms, a bathroom, a kitchen and a living room – and it was in dire need of restoration. But ... oh my God ... did I love it. As we walked around, he told me, how he had bought it to do it up in his spare time and he explained with such enthusiasm what his plans were, that it made me love him even more. He had already knocked down the wall between the kitchen and the living room so it now was one room and all the plumbing throughout the house had been done. But there was still a long way to go. He had ripped out the kitchen so a new one was a must and even though the bathroom had a toilet, a crusty old white porcelain sink and an iron faucet – all which at some point had to be replaced – it was the only room where everything was actually working. There was an old fireplace in the living room and I could see that with some brick work and a bit of paint it could easily be brought back to its original beautiful state. No doubt the doors and windows in the house were from when the house was built and even though they would need to be replaced, they gave the place charm and character. There was no electricity in the house as the whole place needed rewiring and when it came to insulation ... well let's just say the house was built before any was required by law. But, as Luc pointed out, the roof was good although he wanted to eventually replace it with a natural roof on which he would plant grass.

"But other than that, it's liveable," he said and I couldn't help but laugh at his inspiring optimism.

"Well... It's always good to have a project and this certainly is. But when we are done with it, it will look amazing." I smiled at him before I kissed him and it wasn't the kiss that made him look at me in surprise.

"We?" he replied, "Are you going to help me?"

"Of course. You know ... I do know my way around tools. And I'm pretty good at plastering." Luc laughed and wrapped his arms around me.

"I knew there was a reason why I married you," he said and kissed me so deeply that I forgot the world around me.

"Let's go outside and celebrate," he said after letting go of my lips and then he opened the double doors to the terrace. Stepping out on the cobbled stone porch I became lost for words. The view over the valley below us and the forests and mountains on the other side was breathtaking. I didn't know that green could come in so many variants and ... the sound of a pine cone hitting the terrace made me instantly turn my head towards it but there was nothing to see except a frightened squirrel sprinting up the tree next to the house. I had to learn not to jump at every little sound but as they say: Rome wasn't built in a day and it would probably take me a longtime to quit the habit.

Luc had gone inside and reappeared with the basket he had brought from the car. He placed it on an old wooden bench that had been white but due to time and weather now was in a state where its white paint was peeling off, but somehow it didn't matter as it matched the house perfectly.

I could hear the champagne cork popping and the fizzing sound of two glasses getting filled with champagne and a moment later Luc stood beside me handing me one of the glasses. Still gazing at the beautiful scenery that surrounded us I took the glass and could feel his arm around my waist.

"To my beautiful bride," he said as he clinked my glass with his and it was as if the sound of it brought me back from my almost trance-like state. I turned my eyes to Luc and saw he was staring at the mountain tops across the valley.

"Sometimes I forget how much I love this place." His voice was low and I could hear the words came from deep within him.

"It is beautiful," I stated as I leaned into him.

"Do you think you could live here?" he asked, his voice carrying the hope of me saying yes. But it was an easy answer. From the moment we pulled up in front of the house I knew I could and when I told Luc, he turned to me and gave me a smile that forever stayed with me.

"You have an amazing place here ..." I continued and I was going to say some more when Luc interrupted me.

"WE have an amazing place ...," he emphasized as he gazed at me, "not me ... US. This is your place as much as mine." He put one hand in his pocket and took out a key, "This is yours. Your key to OUR house." I stared at it wide eyed as I couldn't believe it. Our Place? This was our place. I looked up at him happiness shining from my eyes and he must have seen it because he cupped his hands around my face and kissed me. When we had kissed, he pulled me in close and hugged me tight. My body was trembling and I couldn't help but tear up a bit. What the hell was wrong with me. I never teared up. And over a key? But where before I would have pulled away from him, I stayed in his arms. This was my home and he was my man and if I couldn't shed a tear of happiness for that I don't know who could.

"I had a feeling you would love it," he said squeezing me even tighter. A little tremble went through my body which immediately made Luc look down at me.

"Hey baby ... are you okay? What's wrong?" he loosened his grip and took a step back so he could see my face properly.

"I don't know what is happening to me. I normally don't sob but I can't seem to stop." I looked up at him with wet and gleaming eyes, "I'm just so happy." Luc smiled at me and wiped away a tear on my cheek with his fingers.

"I'm just happy that I can make you happy," he said lifting my chin up with two fingers so our eyes met, "I love you, Camille, and I will do anything to make you happy. Don't you ever forget that."

"Make us happy," I replied, "We will do anything to make US happy." I wiped my tears away with the back of my hand and then my eyes fell upon the key again and the key chain it was on. The chain was short with the letter D on it in steel and painted red.

"What does the D stand for?" I asked both out of curiosity but also to change the subject.

"Come." Luc said taking my hand and leading me to the kitchen area. In the floor there was a hatch, which I hadn't noticed when I was given the Grand Tour, and when Luc opened it a narrow staircase was visible. He took his phone out of his pocket and turned on the flashlight and as we slowly descended the stairs a large room opened up in front of us. No doubt this was a cellar but it was huge and it was high enough for Luc to stand upright. As we stood at the end of the staircase Luc let his flashlight wander around the empty room and it appeared to be the size of the entire ground floor above.

"I was planning on turning this into a gym with air-con and everything but now ... I think we should build a playroom."

"Playroom?" I repeated not quite sure what he meant.

"Yes. Or Dungeon as you call it. Our own little place where we can explore each other's sexual fantasies." I stared at the empty room and the endless sexual possibilities it suddenly presented to us and then I turned to Luc and smiled wickedly.

"D for Dungeon," I said as I touched the D on the key chain, "You are the most beautiful man inside and out. I fucking love you, Luc and the way you think." He started laughing asking if that was a yes and I kissed him wildly all over his face as I kept repeating the word YES YES YES.

"Come," he finally said laughing and as he took my hand I stopped kissing him, "Let's go upstairs and eat." Laughing and chatting we walked back upstairs and out onto the terrace and while Luc unpacked a delicious feast consisting of baguette, cheese, ham, honey, mustard and grapes, putting it all on the little bench, I took our glasses – that we had left on it before going down into the basement – and filled them with more bubbly champagne.

"When did you get all this?" I alluded to the amazing spread of food. Luc grinned as he broke off pieces of the bread and divided them in the middle so they resembled bread for sandwiches.

"When I went shopping for my wedding suit. Do you want ham or cheese?" he asked pausing his hand above the two white greaseproof pieces of paper containing the two toppings in question.

"Both," I replied smiling, "And with a bit of honey on top, please." Luc smiled as he made me my sandwich. Then he handed it to me and made his own – with cheese, ham and mustard.

As we sat there on the little bench, eating our baguettes looking out over the mountains I had never felt so complete. I was with the man that I loved, in a place that was not only stunning but also ours and totally hidden from the outside world. It was as if I in the last twenty-four hours had been given a whole new life or at least an insight to what I could have if I wanted it. A thought popped up in my mind. Could this be my promised land? I looked at Luc and the way he smiled back at me with a bit of mustard in the corner of his mouth I knew that it was. This was our promised land!

"Does this house have a name?" I asked him as he chewed on his sandwich.

"No. Do you want to name it?"

"YES," I replied promptly, "I want it to be called 'The Promised Land'." Luc choked on the piece of bread he had in his mouth but then his gaze turned serious.

"Well ...'The Promised Land' it is then. I like it. It has a ring to it."

"Let's toast to it. To 'The Promised Land'," I said and raised my glass. Luc swallowed the bread he had in his mouth. And then he lifted his glass.

"To 'The Promised Land'," and for the second time that day we clinked our glasses.

"So, Luc ... what is the plan? We fix up 'The Promised Land' and ...?"

"Well, my original idea was to do this place up, retire and get a dog. A German Shepherd." He put the last of his sandwich in his mouth and started to chew.

"Sounds good to me. I like dogs. When did you plan to retire?" Up till now this question would have been insane to ask because people in our profession do not retire. But sitting here it became a real possibility for us.

"I was planning to use the money I got from Wizard to do this place up and now that I have been promoted to Captain, I get a higher pension so the plan was in a couple of years. But now that I have you, I wouldn't mind retiring earlier." He smiled at me and then he swallowed the last bite.

"The money from Wizard ..." I repeated before sighing.

"Yeah ... they pushed forward my retirement plans so it came in pretty handy." There was a minute of silence between us and it was Luc who broke it, "You do know it was Wizard's idea with the money, right?" I stared at him.

"No I didn't. What do you mean?" Luc snorted.

"I didn't ask for it. He offered it to me." I couldn't believe my ears. Here

I had thought that Luc had demanded money from Wizard in exchange for him keeping his mouth shut about Wizard not being killed in Kandahar.

"What? He gave three million like that?" Luc giggled.

"Well ... kind of. One night we had a fucking lot of JD ... I mean like two bottles and in our drunken wisdom the plan of making Wizard disappear took form. I have always seen Wizard as a friend and I honestly just wanted to help him. Money was not even on the table. Not for me. But when we had planned his 'death' he asked me what all this would cost him. I had no idea what he was talking about. In my mind I was just helping a friend to escape and survive but Wizard made it very clear that silence always had a price. When I said that I didn't want anything he said that HE didn't want to owe anybody anything and that included me so I had to come up with a number. We had a big fight about it so in the end I just said three million. I didn't even calculate. I just blurted the number out thinking that he would object.

But he didn't. So that's when I thought: What the hell ... early retirement and my house ... our house ... done up." I was stunned and could hardly believe what I was hearing.

"So you didn't demand money from him?" Luc giggled again.

"Hell no ..."

"But Wizard always made me believe that you were after his money and that he had only bought three months of silence from you. And then he would be on your kill list again."

"He is a fucking idiot .... He has never been on my kill list. Do you remember how surprised I was two days ago when you asked me to take him off my kill list?"

"Yes."

"That is because he was never on it. I consider him my friend and just as you don't kill mercs I don't kill my friends. Wizard is fucking paranoid."

"Wouldn't you be if you were him? He has been running from pretty much everybody for the past twenty years."

"Yeah ... I guess I would. But he has never had a reason to run from me and never will have." Luc took a sip of his champagne as I ate the last of my sandwich. Even though I didn't want to talk about Wizard on my wedding day I was happy that all this came up. For me it had put Luc in a totally different light as it had showed that he had not been a greedy bastard only thinking about himself but a friend who just wanted to help another friend out of trouble. And the money issue ... well I knew Wizard could be a stubborn ass and if he had got an idea in to his head – like the one that Luc would rat him out if the wrong people paid him the right kind of money – well ... let's just say I fully understood why Luc in the end just had given him a price.

I looked at Luc as he sat leaning slightly forward with his forearms resting on his knees staring at the mountain side across the valley.

"How did you get to know Wizard?" I had never given it much thought but now that we were on the subject of Wizard, it actually puzzled me.

"We met in Libya." Luc leaned back on the bench and tilted his head slightly until it touched the stone wall of the house then closed his eyes, "I never told this to anyone but Wizard actually sprung me from jail." The surprise of hearing this must have been written all over my face because this was something I definitely did not expect. Luc looked at me from the corner of his eyes. I think he just wanted to see my reaction and when he had he closed his eyes again and continued, "The story is: I was young and had just finished my fifth year in the Legion. So pretty much a rookie but a well-trained one." He paused. Then as he tilted his head back to the normal position, he opened his eyes and looked to the mountaintops on the other side of the valley, "My first mission went to Mali and when it was time to go home things got a little cocked up, so the entire platoon ended up in Libya. Of all places. Anyway ... cutting it short ... we got ambushed as we were boarding our helicopter. I was one of the men who gave cover so my team-mates could get on the bird and in the chaos the helicopter departed without me ... leaving me on the ground and in the hands of the Libyan militia. So ... after a couple of hours of interrogation – and without me saying anything basically because I didn't know anything – they brought me to a training camp which evidently was run by them. Wizard was in that camp being trained as a soldier and I got to meet him when they put me through some real nasty interrogation. Wizard never did anything to me during these beatings and ... well you know the drill .... No, he just stood there, leaning against one of the walls with his arms crossed over his chest and watched. Three days into the torture he suddenly commanded the people to stop and then he approached me. So far no-one had spoken French to me – it was all in English or Arabic – but he switched to French and that is when it got really interesting. He told me that he believed me when I said I didn't know anything but that the fuckers who were torturing me didn't, so I should listen very carefully to what he said and only follow his orders from now on. Then he told me not to worry because the idiots didn't understand French and that I should say something in French to him – it didn't matter what it was – and afterwards he would knock me out. So I told him he was an ass and could go fuck himself. The last thing I remember is Wizard's crooked smile and then he punched my lights out. The next evening there was a key in my cell door and on the other side was Wizard. And only Wizard. I could hardly walk but he managed to get me out and into a car. It was just me and him in the car and he drove. I had no idea where he was taking me and honestly, I was shit scared but he took me directly to the airport where a guy was waiting for me with clean clothes, a fake passport and a plane ticket to Paris. Wizard even gave me some money and then he said goodbye. Well ... he actually said: "Hope you enjoyed your stay and no hard feelings." Luc started to giggle, "That fucking idiot ... but honestly ... I think he saved my life because they would have killed me. I didn't see Wizard again until years later when I bumped into him in Egypt. He was having trouble with getting a weapons transport over the border to Gaza – illegal of course – but who the fuck cares. Anyway ... again long story short ... I ended up springing him from the military facility he had been detained in so, I guess you can say, Wizard and I have saved each other's asses." Luc held out his empty champagne glass for me to pour more into it, which I of course did. Then he raised his glass and said, "And that was the start of a beautiful friendship." He took a big sip from the glass while still looking at the mountains. A minute passed. All this new information just had to sink in but eventually I turned to him and caught his gaze.

"Well ..." I said grasping the bottle of champagne and filling our glasses, "Enough about Wizard ... I want to know about the roof." I pointed at it with my glass before taking a sip of it, "You want to plant grass on it?" Luc glanced up at it and giggled.

"Yep ... I think it will look nice ... you know, compliment the surrounding nature and stuff."

"And stuff! You are turning into a right little French farm-boy aren't you?" I giggled back.

"Not really. Goats have never been my thing." Luc chuckled as he once again looked at the mountain tops.

"Well ... you could grow wine?" Luc burst out in laughter.

"I doubt it. I can't even keep a cactus alive." We both laughed heartily and it was liberating.

"Well ... I can't cook but I'm willing to learn ... when we get a new kitchen." Luc leaned towards me and replied,

"Or we could do 'take out'." Then he kissed me and smiled, "I fucking love you, you know that?" he said as he took my free hand and kissed it.

"I know ... and I love you," I replied and moving his hand to my chin and his lips to mine.

How long we sat on the bench I don't know but when we finally put the remaining food back in the basket the darkness had started to descend. The sunset from the terrace had been spectacular to watch and we had both witnessed it in silence as we held each other and finished the champagne.

Back inside I looked around the living room and, in the corner, I noticed an old mattress leaning up against one wall. On the floor next to it was what looked like a folded sleeping bag and that's when I got the idea.

"Luc, why don't we stay here tonight?"

"What! Here? But ..."

"Yeah .... There is a mattress and a sleeping bag. And we could light a fire," I nodded towards the fireplace that by the looks of burned wood and ashes had been used recently.

"We could do but ... why? It's not very comfortable. I've stayed here a few times while working on the place and trust me it gets fucking cold at night."

"So what ... we'll put the mattress next to the fireplace and with the sleeping bag and our body heat ...." I winked at him and he reciprocated with a crooked smile.

"Well ... If that is what you want."

"It is .... If I get the mattress you ..."

"I'll get the wood." Without further discussion Luc went outside and while he was gone, I put the mattress in front of the fireplace. By now it was so dark that I had to use the flashlight on my phone to navigate my way around the room. To avoid having to carry it around I placed the phone so it leaned against the stone wall next to the fireplace. Its cold white flash lit up the entire room as I went to get the sleeping bag but as I picked it up, I noticed a book underneath it. It was a paperback of 'The Three Musketeers' by Alexandre Dumas. I little smile of surprise spread on my lips as I picked it up and flipped through it. I had never seen Luc as a guy who read books and definitely not a book of this calibre. Alexandre Dumas was not for beginners although his stories were incredible. I could hear Luc enter and shortly after deep thumps from pieces of wood hitting the floor filled the room. Still engrossed in looking at the book I walked towards the front door, that Luc had left open, and closed it.

"Have you read this book?" I asked as I didn't want to make any assumptions before diving into his reading habits. But as it turned out I didn't have to. He looked up from preparing the fireplace with the wood and saw me holding the book in my hands.

"Yes. Many times," he answered turning back to lighting the fire, "It is one of my favourites. Although 'The Count of Monte Christo' comes pretty close." I looked up from the book and stared at him.

"Have you read 'The Count of Monte Christo'?"

"Yes. Why? I have read most of Dumas's books. I love them. Love the way he writes. You know ... That was one of the things I was planning to do when I retired ... read all the books I haven't had time to read." Luc had got the fire going and stood up turning to me. I must have looked like I was in shock because he started to giggle as he took his jacket off.

"You look like you have seen a ghost," he added as he folded his jacket neatly and laid it on the mattress.

"No .... No! But I never thought of you as a guy who read." Luc walked over to me and with two fingers under my chin he tilted my head back so our gaze found each other.

"Well ... now you know." He bowed his head down and gave me a kiss, "Do you want to talk books or ...?" He smiled seductively and I could feel how it sparked my inner naughtiness.

"No ... we have plenty of time for that," I replied. I could feel him replacing the book in my hand with his and the moment out lips met he let the book fall to the floor.

"I love you so much, Camille," he said groaning, "So fucking much." And then he led me to the mattress.

* * *

I woke up with my naked back freezing. Luc had swept the sleeping bag aside to get out of bed and he had forgotten to tuck it around me so my back had been exposed to the cold. I turned around and found him in the process of reviving the fire that had almost died out.

"You were not kidding when you said that it gets cold up here," I said in a sleepy voice. Luc was blowing into the embers trying to make them catch one of the small twigs he had put on top of them. As the sticks caught on fire, he put more twigs in and topped it off with a piece of wood. Then he turned to me and I opened the unfolded sleeping bag for him to crawl in. His skin was icy cold but a couple of minutes of a little one-on-one body heat did the trick. My buttocks were dark red going on purple from the strokes Luc had given them with his belt but they didn't hurt. It was more of a pleasant numbness which was more than could be said for the way Luc's back looked.

"I'm sorry if I was too hard on you," I said kissing Luc on the back of his neck. He was lying on his stomach next to me and the red stripes colouring his back ran deep and in some cases hints of blood surfaced in the form of little red pearl-shaped drops.

"It's okay," he replied turning his head towards me, "I didn't mind. I loved it." A content feeling showed on his face.

"You know ... not many people get to do to me what you did last night." I smiled wryly.

"Then thank you for letting me do it. I enjoyed it. Every single stroke." He giggled.

"Not as much as me. I got off on it."

"I remember. And you got off hard." I let my fingers run over the redness on his back and shivers went through his body.

"God ... I love it when you do that," he whispered closing his eyes as he bit his lower lip. I let my lips graze the surface of his wounds as I slowly started to kiss them. He groaned deep in pleasure as I once more awoke every single nerve cell in his body.

"You are getting me hard again," he said in a low sexy voice and my answer to that was,

"Good." I moved my lips up to his ear and whispered softly almost purring in it. "I need to feel you inside my ass. Having your hard cock moving in and out of it slowly so I can feel your hardness. Feel how you fuck me. Feel how you come ... how you make me come ..." I didn't get to finish the sentence before Luc was on his knees and with a firm grip around my hips, he raised me to mine. I could hear how he spit on his hands and rubbed his hardness in it and then ... then he thrust his cock into my ass. I thought I was going to faint but Luc's firm grip in my hair as he pulled it back prevented me from giving in to it and instead, I let the pain consume me. It rolled over me like waves. Waves that broke against the hard cliffs every time he thrust into me. Deeper and deeper for each thrust. And I just couldn't get enough of it. And of him.

When we finally collapsed on the mattress my whole body was trembling from the euphoria of sexual ecstasy he had imposed on me. He curled up and spooned me from behind and while I was coming down from my high, he held me tight and nuzzled me. We fell asleep in each other's arms but not before putting more wood on the fire.

I woke up with my head resting on Luc's chest and his arms around me. His rhythmic heartbeat and steady breathing were so soothing that I think I could have disappeared into a state of meditation but a crackling sound from the fire made me raise my head.

"Good morning," Luc whispered in his dark deep voice, "How are you feeling?" His voice was full of genuine concern and I couldn't really blame him. He had been rough on me last night but I had loved it. Even asked for more which he had delivered. I looked up at his face and smiled.

"I feel fantastic. A little sore but ... that just reminds me of you. Of the things you did. Of how you made me feel ... so ... it's a good thing." I purred the words and was about to continue when his lips met mine and we kissed passionately. When our lips parted Luc leaned back and put one arm behind his neck. The other he kept around me holding me tight. I laid my head on his chest again and looked into the fire.

"When did you first know that it was going to be you and me?" My question just blurted out and I don't really know why I asked it but for some reason I just had to know. Luc took a deep breath as if he just had to think back to when it happened ... if there even was a when. Maybe it had just come gradually.

"First time I met you was in the camp in Afghanistan. You were about to go into the tent to punish a soldier who had been an idiot. But before you left you looked at me with you brown almond shaped eyes and that did something to me. But I knew it would be foolish of me to try anything because you belonged to either Liam or JAC or both ... I couldn't really figure it out."

"I didn't belong to any of them. They belonged to me. They were my bitches. I decided which one I wanted to have sex with. They had nothing to say about it." Luc giggled.

"That's my girl. Having two of the biggest contractors as her sextoys." His giggle moved into a laugh but it soon died out and he continued to talk, "But I really knew the night in the apartment in Amman. When you had broken it off with JAC and crawled into my sleeping bag. You were devastated and I didn't take advantage of you. Normally I wouldn't have given a shit and just have fucked you but I didn't because you meant something to me. I respected you and I don't respect anybody. And then there was the kiss." I glanced up at him.

"The kiss?"

"Yes. The kiss behind the truck before I left for Mosul. That kiss did something to me. It changed everything. I could feel it in my bones. I didn't want to let go of you. And the way you looked at me when I was about to take off in the chopper ... It just went straight to my gut. And that is when I knew. Knew that I just had to have you ... that you were mine."

"That kiss did something to me too. I didn't want to let go of your lips. Didn't want it to end. And I remember looking at you in the helicopter and then looking at JAC in the other chopper and feeling there was nothing. And when I looked at you there was everything." Luc removed his arm from behind his neck and pulled me up to meet his face. Then he kissed me. It was so sensual that it made my toes curl and fingers tingle.

"You know what," he finally said after finishing the kiss, "I'm going to make this my last mission because I want to be with you. Hell ... I need to be with you ... you make me ... ME. Does that sound crazy?"

"No. Not at all because you make me ... ME," I answered and then we kissed again. A very, very long deep kiss that in some way sealed our destiny. We were going to retire when Luc came home from his mission.

"What is the time?" Luc said when our lips finally parted. I looked at his watch that lay on the floor next to the mattress.

"It's almost 7 a.m."

"Shit I have to be in Aubagne at 11 a.m. for briefing. My last briefing."

He smiled and then kissed me.

"That means that we have four hours. Let's make them count," I said and he immediately flipped me on my back and started to kiss my neck.

"You bet," he groaned and then we made love.

* * *

A couple of hours later I walked out of the bathroom. There was no hot water in the house so my morning bath had been reduced to a quick splash of cold water on the most needed parts of my body. There were no towels in the house so I stood in front of the diminishing fire hoping that the last heat from it would air-dry my shivering body. Luc had put on his pants and shirt and had gone outside to the terrace. I couldn't see him but I could hear him doing something. As the flames in the fireplace died so did my hope of getting any drier. With my hands I brushed of the last of the water from my body before I put on my lingerie and my wedding dress from yesterday. Luc was still outside and I was quite curious what he was doing so while trying to brush my hair by running my fingers through it I walked out onto the terrace. The sun had only been up for an hour but already the stones beneath my feet were warm and the air smelled so wonderful of grasses and pine. For a moment I got lost in the sounds and smells of nature waking up but then I heard Luc behind me. I was going to ask him what he was doing but after turning to him I froze Luc was squatting in front of the little bench and from the look of it he was putting the final touches to an inscription he had carved into the wooden back of the bench.

"Done," he said as he got up and we both stood and admired his masterpiece. It was a heart surrounding the date of our wedding.

"Now we will always remember this day. Even when we sit on the bench old, grey and senile we will just have to turn our heads and there it is. Our wedding day." I put my arm around his waist and he did the same with me. It was all so natural. So right. So meant to be.

"Beneath all that hard exterior you are a big softy, aren't you?" I said rhetorically and he gave me a loving squeeze as he kissed me on my hair.

"Yeah ... but don't tell anyone," he whispered and kissed me again on the hair.

"I won't. Your secret is safe with me." I looked up at him and we kissed.

"Come. Let's close up the house and get back to the hotel. I ... we ... need a shower and some breakfast." He took my hand and with a bit of a knot in my stomach I helped him close the house. I didn't want to leave this place. Our place. Our house. Didn't want to leave 'The Promised Land'. And I sensed that neither did he.

* * *

Half an hour later we left the cottage and even though neither of us wanted to. Luc had to attend his last briefing and then find out what the procedure was in regards to retirement. I had to go back to Barcelona and wait for him to call me because there was no reason for me to talk to JAC and Wizard about stepping out of the business before I had something concrete to tell. Concrete being the date Luc would take his retirement.

But first we needed a shower, some clean clothes and breakfast. So, we went back to the hotel but as the shower turned into us making love, we had to skip breakfast for Luc to catch his briefing.

I dropped him off at the Legion's head office in Aubagne and we said goodbye in the car. If his briefing went as planned and if he had found out some more about his exit from the Legion, we might have some time together before he had to leave for his mission. But Luc's briefing took longer than expected and afterwards he had been in several meetings with his superiors about his retirement. When they had finally agreed to having the paperwork for his retirement ready for him when he returned, it had taken so long that we didn't get to see each other again, as he had to stay with his group before their departure the next morning. Luc and I had agreed that before there was a definite return date on his mission, which there currently wasn't, I would not say anything to Wizard and JAC. We would do this together and with as few people as possible knowing about it. So, I drove to the airport where I had to return the car and got a flight back.

Chapter 35

I arrived in Barcelona on the nine-thirty p.m. flight from Marseille. Aslan picked me up at the airport and before we reached the house, I was up to date with everything that had happened while I had been gone. It seemed that the only thing they needed to be up and running was to have the iron gates that I had ordered to be installed. Otherwise, everything was done. However, there was a problem. Castro had shouted so loudly at the men who came with the gates that they had driven off, without putting them on the hinges and since the gates weighed almost a quarter of a tonne each, a crane was needed to do this. Wizard, who had physically separated Castro and the three workers, had subsequently ordered a punching ball for the gym. Whether the ball was intended for Castro's or his own frustrations remained unknown.

With my arrival, the whole team was gathered again and since the mission requests kept rolling in, it was just a matter of deciding what and where we wanted our next mission to be.

But first I had to catch up on what the different team members had been doing the last month. Knox was in love, which made him extremely unbearable to be around, because all he talked about was the fair-haired nurse, Hafía.

Christo, Ben and The Kid had been partying 24/7 in London and their biggest achievement was without a doubt that none of them had developed an addiction. Knox had named them 'The Frogg Team', referring to the fact that everything that could be transformed into a powder-like substance had been 'snorkelled' by them and strangely enough, they did not seem to mind their new nickname.

I kept my new status as a married woman to myself. I had put my gold ring together with my dog tags, so I was sure that Luc would get the ring if something happened to me. He had done the same thing with his ring.

The following evening, we gathered in the living room to discuss what mission we should accept which didn't take long. The company we had worked for in Jerusalem had won several new contracts and therefore wanted to hire us again for a three-month period. Everyone voted for it, as we knew both the area and the terms of the assignment, so we were pouring JD into glasses after just fifteen minutes of discussion. We had a month before we were due to be in Jerusalem, so Aslan got stars in his eyes at the thought of all the diet and exercise plans he had the opportunity to put us through before departure.

We started our training the very next day. No doubt 'The Frogg Team' was in the greatest need of it, and Aslan worked them hard. He was so harsh on them that Ben proclaimed that he was seriously considering becoming a Muslim, for the sole reason that then he would be given extra breaks when he had to pray. His statement, however, bought him a hundred and twenty-five extra pull-ups that day.

My days were planned so I worked out in the gym in the mornings and in the afternoons I worked alongside Wizard, Knox and Castro. We were preparing for a six-kilometre running track within the perimeters as well as building a shooting range. 'The Frogg Team' had been given the task of fitting the gates, and their frustration about this was clear: Barcelona was not so big so the news of Castro's behaviour had travelled amongst the companies like a forest fire and no one in the area, that had a crane, would therefore come and help us. After eleven days 'The Frogg Team' managed to persuade a small local contractor in Sitges to come and assemble the gates. On the day the assembly was to take place, Castro was told to stay away, because if he got in a fight with this contractor, 'he could lift the fucking doors himself', as Christo so succinctly put it.

Fortunately, everything went according to plan. The gates were fitted and electrified, we were getting super-fit and there were twelve days before we had to leave for Jerusalem. Then something happened: One morning Castro came running down from his room and he went straight into the library. Wizard was sitting at the desk working on his tablet, Aslan sat in a tailor's position in one of the large chairs in the corner opposite Wizard with the laptop adjusting calorie tables and I was about to light the fire in the living room. With Wizard's and Aslan's eyes staring quizzically at him, Castro turned on the large flat screen that hung on the wall of the library, tuned in to CNN, and turned up the volume. I got up from the living room floor and walked into the library because what could be so important?

Breaking news ran across the screen and I froze. An attack on the city of Mosul in northern Iraq, led by the International Coalition, had resulted in heavy losses, and ISIS, who controlled Mosul, had released videos of captured soldiers from the international forces. There were Americans, Brits and French among them. From the images of the captured soldiers, released for CNN to show, I tried to see if I could see Luc, but no.

Aslan took the laptop and found the videos ISIS had released and projected them up on screen, so they ran simultaneously with CNN's coverage of the events in Iraq.

"Freeze!" I suddenly shouted to Aslan, who immediately paused the video. "It ... it's Luc." My voice was almost a whisper. I couldn't see his face as he had a hood over it but I recognized the tattoos on his arms and his dog tags – because there was our ring. It was as if I stopped breathing. A fear I had never known rose in me. My knees wobbled and as they hit the floor a thick thumb was heard. My throat tightened and threatened to suffocate me.

"No." I raised my hands up in front of my face as if I wanted to pray and I could feel my neck tightening. Suddenly it was as if I could breathe again but it wasn't just air that came out of my mouth. It was screams,

"NO, NO! NO!!"

I screamed and screamed and screamed while Aslan beeped the rest of the team to come to the library. In a few minutes they were all gathered in front of the flat-screen in the room and their glances went from the news to me and back again.

"The fucking Islamists got Luc," I shouted, "I'm going to kill them. Kill them!" I stood up and started pacing around the floor and suddenly I felt a lump in my throat. It snagged everything and made me feel like I was being strangled. I ran to the living room where I stood gasping for air. Knox and The Kid came after me, but neither of them dared approach me.

"Fuck ... I'm going to kill them," I hissed as I tried to control my breathing. I could hear on CNN that there were talks going on between the governments of the captured soldiers, but everyone knew that no government would enter serious negotiations with ISIS, and that it was just a matter of time before the first heads would roll – literally.

All my logic was gone. All I wanted was to take the first flight to Mosul and free Luc. I had to. I exploded back into the library.

"Wizard, count me out of the mission in Jerusalem," I said loudly and I could feel my rationality and logic was back. Then I turned and made eye contact with Aslan, "Get me to Mosul, via Amman and give me the code for the warehouse," I said, pointing at him and the laptop.

"Just a moment," Wizard's voice was calm and hard, "What are you going to do? Go to Mosul yes ... and then what? Storm into the city like a one-man army and free him? There are twenty thousand – thirty thousand ISIS soldiers in Mosul – give and take the few hundred that the international forces have killed today. You don't stand a chance."

"Do you want to bet?" I said slamming both my hands down on the table in front of him, "I have JAC and his Kurds."

"They can't do shit. They are poorly equipped and are no match for ISIS. And why do you think JAC will help you free Luc?"

"Because he will have the opportunity to kill ISIS soldiers and I will give him the weapons to do it."

"And how are you going to do that? Even if you took what's in the warehouse in Amman, it's like a drop in the ocean. You need Stinger missiles, anti-tank missiles, ground to air guns and God knows what else just to have a minimal chance of anything. Where the hell are you going to get all that from?"

"I don't have to kill thirty thousand Islamists. I just have to kill enough to free Luc," I hissed, "I just have to locate where he is and then I'll get him out. I'm a woman and as you know, Islamists don't want to be killed by a woman, because then they will go straight to hell, so they will avoid me."

"Or shoot you." Christo replied.

I heard what he said, but I deliberately chose to ignore his comment, because being shot was always a real possibility for us.

"And secondly?" asked The Kid, who stood with his arms crossed next to Christo.

"I have the French Foreign Legionnaires who are in the area on my side."

"And what do you think will happen? They will fight for Luc if they are told to, but you are not one of them, so they will not lift a finger for you." The Kid said.

"I'm married to Luc ... that makes me one of them." I threw my dog tags on the table and the wedding ring was shining unmistakably between all the metal tags.

There was complete silence in the library and the only thing that could be heard was the voice of the CNN reporter, who just said the same things over and over again.

"You are married to Luc?" Wizard asked sceptically, "Since when?"

"Since I was in Aubagne last month."

Everyone's eyes rested on me and I was well aware that now the cat was out of the bag, they would not let me go that easily. I therefore briefly and accurately told them about our wedding. How several officers of The Legion had borne witness. That we subsequently had lunch with them and that I had become good friends with all the participants and that they had sworn to me that now I was part of their 'family'.

"It does not mean they will go to war for you." Ben said dryly, who with his past in the Legion knew what went on behind their walls.

"They are not going to war for me, but for Luc and I will join them."

"Jesus," Ben said, shaking his head, "You're not going anywhere with them. They will not touch you. And if they do it won't be to go to war with you."

"We'll see." I was so tired of them all. It was not as if I was asking them to go to war with me. But I had to save Luc, and all this talking was simply a waste of my time. And with ISIS, time was of the essence.

"Book me on the fucking plane, Aslan, and then give me the damn code to the warehouse." I looked at him firmly and aggressively, and could see that he and Wizard exchanged glances. Then Wizard nodded once to him and that was my cue. Like a gazelle, I jumped up the stairs and started packing my equipment. Never had I packed so fast and less than three minutes later, I dropped my bag on the stone floor in the hall.

The team was still in the library when I entered. Wizard had got up and, as I was making my entrance, he threw a passport on the table. It was for me. There was a strange depressing mood, but it was not something I was going to do anything about. ISIS had the man I loved – in fact the only man I had ever loved – the man who could give me the best of both worlds – the man who could give me a life full of love and happiness – so I had to leave.

I had to save him, save us ... save myself.

"OPUS, it's not because ..." The Kid began, but I stopped him.

"It's not your war," I said calmly, "and I would never ask you ... or for that matter any of you to come with me." I paused for a moment and then turned so I could see all of them except Wizard.

"I probably won't survive, but I have to do this. He would come for me. I know that."

"You're crazy," Christo said, "but I would do the same if I was you."

"You really love him, don't you?" The question came from a wondering Ben and his frown showed that if my answer was yes, then it was rather incomprehensible for him.

"Yes, Ben ... I do ... I love him with all my heart, so therefore ..."

I turned and looked at Wizard, because of the entire team, he was the one who meant the most to me, although not even he could stop me from leaving – and he knew it.

"Don't forget your dog tags," he said with a stoney face, "They must have something to identify you by when your head is missing."

He avoided making eye contact with me when he said it and just nodded in the direction of the chain lying on the table. I took the tags and hung them around my neck. At the same time Aslan appeared with the ticket. He looked at me seriously but understandingly as he handed it to me as well as the papers with the special permits for all my equipment.

"I've sent the warehouse code to your email," he said, nodding almost imperceptibly a few times to me. Calmly and thoughtfully, he began to explain that he had arranged 'a special transport' from Amman to the north of Mosul, and if there were problems, he had sent a secondary phone number of another pilot to my cell phone. Out of the corner of my eye I saw Wizard taking the car keys and without as much as a glance in my direction, he walked out of the library. It was time to go, so after thanking Aslan, the hard part came – saying goodbye to the team.

"See you, boys," I said, looking at them for the last time. Like an artist assessing a person for a portrait, I tried to imprint every little detail of their individual faces. And slowly it dawned on me that I may never see these amazing people again. My incipient melancholy was miraculously interrupted by The Kid.

"Fuck you," he said suddenly and at the same time he stepped forward and gave me a long sincere hug. It was nice to feel him and how he hugged me. Whether he knew, I'm not so sure, but he had always had a special place in my heart.

The Kid's' emotional gesture apparently set the precedent for just as quietly the rest of the team came up to me and one by one, they hugged me. It was both strange to have to say goodbye to them, but also incredibly life-affirming to feel their arms around me, even though it was only for a short time.

"Take care of each other ..." I said when the goodbye hugs were over, "and remember ... in my own distorted way I have always loved you." Then I winked at them and went out to Wizard, who was sitting in the car waiting.

For the first few miles we did not say anything, but then Wizard broke the silence.

"I'll get JAC to pick you up in Mosul and as soon as I know the co-ordinates of the drop-off site, I'll text them to you."

I looked at him and a brief moment of grief washed over me.

"Thank you, Wizard," I said quietly, most of all wanting to hug him.

He was one of the very few people I trusted and it hurt me that we may never see each other again.

"You're crazy, but I would have done the same if ..." He was silent; for there was no doubt that the thought of it being Imeni and the children was not one he wanted to put into words.

"I know," I replied and besides the faint rumble from the car engine, the rest of the trip passed in total silence. We could have tried to put more words to all the emotions we had right there, but why? It could risk sounding fake and pathetic and neither of us wanted that.

When we arrived at the airport, Wizard parked the car and went in with me, and after checking in, we hugged each other but we did not say a verbal goodbye. As I went up the stairs I purposely did not look back. Somehow it would have been too definite. I could feel Wizard's eyes following me until I was out of sight and I felt a weird feeling of emptiness in my chest as I walked towards the security area.

On the trip to Amman, I was unbelievably restless. Here I was sitting on a plane while Luc was somewhere in Mosul – blindfolded, gagged and tied up. The fact that he had been promoted to Captain could actually be an advantage for him, as it made him more valuable to them, and could therefore buy him extra time – which was to my benefit – before being beheaded. But on the other hand, ISIS could also choose to kill him as one of the first ones to show the world, and not least their own soldiers, that not even being an international coalition Captain could save you.

Throughout the trip, I followed the news on my phone and fortunately there were no developments in the story. Nowhere else on the net did it appear that any prisoners had been killed either, so Luc was still alive – I hoped.

I have never left an airport so fast as I did that day in Amman. I contacted the pilot who was to fly me to Mosul and asked him to have the plane ready in two hours and then I took a taxi to the garage, where the Hummer was parked. The garage was a fifteen-minute drive from the storage facility and I arrived without any traffic delays.

In the storage room, Aslan's systematic and structured mind was apparent. Everything was categorized and boxed, so it only took me ten minutes to load the Hummer with everything I needed: exclusively weapons and ammunition. With exactly half an hour until the plane took off, I rolled down the sliding door to the storage room and locked it.

On the way to the plane, my phone beeped. It was Wizard with the co-ordinates of where the plane was to land.

I drove to the small airport we had used when we sent Luc and his team to Mosul, and where Luc and I had kissed behind the truck sealing our faith and bond to each other, and it seemed like an eternity since that happened, even though it had really only been a few months ago. The pictures of him kissing me played in front of my eyes but I had to blink them away. The pilot who had his own little twin-engine plane was already waiting for me.

I had parked the Hummer next to the runway, and after a brief conversation with the pilot, he was given the keys as well as a money transfer to move the car upon return. Within ten minutes we had thrown all the equipment into the plane, I'd given him the landing co-ordinates and then we took off. When the plane was in the air, I sent Wizard the message that I was airborne.

The trip to Mosul could not go fast enough. Never in my entire life had

I wanted to go into a war-zone so badly. I had to save Luc. There was no other option. He had given me everything. Made me see that there was a life besides this. How he and I could build a world full of love and happiness. He had given me hope and shown me that there is a way out of this hell. He had not only shown me 'The Promised Land'. He had physically found it and together we were going to live there. I loved Luc more than anything and anyone. He was the air that I breathed and my very reason for existing. And no fucking terrorists – ISIS or anybody else – would take him from me.

The rage in me boiled. Like a volcano that had lain dormant for thousands of years and now finally was erupting. I was going to kill every single one of those Islamic fuckers because I was going to get my man home.

The co-ordinates Wizard had given me were twenty-five kilometres north-east of Mosul. It was a very dangerous airspace, and the pilot knew it, so he had taken his payment up front. We flew relatively high and after three and a half hours, we landed on a fairly flat piece of desert. The plane did not come to a stop – the area was simply too dangerous for that – so just before it turned around to take-off from the somewhat improvised runway, I threw all the equipment out and then jumped out myself. JAC and a couple of his militia were there waiting for me, and I honestly do not think they had expected me to be carrying that much luggage, because they seemed rather surprised at the number of bags that came flying out of the plane.

The sun was about to set and as the plane disappeared over the horizon it was accompanied by the sound of distant grenades and gunfire.

It was war: Worse for some, better for others. For me, it was something that did not affect me very much. I had one goal and one goal only: To get Luc home.

While the men from the militia gathered all the equipment, JAC and I hugged each other. There was no time to exchange more than that, because the vehicles were already loaded with all the gear, so we had to get going.

As JAC sat there in the front seat, dressed in the same outfit as the militia, he looked like a partisan warrior, and strange as it may seem, it actually suited him. Although it was nice to see him again, I knew that my feelings towards him were not the same, and since our time together here in Iraq would be limited, we would probably not have the opportunity to elaborate on what we felt for each other. That suited me just fine because what was there to say? It was over – at least for me.

We drove twenty kilometres through a relatively hilly terrain and the engine noise made it completely impossible to talk, so there was no conversation between us, and, strangely enough, it felt perfectly okay.

By an old dilapidated barn that would have been state of the art in 1880, we parked the vehicles, and I saw a small house next to it. Maybe it was more appropriate to call it a shed, because it was basically not much bigger than that. I could see a couple of militia sitting inside around a small fire they had made on the floor, eating, but how many were in the shed I could not say. JAC and I went over to it and while the equipment was being unloaded, I greeted what was a mix of local patriots and professional soldiers. It amazed me that there were so many foreign contractors present presumably fighting voluntarily and unpaid as JAC was. It seemed completely absurd, but nonetheless, it was the case.

One of them, a former U.S. Marine, had heard of me from his time in the corps, and he therefore started the usual bullshit about it being an honour to meet me. I ignored him as I noticed something much more interesting. While he was letting all sorts of positive phrases rain down on me, I had spotted a couple of young women sitting at the back of the building. They were in full partisan kit and by their side lay some old AK 47 rifles.

I turned to JAC interrupting the American's flow.

"Tell me about those girls. Can they shoot?" I asked and while my change of subject came as a total surprise to the American soldier, it seemed quite natural to JAC. In a way, I think he was expecting it, because he knew how little someone else's verbal recognition meant to me.

"Yes, they are okay. Naseem is the best. She's one of our snipers," he replied, nodding in the direction of the one sat on the right, "What do you want with them?"

"To send as many Islamist fuckers as possible straight to hell," I replied coldly without looking at him.

"So just another day in our version of paradise here?" he replied but I didn't comment.

"When are we going to Mosul? I don't have time for this fucking tea party." JAC's phone beeped.

"In ten minutes," he replied looking at the message on the phone. I signalled to the girls to come with me and they got up and followed me out of the shed.

The bags with the equipment were next to the vehicles and I went and found the bag containing the Dragunov rifle. It was the rifle that Knox had with him when he arrived in Damascus, and which I now handed to Naseem. I nodded to her that she should take it and with a mixture of astonishment and scepticism she did.

"Do you understand English?" I asked, sincerely hoping she did since my Kurdish was non-existent.

"A little bit," she answered while her eyes were fixed on the new weapon she had just received.

"Take it. It's yours. Do you know how to use it?" She shouldered it and looked through the telescopic sight. "Good," I continued handing her a carton of bullets. Then I took a new AK 47 and gave it to the other girl. "It's the same as yours, but newer." The girl's face lit up as she took the rifle, and it was clear that she knew how to operate it. The girl didn't speak any English so Naseem translated what I had just said. The girl smiled and thanked me. At that moment, JAC came over and squatted down next to me.

"You just turned two women into really good soldiers," he said smiling as he touched one of my hands.

"Be realistic," I replied removing my hand, "These two are not soldiers. They're warriors and right now that's what I need. Warriors with a cause."

"I forgot how lovely and cold you are." JAC said as he smiled stiffly. Normally I would not have cared about such a comment, but right now it actually touched me. I might have seemed cold, but it was a *façade*. I was desperate and unbelievably terrified that I would not see Luc again.

A Jeep came driving at breakneck speed around the corner and forced us to jump aside to avoid being hit. When it stopped, a French legionnaire jumped out and came straight to us.

"Where do I find JAC?" he asked in a strong French accent and without showing the slightest sign of offering an apology for almost running us over.

"It's me – the one you almost killed." JAC snarled, but the legionnaire was in no way embarrassed by JAC's comment.

"I'm here to pick up cargo," he replied, staring at us.

"What the hell are you talking about? What cargo?" JAC asked visibly annoyed by the legionnaire's total disregard for him.

He looked sceptically at JAC and out of sheer reflex I put my hand on my Glock. If you knew JAC – which the legionnaire did not – then you also knew that such behaviour could trigger him and there was no need for that right now.

"I'm here to pick up OPUS," the legionnaire said looking JAC straight in the eyes.

"Do you have 'my cargo'?" JAC replied rather condescendingly, but again the tone completely bounced off the legionnaire. Forcefully he walked over to the back of the Jeep and lifted a tarpaulin. JAC and I followed – and there – were two boxes of stinger missiles. JAC waved four militia guys over and told them to take the boxes.

"Where is OPUS?" the legionnaire asked looking at JAC, who was about to light a cigarette.

"Next to you," he replied, inhaling, "Her cargo is over there." He nodded toward the bags as he exhaled smoke through his nose.

I stared at JAC and was honestly in doubt about what to think of the situation.

"Did you just sell me for two boxes of stinger missiles?" I asked quietly and to my relief he shook his head as his lips formed a smile.

"Tempting but no. I just bought two boxes of stinger missiles, but since the delivery service is a bit unstable in these parts, the legionnaires in the camp agreed to bring them when they were picking you up." He winked at me and took another puff of the cigarette before crushing it underfoot. He then went over to the vehicles and gave an order regarding the missiles to some of the militia men.

For a brief moment, it occurred to me that Aslan had probably been right about JAC's account being empty before long, but right now I couldn't be bothered. It was his money and if he wanted to spend it on financing somebody else's war it was his choice.

At the sound of the legionnaire slamming the door of the car, I was torn out of my thoughts. While I had been engrossed, he had thrown all my bags in the Jeep, and that could only mean one thing. We were ready to go. I jumped in next to him as he started the engine and selected a gear.

"Stop!" I shouted as he accelerated and he immediately braked.

"We have to take two girls with us," I told him before waving the two women over. They were a little uncertain and it was only when JAC signalled to them that it was okay that they jumped in the back. The legionnaire looked at them in the rearview mirror, and it was only when they had sat down, he floored the accelerator and we disappeared into the darkness.

Chapter 36

The barren, rocky and uneven terrain that we drove through made the jeep shake and rattle like it was going to fall apart. To keep my balance, I constantly sat with my hands on the dashboard in front of me, and the vibrations from it made my whole body tremble. Sometimes the car tilted so much, due to the hilly roads, that I wondered if the two women and all the equipment were still in the back of it.

After twenty minutes we arrived in front of a tent at a military camp, which appeared to house a whole division of legionnaires. Strangely enough, when I entered the tent, no-one seemed to take any notice of my presence. A corporal approached me after a while but the situation had already generated a violent irritation in me that reflected on my attitude.

"What the hell am I doing here?" I snarled as I stared at him, "Where is Command OP?"

"Hold it," he said condescendingly while smiling wryly, "Camouflage clothes. Wow. You must be Luc's wife." He shook my hand and looked indulgently at me.

"Camouflage clothes? What the hell is that supposed to mean?" I hissed and was about to lash out at him when a familiar voice distracted me.

"He has no idea who you are." The words came from behind me and made me spin around. And there, at the entrance to the tent looking as calm and well-balanced as ever, was Wizard.

"Wizard, how ... what ..." Words failed me completely.

"Later," he said, looking at the corporal, "If you don't mind, I'll just snatch her, okay?"

He nodded towards me with his usual stoney face. The corporal didn't seem to care as he just shrugged.

"Be my guest," he said cheekily, smiling indifferently at us. Wizard did not let himself be influenced by it, and together we left the tent.

"What the hell are you doing here?" I said when we got outside.

"We are a team," he said as we began to descend toward Command OP,

"We can't just let you go to war on your own."

"We?" I said.

"Yes," he replied and then he steered me towards a tent that was opposite Command OP. He pulled the tent flap aside and revealed the whole team. I smiled broadly.

"Fuck, you don't know how happy I am to see you," I shouted and then I began to laugh in relief that they were here.

"We had nine days we didn't really know what to do with. And since there was room for us on transport to Mosul, we thought we might ..." Knox winked at me as he sent me a telling smile. I went over to him and we hugged for a long time.

"You guys are amazing."

"Yep," Ben replied, before he blew a bubble with his chewing gum. As it burst he chuckled, "We are fucking amazing."

"Love to chat, guys, but I have to go to Command OP," I said seriously, because there was no time to waste. I had to figure out what was happening, because as I saw it, things were going too slowly. Wizard nodded and then he looked at the team.

"And while we're gone, you sort out the equipment." His order and gaze were decisive and did not leave any room for objections. So, after giving it Wizard and I left the tent.

It was nice that he was there because it made me feel extra safe and I definitely needed that now. I was heading into an inferno of violence and hatred between two enemies – the coalition and ISIS – so it was nice to have Wizard and the team as my back-ups.

We entered Command OP and as expected there was a lot of activity in the tent. After a quick look around, my eyes fell upon two soldiers with FAMAS rifles guarding a door in the back.

We started walking in their direction, but we only got a few steps before we were stopped by a sergeant. I told him who I was and then he escorted us down to the guarded door. Here he asked us to wait, and then he disappeared through it. A few minutes passed before he returned and this time he was with another soldier who I recognized immediately, as being one of the witnesses to Luc's and my wedding, and, since he was a Major, he demanded an immediate salute from the two guards at the door. He invited me inside, but the gesture was only meant for me and not Wizard, so he had to stay and wait.

I was faced with the collective military leaders of the International Coalition, when I entered. They were gathered around a white board and discussing possible scenarios for a liberation attack and they did not take much notice of my arrival.

"Is he alive?" I whispered to the Major, dreading the answer.

"Yes." Despite trying to hide my sigh of relief, I did not really succeed and no doubt the Major noticed it.

"Do ISIS know he is a Captain?"

"We don't know. I don't think so, but you never know."

He joined the other officers and after saying a few words to them, a couple of them looked at me but nothing else happened. I stood for a while studying the drawings on the white board and, without thinking, I asked, where in Mosul, the building with a blue ring around, was located. There was silence as the officers turned towards me.

"North – northeast," one of them replied, and then they all focused on the white board again. I stood for a while looking at them and the white board, and I must have seemed a little bewildered, because the Major came over to me again.

"You better go," he said seriously, "I'll keep you informed. I promise." Despite the fact that he tried to be kind, the smile he sent me, did not reach his eyes.

There was nothing more for me to do there so I thanked him and left the room as quietly as I had entered it. Wizard was standing where I had left him a few minutes ago and together we walked out of Command OP and over to our tent.

"They apparently know where he is and most importantly – he is alive." Saying the words was a relief to me, for as long as he was alive, there was hope.

Wizard did not say anything, but put one arm around my shoulders and squeezed them a little. Had it been JAC, he would have tried to comfort me by reassuring me that they were going to find Luc, but it was Wizard, and a hug from him was his way of expressing cohesion. We walked the few metres back to the tent and here a surprise awaited us.

I think we both had imagined that there would be seven people in the tent, and not a dozen or so as was the case. From their clothes they were clearly militia, but also the noise was significantly higher than we had expected. They were talking and laughing, and one of them stood in the middle of the floor, singing and dancing, while his audience of six or eight militia men clapped and stomped on the ground to make up for the missing music.

"What the hell is going on?" Wizard shouted and his voice made the whole party stop abruptly.

"Hey," JAC greeted us from the back of the tent and started fighting his way up to us. When he reached us, he and Wizard gave each other a hug.

"Damn, it's good to see you." JAC said smiling.

"You too," Wizard replied sounding somewhat surprised looking JAC up and down, "What the hell are you wearing?" JAC immediately spread his arms.

"Stylish, isn't it?" he said laughing.

"You look like an idiot, when are you done playing a partisan?" JAC laughed.

"You still don't get it." He looked around the tent, "All these partisans need guys like you and me to fight the evil." He nodded and pointed at all the militia who stood mortified.

"No, JAC. You're right. I don't get it and I don't give a shit about why you are fighting alongside them. It's not your war." Wizard wriggled himself free of JAC's arm that was across his shoulder.

"Go ahead, kill the Islamists if that's what is what it takes, to get whatever it is, out of your system."

"Dashers ..." JAC shouted, "we kill Dashers." He raised both arms in the air and the militia cheered and shouted,

"We kill Dashers."

Wizard and I stood as if stunned, watching how the cheering over these words turned into song and dance again. The rest of the team, slowly moved so they covered every angle of the tent. Except Ben and Christo, who sat discreetly on the two beds with our equipment bags.

"Get those militias out of here, Wizard," I said quietly, "This thing could easily turn ugly." I could sense that Wizard agreed with me.

"STOP!" he shouted and the cheers quickly died out, "Get the fuck out of our tent. It's not a party or a demonstration. This is damn serious. Get out."

In the wake of his announcement, there was complete silence in the tent. I could see JAC and Wizard staring at each other and then suddenly JAC shouted something in Kurdish. Slowly the militia started to leave the tent.

"You disappoint me, Wizard," JAC said calmly with a strange astonishment in his voice, "This is what we do to forget it all. We celebrate ... celebrate life ..." Wizard interrupted him.

"I do not give a fuck, JAC."

As the last militia left the tent JAC looked at Wizard, but this time there was no kindness in his eyes.

"Do not expect ..."

Wizard took a firm grip in JAC's upper arm.

"I expect you to be here if we need you," he said, staring intently at JAC, "Not for me but for her." He nodded towards me and without a word JAC wriggled himself free and left. We all stood still for a moment relieved that this spectacle was over. Slowly the mood of the tent returned to normal.

"Holy shit." The words came from The Kid, "Our dear JAC has definitely changed."

"He will come back. He just needs a reason." Wizard said and I had no doubt that he was right. JAC might be a 'freedom fighter' right now, but he will not continue to be. A beep from Wizard's phone put a stop to my thoughts about JAC. It was from Aslan.

Christo and Ben started distributing the bags of equipment, and we all began to open the bags that had been thrown onto our respective beds.

"Here." Castro shouted, throwing OPUS over to me plus a case of bullets. I grabbed both and laid them on my bed. There was a nice relaxed mood between us that reminded me of the time in East Jerusalem. But then ...

"What's up, Wizard?" Christo's voice made us all look at Wizard. As he stood there staring at the phone display, I almost stopped breathing.

"Wizard?" I said quietly, "Is that Luc?" He looked at me without saying anything, but I could see in his eyes that it was. Instantly I felt completely empty followed by an extreme nausea.

"No, no! No!" I exclaimed desperately as I hurried up to him and ripped the phone out of his hand. There was a play button on the display and for a moment I hesitated to press it. If I did not do it, then whatever was on the video had not really happened yet.

"Don't say he's dead, Wizard? Please, Wizard. Please!"

Still staring at the play button, the corners of my mouth began to tremble and my voice cracked. My eyes began tearing up and through the mist I could see Wizard put his hands on his hips while he looked down at the floor. Then he looked up and our eyes met.

"He can't be dead. He just can't. Please?" I started sobbing and then I pressed play.

On the display, Luc appeared looking beaten and abused. He sat kneeling on a concrete floor with his hands tied behind his back. Either side of him stood a hooded Islamist, each with a rifle. One began shouting oaths and curses concerning the Western World, western culture and the United States while the other placed his gun on the floor and began to recite the Koran in a monotonous tone of voice. As the oaths escalated, the recitation got louder and louder, and eventually the one who recited picked up a machete and took hold of Luc's hair. In a verbal inferno of Arabic oaths and the sacred words of the Koran, he began to behead Luc.

"Allahu Akbar – Allahu Akbar – Allahu Akbar," the hooded men chanted, while Luc screamed in pain as the dull blade of the knife began working its way through his throat at all too slow a pace. It was as if his executioner made a virtue out of torturing him. He started by slowly cutting into the flesh of Luc's throat then hacked and ripped with the blunt blade. The quick jerks with which he cut his way through Luc's throat made me scream. How could he do that to this beautiful man? To the man I loved? I could hear Luc screaming. Screaming in pain. In powerlessness ... and then it came. My name. He screamed my name ... I froze completely and while the tears ran quietly down my cheeks I forgot to breathe.

I think my name had put an end to his pain, for no more screams came from him, only a soft rattle as the blood pulsed out of his throat. His lovely mouth, from which the most wonderful words had come, was now filled with blood, and as if it were a dam that burst, the blood now spilled out of it and down over his soft lips. The fundamentalist with the knife held Luc's head and the body slowly collapsed – and the video stopped.

It was as if my body had turned to stone.

What was I supposed to do? He was dead ... he was ... I took a few steps back and backed into Knox, who had been standing only a metre or so behind me. As a natural reaction on his part, he wanted to grab me, but I shrugged him off and took a few steps forward. Suddenly I stopped and screamed. I screamed and screamed and screamed ... screamed until I was out of breath and just stood gasping. It was as if I was being strangled. As if all my strength was gone. My legs gave away beneath me and I fell to my knees. I gasped for air but then, suddenly I could breathe again.

"I'm going to kill them," I hissed quietly while still gasping, "I'm going to kill them. Each and every one of them. The fucking ISIS. I'm going to send them all straight to hell." My voice was almost whispering and my body consumed with so much hatred that I had never felt anything like it before. I got up slowly and on the way I wiped my eyes and mouth.

"They killed him, Wizard," I said and his and my eyes met, "They killed him while the fucking partisans were singing and dancing in here." I turned my head towards the door, "I hate them. Hate them," I screamed, "And what the hell are all the high-ranking assholes doing over there? Not fucking shit. They talk and talk, while the others kill ... They killed him. Fuck ... They killed him." I turned my head slowly and looked at the team. None of them moved or said a word.

I do not know where it came from but suddenly, I felt energised and I knew exactly what to do. I went over to my bed, took OPUS, and filled my pockets with bullets. Then I went to Ben who had the bag of AK 47's and took one of them as well as extra magazines and finally I went to Wizard and gave him back his phone.

"I'll be in Command OP," I said loudly and then I disappeared out the door. I actually did not sense it but Wizard and the rest of the team were right behind me. There was only me and me alone in the camp. All around me were props that could be dispensed with. I sensed only indifference surrounding me and this all-consuming lust for revenge. I had never felt it before, but it was like a power plant that just fed me energy.

When I reached Command OP, I ripped the door open and marched down to the two legionnaires. At the sight of me they took charge of their FAMAS, but it was too late. I had already pulled my Glock, and before they could raise their rifles, I had shot each of them in the shoulder. Now that there was free passage to the room with the officers, I pushed open the door and, with my Glock in my hand, I made my entrance.

"Now you have talked long enough," I hissed, scowling at the officers, "What are you going to do about the fact that those pisshead jihadists just killed Luc?" There was complete quiet in the tent and after a short while the Major from the Foreign Legion replied,

"We have just heard that he is dead and we are so sorry, but you have to let us do our job." He looked serious but at the same time his voice was incredibly condescending.

"Do your job?" I said hatefully and full of mistrust, "You are not doing shit. Have you really not understood how this works? You can't win this war by negotiating with these fuckers. Diplomacy doesn't work. They are not interested in negotiating. They are fanatics. Crusaders of our time and what happened to the first crusaders?" There was complete silence in the tent and for a brief moment I doubted as to whether this bunch of officers were at all able to understand what I was saying to them. "My God, are you a bunch of imbecile idiots? Do to the Islamists what they are doing to you. Have you captured any of their soldiers?"

A couple of the officers smiled indulgently at me.

"Yes, we have captured some of their soldiers and we are trying to arrange a prisoner exchange right now," said one of the British officers, "But it's not something you have to worry about."

"And while you are planning and arranging, they are cutting off the heads of their prisoners – your soldiers – my husband," I shouted, "Give me a couple of the prisoners you have, and then I will guarantee you that there will be a shift in the dialogue you have with them."

"We can't give you any prisoners," a U.S. officer interrupted, "And besides, we must abide by the Geneva Convention on Prisoners of War."

"Maybe you have to ... but I don't, because I do not belong to any conventions. I'm a contractor – a mercenary." Again complete silence in the tent, but this time there were no indulgent smiles on their faces.

"This is going too slowly," I yelled aggressively, "If you do not want to give me some of your prisoners, I'll go and get some myself. What will it be?"

Not surprisingly there was no answer.

"Fine." I turned and there, right behind me, stood Wizard and Knox.

"It seems like we have to fend for ourselves," I said to them and started walking out of the tent.

"What's new." Knox replied quietly as I passed him. And he was right.

When things got tough, we were basically always left to ourselves. No help. No friends. No one to claim knowledge of us. We were alone.

On the other side of the canvas door 'The Frogg Team' and Castro were holding the rest of Command OP at gun-point. The two foreign legionnaires I had shot were not to be seen anywhere, but that did not really matter.

"Fuck the International Coalition," I proclaimed, "I would advise all of you to learn Arabic and read the Koran, because, before the I. C. gets its head out of its ass, ISIS will have taken you by surprise and either beheaded you or you have been sent to a Koran school." I looked around at the soldiers who were in the tent, and shook my head. Then I left Command OP.

Wizard was right on my heels and he only caught up with me when I opened the flap to our tent. He did not comment on what had just happened, which was probably also for the best. If you looked at it from a collaborative point of view, it was not the most constructive thing I had done, but I did not care. If I had to go to Mosul alone and find some 'Dashers', as JAC called them, I would do it.

As soon as everybody was back in the tent, Wizard asked me to sit down and despite my level of anger and aggression, I did. When Wizard's tone of voice changed to a lower key, like it did now, one listened. He took off his jacket and threw it over a chair. Then he looked me straight in the eye.

"Do you really want to do this? Do you really want to get hold of some fundamentalists? If you want, we will do it, but it must not only be to reciprocate. It must be to set an example and it must be done methodically and respectfully."

"As long as I'll be in charge of the interrogations, it will be quite methodical and respectful," I replied hissing with an elated look at him. Wizard looked at me for a long time before raising his head.

"Okay, here's what we do," he said, and suddenly I could see that the military leader from the Balkans was back. He no longer led a team, but an entire battalion, and the team – they did not ask any questions.

On Wizard's command Knox disappeared out the door to pick up JAC while The Kid was told to get a vehicle. 'The Frogg Team' had twenty minutes to procure all the C4 and detonators that could be found in the camp.

"What do you need for the 'interrogation'?" Wizard asked turning to me. He was standing with his hands on his hips and I could not help but think that if you ever wanted to portray him, it would have been in that way. I sat for a while thinking.

"Zip ties, metal wire, hand winch, a Koran, a Bible, a bucket, three ski masks and the two militia women, who arrived with us." I looked up at Wizard, but he was too busy taking notes, "And then I want it all videotaped and posted online."

* * *

He nodded a few times and then he called Aslan. While waiting for Aslan to pick up he told Castro to find metal wire and a hand winch and immediately Castro disappeared out of the tent. Wizard got a hold of Aslan at the same time as Knox arrived with JAC.

As expected, JAC came directly to me. He sat down in front of me and we hugged.

"I'm so sorry. Knox just told me what has happened." It was the first time in all this that someone had touched me and it made me realize how much I needed it. The realization of this made me hug him even harder. We sat like this for a long time and even though I could hear Wizard talking to Aslan, I could not understand the words. It was as if they became lower and lower until they were just a mumbling.

"I promise you we'll get them. I promise you." JAC whispered in my ear and I had no doubt that he meant every single word. I honestly don't think he wanted to get them to revenge Luc. He was in it for the killing. But at this point his reasons didn't matter to me. As long as we got the fuckers.

His touch and his voice made the knot I had in my stomach form a lump in my throat, and suddenly I had no control any more. I started to cry. JAC sat still and just held me while I let the tears flow. Wizard looked over at us a few times, but he let us be, and concentrated instead on organizing the different tasks. Knox was sent out again, this time after a cable that could connect Wizard's phone to his tablet. Suddenly 'The Frogg Team' was back with the explosives and shortly after they left again. This time they were ordered to find a copy of the Bible and the Koran. I think I could have sat in JAC's arms for hours just crying, but I was well aware that if we were to complete the mission, I had to get going. Slowly I therefore released my grip of JAC, wiped my eyes and nose free from tears and snot, and looked at him. He sent me a little smile and then kissed my forehead.

"JAC?" It was obvious that Wizard needed JAC's attention. However JAC, who was sitting with his back to him, looked at me first and it was only when I nodded to him, he got up and went to Wizard.

"Can I see the video?" JAC asked. Wizard looked at me as if to check if it was okay. I signalled to him that it was. Wizard handed him the phone and I could hear the voices from the video again. Hear Luc screaming my name. JAC did not comment on the video but played it several times but muted.

"They are north-east of Mosul." Wizard said casually referring to the location in which the video was recorded.

"Hell, they're not," JAC replied harshly. "Who the fuck told you that?"

Both Wizard and I stared at JAC.

"Command OP." Wizard replied.

"Yeah, fuck them ... they have no idea about anything," JAC snorted, "This ... I wish we could get a better picture ..." he said starting to fiddle with the phone. At the same time, Knox appeared with a cable and Wizard almost ripped it out of his hand. "Two seconds," he said as he connected the phone to the tablet. The video appeared on the tablet screen. "Look," JAC said, pointing to the tablet. I got up quietly and walked over to them. Wizard looked at me, but I nodded to him to assure him that I was okay in watching the video again. JAC played it again. "Look, there," he said suddenly, freezing the picture, "The background wall is not white. It is made of wood. Not concrete." The picture showed a wooden wall that they had plastered and painted white so that it would look like concrete. Evidently, they had not set the camera correctly and, as JAC pointed at it, we all looked at a spot in the far corner where there was a small area where the wooden wall was visible. "Mosul has a lot of everything, but wooden walls in houses are NOT one of them." JAC said, taking a deep breath.

"Play the video again." This time the words came from Knox, who had been standing looking at the tablet over Wizard's shoulder. JAC played the video again and Knox pointed to Luc's subtly moving lips: "Fourteen minutes ... I love you C ... fourteen minutes ... I love you C ... fourteen minutes ... I love you Camille ... fourteen minutes ..."

JAC stopped the video at the same time as the ISIS soldier swung the knife. There was no reason for us to watch the last seconds of the video. We all knew how it ended.

"That's damn good spotting, Knox." JAC's compliment was accompanied by a crooked smile.

"I didn't know you could read lips." Wizard said quietly and there was actually a rare admiration in his voice.

"I can," Knox replied still with his eyes glued to the screen, "And in two languages."

"Fourteen minutes," I said and we all looked at each other, "Luc must have given us the time they took to transport him."

"Shit ... you're probably right," Wizard replied, "JAC?"

"Let's find a satellite image of the area."

"Fourteen minutes by road, presumably from where they were captured, which according to my sources was here," JAC pointed to western Mosul, "Let's assume that the driver knows his way around and that he would be able to drive at an average speed of forty kilometres per hour – he has to get out of Mosul first and it takes time."

JAC drew an invisible circle on the tablet with his finger.

"Somewhere along this line, Luc was ..." He stopped talking, "We will find Luc's executioners along this line."

There was silence for a moment, but then Wizard broke it.

"Okay, find a house with wooden walls located near this line. Luc did everything he could to give us this information, let's credit him by finding and capturing his executioners." At the same moment, 'The Frogg Team' came back and they did not have two books with them but a whole stack.

"Here we go," Ben proclaimed as they laid them down on one of the beds, "Now there are a few to choose from. And if we want help, the legionnaires are more than willing to step up – unofficially of course – even if you did send a couple of their team mates to the infirmary."

JAC looked up from the tablet. He looked at Ben and then he looked at me, after which he smiled and shook his head a little.

"You do not want to know." Knox whispered to him.

"Probably not," he replied while continuing his scrutiny of the imaginary line he had drawn on the tablet.

"How much C4 did you get?" Castro asked as he looked at Christo.

"Ten kilos." Christo replied.

"We have five kilos in one of our trucks," JAC said, "Just go over and get it and say that 'Heval Ari' has given the orders for you to pick it up."

'Heval Ari' was JAC's Kurdish nickname and with my sparse knowledge of the language, I was sure it meant 'White Friend'. In my opinion they could have called him 'Black Enemy' so long as they did what he said and we got the C4.

"And bring Naseem and her friend back with you," I added. It was time for them to be involved in the plan I thought so they might as well be here.

Immediately, Christo and The Kid left the tent, leaving Castro standing by the boxes with the C4.

"Tell me if you need anything." Wizard said to him and he was about to give Knox a command when JAC exclaimed,

"Here. This is where they took him." He handed Wizard the tablet.

" You are sure?"

"Yes. It's the only logical place: A cluster of small houses in a relatively hilly terrain with a location that allows them to see if uninvited guests should approach. It's there, Wizard. I promise you." Wizard looked at the picture on the tablet and then he looked at JAC.

"Let's get the sons of bitches, then," he said and in such a low voice that only JAC and I could hear him. JAC smiled as he patted Wizard on the shoulder, and, as if it was the starting shot, they both went to one of the beds where they sat down with the tablet between them ready to plan the attack.

It took twenty minutes and about the same time as they got up off the bed again, Christo and The Kid came in the door with five kilos of C4 and the two women. Both women were the same height as me so they had no trouble fitting into any of my camouflage clothes. It would be safest for them if they posed as 'real' military people and not as militias, because the retaliation for what we were about to carry out would undoubtedly be massive and the militia – no matter how many they were – would not be able to withstand it. After all, the international forces had a few more options, not to mention better weapons. Wizard, who had left our tent with the tablet, now returned.

"The legionnaires are with us," he said and it sounded more like a statement than an actual piece of information for us.

"Super. It's nice to be back in some ordinary clothes again." JAC had changed into camouflage clothes and was now sitting lacing up his boots.

"Nobody asked you to dress like a Bedouin," Wizard replied dryly as he looked around the tent, "We're leaving in five minutes, so let's review the plan." He went to one of the beds and sat down and, like moths to a flame, we gathered around him. With the pictures on the tablet as a colourful backdrop, he now told us about the plan and, after reviewing it, we found our headsets and set the frequency so we could communicate. JAC had already left the tent and at a hand signal from Wizard we followed his example.

We drove out of the military camp, to meet up with the legionnaires at a checkpoint. JAC had instructed the two female militias how to work the headsets, but on Wizard's order, their microphones were muted. It might be that they were fighting with us, but they were unknown to us, so they just had to carry out orders and contribute without comments.

We had to drive in an arc around Mosul to get to the checkpoint, which was two kilometres from the houses, and the twenty-five minutes it took to get there, gave me just enough time to play the video with Luc fifteen times. The purpose of this was to find characteristic features on the two executioners so that I would be able to identify them among the soldiers we encountered.

And characteristics were found: One had a tattoo on the inside of his wrist. It was very unusual for an ISIS warrior to have that as tattoos were not allowed. However it was there, even if it had only appeared in the fraction of a second, when he took the knife to Luc's neck. But it was long enough for me to be able to identify him.

The other wore a white t-shirt under his shirt and a few times you could see something black on it – probably the top of some letters or a design of some kind. Whether he would still be wearing it was uncertain, but that was all I had on him, so that was what we had to go on.

I sent a picture of the two executioners to everyone in the team and described their characteristics. Then everyone knew what we were looking for and whom NOT to kill.

In addition, I wrote a separate message to Wizard, in which I asked him to inform the legionnaires of my findings and how to deal with them. As expected, he confirmed the message after a few minutes. The legionnaires had been informed.

Each time that I watched the video, I stopped it before they killed Luc and a couple of times I sat for a while just looking at him. He seemed to be very clear regarding the situation and not really scared. Or at least I hoped that was the case. Before I switched off the phone, I kissed his face on the display and Christo, who was sitting next to me, saw it and patted me gently on my knee.

"We will get them," he said determinedly, "I promise you." And then he gave my knee a few encouraging slaps. I had no doubt that he meant it and mentally I repeated his words. But they were not for myself. They were for Luc. And only for Luc. The words became almost a mantra and with the help of them I slowly went into combat mode.

The legionnaires were already waiting for us when we arrived at the checkpoint. They came in three vehicles so with them we were thirty-five highly trained soldiers – and two militia women. We drove in procession towards the goal and as soon as the small cluster of houses became visible, 'The Frogg Team' stood up and tore the tarpaulin off the jeep. Next, Ben inserted the top part of the single pivot gun-mount into the baseplate that the boys had bolted in place earlier and then attached his AK 47. The Kid and Christo lined up so they flanked Ben, with raised rifles.

"Lock and load," Christo shouted when we were fifty metres from the houses and then all hell broke loose.

* * *

From all sides ISIS soldiers came running and the sound from machine guns and fully automatic handguns filled the air.

There were five houses, so each vehicle had its own target. It may sound a bit random, but it was actually agreed in advance.

We had the honour of the house, which was the largest and centrally located in the crescent shaped settlement. In the event that ISIS had any other prisoners on the site, we had planned to throw tear gas through the windows of the buildings, but since they had been nailed shut by boards it was not possible. We could easily have blown all the buildings up, but that was not the plan – and it would not have been very constructive in relation to finding the perpetrators.

* * *

After fighting our way to the door, Knox and JAC were the first ones to go in. When they had cleared the entrance of ISIS soldiers, Christo and I followed.

We then divided the house between us. And as we went from room to room, we secured the location. Christo and I took no prisoners. Not because no one surrendered, several did in fact, but as soon as I had checked that they were not the executioners, they were either shot in the temple or directly in the forehead. I killed them, while Christo kept them at gun-point. It was pure assassination but who fucking cared. If anything, we felt we did everybody a favour by getting rid of some the world's most horrible religious fanatics.

One can discuss whether the way they spread death and destruction was so much different from what we did that night, but at least we worked methodically and that was one of Wizard's criteria for the mission.

In the middle of one of my executions, Wizard entered the room. He came just in time to hear me say 'Allahu Akbar' to an ISIS soldier before my bullet sent him straight to hell. Without any objections, Wizard disappeared again, and Christo and I were off to the next room.

Ten minutes after our arrival there were no more shootings. The majority of the ISIS soldiers were dead and the remaining fifteen were our hostages.

While Knox, Ben and some of the legionnaires loaded them into the vehicles, The Kid called for me. They had found the room where Luc's execution had taken place. JAC, Castro, and three legionnaires were inspecting the room as I entered. It was clear that this was where the murder had taken place; blood on the floor and blood splatter up and down the walls, also there were clear blood trails, where they had dragged Luc's dead body from the crime scene. I started following the trail of blood and not surprisingly it led to a back exit. The door was open, and as I approached it, Wizard appeared in it.

"Don't go out there," he advised me without emotion.

"Is he out there?" I asked very quietly and he nodded. I took a step forward, but he grabbed my arm and looked at me.

"I have to, Wizard. I have to see him." Wizard stood for a while but then he let go of my arm. My mind was blank and yet, I had never had so many thoughts within the few seconds it took for me to walk through that doorway.

Outside stood five legionnaires. They had put Luc's dead body and his head in a black body bag and were about to zip it closed. At the sight of me they stopped. I went and knelt down by the body bag and looked at Luc. How I wished I could put him back together. Make him whole. Make him warm and alive. Feel his arms around me and feel his kisses on my neck.

I placed my hands around his head and lifted it up. His eyes were half closed and his mouth was slightly open, and there was something peaceful about him, which made me strangely at ease. How could they do it? How could they chop the head off the man I loved? I clutched his head to my heart.

"I love you," I whispered as I started to cry silently, "I love you."

One of the legionnaires said something to me in French and gently tried to take Luc's head away from me, but it just made me hold it even closer and suddenly I heard myself scream.

Wizard immediately came out the door with JAC, and while Wizard got me up, JAC talked to the legionnaires. Calmly, Wizard escorted me to our jeep, while Luc's head was still in my arms.

"We're leaving now." Wizard shouted, and then I don't recall much more.

The next thing I remember is sitting between Wizard and JAC in the jeep, which was bumbling on the uneven road. Wizard drove and JAC sat with one arm around my shoulders. I held Luc's head close to my chest and, in the background, there were some huge explosions as the buildings behind us were blown up. The light from it illuminated the sky above us for a while, but then all went black again. My mind was hollow and dark like never before and had I had a rational thought, it had been blown away with the blast.

When we arrived at the camp, we parked in front of our tent and, as expected, the legionnaires were right behind us. Wizard jumped out, but JAC remained seated next to me. Neither of us spoke. I could hear the team moving around behind the jeep and then there was silence. How long we sat there, I do not know, but suddenly Wizard opened the driver's door.

"Come," he said in an extremely calm and almost mesmerizing voice, which at that moment seemed appropriate. Our eyes met, and maybe, because of my state of mind, for a moment I thought there was something mild about him, something I had NEVER seen before. Normally, such an emotional display on Wizard's part would have provoked alertness in me, but not now. In fact, it was as if a veil of security fell upon me and it felt nice. Soothing.

Wrapped in an almost trance-like state, I slid along the seat, and while JAC stepped out the other side Wizard helped me out. The three of us walked into the tent and here a surprise awaited.

The team had clearly been busy. The whole tent had been cleared of beds and along one of the walls, the prisoners were kneeling on the floor and, as I stood there looking at them, the fog in my mind began to lift.

Strange as it may sound, my vision throughout this whole process had been incredibly tunnel-like. Everything had been faintly blurred or black except for what was directly in front of me. Even the details had been out of focus, if they had been there at all. But now. Now it was as if they came back with a force that was tenfold.

As my haze slowly disappeared, everything in the tent became razor sharp to me. My gaze slid from one person to another, and everything I observed was stored in my obscene mind.

I noticed that the team as well as a dozen legionnaires and a couple of officers from the International Coalition were among the spectators and I could see that there was a bit of whispering among the officers when they caught sight of Luc's head in my arms. Suddenly it was as if I woke up from my trance. I was now back.

Quietly – and in a very calm voice – I asked for a chair and a few seconds later one was put next to me. With Luc's head under one arm, I lifted the chair with the other and went and placed it in the middle of the room. Gently I put Luc's head on the chair so that it faced the row of prisoners, and then I turned to them. Most stared at me, some in fear, others vacantly and one just looked down at the floor. I slowly took off my jacket and tossed it over to The Kid. He grabbed it and at the same time I switched to Arabic.

"Which one of you did this?" I pointed to Luc's head,

"Which one of you cowards cut off his head?" There was no answer.

"You might as well speak, for those who are innocent, I will spare them from going to hell. Yes, you heard right. I intend to kill you, but if you speak – and if you speak the truth, I will be so merciful as to let a man kill you. Think about it. I offer you heaven with seventy-two virgins instead of hell. Seventy-two virgins to serve you."

There was complete silence in the room and as my gaze wandered from one prisoner to another the tension in the tent increased.

Unexpectedly, there was no response from the fifteen prisoners, so without further explanation I went ahead with my plan.

With a copy of the Koran in one hand and the Bible in the other I went towards the prisoners.

Armed with these two holy scriptures, I moved along the row of the kneeling faithful.

"What will it be? Heaven?" I shouted and raised the hand in which I was holding the Koran, "or Hell?" whereupon the Bible was raised. There was still no one who spoke out.

"If none of you want to speak, I have to find out for myself." I put the Bible aside and walked over to the ISIS soldier who was sitting furthest away from the door. I ripped his shirt open, to check if he had a t-shirt under it, but that was not the case.

"Bend forward," I commanded, but he remained seated without reacting, "It's going to be a long night if you don't obey me!" I said softly and then I slapped him on the back of the head with the Koran so he fell forward. I could clearly see his wrists and there was no tattoo. So, I moved on to the next one who got the same treatment. I continued until I got to number five. He was wearing a t-shirt that could possibly be the one from the video, but I saw something far more incriminating ....

"What the fuck?" I said as I looked at Luc's dog tags. The soldier had tried to conceal them under his t-shirt and that fact made my contempt for him even more intense – if that was possible. Not only was he Luc's executioner but this obvious cowardly act made me despise him even further. Rule number one is never to underestimate your enemy, and he had certainly done that. Thinking I would not find the dog tags was foolish. Stupid!

A couple of the legionnaires distracted me as they took a few steps forward. Judging by their facial expressions, they were more than ready to kill the ISIS soldier, but I stopped them.

"Back off," I said loudly and they did. Then I tore the chain off the soldier and threw it to Wizard. Out of the corner of my eye I saw that without so much as looking at it, he put it in his breast pocket. With it safely tucked away, I waved Naseem and her friend over. There was no need for words, a few mutual glances were enough and the girls removed the ISIS soldier from the row.

Then I went on to find the second executioner and number fourteen had exactly the tattoo on his wrist that I was looking for. Naseem and the girlfriend removed him too. Then I turned to the assembly of spectators.

"I only want these two. Any of you who want the rest?" There was quiet in the tent, "None?" Not a word was said, so I turned to the ISIS soldiers again.

"It doesn't seem that anybody wants to save you, so look at your friends there. You will get the same treatment as they are going to get. Gag them!" I said harshly, looking at The Kid. Immediately he and Ben gagged the thirteen prisoners. The two ISIS soldiers that Naseem and her friend had removed now became my focus and, as I quietly turned the chair with Luc's head on it so that it had the prime position to view the rest of the 'interrogation', my hatred towards the executioners grew. The three ski masks, which lay on a table by the door, now came into use, as the girls and I each put one on.

"Let your hair hang loose so they can see that you are women," I ordered, and they promptly took their elastic bands out of their hair before pulling the masks down over their faces.

"Turn the camera on," I commanded and Castro, who had been given the honourable job, immediately pressed 'start' for the video on Wizard's phone.

I went over to the ISIS soldier who had cut Luc's throat. The soldier was kneeling on the floor reciting verses from the Koran.

"Just keep going," I said without any feeling, "It doesn't help you. You will go straight to hell, but first I'm going to halal slaughter you."

I could see the eyes of some of the officers and legionnaires reacting, but I did not care. If they had any problem with it they could just fuck off.

Resolutely, I took the winch and threw the support rope over the load-bearing ceiling beam in the tent and fastened the winch cable to the soldier's zip tied ankles. I signalled to the girls to hoist him up, which they did immediately. The tent filled with the clicking of the winch locking mechanism and the soldier's monotonous recitation of the Koran, which got louder and louder with each click of the hand winch. It almost sounded like a 'countdown to the inevitable'. As he hung there with his head toward the floor, he almost screamed the Koran verses out in terror.

I approached him and I could hear that he had started reciting the verses over again.

"Out of respect for your faith, I will let you finish the passage you are reciting," I said calmly and stepped back to allow him to finish.

The soldier screamed and cried his way through the passage and when he was done he went straight on to another verse. With calm and determined steps I placed myself behind him and slowly I took out my hunting knife.

"Like a lamb you were led to the scaffold, but you are going to be slaughtered like the pig you are," I said, half-whispering, grabbing his hair. I forced his head and neck backwards and slowly I sliced his artery. The blood began pumping out of him and he screamed while reciting the Koran. Slowly I wiped off the knife on my pants and put it back in its scabbard. I then pointed to the bucket by the door and one of the girls immediately brought it to me. With an elegant motion I put it under the soldier and while the blood ran from him and into it, I walked silently and quietly around him. As more and more blood drained into the bucket, his voice became weaker and in the end it was just a faint rattle. At that point, I grabbed his wrist with the tattoo and checked his pulse. There was almost something poetic in feeling the life in the hand that killed Luc running out. The pulse was faint, but it was there, so I let go of the ISIS soldier's wrist and let it hang while I waited for the blood flow to slow down even more. A minute later no more sounds came from him, and the blood now no longer pulsed, but ran in a quiet stream over his face and down into the bucket.

I took his pulse again and this time it was gone.

Then I looked directly at the phone that was recording.

"This is how you slaughter an ISIS pig and send him straight to hell," I said, "And I can promise you that one more will be slaughtered again in the next twenty-four hours if you do not release the prisoners," I told Castro to turn off the phone, which he did.

"This is how you negotiate with ISIS." I put my hands on my hips as I turned to the officers, "And if you don't have an agreement with them in twenty-four hours,

I'll slaughter another one and I will continue till there are no more prisoners. And now get the fuck out."

Silently everyone left the tent except the team, JAC and the two militia women.

When they were gone, I squatted down in front of Luc's head. Then I gently stroked his hair.

"I got your executioner and I'll kill the other soldier too," I whispered, "but now you need to have peace, my darling. I love you – never forget that. Never ever."

I kissed him on the hair and got up. My eyes were filled with tears. Tears I just wished he would be able to kiss away. Wished to hear him say that he loved me and that we would be together. But that would never happen.

Luc would never speak again so in the midst of my desperation and sense of powerlessness never to see him alive again, to be able to touch him and to feel him, I wiped my eyes before lifting his head into my arms.

With steady steps I headed for the door and as I passed Wizard, he followed me. I walked to the legionnaires' tent and as I stepped into it a silence fell. Not knowing who to talk to, I addressed all of them.

"Where's Luc's body?" I asked, choking on tears, and Wizard standing next to me put his arm around my shoulders. One of the legionnaires discreetly pointed in the direction of their rear exit and a few seconds later I was standing next to a black body bag that was slowly being zipped open for me.

Gently, I laid Luc's head next to the rest of his body.

"See you, my love," I said quietly, "See you – I love you." The ensuing silence only emphasized the enormous emptiness that I felt, and the final goodbye, as it was, only became more definitive when the sound from the closing zipper, hit me.

As if in slow motion I got up still facing the body bag. I really wanted to say something, but words failed me. I turned to Wizard and felt how he pulled me in to him and, without exchanging a single word, we stayed like that for a long, long time. When we finally let go of each other we walked back to our tent in silence.

Upon my return, I could see that the team had not wasted any time. Not only had they removed the body of the slaughtered soldier and brought the tent back to its original state, but they had also had the remaining prisoners escorted to the legionnaires' quarters. Apparently they had volunteered to 'take care of them', and I was completely indifferent to what they had in store for them, as long as they did not touch the soldier that took part in Luc's murder because I planned to slaughter him the following day. Christo assured me, that he had explained it to them, and I had no doubt, that he had got the message communicated properly.

JAC had disappeared together with the two militia women, and I had to face the fact that I had scared them well and truly, but then again, it is not every day that you halal slaughter a human being.

The bucket of blood had been left standing on the floor and for a time I kept staring into it. The blood seemed completely black and for some reason I expected there to be more. The idea that the contents of this bucket had recently given Luc's executioner life was strange. Although it would never run through this man's veins again and therefore ensured that he did not cut off any more heads, it was a small consolation. For a brief moment, I considered kicking the bucket so his blood could run out onto the floor and into the ground. What had given life to such a man deserved no better than to be poured onto the barren earth, but it was somehow too easy and not honourable.

It might seem strange to talk about honour especially after what I just done to him but for me it was the right thing to do. The blood that had given life to such a monster deserved to be returned to the people that fostered this evil behaviour. They deserved to see his lifeless body next to the bucket containing the blood that had once given it life. They deserved to feel the same as I had felt when I held Luc's decapitated head in my arms. I had separated the blood from the ISIS soldier's body as he had separated Luc's head from his. And just as I wanted Luc to be buried intact, the family of the dead ISIS soldier should have the same opportunity. A monster took Luc away from me and undoubtedly the ISIS soldier's loved ones felt the same about me. But that is what war is. There are monsters on both sides. We are turned into enemies and in this case into monsters. But at least in death we can give each other some dignity. Show each other a bit of honour.

"Leave the soldier's body outside the camp and place the bucket next to him so they can pick him up," I said tiredly, "and then co-ordinate with Command OP when you post the video."

"It's already posted," Wizard replied looking at me, "When was the last time you slept?"

"It's been two days," I said quietly while lighting a cigarette.

Without further comment, we went outside and sat by the tent.

"You'd have done well in the Balkans," Wizard said coolly, "Halal slaughter. I hadn't seen that coming. And then to call him a 'pig'." He snorted. For a while we just sat in silence, but then Wizard continued, "But at least you let him recite the verses from the Koran. I call that respect." He took the cigarette from me and took a puff. We sat like this for a while until he suddenly took Luc's dog tags out of his pocket. I sat for a while staring at them as they dangled from his hand. In a few days they would be the last thing left of Luc. The last physical proof that he had existed. The rest would be cremated and buried. With the tags in my hand, I took one of them and his wedding ring, and put them on my own chain. Then I gave Luc's chain back to Wizard.

"Will you give it to the legionnaires?" He nodded and blew smoke from the cigarette out through his mouth, "His ashes are to be buried in Antwerp next to his brother Lenard," I said calmly, staring blankly into the night, "Will you make sure that happens?"

Actually, I wished he could be buried near Barcelona, but I knew he would have appreciated being in the same place as his brother. Maybe then he could get the forgiveness from him – for not having brought him with him to the Foreign Legion – which he had needed all these years. Wizard nodded in silence at my request.

"When I'm done here, I think it's best if you send me away for a while." I did not look at Wizard as I said it, but just kept staring into the night.

"You're probably right," he replied quietly and not surprisingly.

"Can't you get Aslan to give me some assassin assignments?"

"Yes." Wizard replied, taking another puff of the cigarette before handing it back to me.

We sat for a while without saying anything.

"You just have to promise me that you will contact me if there is anything – no matter what – and when you are ready to come home again, just do it."

"Even if I am too damaged?" I didn't look at him as I took a puff of the cigarette. We both knew what I meant and honestly ... who would want a broken soldier?

"Even so," he replied, "Just come home." I nodded slightly then I put out the cigarette. I was so empty inside. So hollow. I had no idea how I would survive without Luc. I tried to find something to cling to, just the smallest thing. But there was nothing. No light. No purpose. Just the echo of him screaming my name. My heart dropped to my stomach and I began to tremble violently while I gasped for air. Wizard took hold of me but I tilted into his lap shaking and rattling. As saliva and snot poured out of my mouth and nose I clung to his thighs and I could feel him holding me tight.

"I can't live without him, Wizard," I whispered and then I started to cry. It wasn't a normal cry. No. It was an uncontrolled stream of tears that just kept pouring out of my eyes. No sound accompanied them. It was just tears. Thousands of tears.

"You can. And you will. It will just take time." Time, I thought. Fuck Time. The only time I needed was with Luc. We were supposed to have the rest of our lives together. What was I supposed to do now? He was my everything. I had lost my everything. There was nothing left. Nothing but the next kill.

Chapter 37

The next few days are a bit unclear to me. I remember slaughtering the other ISIS soldier, but not much more before sitting on a plane between Knox and The Kid. When I asked them where we were going, I remember The Kid replied that we were on our way home to Barcelona and what happened next only comes in glimpses. I do remember, though, that at one point I was in the house in Barcelona sitting and eating with Knox, The Kid and Aslan, but for the most part I think I was asleep.

How long I was in this state of mind, I do not know, but one morning I woke up and felt fresh. My body was a little tired, but otherwise I was fine.

The house was completely quiet. Not even in the kitchen was there a living soul. Normally it was the place where you were certain to find at least one of the team, but not this time.

The fridge was full of food and, judging by all the dishes, Imeni must have been here. I scooped a plate-full of the food from the pot on the stove and put it in the microwave. While it was heating up, I went upstairs to pick up my Glock. I had completely forgotten to bring it with me, so I was certainly not okay yet. The Glock was nowhere to be found in my room which made me a little uneasy. As I returned to the kitchen Imeni was standing at the counter pouring herself a cup of coffee.

"Well, I thought I heard someone out here," she said, smiling, "How are you today?"

It was quite nice to see her friendly and gentle face again.

"Really good," I replied, "It's a bit like I've slept for a hundred years like in 'The Sleeping Beauty' and just woken up from the prince's kiss."

Imeni laughed heartily. "I have to tell Aslan that."

"What are you going to tell me?" Aslan's voice came from the doorway. He stood in the middle of it with a can of Coca Cola in one hand and smiled, "Good morning," he said winking at me.

"Good morning," I replied, "Where are the others?"

"They are in Jerusalem." He took a sip of the red-and-white can and walked towards Imeni and me.

"How long have they been gone?" I asked looking at him curiously. It was not because it really interested me, but it was a way to figure out how long I had slept.

"Uhh ... a little over a month," he replied, "Fortunately, I have had Imeni to help me with you." He took another sip of the cola.

"Have I been so difficult that it needed two to handle me?" It was said with a twinkle in my eyes because how bad could it have been? I had been sleeping most of the time. However, the serious glance that Aslan and Imeni sent each other quickly got me thinking differently.

"Can't you remember anything from the last month?" Aslan asked with a fierce concern in his voice.

"No ... not really ... only fragments ... why? Have I been bad?"

He nodded.

"You have alternated between being totally withdrawn – almost apathetic – and then being completely psychotic. At one point, it took three of us to hold you down, and even then we had a hard time controlling you, so you didn't hurt anybody."

It seemed completely unrealistic that I had been so insane that it took three from the team to gain control of me.

"I'm so sorry. I can't remember it at all. Have I injured any of you?"

Aslan smiled, "Ben has a scar on the back of his head after you hit him with a fire extinguisher, but otherwise everyone is okay. Maybe there's a little hurt pride in some of them because they physically didn't cope when you freaked out. And I have no idea how many times Wizard had to knock you out so we could have some peace and quiet. Believe me. He felt miserable doing it, but sometimes there was no other way, because otherwise you would have done harm to us or yourself." Aslan smiled and took a sip of his cola again.

I was pretty shaken up to hear all this, because I really could not remember anything. It might as well have been a completely different person we were talking about. It seemed so absurd that I had behaved like this.

Aslan's nostrils vibrated.

"Is it lunch time?" he said looking in the direction of the microwave. Imeni laughed heartily again and within five minutes we were all sitting and eating at the dining table in the kitchen. The talk went from the team to princes and princesses and it was liberating to finally be back in the real world again.

The next couple of days, I just relaxed with Imeni and Aslan.

Of course, Aslan had contacted Wizard, and he and I had had a two-hour conversation over Skype, where I also had the opportunity to apologize to everyone on the team for being an ass to them, but there were no hard feelings. They were just happy that I was back again.

One night I had a serious talk with Wizard. I had started to get restless and wanted to go back 'in the field', but he was not keen, however after a long conversation with Aslan he decided that if I went through a physical rehabilitation programme with Aslan and otherwise was fine, then I could be reinstated.

What I didn't tell Wizard was the real reason for wanting to come back. My heart was so broken from losing Luc that I needed a purpose to live. They had been right in removing my gun from my room because some nights when the longing for him was at its highest it seemed like the only valid option I had left. It was so crazy to think that of all the things I had done in the real world it would be the normal world and the love I felt in it that would kill me. But the fact was that when Luc left this world he took my soul with him. So now all there was left was an empty shell with the ability to kill. And maybe ... just maybe ... getting back in the game would heal some of me. Just like it did when I returned from Belize.

So for the next two weeks I therefore worked like a horse in the gym with Aslan. Out of all of them, he was the best man to whip me into shape. I went through various programmes, six hours a day, and I think he enjoyed that I did not at any point object to anything he put me through. If that would get me back in the game again, so be it.

When I was not sweating with Aslan, I was on the shooting range and fortunately my precision skills had not been damaged by my 'rest period'.

Now that I was much better, Imeni went home to the boys, and there was almost something symbolic in the fact that I passed the physical test on the day she left.

Whether Wizard really wanted me to go back to work again, I do not know, but he had no choice as he had given me his word. After another long conversation between us, he agreed to send me on a 'trial mission'. Through one of his old contacts in the Balkans, he had been able to find an assassin assignment for me, so two days later I was on a plane on my way to Pristina.

* * *

But it was too soon for me to come back, because as I sit here, shot, on a cold concrete floor in Bosnia, I can only remember fragments from the time I left the plane in Pristina until now.

I have to get back to Barcelona. So I can heal ...

It's so fucking cold. I cannot really feel my body. My arms will not obey me. They shake. I'm drained of energy.

I can see that I have my hand on OPUS, but I can no longer feel its contours.

It is as if the light disappears; whether it's my eyelids that have slid down, I'm not sure. Slowly everything gets dark.

It is quiet. Completely quiet. It is nice. I'm not scared – on the contrary.

I miss Luc so much.

I miss …

Epilogue – *JAC*

It was three p.m. and Wizard and I had been searching for hours. The district she was supposed to be in was an old industrial area. Empty and deserted office and factory buildings stood side by side as hollow shells testifying to the bitter reminder of the war. Two decades of dust and the decay from the weather had left its foot print everywhere. Rubble, rusty armour and broken concrete blocks lay scattered over the stairs and floors. Dangling garlands of old electrical cords hanging from almost every ceiling. Most of the doors and windows had been blown to pieces by blasts from grenades. The lack of them made the façades of the buildings look like grey monsters with big black piercing eyes. I had seen it a thousand times before but this time it was different.

Somewhere in one of these monsters was OPUS. I had no idea what condition, physical or mental, she would be in. Best case scenario was that she was still alive – and my God I hoped so. I tried to convince myself that the reason she had broken contact with us was that her phone had been lost or damaged but deep down I knew OPUS would never break contact for more than a day or two and it had been a week since she last checked in.

Wizard's friend Jowan, who lived in Pristina, had been her contact person and he was the one who had alerted Wizard of her being missing. Wizard's call had made me drop everything and leave Erbil.

It didn't matter what had happened between us. In my heart she was still mine even if just as her friend. Our bond of trust and loyalty went beyond a stupid crush. It went beyond everything. I had told her that I would always be there for her and I would. No matter what.

I had been such a fucking coward when I had left Mosul. She had just lost Luc and I knew she was broken in every sense of the word. And still I left. I should have stayed. Helped her. But I didn't. I was too caught up in myself. Some friend I was.

Maybe I did what I did because I knew she had Wizard. If anybody could straighten her out it was him. But I should have called. Should have checked up on her. I thought about it but as time passed it just became more difficult to do. 'No news is good news' became my mantra when I thought about OPUS and it legitimized my action. But honestly ... she never left my mind.

It was almost a relief when Wizard called telling me to get my ass to The Balkans to help find her. My own private redemption was served to me on a platter and I eagerly took it. It was as if I was offered a second chance. I blew the first one and damned if I was going to do that again. Even if it cost me my life. Because, as Wizard explained, there was a real chance that she had snapped. If so, she would likely see us as a threat – as an enemy – and given the chance she would kill us. But I didn't care. I took the first available plane and well ... Here I am searching for her. And I am not leaving without her.

Wizard and I have split up to cover more ground and we communicate by our headsets so ....

* * *

Fuck ... She is here.

"Wizard I've found her!" I shout. She is sitting up against a pile of stone and bricks. She is barefoot and she has one hand on her rifle. Her head is hanging forward so her chin is almost touching her chest. My worst fear seems to have come true. She has been shot. Killed? I squat down next to her and take off my gloves. Desperately I try to find a pulse on her neck but I can't.

"Fuck Wizard, she is ... No ... I got a pulse. I got a pulse," I scream excited. It is faint but it's there. Out of the corner of my eyes I see Wizard enter.

"She is alive," I say and relief rushes over me like a Tsunami. Wizard stares for a brief second at OPUS and then he changes channel on his headset.

"Bring the car around, Jowan," he says in a hard commanding voice, "We found her." Then he squats down next to me as I lift her head up. Her eyes are open and her stare is cold and lifeless. But she has a pulse.

Without any words being said I lift her up in my arms. Her body is limp and without any strength.

"I'm here, baby," I whisper to her, "I got you. You're safe." Although my focus is on her I register Wizard picking up her rifle.

"Hang in there, you hear? Hang in there," I repeat as I hurry down the stairs, Wizard right behind me. Jowan is already waiting outside in the car and I get in on the back seat still with OPUS in my arms. I'm not letting go of her. Not again. Not ever.

As we rush to the hospital I hold her tight, her head leaning against my chest. I kiss her on her hair and I can feel my eyes welling up. I can't lose her. I can't. I look at her and bow my head down to her. She feels so lifeless.

"I'm so sorry," I whisper as my voice cracks. I squint but the tears find

their way out anyway, "Come back to us, do you hear? Come back." My voice fails me and I can't stop crying silently.

"Please don't die," I plead, "I can't live without you." I hug her tight as my body trembles, "Please don't die. Please."

* * *

I hear Wizard saying, "We are here" and seconds later he opens the door to the backseat and takes her from my arms. I wipe my tears away on my sleeve and snort a couple of times. Then I rush inside the hospital to find her.

I'm not leaving her.

Not this time.

Acknowledgements

I have been very fortunate to have been assisted by a number of people.

My thanks to you all, especially:

To my incredible editors Rodger and Corinne Attaway. Working with you is such a privilege.

To Ditte L. Pedersen, Anja Meyer Jacobsen and Karina G. Thomsen for being my Alfa-readers. Your feedback and input were invaluable to me.

To all my Beta-readers. Your comments and constructive criticism were greatly appreciated. Thank you all for believing in me and my book.

To David Bonham for the first proofread as well as identifying specific English phrases and sayings.

To Matas Krivickas for his incredible work in creating my website.

To Jem Butcher from Jem Butcher Design for creating the fantastic book cover.

And, finally, to all the people that helped to verify specific paragraphs in the book so it comes across as believable. You know who you are and I honour and respect your wishes to remain anonymous.

Author's Bio

Lee Shye's lifelong ambition was to become an author and OPUS is her first published novel. Danish but now living in Spain, she has completed the second in this series of five books which psychologically explore the main characters introduced in OPUS through their dark and extreme lives as mercenaries.

Lee devotes her spare time to actively supporting local animal rescue charities.

'Phoenix'

is my second book in this series
Please keep checking through my social media:

Website: www.leeshye.com

Instagram: #leeshye_author

Tik Tok: @leeshye_author

Facebook: Leeshye_author

Printed in Dunstable, United Kingdom

78403316R00259